CONQUER

THE STORY OF NINTH ARMY

CONQUER

The Story of

Ninth Army

1944-1945

WASHINGTON
INFANTRY JOURNAL PRESS

First edition

April 1947

Reprinted by
THE BATTERY PRESS, INC.
P.O. Box 3107, Uptown Station
Nashville, Tennessee 37219 U.S.A.
Fifth in the Combat Arms Series
1980
ISBN: 0-89839-027-3

PRINTED IN THE UNITED STATES OF AMERICA

CONTENTS

MAPS

MAP SYMBOLS

CAPITAL OF COUNTRY BERLIN

CITIES 100,000 UP HANNOVER

CITIES 25,000 TO 100,000 HILDESHEIM

CITIES UNDER 25,000 ● ZERBST

INDUSTRIAL LOCALITIES

INTERNATIONAL BOUNDARIES

ROADS

AUTOBAHNS AUTOBAHN

RAILROADS

LAKES AND OCEANS

RIVERS

MILITARY BOUNDARIES (DIV, CORPS, ETC) ——— xxx ———

DIVISION SYMBOLS

| XX ⊠ INFANTRY | XX ▭ ARMORED | XX ⊠ AIRBORNE |

CORPS SYMBOLS

| XXX XIX CORPS | XXX ·▫· XIX CORPS ARTILLERY |

ARMY SYMBOLS

| XXXX NINTH ARMY | XXXX NINTH ARMY COMMAND POST |

ENEMY UNITS

| XX [×] INFANTRY DIVISION | XX [○] PANZER DIVISION | XX [⊗] PANZER GRENADIER DIVISION |

NINTH ARMY ADVANCES

INFANTRY OR INFANTRY AND ARMOR

ARMOR

OTHER ALLIED ADVANCES

STABLE FRONT LINES PATROLLED FRONT LINES o·o o o o o o

SIEGFRIED LINE OTHER FORTIFICATIONS

FOREWORD

CONQUER: THE STORY OF NINTH ARMY is intended to present in broad form a brief account of that Army's activities—tactical, administrative, and logistical. Considerations of space, time, and proportion have generally limited the mention of individual units to divisions and larger. In Ninth Army, however, as in any modern American army, these were only one-half of the troop strength. The other half comprised the large number of corps and army troops—cavalry, antiaircraft, engineer, chemical, field artillery, medical, military police, ordnance, quartermaster, signal, tank, and tank destroyer—the "supporting" troops, without whom the job could not have been done. And it is to these, most of whom wore the Ninth Army shoulder patch, that I wish to pay particular tribute here, without detracting in any way from the fine performance of the larger units.

To the individual soldier I give final and highest praise. Whether in a front-line line unit—often cold, wet, tired, and miserable, always exposed to the hazards of mines, shell fire, sniping, and strafing—or in a rearward position, performing hard and frequently monotonous and dull tasks without glamor—it was only through his spirit, courage, and ability, working in a team with his fellow soldiers, that our armies were victorious.

To all Ninth Army men I say again:

Command of the Ninth Army I consider a privilege; service in it, along with you, a great honor.

W.H. Simpson

Lieutenant General, United States Army

INTRODUCTION

"The book should enable you to say, when your wives or other relatives and friends ask you what the Ninth Army did, 'Here, read it for yourself.' It should be written in language that the non-military person can understand and should cover the mistakes as well as the more creditable accomplishments."

With this directive from Major General James E. Moore, Ninth Army Chief of Staff, immediately after the cessation of hostilities in Europe, a committee composed of Brigadier General Richard U. Nicholas, U. S. Army, Chairman; Colonel Harold D. Kehm, General Staff Corps; Colonel William J. Thompson, Field Artillery; Colonel Clifford A. Kaiser, General Staff Corps; and Colonel John R. Beishline, General Staff Corps, was formed to supervise the writing of a history of the Ninth Army. Later, Brigadier General Armistead D. Mead, Jr., U. S. Army, and Colonel William E. Shambora, Medical Corps, were added to the committee upon Colonel Kehm's transfer and Colonel Thompson's detail as author.

The first draft of the major portion of CONQUER: THE STORY OF NINTH ARMY was prepared by Colonel Theodore W. Parker, Jr., General Staff Corps. After Colonel Parker's transfer, the project was completed under the supervision of Colonel Thompson. The initial drawings for the maps and chapter heading illustrations were prepared by Lieutenant Colonel Henry S. Parker, Medical Corps. First Lieutenant Henry M. Parker, Signal Corps, assisted in the selection of photographs.

Principal assistants to the authors included Lieutenant Colonel Ellsworth A. Cragholm, Infantry; Lieutenant Colonel Wayne E. Downing, Corps of Engineers; and Major Robert E. Burke, Infantry. The authors made use of the outline history of the Ninth Army prepared by the 4th Information and Historical Service; official records pertaining to the Ninth Army; and narrative accounts prepared by representatives of the general and special staff sections of Headquarters Ninth Army. Valuable contributions, comments, and constructive criticisms were received from numerous individuals.

The editorial committee wishes to express its sincere thanks and appreciation to all those associated with the preparation of the book, without whose unfailing efforts it could not have been completed.

CONQUER

THE STORY OF NINTH ARMY

CHAPTER 1
THE BEGINNINGS

"CONQUER" was the code name, and this is the story of the United States Ninth Army, which came into being at Fort Sam Houston, Texas, May 22, 1944. Since the Commanding General and staff of the newly activated Army Headquarters were transferred in toto from Headquarters Fourth Army, where they had been working together for some months, it is necessary to go back a bit to get the whole picture.

In September, 1943 the Fourth Army was separated from the combined Headquarters Western Defense Command & Fourth Army at the Presidio of San Francisco, California, and was designated as a training army under the Army Ground Forces, with headquarters at San Jose, California. Major General William Hood Simpson, who had made an enviable record as the commander of the 35th Infantry Division, the 30th Infantry Division and the XII Corps, was selected as the commander of the Army and was invested with the rank of lieutenant general.

A nucleus for the new staff, particularly in junior officers and enlisted men, was furnished by the Western Defense Command, but the senior officers were nominated from the service at large, and all were personally approved by General Simpson prior to their assignment. With comparatively few changes, the chiefs of the Army staff sections who were assembled on the West Coast in the fall of 1943 were present with the headquarters when the Ninth Army was inactivated after the war's end, almost exactly two years later.

On October 13, 1943 when General Simpson assumed command of the Fourth Army, already assembled at San Jose were, among others: Colonel John Weckerling, Assistant Chief of Staff, G-2 (Intelligence) and Colonel Roy V. Rickard, Assistant Chief of Staff, G-4 (Supply). From the XII Corps General Simpson brought with him his Chief of Staff, Colonel James E. Moore, who had served with him in a similar capacity in the XII Corps and the 35th and 30th Divisions. A few days later these section heads were joined by Colonel Philip D. Ginder, Assistant Chief of Staff, G-1 (Personnel); and Colonel Armistead D. Mead, Jr., Assistant Chief of Staff, G-3 (Operations and Training).

15

During the remainder of October the headquarters made plans for its future operations as a training army. From the outset it was made clear by the chief of staff that the methods of staff functioning which had been taught in our service schools, as laid down in our field manuals, would be followed exactly, and that all developments of operational procedure would be tested by the question: "Would it work effectively in combat?" Trick ideas for the organization and functioning of the headquarters, even though it appeared that they might be temporarily effective, were rejected in favor of the normal methods of procedure. That such procedure was sound was proven in combat.

On November 1 the headquarters, unable to find adequate office space and housing facilities in San Jose, moved to the Presidio of Monterey, California. On this date, also, Fourth Army became operational with the mission of training all Ground Force troops on the West Coast and processing certain units for shipment overseas. Since no corps headquarters were now assigned to the Army, the conduct of the many training tests and field exercises, normally performed by corps, became a responsibility of the Army Headquarters. This fact proved to be of great value in the basic training of the staff itself, giving the members additional familiarity with the problems and procedures of units the size of a division and smaller. The preparation for overseas movement of the headquarters also was started at Monterey, with the thought that, although it was the newest army formed, it should be ready for overseas duty when and if the call came.

In January, 1944 the Army Headquarters was moved to Fort Sam Houston, where it succeeded to the training mission of the Third Army when that unit moved to the European Theater of Operations. There were assigned to the Army three corps and the usual army troops, plus the mission of operating the Louisiana Maneuver Area, where exercises involving large masses of troops were conducted with all the realism possible outside of an actual combat zone. By rotation of staff officers between Fort Sam Houston and the Louisiana Maneuver Area much valuable practical experience was gained for the headquarters.

In the early spring of 1944 Headquarters Fourth Army received successive augmentations of personnel to permit the formation of an additional army headquarters at Fort Sam Houston, so that the headquarters commanded by General Simpson could proceed in the near future to the European Theater of Operations. On May 5, when the augmentations of personnel were complete, Headquarters Eighth Army (eventually to be renamed the Ninth) was activated at Fort Sam Houston, and the Fourth Army staff was transferred thereto. The augmentation group then became Headquarters Fourth Army and took over the training mission of that army.

For approximately a month, while the new Fourth Army staff was taking over its duties, the headquarters engaged in a map exercise devised to instruct the staff in combat operations and to provide an opportunity for working out a standing operating procedure for the headquarters. Major General William H. H. Morris, Jr., commander of the XVIII Corps, which had just completed maneuvers in Louisiana, acted as the director for the exercise. He was assisted by members of his corps staff. Since the Army Headquarters had been unable to take part in a maneuver as a unit, this exercise proved to be a great benefit, focusing attention on a number of problems the solution to which made future staff operations much smoother.

Certain changes had taken place in the chiefs of staff sections since the original organization. Colonel Daniel H. Hundley had become the Assistant Chief of Staff, G-1; and Colonel Charles P. Bixel, Assistant Chief of Staff, G-2.

The first movement to the European Theater of Operations began on May 11, 1944 when General Simpson, with a number of his staff section chiefs and certain other selected key personnel, took off from Washington, D. C., in three four-motored C-54 Army transport planes. The advance party arrived in the United Kingdom on May 12 and proceeded to London, where the members immediately began to acquaint themselves with the methods and procedures of operations and supply in the European Theater and to make preparations for the reception of the main body of the Army Headquarters. A short time later Headquarters Eighth Army was redesignated Headquarters Ninth Army, at the request of the Supreme Allied Commander, General Dwight D. Eisenhower, to obviate any possibility of confusion with the British Eighth Army.

With this change in designation, it became necessary to design a new shoulder patch. Since Headquarters Ninth Army was essentially Headquarters Fourth Army under a new name, the new shoulder patch reflected that origin. The white heraldic rosette, standing out vividly on the red nonagon of the Ninth Army emblem, was a conventionalization of the white four-leaf clover of Fourth Army. At this time, too, the code name "Conquer" was selected for the headquarters.

From London, the advance party made visits to the headquarters of the First and Third Armies, as well as to a number of corps and divisions, all of which were then preparing for the coming assualt on the Continent. The staff was fully acquainted with the battle plans for the invasion. Visits to the various base sections of the Communications Zone, European Theater, also were made, and the systems of supply and administration in use, and to be used during the attack, were studied.

Until the arrival of the main body, the advance party had its headquarters with the First U.S. Army Group, later to become 12th Army Group, in London, where contacts with higher headquarters were easily maintained and, after D-day, June 6, the progress of the invasion could be closely followed. In the meantime, plans were made to establish the headquarters, on arrival of the main body, at Clifton College in Bristol, where the First Army Headquarters had been located while planning the invasion.

The main body of the headquarters, under command of Colonel John G. Murphy, Army Antiaircraft Officer, sailed from New York on the great British liner *Queen Elizabeth* on June 22. Disembarking at Gourock, near Glasgow, on June 28, the main body moved by train to Bristol, where the two echelons of the headquarters were reunited. The friendly people of Bristol gave the headquarters a cordial welcome. The historic old city, heavily blitzed in the early days of the war, and Clifton College, with its beautiful buildings, tall trees, and broad sweep of green cricket fields, was the home of headquarters for the next two months.

Here in Bristol Ninth Army received its first mission in the European Theater of Operations—that of supervising the reception of units arriving from the United States, and their equipping, training, and preparation for shipment to the Continent. Since the flow of troops from the United States to the United Kingdom continued unabated, the headquarters immediately became active in furtherance of its mission. Units from the size of battalions to divisions were received and processed. Advance parties reported to Army Headquarters, where they were oriented on supply, equipment, and training. Prior to the arrival of the main body, Army Headquarters arranged for living accommodations and training areas, and supervised reception measures. It was recognized that incoming units would often be tired and dispirited from a long and hazardous ocean voyage by slow convoy, and that they were arriving in a strange and foreign country, often during complete blackout and in the chill and rain of a typical British summer. Assistance was given, therefore, from other troops to insure that incoming units, no matter what the hour of the day or night, were provided with a well prepared hot meal and with clean and adequate quarters. Representatives of general and special staff sections met major units to provide assistance to the commander. Reconnaissance parties from Army Headquarters traveled all over southwestern England, familiarizing themselves with the available accomodations, the training areas, and the supply establishments, to insure that every possible step was taken for the orderly and comfortable reception, equipping, and training of the incoming troops.

At the same time active contact was maintained with operations on the Continent, and the headquarters was augmented to meet anticipated needs, pending the day when Ninth Army would go into combat. The G-5 Section (Civil Affairs and Military Government) was added to the general staff, with Lieutenant Colonel Carl A. Kraege as Assistant Chief of Staff, G-5. To the special staff were added the Armored Section, and the Publicity and Psychological Warfare Section. Other sections were augmented to meet anticipated needs. To both G-2 and G-3 were added Air Sections, together with Office of Strategic Services detachments. Certain other specialist teams also operated under G-2. Under G-4 was established a Traffic Control Headquarters, a far-reaching measure of major importance, based on the experiences of units in combat. The 4th Information and Historical Service was added to the special troops. At this time there also became associated with the headquarters two air force units that were to remain with it throughout the war—the 125th Liaison Squadron, which provided light airplanes for messenger and courier service, and the 50th Mobile Reclamation and Repair Squadron, which supplied special maintenance and repairs for all light aircraft with the Army.

To gain first-hand views of methods of operations on the Continent, the Army Commander and the chiefs of general and special staff sections visited and observed units in combat. This opportunity was used to check procedures already developed in the Army Headquarters, particularly as they affected lower echelons. Staff officers visited units of all sizes and saw how methods contemplated by Ninth Army would work out in combat.

At this time the headquarters held a map exercise, using as a general area the European Theater of Operations and as a specific area the region of Metz. Available major units subordinate to the Army in the United Kingdom participated. In the course of the map exercise, the Army standing operating procedure earlier developed at Fort Sam Houston was checked against information obtained from staff visits to units on the Continent. The procedure thus arrived at was kept without material change throughout the course of Ninth Army's participation in the war.

An intensive program of evening schools was carried out for all members of the staff. Observers returning from the Continent presented in detail their views of the operational and supply practices in use there. Officers from Theater Headquarters discussed the Theater organization, its methods of operating, and its plans.

Late in August came the word that Headquarters Ninth Army was to move to the Continent and pass to the operational control of the Commanding General, 12th Army Group. The XIII Corps, commanded by Major General Alvan C. Gillem, Jr., was made the Ninth Army agency for executing the Army's troop-processing mission in the United Kingdom. The Army Headquarters, in two echelons, forward and rear, sailed from the port of Southampton, England, and landed on the continent of Europe over Utah Beach in Normandy on August 29 and 30. The forward echelon, "Conquer," set up its temporary command post in Normandy at St-Sauveur-Lendelin in a tent camp along avenues of magnificent old trees leading to a château. The rear echelon, "Conquer Rear," occupied a school building at Périers, a few miles north of St-Sauveur. In anticipation of taking over operations in Brittany and along the river Loire, the headquarters moved again, on September 3, to the hamlet of Mi-Forêt, just northeast of Rennes, Brittany, where both "Conquer" and "Conquer Rear" went into tent camps in the forest preserve surrounding Mi-Forêt. Headquarters Ninth Army was on the Continent and ready for its first operational mission.

CHAPTER 2
BREST AND THE BRITTANY PENINSULA

T HE operational life history of Ninth Army began on September 5, 1944. At noon on that date General Simpson took command of all the forces in the Brittany Peninsula which had been operating under the Third Army. His mission was to complete the reduction of the Brittany Peninsula and to protect the south flank of the 12th Army Group along the Loire River as far east as Orléans. (*Map No. 1.*)

The situation in this area as it existed when Ninth Army assumed responsibility had developed in the following manner. The invasion of Normandy had begun June 6, 1944, by the U.S. First Army, under Lieutenant General Omar N. Bradley, and by British and Canadian forces. The initial successful beachhead landings had been followed by many weeks of hedgerow fighting with very slow progress and numerous bloody battles. The names Caen, Carentan, La-Haye-du-Puits, and St. Lô are well known to all who lived through those tense days. Late in July the now famous breakthrough at St. Lô was effected by First Army, and early in August Lieutenant General George S. Patton's newly operational Third Army drove through the bottleneck at Avranches and struck to the east, the west, and the south. On August 1 the 12th Army Group Headquarters became operational, with both First and Third Armies, under the command of General Bradley, and Lieutenant General Courtney H. Hodges took command of the First Army. Following the breakthrough at St. Lô and the drive southward, American armor and motorized infantry raced rapidly forward in independent, daring advances. So rapid and so demoralizing were these sudden thrusts that German defensive plans and defensive lines became useless, and the enemy had to resort to concentrating what forces he could at key points and holing up in such fortresses as would afford him the opportunity for a long-term defense and the denial to the Allies of the most important facilities for carrying on their campaign. Accordingly he chose such ports as St. Malo, Brest, Lorient, and St. Nazaire, and garrisoned these cities with all the manpower and matériel he could salvage.

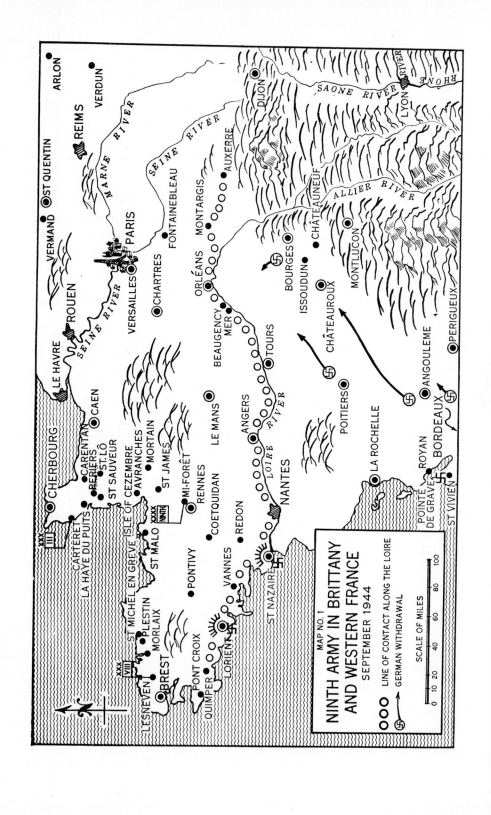

NINTH ARMY IN BRITTANY
AND WESTERN FRANCE

MAP NO. 1

SEPTEMBER 1944

OOO LINE OF CONTACT ALONG THE LOIRE

⟶ GERMAN WITHDRAWAL

SCALE OF MILES

0 10 20 40 60 80 100

A brief stand was made at Rennes, ancient capital of Brittany Province, but this was short-lived. St. Malo was reduced by Major General Robert C. Macon's 83d Infantry Division while still operating under Third Army. The Ile de Cézembre, guarding St. Malo's port, capitulated after it had been subjected to fire by heavy artillery at close range, as well as the first tactical use of jellied gasoline bombs dropped by the United States Army Air Forces. By-passing St. Malo and pushing out west through the Brittany Peninsula, the main forces of the VIII Corps, under the command of Major General Troy H. Middleton, had made rapid progress until the Germans finally dug in, in and around Brest, to fight it out for that worth-while prize. This, then, was the situation when Ninth Army became operational.

The city of Brest, with a pre-war population of some 85,000, began its connection with the United States Army when it was developed as the chief American port in France during World War I. Most of the American troops and supplies used to break the might of German aggression twenty-six years previously had entered France through Brest. In subsequent years the French Navy continued the development of Brest until, at the outbreak of World War II, it was France's chief naval port. When, in 1940, the German *Blitzkrieg* swept across Western France, Brest was one of the first-class plums that fell to the enemy, for in its magnificent harbor the Germans were able to develop one of their most important submarine bases with tremendous concrete-covered submarine pens which withstood every Allied attempt to knock them out from the air.

The enemy was fully aware of the usefulness of the port of Brest to the Allies in the continuation of their European campaign. The estimate of the Allied planners of the invasion was that operations could be sustained by supplying over the beaches and through the limited port facilities of Cherbourg until early September, but after that the port facilities of Brest must be in Allied hands in order to continue the impetus of the offensive throughout the winter. This estimate was based particularly on the weather conditions which were expected to reduce drastically the tonnage which could be successfully handled across the beaches. That it did not prove entirely accurate is beside the point. In planning operations for late summer of 1944, one mission stood out boldly in the minds of Allied leaders—Brest must be taken.

VIII Corps had begun operations in the actual battle of Brest in mid-August, and it was expected at that time, that the capture of the city would be accomplished within one week. However, it was to be nearly a month later before the tenacious defenders finally surrendered the city, which by then had been virtually destroyed by Allied planes and artillery.

Ninth Army's first battle mission was defined in the first paragraph of 12th Army Group's Letter of Instructions No. 7, dated September 5, 1944.

> The Ninth Army, effective at 1200 hours, 5 September 1944, assumes command of the VIII Corps, as now constituted, with the mission of reducing the Brittany Peninsula and protecting the south flank of 12th Army Group along the Loire River from its mouth to Orléans exclusive. Ninth Army will prepare for further action to the east on the right (south) flank of the Third Army.

Actually this mission was given to the Army Commander on the previous day. Leaving the tents of his command post in the forest of Mi-Forêt near Rennes on September 4, General Simpson had reported to General Bradley at 12th Army Group Headquarters, which by contrast was then located at Versailles. There General Bradley informed him of his mission and urged the speediest conclusion possible to the campaign for Brest.

A curious incident arose in regard to the hour of the day at which Ninth Army became operational. Returning to his command post in the early evening of September 4, General Simpson issued the necessary instructions to effect the assumption of his new role on the following day. It was then discovered that the Army Group Commander had not named a specific hour. Owing to communications difficulties it was impossible to contact Army Group Headquarters to ascertain the definite hour. General Simpson, recalling that General Bradley had used the phrase, "tomorrow morning," said that morning meant six o'clock to him, and so it was that Ninth Army's first situation report recorded the fact that the Army had become operational at 6:00 A.M. When the 12th Army Group letter of instructions was subsequently received, directing the assumption of command at 12:00 o'clock noon, corrections "for the record" had to be made and Ninth Army's operational life was cut short by six hours.

The forces which came under Ninth Army command on September 5 were the VIII Corps with its supporting combat and service troops and with four infantry divisions—the 2d, commanded by Major General Walter M. Robertson; the 8th commanded by Major General Donald A. Stroh; the 29th commanded by Major General Charles H. Gerhardt; the 83d, commanded by Major General Robert C. Macon—and one armored division, the 6th, commanded by Major General Robert W. Grow. The VIII Corps Artillery, commanded by Brigadier General John E. McMahon, Jr., included some five group headquarters and seventeen artillery battalions, principally of medium and heavy calibers. Attached to the VIII Corps Artillery was Brigadier General John F. Uncles' 34th Field Artillery Brigade, which was destined to be the Ninth Army brigade of army artillery.

The disposition of these troops was as follows (*Map No. 2*): the 29th, 8th, and 2d Infantry Divisions formed an arc around the city of Brest with the 29th on the right (west), the 8th in the center, and the 2d on the left (east). This arc stretched from the Conquet Peninsula around to the Elorn River east of Brest proper. Occupying the bases of the peninsulas to the south and southeast of Brest and completing the encirclement of the fortress were two task forces. Task Force A on the Crozon Peninsula, under Brigadier General Herbert L. Earnest, commanding the 1st Tank Destroyer Brigade, included a tank destroyer group headquarters, a cavalry group headquarters and two cavalry squadrons, an infantry battalion, and elements of a tank destroyer battalion and of a combat engineer battalion. Task Force B on the Daoulas Peninsula had already completed the clearing of that area and now consisted of small infantry elements to prevent the Germans from infiltrating back onto the peninsula from either Crozon or Brest. Also in the Daoulas area was a group of corps artillery whose battalions could fire across the harbor and pound the enemy batteries on Crozon and the rear of the defenses around Brest.

The siege of the city was twelve days old when Ninth Army assumed command, and it was well established at the time that the defenders had no intention either of capitulating or of evacuating, but were intent upon holding their positions to accomplish a maximum delay in American occupancy of the port.

The 6th Armored Division, which had led the race westward through the Brittany Peninsula to Brest, had been withdrawn

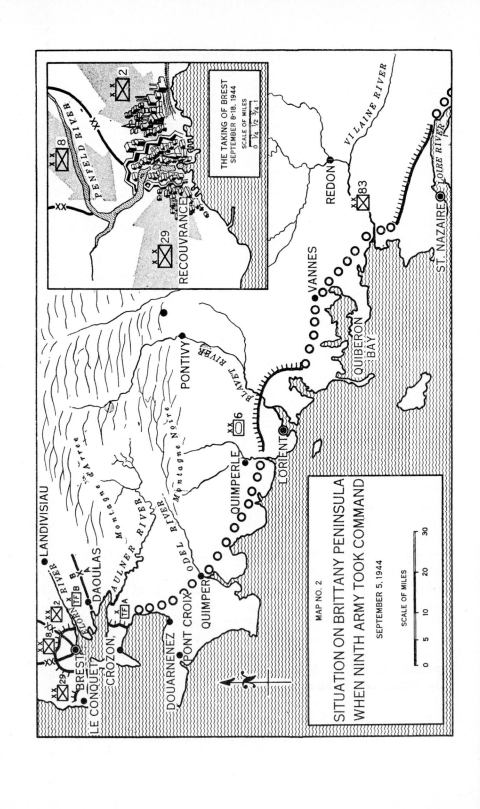

SITUATION ON BRITTANY PENINSULA
WHEN NINTH ARMY TOOK COMMAND

SEPTEMBER 5, 1944

MAP NO. 2

SCALE OF MILES

0   5   10   20   30

THE TAKING OF BREST
SEPTEMBER 8-18, 1944

SCALE OF MILES

0   ¼   ½   ¾   1

PENFELD RIVER

RECOUVRANCE

2

8

29

BREST

LE CONQUET

CROZON

DAOULAS

LANDIVISIAU

ELORN RIVER

TF B

TF A

29

8

2

B

A

PONT CROIX

QUIMPER

DOUARNENEZ

ODEL RIVER

AULNER RIVER

Montagne d'Arrée

Montagne Noire

QUIMPERLE

QUIMPER

6

PONTIVY

BLAVET RIVER

LORIENT

VANNES

QUIBERON BAY

REDON

VILAINE RIVER

83

ST. NAZAIRE

LOIRE RIVER

once the siege had begun, in order to permit infantry work to be done by infantry, and now it was engaged in containing the enemy pocket at Lorient and patrolling the Vannes area in the vicinity of Quiberon Bay. Continuing the flank protection to the south and east the 83d Infantry Division, having completed its task at St. Malo, was containing the large German pockets at St. Nazaire and Nantes (*Map No. 1*) and patrolling the Loire River as far east as Orléans. Plans made long before for the invasion had designated the Loire River as the southern limit of advance of Allied forces. There was no intention to disperse the effort aimed at the heart of Germany by embarking on a campaign in southern France. However, the security of this long, exposed flank of the Army Group was of extreme importance, and the limited number of troops engaged in its protection were pressed to the utmost to accomplish their task. In fact, had it not been for the able assistance of the loyal French Forces of the Interior, it is doubtful that the mission could have been executed so economically.

In the Brest area the enemy forces under Major General Hermann Bernhard Ramcke, an able, courageous, and fanatic Nazi who had commanded the German airborne invasion of Crete, were disposed in two pockets—the larger one in Brest proper and smaller one on the Crozon Peninsula. The core of the German defensive organization was three regular divisions—the 266th Infantry, the 343d Infantry, and the 2d Parachute Divisions. The parachute division was an élite unit of the German Army, but it was estimated that losses without corresponding replacements had reduced the parachutist strength in its infantry companies to about thirty-five percent of normal. Reinforcing the three regular divisions was a heterogeneous collection of battle groups comprising all manner of personnel. In addition to members of the static coastal garrison, there were odd-lot army individuals and naval and marine units, all of which had been trapped by the besieging American forces. The defenders even utilized members of the customs service and the navy meteorological service in their desperate attempt to hold out.

By September 5 the attack on Brest had been slowed almost to a stop. The strong natural defensive features of the area, the skillfully constructed German defenses, and the desperate, well coordinated effort of the defenders proved a difficult problem to overcome. The key to the situation for the attackers was over-whelming artillery support, and therein lay the reason for the slowing down of the operation. Although adequate artillery was present in the battle area, there was a critical shortage of ammunition, particularly of heavy caliber. Supply lines were long and the speed of the attack on the Peninsula had given rise to the hope that a siege of Brest would not be necessary; that it could be taken quickly before the enemy had time to prepare an effective defense. By September 5 steps had already been taken to accelerate the ammunition supply, and further artillery operations were curtailed in order to permit a build-up of three units of fire[1] for all types of artillery ammunition, a level estimated to be necessary to support an all-out coordinated attack. General Middleton, the VIII Corps commander, already had completed his plans for the contemplated attack and after study General Simpson approved them.

Working in conjunction with the Communications Zone of the European Theater of Operations, the agency charged with the delivery of ammunition to the Continent, the Army Assistant Chief of Staff, G-4, Colonel Roy V. Rickard, and the Ordnance Officer, Colonel Walter W. Warner, were particularly concerned with getting artillery ammunition to the VIII Corps. Direct unloading of ammunition ships across the beaches in the vicinity of Morlaix was already in progress. During the two weeks beginning September 5, 40,000 tons of ammunition were delivered across these beaches; the ammunition depot for the supply of the VIII Corps was built up to an average stock of 10,000 tons, with a turnover of 1,000 to 1,500 tons per day. Ammunition was transported to Morlaix from the United Kingdom and from Normandy in landing craft and small coastal vessels, with a small amount coming direct from the United States. A few critical items were hauled by truck from the dumps on the Normandy beaches.

The ammunition supply picture was complicated by the di-

---

[1]A unit of fire of artillery ammunition is a specific number of rounds of ammunition for each type of weapon, based on average expenditures of the various calibers of cannon in typical operations. As used in this book, units of fire are those of the European Theater of Operations in round numbers, not including certain additions for various special types of ammunition and fuzes, and are as follows: 105mm howitzer, 125 rounds; 4.5 in. gun and 155mm howitzer, 75 rounds; 155mm gun and 8 in. howitzer, 50 rounds; 240mm howitzer, 25 rounds; 8 in. gun, 35 rounds. The unit of fire is useful in considering ammunition requirements for specified operations and in planning over-all ammunition stock-piling, but all allocations to units for expenditures are habitually made in terms of total numbers of rounds of ammunition.

The 2d and 8th Divisions pressed forward, gaining nearly a mile on September 9. They were now well into the built-up area of Brest proper, and their battle became that of destroying a city. The advance which squeezed the life from the encircled fortress was not made down the streets of the city but rather through the buildings, block by block. Pillboxes, positions dug in at intersections, and small embrasures cut in buildings at street level permitted the enemy to sweep the streets with such intense fire as to deny their use to the attacker. The doughboy and engineer teamed to go through the buildings, blasting a path and capturing the defenders from the bottom floor, a houseful at a time. Concrete air-raid shelters were strongly defended and difficult to take. Open spaces such as cemeteries, parks, and railroad yards had to be by-passed because they were covered with crossfire from the surrounding buildings. The Germans also made maximum use of the extensive network of tunnels in the city. They employed them as hospitals, headquarters, and troop shelters, and, in addition, utilized them to facilitate movement of troops from one quarter of the city to another in comparative safety. Slowly, however, and with considerable cost, the German garrison was being strangled.

On September 11 the 2d and the 8th Divisions again pushed ahead with gains up to one-half a mile, while the 29th Division made little or no progress in the Recouvrance sector. In Brest proper the old wall and moat which surrounded the medieval fortress in the center of the city had now been reached. This was a formidable obstacle and it was strongly defended. Initial efforts to scale the wall were repulsed. The ditch or moat was some 45 to 60 feet wide and some 18 to 45 feet deep, and in general followed the contour of the fortress wall. The wall varied from 25 to 45 feet in height. All entrances were blocked and heavily defended. Along the wall and on top of it the enemy was firmly entrenched. Efforts to breach the wall with artillery, including heavy and super-heavy weapons, proved useless. Eight-inch howitzers, 8-inch guns, and 240mm howitzers all had a turn at trying to make a hole for the infantry—but to no avail. Although the upper portion of the wall was breached in several places, the lower part, forming the rear wall of the moat and hence defiladed from direct artillery fire, remained undamaged.

With the Conquet Peninsula cleared and Brest penetrated as far as the old wall it was now decided to withdraw the 8th Di-

version of large vessels from Normandy to the Brittany Peninsula. These ships, loaded in the United Kingdom and scheduled to discharge on the Normandy beaches, had been bulk-loaded with the separate components of heavy artillery ammunition, the shells in one ship, the propelling charges in another, and so on. Hasty diversion to an emergency port caused considerable difficulty, for it was impossible to keep balanced stocks. Many a heavy-caliber shell lay unfired for a long time for want of the proper propelling charge to deliver it to the enemy. Another interesting difficulty arose to plague the supply services. To conserve combat troops it was necessary to employ French civilian labor to unload and handle the greatly increased ammunition stock. Money, which could buy little, was scant inducement to the French laborers, but food was a luxury not to be scoffed at. To obtain the much needed labor, then, it was necessary to feed these people, and so the supply problem grew; more food in order to provide more ammunition.

Since there was no tactical air command yet organized for operation with Ninth Army, the XIX Tactical Air Command, which operated with Third Army, was assigned the mission of performing close cooperation missions in the Brest battle and along the Loire River. There was a very heavy air bombardment of Brest September 5, when eleven groups of medium bombers, reenforced by heavy bombers of the Royal Air Force and both heavy bombers and fighter-bombers of the United States Eighth Air Force, performed a widespread attack on the German installations. Subsequent to that attack, only intermittent air effort supported the Brest operations. There were two reasons for this: first, the airfields of the fighter-bombers supporting First and Third Armies were being moved eastward to keep up with these advancing armies; and second, as the attacking forces closed in around the city of Brest there was insufficient room between targets and friendly forces to permit bombing effort. Similarly, the forward movement of airfields, and the lack of adequate signal communications over the great distances involved, precluded continuously effective aerial reconnaissance, and the Army Commander was forced to depend almost entirely on ground sources for information pertaining to enemy activity around Brest.

On September 14 at Vermand, France, the XXIX Tactical Air

Command, with Brigadier General Richard E. Nugent commanding, was activated and assigned the mission of providing close cooperation with Ninth Army. This was the start of an extremely successful Army-Tactical Air Command relationship which lasted to the conclusion of hostilities in Europe. XXIX Tactical Air Command was formed by merging the 84th and 303d Fighter Wings into one headquarters. Four fighter-bomber groups were assigned to its command, and although initially it continued to operate on the basis of a wing, relaying missions to the units under its command and reporting the results of these missions, it was to develop by October 1 into a full-fledged, separate Tactical Air Command and from then on furnished close air cooperation to the Ninth Army.

The final battle for Brest began at 10:00 A.M. on September 8. (*Map No. 2.*) At that time the 29th Division was two to four miles west of the city, the 8th Infantry Division two miles to the north, and the 2d Infantry Division three miles to the east. Task forces, already described, were operating on the small Daoulas Peninsula south of the city and the larger Crozon Peninsula farther to the south. A twenty-minute artillery preparation, now possible with the newly arrived stocks of ammunition, preceded the jump-off on the morning of September 8. All three divisions attacked simultaneously.

The Penfeld River, running south along the western edge of Brest proper, divides Brest from its smaller companion city of Recouvrance. This river had been the location of the great French naval establishment, but now it was merely a very difficult obstacle, for it tended to divide the efforts of the 29th Division on the right (west) from those of the 8th and 2d Divisions on the left (east). It was planned, therefore, that the 29th Division clear the Conquet Peninsula and drive east to the Penfeld River while the 8th and 2d Divisions closed in on Brest proper. In the final stages, the 8th Division would be pinched out for lack of room, and the mopping up of the city would be done by the 2d Division. There was no room whatever for large-scale maneuvering and, in fact, very limited small-unit maneuvering was possible. Moreover, the beaches in this vicinity were studded with steel rails and well wired; coastal guns of calibers up to fourteen inches covered the sea approaches—they covered the land approaches, too, for they were capable of all-around traverse—and promised

terrific losses for any attempted amphibious flanking In general, it had to be a head-on attack against a stubb

Resistance was very stiff during the first day, par the Conquet Peninsula and in the Recouvrance area. northeast of the city gains of up to half a mile were ac The enemy was using every device at his disposal to i mum delay. Pillboxes and strongpoints were hotly de mines and booby traps were used in great numbers. I time in this area the enemy used miniature tanks, radi and carrying a charge of high explosives. His air powe was practically nonexistent, as it was throughout the Brest. Only two small-scale bombings were recorded caused neither casualties nor damage.

Rather amusing incidents occured when two of the air supply missions miscued and resulted in showering troops with quantities of German rocket ammunitic codes, and Iron Crosses. It is perhaps appropriate to sa displays were matched in a way when some of our dropped leaflets intended for the Germans almost dire 2d Division command post.

The Brest operation was really unique in the resp was the first operation of the Allied armies in northern be almost completely free of enemy air attack. Figh American Ninth Air Force were able to carry out cooperation with the ground forces with practically ference from enemy interception; the attacking troop from enemy air attack, particularly the harassing nig commonly used by the Germans; and, except for a mi alert personnel, the power of five AA artillery battalions able in its secondary role to reinforce the infantry-artil

On September 9 and 10 fighting continued along muc pattern. In the Conquet Peninsula area the 29th Div gressing in the face of heavy opposition, secured the su the commanding officer of the troops in this area on t though the mopping-up met stubborn resistance. Isola refused to acknowledge their commander's surrender an as individuals only after another day of fighting, but 10 saw the last enemy cleared from the Conquet Penins 29th Division. In the Recouvrance area, however, th made little or no advance.

version of large vessels from Normandy to the Brittany Peninsula. These ships, loaded in the United Kingdom and scheduled to discharge on the Normandy beaches, had been bulk-loaded with the separate components of heavy artillery ammunition, the shells in one ship, the propelling charges in another, and so on. Hasty diversion to an emergency port caused considerable difficulty, for it was impossible to keep balanced stocks. Many a heavy-caliber shell lay unfired for a long time for want of the proper propelling charge to deliver it to the enemy. Another interesting difficulty arose to plague the supply services. To conserve combat troops it was necessary to employ French civilian labor to unload and handle the greatly increased ammunition stock. Money, which could buy little, was scant inducement to the French laborers, but food was a luxury not to be scoffed at. To obtain the much needed labor, then, it was necessary to feed these people, and so the supply problem grew; more food in order to provide more ammunition.

Since there was no tactical air command yet organized for operation with Ninth Army, the XIX Tactical Air Command, which operated with Third Army, was assigned the mission of performing close cooperation missions in the Brest battle and along the Loire River. There was a very heavy air bombardment of Brest September 5, when eleven groups of medium bombers, reenforced by heavy bombers of the Royal Air Force and both heavy bombers and fighter-bombers of the United States Eighth Air Force, performed a widespread attack on the German installations. Subsequent to that attack, only intermittent air effort supported the Brest operations. There were two reasons for this: first, the airfields of the fighter-bombers supporting First and Third Armies were being moved eastward to keep up with these advancing armies; and second, as the attacking forces closed in around the city of Brest there was insufficient room between targets and friendly forces to permit bombing effort. Similarly, the forward movement of airfields, and the lack of adequate signal communications over the great distances involved, precluded continuously effective aerial reconnaissance, and the Army Commander was forced to depend almost entirely on ground sources for information pertaining to enemy activity around Brest.

On September 14 at Vermand, France, the XXIX Tactical Air

Command, with Brigadier General Richard E. Nugent commanding, was activated and assigned the mission of providing close cooperation with Ninth Army. This was the start of an extremely
successful Army-Tactical Air Command relationship which lasted
to the conclusion of hostilities in Europe. XXIX Tactical Air
Command was formed by merging the 84th and 303d Fighter
Wings into one headquarters. Four fighter-bomber groups were
assigned to its command, and although initially it continued to
operate on the basis of a wing, relaying missions to the units under
its command and reporting the results of these missions, it was to
develop by October 1 into a full-fledged, separate Tactical Air
Command and from then on furnished close air cooperation to
the Ninth Army.

The final battle for Brest began at 10:00 A.M. on September
8. (*Map No. 2.*) At that time the 29th Division was two to four
miles west of the city, the 8th Infantry Division two miles to the
north, and the 2d Infantry Division three miles to the east. Task
forces, already described, were operating on the small Daoulas
Peninsula south of the city and the larger Crozon Peninsula farther
to the south. A twenty-minute artillery preparation, now possible
with the newly arrived stocks of ammunition, preceded the
jump-off on the morning of September 8. All three divisions
attacked simultaneously.

The Penfeld River, running south along the western edge of
Brest proper, divides Brest from its smaller companion city of
Recouvrance. This river had been the location of the great French
naval establishment, but now it was merely a very difficult obstacle, for it tended to divide the efforts of the 29th Division on
the right (west) from those of the 8th and 2d Divisions on the
left (east). It was planned, therefore, that the 29th Division
clear the Conquet Peninsula and drive east to the Penfeld River
while the 8th and 2d Divisions closed in on Brest proper. In the
final stages, the 8th Division would be pinched out for lack of
room, and the mopping up of the city would be done by the 2d
Division. There was no room whatever for large-scale maneuvering and, in fact, very limited small-unit maneuvering was possible.
Moreover, the beaches in this vicinity were studded with steel
rails and well wired; coastal guns of calibers up to fourteen inches
covered the sea approaches—they covered the land approaches,
too, for they were capable of all-around traverse—and promised

terrific losses for any attempted amphibious flanking
In general, it had to be a head-on attack against a stubb

Resistance was very stiff during the first day, par
the Conquet Peninsula and in the Recouvrance area.
northeast of the city gains of up to half a mile were ac
The enemy was using every device at his disposal to i
mum delay. Pillboxes and strongpoints were hotly de
mines and booby traps were used in great numbers. I
time in this area the enemy used miniature tanks, radi
and carrying a charge of high explosives. His air powe
was practically nonexistent, as it was throughout the
Brest. Only two small-scale bombings were recorded
caused neither casualties nor damage.

Rather amusing incidents occured when two of the
air supply missions miscued and resulted in showering
troops with quantities of German rocket ammunitic
codes, and Iron Crosses. It is perhaps appropriate to say
displays were matched in a way when some of our
dropped leaflets intended for the Germans almost dire
2d Division command post.

The Brest operation was really unique in the resp
was the first operation of the Allied armies in northern
be almost completely free of enemy air attack. Figh
American Ninth Air Force were able to carry out
cooperation with the ground forces with practically
ference from enemy interception; the attacking troops
from enemy air attack, particularly the harassing nig
commonly used by the Germans; and, except for a mi
alert personnel, the power of five AA artillery battalions
able in its secondary role to reinforce the infantry-artil

On September 9 and 10 fighting continued along mud
pattern. In the Conquet Peninsula area the 29th Div
gressing in the face of heavy opposition, secured the su
the commanding officer of the troops in this area on t
though the mopping-up met stubborn resistance. Isola
refused to acknowledge their commander's surrender an
as individuals only after another day of fighting, but
10 saw the last enemy cleared from the Conquet Penins
29th Division. In the Recouvrance area, however, th
made little or no advance.

The 2d and 8th Divisions pressed forward, gaining nearly a mile on September 9. They were now well into the built-up area of Brest proper, and their battle became that of destroying a city. The advance which squeezed the life from the encircled fortress was not made down the streets of the city but rather through the buildings, block by block. Pillboxes, positions dug in at intersections, and small embrasures cut in buildings at street level permitted the enemy to sweep the streets with such intense fire as to deny their use to the attacker. The doughboy and engineer teamed to go through the buildings, blasting a path and capturing the defenders from the bottom floor, a houseful at a time. Concrete air-raid shelters were strongly defended and difficult to take. Open spaces such as cemeteries, parks, and railroad yards had to be by-passed because they were covered with crossfire from the surrounding buildings. The Germans also made maximum use of the extensive network of tunnels in the city. They employed them as hospitals, headquarters, and troop shelters, and, in addition, utilized them to facilitate movement of troops from one quarter of the city to another in comparative safety. Slowly, however, and with considerable cost, the German garrison was being strangled.

On September 11 the 2d and the 8th Divisions again pushed ahead with gains up to one-half a mile, while the 29th Division made little or no progress in the Recouvrance sector. In Brest proper the old wall and moat which surrounded the medieval fortress in the center of the city had now been reached. This was a formidable obstacle and it was strongly defended. Initial efforts to scale the wall were repulsed. The ditch or moat was some 45 to 60 feet wide and some 18 to 45 feet deep, and in general followed the contour of the fortress wall. The wall varied from 25 to 45 feet in height. All entrances were blocked and heavily defended. Along the wall and on top of it the enemy was firmly entrenched. Efforts to breach the wall with artillery, including heavy and super-heavy weapons, proved useless. Eight-inch howitzers, 8-inch guns, and 240mm howitzers all had a turn at trying to make a hole for the infantry—but to no avail. Although the upper portion of the wall was breached in several places, the lower part, forming the rear wall of the moat and hence defiladed from direct artillery fire, remained undamaged.

With the Conquet Peninsula cleared and Brest penetrated as far as the old wall it was now decided to withdraw the 8th Division for recommitment on the Crozon Peninsula. There was not sufficient room east of the Penfeld River for two divisions to operate and in addition the establishment of a division on the Crozon Peninsula before Brest fell would insure that no large number of German troops could escape from the city through Crozon, where Task Force A was containing, on order, a strong line of enemy resistence. On the night of September 11-12, therefore, the 8th Division withdrew its lines 1000 yards and prepared to move.

By September 13 the 29th Division had taken over the zone vacated by the 8th Division, and the 8th Division was completing its move to the Crozon Peninsula. The 29th Division also, in spite of continued strong enemy resistence, had taken Forts Keronroux and Portzic, west of the city, and stood before Fort Montbary, the strongest of the strongpoints. The 2d Division was still stopped by the massive wall of the old fortress.

During operations on the Peninsula, SHAEF (Supreme Headquarters, Allied Expeditionary Forces) and 12th Army Group joined in a psychological warfare campaign against the surrounded garrisons. This campaign concentrated on giving the Germans news of the difficulties in their situation on other fronts and of trials and tribulations in the German homeland. The hopelessness of the situation in the various pockets of resistance was stressed. The ground had been prepared, therefore, when on September 13 General Middleton sent Colonel A. R. Reeves, his Assistant Chief of Staff, G-2, as *parlementaire* to General Ramcke, the commanding general of the German forces at Brest, to demand the surrender of the city. General Middleton outlined the German defenders' position as being hopeless, and he urged Ramcke as a professional soldier, to consider the proposal. Even though he must have realized the hopelessness of his position, General Ramcke declined to surrender. General Middleton then addressed an order to all the troops of his command directing that they "enter the fray with renewed vigor; let us take them apart and get the job finished." The facts of the presentation of the demand and General Ramcke's refusal were communicated to the besieged garrison by leaflet and radio.

The next three days saw little progress. The German defense was desperate, and their use of the built-up city was particularly effective. Fort Montbary withstood terrific punishment before it finally capitulated to the 29th Division on the afternoon of the 15th. This old French casemated fort had earth-filled masonry walls 40 feet thick and was surrounded by a moat 40 feet wide and 15 feet deep. Its gun positions, facing to the northwest, were protected by a minefield composed of 300-pound naval shells equipped with pressure igniters. It garrisoned an estimated 200 to 250 troops. Once the infantry reached the sunken road along the western side of the fort they found themselves pinned down, and the reduction of the fort became a problem requiring help for the doughboy. At this point, a British unit equipped with flame-throwing tanks was brought into the battle. On two successive days these tanks flamed the fort, its walls, and the moat, and after exhausting their fuel, remained in position while the crews employed white-phosphorus hand grenades in support of the assault by the infantry. It was a bloody battle and when the garrison finally capitulated, only eighty Germans remained alive to be taken prisoner.

By now the relentless pressure was having a telling effect on the Brest garrison. On September 16 and 17 the artillery maintained continuous fire into an area only 900 yards wide paralleling the waterfront, and into the walled city itself. Although the German antiaircraft guns were now serving as field pieces, the intensity of the enemy artillery fire had diminished considerably. On the Crozon Peninsula the 8th Division had taken over Task Force A and, supported by the principal elements of five battalions of medium and heavy artillery under the attached 34th Field Artillery Brigade, advanced nearly three miles to the west against scattered resistance. The important turn of events came on the 17th, when the enemy situation deteriorated rapidly. During the day the 29th Division broke through the Recouvrance defenses and occupied the entire area west of the Penfeld River. At the same time the 2d Division was able to breach the fortress wall in two places and was pouring its infantry into the old fortress itself. Meanwhile the 8th Division was moving another three miles to the west on the Crozon Peninsula, steadily shrinking the area that the Brest defenders might have hoped to occupy for a last stand.

Brest fell to the forces of the VIII Corps on September 18. On that date the 2d Infantry Division completed the capture of the fortress and cleared the area east of the Penfeld River while the 29th Division completed mopping up in the area west of the river.

Included among the prisoners captured were *Generalmajor* (Brigadier General) Hans von der Mosel, Chief of Staff of the Brest fortress garrison, *Oberst* (Colonel) Hans Kroh, commander of the 2d Parachute Division, and Rear Admiral Kahler of the German Navy.   General Ramcke, the commander, had escaped to the Crozon Peninsula, but it was a precarious future he enjoyed there, for the 8th Infantry Division had cleared the entire peninsula with the exception of a small area known as Pointe des Espagnols. On the 19th the 8th Division finished the job on the Crozon Peninsula, capturing a considerable number of Germans still remaining there, including General Ramcke, and on the next day, September 20, the Brest campaign was wholly completed when a small pocket of resistance on the Pont Croix Peninsula, across the bay to the south of Crozon, was finally eliminated.

Ninth Army's phase of the Brest campaign netted a total of some 28,000 prisoners of war, with an additional 4,000 enemy estimated killed. The total of prisoners captured by VIII Corps during the entire Brest operation, including the period prior to Ninth Army participation, was 37,888. Of this number approximately 20,000 were actual combat troops, including naval personnel; the remainder were civilians who had been put in uniform and armed to assist in the defense. From September 5 through September 20 Ninth Army casualties, incurred almost entirely at Brest, totaled 2,952, including 436 killed and 2,286 wounded.

It was bitterly ironical that the port for which this bloody campaign had been waged was rendered entirely useless in the taking and proved valueless as a port to the Allies throughout the war. In fact, the terrific destruction brought upon Brest by the desperate resistance of its trapped German defenders was the worst suffered by any major city of the invasion up to that date, and left the French nation with the difficult decision as to whether it was even worthwhile to rebuild the city in the same location.

With the surrender of Brest, the Army Surgeon, Colonel William E. Shambora, faced for the first time a medical situation which was to be met again on a larger scale in Germany. On September 18 a preliminary report indicated the presence within the city of 5,500 German wounded. The next day a more complete survey indicated the figures to be 5,982 in Brest and 1,900 in Recouvrance. All sources stressed the deplorable conditions under which these patients were being treated. The majority of the installations were underground and lacked adequate lighting and ventilation. They were damp, grossly overcrowded, and suffered a severe shortage of attending personnel. Outside of Brest there were also large numbers of enemy wounded.

At this time an Army medical clearing company was operating as a holding unit at an air strip at Morlaix, and a Communications Zone field hospital was located at Plestin for casualties to be evacuated by landing craft from St. Michel-en-Grève. (*Map No. 1.*) Patients ready for evacuation to the United Kingdom were transferred to one of these units. All possible Allied personnel were evacuated by air; the remainder and all prisoner of war wounded were evacuated by sea. The air-holding unit had a limited capacity, and when the number of planes arriving was small, as it frequently was, this unit could take no more patients; in order to clear the evacuation hospitals, it was therefore necessary to send Allied personnel to the shore-holding unit. Moreover, evacuation by air was very erratic owing to the frequency of bad weather and to the need for planes in northern France. Landing craft unloading supplies on the beach were utilized for the return of casualties to the United Kingdom, but very few arrived with medical personnel aboard, and the loading was limited by tide and weather. Hospital trains occasionally relieved the situation by transporting the patients from Army hospitals to the more extensive port facilities of Cherbourg.

In spite of the prospective high overload on these medical facilities, all available medical troops and vehicles were marshalled for the rapid removal of the wounded prisoners from the ruined city of Brest to Army evacuation hospitals. Many with minor wounds were treated and sent to the prisoner-of-war inclosures. Within twenty-four hours the census of one enemy hospital had been reduced from 1,184 to 620. The transfer to American military hospitals was accomplished quickly, but the evacuation to the United Kingdom was difficult, and hospitals which were needed elsewhere were immobilized until they could be cleared. But, as a result of intensive efforts to obtain additional trains, vessels, and aircraft, the load was soon reduced. For example, 1,357 casualties, for the most part enemy, were evacuated on September 24. By the same date only forty patients remained in Brest, and these were in such condition that they could not be moved.

During the operations in Brittany the Army operated two

cemeteries at St. James, north of Rennes—one for American and Allied dead, the other for enemy dead. An additional enemy cemetery was located at Lesneven, near Brest. These cemeteries were transferred to Army control on September 9, and were operated until September 30, when they became a responsibility of Normandy Base Section of Communications Zone. During this period 1,457 Americans, 41 Allied, and 314 enemy were buried. Of the 1,498 Americans and Allies, only some four hundred were killed during the Brest operation. The others were disinterments of isolated burials or bodies recovered subsequent to the breakthrough at St. Lô and the fast-moving operations through the Brittany Peninsula.

Although the number of all types of casualties was relatively small during the Army's operations in Brittany, prior planning for the establishment of a rapid and accurate system of casualty reporting proved itself in this initial operation of the Army and in all later operations when the Army became much larger and casualties more numerous. In view of the great importance of accurate and prompt reports, a casualty division had been established by Colonel John A. Klein, the Army Adjutant General, immediately upon arrival of the headquarters in the United Kingdom. Since War Department tables of organization failed to provide for the establishment of such a division, a small cadre was drawn from personnel of other divisions of the Adjutant General's Section. It was not practicable to augment this cadre prior to departure from the United Kingdom, and the division had to be expanded, trained and operated simultaneously with the beginning of tactical operations of the Army in France.

No training or instruction in the United States even remotely covered the practical aspects of casualty reporting. The casualty division began the task of studying the directives and procedures used by other headquarters actively engaged in combat. At the time the Army Headquarters arrived in the United Kingdom the casualty division of First Army had not joined its forward elements on the Continent, and this permitted observation of procedures prior to its departure. Procedures used in the casualty division at Theater Headquarters were likewise studied, and an officer was placed on temporary duty with Third Army on the Continent to obtain practical experience.

Upon the basis of these studies, a casualty reporting directive was prepared in great detail, since most of the units which would be assigned to Ninth Army would not have had previous casualty reporting experience. Personnel of division and corps headquarters directly concerned with processing casualty reports were ordered to Army Headquarters for instruction and orientation. They were then authorized to work with casualty divisions of similar headquarters which had been committed to action for some time.

A gain of one day in casualty reporting was achieved by departing from the usual channels of communication and by-passing corps headquarters, except for corps troops, in the processing of reports. This system relieved the corps headquarters of an administrative burden and, in view of frequent changes of assignment of divisions, not only between armies but between corps, permitted a more uniform operating procedure and obviated transfers of casualty card files between corps machine-records units.

The first casualty report processed and submitted by Ninth Army to Theater Headquarters was handled in record time. As the casualty division gained more experience, the average time lag (from date of incurrence of casualty to date of receipt of the report at Theater Headquarters) was still further reduced until an average of six days was attained for the entire period of operations of the Army in Europe. Many reports reached Theater Headquarters within a period as short as four days.

Considerable regrouping of forces took place during the few weeks that Ninth Army operated on the Brittany Peninsula. In the first place, upon assuming command of the zone on September 5 General Simpson perceived the difficult situation faced by General Middelton, the VIII Corps commander. The situation which had faced General Patton, commanding Third Army, and which was the cause of Ninth Army's introduction into operations— that is, the responsibility of fighting two separate battles—was repeated on a smaller scale in the case of the VIII Corps. General Middleton, with three divisions and supporting troops, was fighting the battle of Brest, his chief mission, and concurrently he had command of two other divisions and the responsibility of protecting some 310 miles along the southern flank. Therefore, on September 10, General Simpson transferred the 6th Armored Division and the 83d Infantry Division from VIII Corps and placed them directly under Army control. This permitted VIII Corps to devote its entire energies to completing quickly the battle for Brest.

Almost immediately instructions were received from 12th Army Group which required further regrouping of forces. The tempo of the battles in the east, where First and Third Armies were pressing their advance, and the rapid progress of the Seventh Army moving up the Rhône Valley from the south, created an opportune situation whose possibilities would be enhanced if more troops could be made available from the Brittany area. Twelfth Army Group therefore issued instructions that both the 6th Armored Division and the 83d Infantry Division were to be released to Third Army at the earliest possible date and that these divisions would be moved with all haste to their new command. Ninth Army reacted quickly to this directive and released Combat Command B of the 6th Armored Division to Third Army on September 11. On the same date 12th Army Group further strengthened Third Army's power by relieving it of the responsibility of flank protection along the eighty mile stretch between Orléans and Auxerre and turning over this mission to Ninth Army. (*Map No. 1.*) The extension of the boundary spread Ninth Army forces very thin along the southern flank. However, the nature of the enemy troops to the south and their scattered dispositions made this risk well worth taking in order to strengthen Allied offensive power further to the east. To replace the 6th Armored Division, Ninth Army on September 11 issued instructions to the 94th Infantry Division, commanded by Major General Harry J. Malony, which was then en route from the United Kingdom to France, to accelerate its movement and proceed from the beaches directly to positions containing Lorient and St. Nazaire.

By this time the Army had been informed by 12th Army Group that the German pockets of resistance at Lorient, St. Nazaire, and south of the Loire were not to be the object of any aggressive offensive action. Plans had been developed for the reduction of both Lorient and St. Nazaire, but it was considered much more economical in troops merely to contain these pockets, thus permitting stronger concentration of forces for the campaign into Germany. It was estimated that some 15,000 troops were contained in the Lorient pocket and another 10,000 in the St. Nazaire area. Both of these forces, as well as a third pocket in the vicinity of Pointe de Grave, northwest of Bordeaux, remained holed up until the end of the war. The troops garrisoning these German "islands of resistance" provided an interesting conglomeration of assorted services. German army, navy, antiaircraft, and air corps personnel, under army officers and noncommissioned officers, made up the bulk of the strength. Some deserters captured by American forces proved to be Russians and Poles—strange bedfellows! The activities of the pockets contained by Ninth Army were largely confined to minor patrolling and light harassing artillery fire. Never did these German forces make any serious coordinated effort to break out.

Progressive relief of the 6th Armored Division continued, with the relieved elements moving east and assembling in the vicinity of Auxerre as elements of the 94th moved in from the beaches. By September 16th the 94th Infantry Division had taken over the responsibility for containing the enemy garrison at Lorient and of patrolling and securing the Army south flank from Quimper to Redon. At 2:00 P.M. on that date the 6th Armored Division passed to the control of Third Army. Regrouping continued as the 94th Infantry Division extended to the east in order to relieve the 83d Infantry Division. By September 22 the 83d Infantry Division was assembling at Montargis, and it began its move east on the 23d. The 94th Infantry Division completely relieved the 83d, and this one division was now protecting the entire south flank over a distance of almost four hundred miles!

In accomplishing his far-flung containing and security mission, General Malony, commanding the 94th Division, made highly effective use of the various elements of the Resistance movement and the French Forces of the Interior in his area. These comprised the equivalent of a division in strength and were armed with all varieties of small-caliber weapons of German, French, Russian, Czech, and miscellaneous manufacture. General Malony had served extensively in France during World War I and spoke French fluently, as did many members of his staff. He quickly established close cooperation with the French forces, assumed responsibility for furnishing them the major portion of their supplies, and integrated their elements into his own sector commands. Soon some of the French were even wearing the shoulder patch of the 94th Division. Through these energetic and tactful measures and with the fine cooperation of the French, the south flank security mission was accomplished with maximum economy of troops.

The 94th Division found numerous occasions when air support would prove beneficial. The difficulties of air cooperation in this area, when the main battle of Europe was rapidly moving hundreds of miles to the northeast, have already been mentioned. In an effort to provide additional air support, Ninth Army accepted the services of a French squadron of medium bombers under the command of *Commandant* (Major) Jean Lagoir. Lagoir and his unit, which he called *Groupe Patrie,* had seen service during the campaign in North Africa and were anxious to continue the fight against the Germans on the soil of France. Acceptance of the support of *Groupe Patrie* involved acceptance of accompanying problems, for there were difficulties in securing proper airfields, adequate spare parts, and supplies, and in administering a unit which had no definite organizational position. It was not until October 5, after Ninth Army Headquarters had moved from the Brittany Peninsula, that *Groupe Patrie* became fully operational. Then, weather permitting, it flew one mission per day in support of the south flank security forces. Generally, its targets were spotted by agents of the French Forces of the Interior operating in enemy territory, and considerable time was spent in studying targets and planning the attack upon them. If possible, a French agent was posted near the target during the bombing to report upon the results obtained. The targets consisted mainly of ferry boats and landing sites, railroad trains, and enemy installations such as command posts and troop barracks. Its elaborate and time-consuming pre-attack measures were taken in an effort to conserve the limited supplies of gasoline and bombs available to this irregular force. It carried on until November, when the squadron joined the French forces on the Western Front. The activities of *Groupe Patrie* were typical of the patriotic efforts of the French and the expedients they used to combat the enemy.

In general, all Ninth Army supply activities during the Brest campaign were greatly influenced by the same factors that made the reduction of Brest so important—the need for a major port to supply the vast American invasion forces and, in the absence of adequate port facilities, the necessity for continuing the use of beaches in lieu of ports. Coupled with this was the spiraling transportation problem; time had not permitted the full rehabilitation of the bomb-shattered French railway system, and the other two armies of 12th Army Group, now racing for the German border, had first call on truck transportation and gasoline —and, indeed, on most supplies coming in over the beaches. For example, certain quartermaster supplies, under Colonel William E. Goe, the Army Quartermaster, were received at the Army railhead at Landivisiau, where they had been delivered from depots of the Normandy Base Section, Communications Zone, over rails operated by the French authorities. Railways in Brittany, however, had not been rehabilitated fully, and it was necessary to supplement the flow of quartermaster supplies into the Brest area by the employment of direct barge and landing-craft shipments from England to the Morlaix beaches. This expedient resulted, as it had in ammunition, in unbalanced quartermaster supplies—rations, clothing, and equipage—since the supplies were originally intended for Base Section depot stocks and often were not appropriate to the requirements of the Brest campaign. The resulting surplus stocks of unbalanced quartermaster supplies in the Brest area were later moved by motor and rail to the Army's new area in southern Belgium.

For the immediate and pressing needs of the Army in the reduction of Brest, however, beachhead supply did work, and most successfully. In quartermaster supplies the following quantities were issued and consumed during the period September 5 to October 1; 3,271,943 rations, representing 9,599 tons; 1,095,-965 gallons of gasoline, representing 6,860 tons; and 29,011 gallons of Diesel oil, representing 115 tons. To provide every possible drop of gasoline for the fast movement of First and Third Armies, it was necessary to limit Ninth Army consumption to an absolute minimum. During the major portion of the operations in Brittany, rations issued were the "operational" or "canned" types—C, K, and 10-in-1, the latter a combination package designed for feeding ten individuals. However, considerable quantities of type B ration—involving more palatable food components—were received and issued during the latter part of September. The nutritional and morale value of the type B ration was greatly enhanced by the introduction of fresh meats and butter, for by this time sufficient perishable meat components were in the "pipeline" (as the system of automatic continous supply came to be called) to permit the issue of a minimum of one fresh meat component daily.

Signal supplies were being provided VIII Corps by the Brittany Base Section of Communications Zone when the Ninth Army arrived, although the quantity was insufficient and many items were not available. The Army took over the operation of a signal supply depot at Lesneven with the stock previously placed there by Brittany Base Section and immediately opened a signal depot at Rennes to begin accumulation of stocks to support further operations. Since the only source of material was on the Normandy beaches and there was little or no transportation available, truck convoys were arranged by requiring each signal corps unit to send all trucks available to haul the supplies. Trips were arranged as often as a convoy could be assembled, and an Army representative remained at the beaches to locate the supplies and obtain the necessary releases from the Communications Zone. Arrangements were under way to have signal supplies landed on the Morlaix beaches, but these were canceled upon the fall of Brest and the subsequent move to the east.

Captured stocks, especially engineer supplies, did much to alleviate critical shortages in the Brest campaign, and electrical supplies captured in the Brest area were of use in later campaigns. German demolition supplies were uncovered in considerable quantities throughout the Peninsula. The French Forces of the Interior, working in conjunction with service troops, assisted materially in locating and securing abandoned German matériel and equipment.

Units had no serious shortage of weapons and vehicles in the battle for Brest, but there were few replacements for battle losses. This shortage of replacement items did not affect the final outcome of the battle, but necessitated refitting the organizations later when they were moved to the east. Ordnance repair parts were obtained from the basic load of one ordnance medium maintenance company and the depleted stock of one depot company, which had been supporting the VIII Corps. Ninth Army had low supply priority on parts and vehicles, because of the pressing needs of the First and Third Armies, and the base depots of Communications Zone were not yet sufficiently organized to be of any assistance. These supplies were coming over the beaches slowly, and their warehousing and issue were progressing even more slowly.

In establishing adequate signal communications Colonel Joe J. Miller, the Army Signal Officer, had one of the most interesting as well as difficult problems at the outset of Ninth Army's operational period. 12th Army Group and VIII Corps Headquarters were located in opposite directions from Army Headquarters near Rennes. 12th Army Group Headquarters was at Versailles, some 200 miles to the east. VIII Corps Headquarters was near Lesneven, some 130 miles to the west, and along the routes connecting Rennes and Lesneven there was almost complete destruction of existing wire and cable facilities. Aggravating this condition was the fact that signal supplies were among the most critical shortages existing in the Theater and little priority could be given to a newly established army operating on a comparatively secondary front. However, communications between Army and VIII Corps had to be established quickly if the Brest campaign was to be brought to an early conclusion.

Rehabilitation of an existing damaged underground German military cable was chosen as the best possible solution. The principal difficulty was that the cable was made of aluminum conductors, not commonly used for communication purposes in the United States, and presented technical difficulties in the soldering or welding of splices. Local French telephone officials stated that a "secret powder" for welding the aluminum conductors was used by the Germans and that they expected to have some of it soon. In the meantime, investigation was begun in the proper method of aluminum welding. It was discovered that ordinary welding technique could be adapted to repairing the cable, and this proved to be completely effective, using a standard aluminum soldering flux, stored and issued by our Ordnance Department— the equivalent of the German "secret powder." VIII Corps already was operating a section of the cable from Pontivy to Lesneven, and Army cable-splicing teams were now dispatched to locate and repair all interruptions between Pontivy and Rennes.

From the beginning the utmost help and cooperation were received from civilians and from French Forces of the Interior. The Resistance forces had interrupted the cable in many places after the Normandy invasion, and in some towns the cable-repair teams were able to locate the persons who had caused the damage, and were shown where to make the repairs. Civilians and resistance members pointed out places where the Germans had planted mines to prevent sabotage. Where formerly men and women of the resistance movement had crept in the dark of night at risk of their own lives and those of their families to sabotage the German military cable, the patriots now led American signalmen to the same spots to repair the breaks. Within two days, and before the renewed attack on Brest jumped off on September 8, seventy-two temporary splices had been made, and the cable was in service, providing reliable teletype and telephone communication to the VIII Corps, as well as to the 6th Armored Division near Lorient.

Equally perplexing was the problem of establishing proper communications with 12th Army Group Headquarters, some 200 miles away at Versailles. It was not until September 8 that the first telephone circuit to 12th Army Group was established. While this circuit was maintained the remainder of the time the Army was in Brittany, it was in trouble approximately fifty per cent of the time because of the long distance, hasty repairs, and maintenance by French civilians, who could not understand the necessity for full-time communications. The first teletype circuit from 12th Army Group, established after the Army advance detachment had departed for the new headquarters site in Belgium, suffered from the same maintenance difficulties as the telephone line. It was in service only ten percent of the time. In the meantime motor messenger service, operating over 200 miles of poor and heavily congested roads to Versailles and taking approximately ten hours to make a one-way trip, provided the only sure, all-weather communication between Ninth Army and 12th Army Group Headquarters. This messenger service was operated by the Army, since 12th Army Group did not have sufficient personnel to assume the responsibility.

While the battle for Brest and the establishment of a firm guard along the 12th Army Group south boundary progressed, Ninth Army was conducting another "operation" which, although not spectacular, played a vital part in the future winning of the war. The Army was charged with the responsibility for the reception, processing, and training of all units arriving in western France which would eventually be assigned to any one of the field armies of 12th Army Group. III Corps Headquarters, under command of Major General John Millikin, was established on the Cherbourg Peninsula and on September 5 was assigned the mission of conducting the program under Army direction. Additional major units assigned to the Army for processing under this program included the XVI Corps, the 26th, 44th, 84th, 95th, 99th, 102d, and 104th Infantry Divisions, and the 9th, 10th, 11th, and 12th Armored Divisions.

In addition, a large number of incoming supporting combat and service troops were under the Army's command for processing. Army supply agencies and the logistical staff faced a particularly complicated situation, since many of the units still were arriving in Europe via the United Kingdom, thereby requiring the Army to function on both sides of the English Channel. XIII Corps Headquarters, augmented by some personnel from Ninth Army Headquarters, already had been charged with the responsibility of receiving, processing, and training all units staging in the United Kingdom en route to the Continent. Moreover, on the Continent, Communications Zone had assumed area responsibility for a major portion of the Brittany Peninsula, which under normal operating conditions would have been the Army area. Communications Zone installations were thus supplying and maintaining the forces besieging Brest and protecting the Allied southern flank. They continued to do so as the Army assumed command, and thereby decreased the heavy logistical burden necessarily shouldered by the new operational army. Communications Zone facilities, however, were operating under the same supply difficulties as was Ninth Army, and were able to furnish very litle ordnance equipment and parts and no ordnance maintenance support.

Moreover, the extremely wide front occupied by units along the Loire River required an abnormal dispersion of supplies. Communication equipment, particularly field wire, was needed there in large quantities. Also, to supplement basic ammunition loads in case of sudden need, an additional unit of fire of ammunition was required for stock-piling along the Loire, where it would be readily available. There was available only one ordnance medium maintenance company to support the 94th Division over its front of nearly four hundred miles, and no additional shop maintenance facilities were available either in the Army or in the Communications Zone.

After the Normandy breakthrough the unexpected lightning progress of First and Third Armies across France and into Germany developed a situation which had a direct influence on Ninth

Army's role in the war. Repair of rail facilities, particularly the rail bridges destroyed by the Germans as they retreated, could not hope to keep pace with the advancing armies. In order that the operations might not be stalled by the lack of supplies, chiefly gasoline and ammunition, a typical American institution was established. The famed Red Ball Express, a truck supply organization operated by Communications Zone, was instituted in the middle of September and continued for some six weeks until rail facilities had been rehabilitated and the attacking armies had come to a halt in front of the German Siegfried Line. It operated cargo trucks day and night over highways restricted to its use. Acting quickly upon 12th Army Group's instructions, Ninth Army provided cargo trucks, personnel, and housekeeping detachments to assist in the operation of this truck line, by stripping the 26th, 95th, and 104th Infantry Divisions of their organic 2½-ton trucks and by withdrawing fifteen hundred additional trucks of similar capacity from field artillery, tank destroyer, and antiaircraft units to form a total of forty-two provisional truck companies. The units furnishing the trucks were, of course, thereby immobilized, and temporarily they could only bivouac, maintain themselves on a minimum scale, and conduct an abbreviated training program.

From a purely Ninth Army viewpoint, this emergency measure imposed a severe handicap upon the reception, equipping, and processing of units slated for its operational command in the future, but from a broader point of view it provided the only means of delivering the supplies needed by the attacking armies to maintain the impetus of the offensive, and hence it played an important part in the over-all campaign against Germany. The general Ninth Army supply situation, already in difficult straits, was further aggravated by this stripping of unit transportation, and during this period supplies which arrived at the beaches had to be left there for lack of trucks to haul them to Army depots. The rapid organization of provisional truck companies which formed part of the Red Ball Express was, however, a worthy accomplishment in the Army's history, and the entire Red Ball Express system was a unique chapter in the annals of warfare.

Concurrently with the battle for Brest, there occurred an incident, unusual in military history, and so interesting in its detail that it is recounted here at some length. On September 9, the day after the renewal of the Brest attack, word was received from the 83d Infantry Division that a German force of some 20,000, located south of the Loire River, was desirous of surrendering to American forces. The events leading up to this bloodless victory were unknown to Ninth Army at the time. Subsequent information brought out the story. (*Map No. 1.*)

Soon after the landings of Allied forces in southern France, when the Seventh Army started its sweep northward to join the Third Army, the Germans began to realize the precarious situation into which their troops in southwestern France were being forced. They decided to evacuate the area in an orderly fashion and move toward Germany. The machinery for the evacuation was organized by an order of the German LXIV Infantry Corps on August 18. In an effort to maintain high morale, the order was worded so as to make the withdrawal seem to be a military operation to clear the Tours–Bourges–Montlucon–Périgueux area of all resistance. All German troops and civilians, with the exception of two garrisons to be left behind to cover the rear, were to take part in the "campaign." This massive and unwieldy collection of units and individuals was formed into three major groupings: Group South, Group Middle, and Group North.

The order activating the groups assigned them to specific areas and indicated their march routes. Group South was to assemble north of Bordeaux, Group Middle north of Angoulême, and Group North immediately north and east of Poitiers. The order also set up a security detachment to provide reconnaissance and flank protection for the columns on their trek homeward. All equipment and supplies that could not be transported with the march groups were ordered destroyed according to a detailed plan of demolitions. Original plans called for the security unit to proceed to the sector south and southeast of Orléans and clear it for Group North, which planned to establish a holding force there. As soon as this had been carried out, the other two groups were to start their move, going by way of Bordeaux, Angoulême, Poitiers, and Châteauroux.

The first part of the plan was carried out as directed. The security detachment moved to a sector below Orléans, and Group North established a defensive position on an arc bisected by Tours and Poitiers. Meanwhile, however, the American armies were gradually closing the gap through which the German units had planned to pass, and a change in plan and formations was necessary. Accordingly, new orders were issued on August 27, calling for a subdivision of the groups into units of fast-moving vehicles, slow-moving vehicles, and foot elements. The first two units were to consist of combat troops, and the last one, was to consist of civilians and men not fit for combat; their food and ammunition were to be carried in horse-drawn carts and wagons. The three march groups attempted to carry out these instructions while moving, but a naval group, which had attached itself to Group South, did not receive its orders in time. As a result, its vehicles were never turned over to the motorized units.

New plans made on August 28 called for the abandonment of the original march groups and the formation of two motorized serials and one foot column. This latter organization adopted the name of Foot March Group South and was under the command of Brigadier General Botho Henning Elster. General Elster's group, moving as rapidly as possible to reach the Loire River before it was cut off, arrived at Poitiers on September 3, 1944. Two days later, no longer in contact with the motorized elements, the group was strung out along the route between Poitiers and Châteauroux. In this vulnerable position, the column suffered two air attacks which caused numerous casualties and severe damage to supplies and ammunition. It was also subjected to incessant harassing action by the French Forces of the Interior and French civilians. Abandoned by the first two serials, without communications and without supplies, and faced with the prospect of more determined Allied action, General Elster decided that it would be futile to continue the march.

During this same period the 83d Infantry Division was covering an area north of the Loire from the mouth of the river to Orléans. Operations did not extend beyond the south bank of the river, but patrols were constantly being sent across the river to reconnoiter the German positions. During the first few days of September, the Intelligence and Reconnaisance Platoon of the 329th Infantry, under the command of Lieutenant Samuel W. Magill, slipped south of the Loire and made contact with members of the FFI who had been harassing General Elster's column. These French Forces of the Interior reported that Foot March Group South was in the vicinity of Issoudun and would probably consider terms of surrender if approached by the Americans.

Lieutenant Magill made contact with General Elster at Châteauroux. The General wanted to surrender, but he requested a token battle, by way of easing his conscience. He asked the Americans to prove that there were at least two Allied battalions south of the Loire River. At this particular time, there were only eighteen regular Allied soldiers within seventy miles of the Germans, but the Americans convinced General Elster that unless he surrendered, Foot March Group South would be bombed out of existence. The General decided to capitulate and said he would meet Allied officers in Issoudun on the afternoon of September 10.

When General Macon, commanding the 83d Division, was informed of the situation, the XIX Tactical Air Command was requested to fly a mission, prepared to bomb and strafe on panel signal, over Issoudun at 2:00 P.M. on September 10. General Macon personally presented surrender terms to General Elster at the German headquarters on September 10. General Elster was ordered to stop the movement of his column out of the Châteauroux–Allier River territory, to withdraw his troops between the Allier and the Loire, and to proceed to the Beaugency Bridge where the formal surrender would take place. His men were to be permitted to retain all their arms and equipment until they reached the north bank of the river. While the conference was in session, planes of the XIX Tactical Air Command flew overhead as requested, and General Elster, who had been hesitating over terms, quickly turned to acceptance.

The terms further provided for the movement of the Germans north to the Loire River in three columns—one to Orléans, one to Beaugency, and one to Mer. The northwest movement of the three columns began as scheduled on the morning of September 13. Minor incidents of clashes with French Forces were reported, but no serious accidents or disorder resulted.

On Saturday, September 16, General Elster formally surrendered himself and his command in a brief ceremony at the Beaugency Bridge to General Macon, who represented General Simpson. By 8:30 on the following morning all three German columns, totalling 754 officers, 18,850 men, and 10 women, had passed into the hastily constructed prisoner-of-war inclosures erected just north of the Loire River. The fabulous tale of General Elster and his 20,000 Germans was completed.

The first casualty in Ninth Army Headquarters occurred in

connection with the surrender of General Elster's forces. Lieutenant Colonel William M. Spinrad, Ordnance Department, who was Chief of the Technical Sub-Section of the Army Ordnance Section, proceeded to Beaugency to supervise the taking over of ordnance equipment surrendered by General Elster's forces. On the night of September 22, Colonel Spinrad was having dinner in a hotel in Beaugency when seven shots were fired through an opaque-glass window of the dining room. Colonel Spinrad was killed instantly by bullets from a German pistol in the hands of an unknown person. A complete investigation revealed no trace of the assailant—presumably a German sympathizer or collaborationist taking blind revenge, or an enemy soldier who had remained concealed when the tide of battle passed.

As General Elster's command was fading out of the war, an unconfirmed report was received that some 15,000 German troops located in the vicinity of Pointe-de-Grave, northwest of Bordeaux, were desirous of surrendering to American forces. Sensing the possibility of another mass surrender, the Army Commander directed that an intelligence officer from his headquarters make contact with the organization reputedly willing to surrender. The German force involved was denying the Allies the use of the harbors of Royan and Bordeaux, and hence its capitulation would be extremely welcome. Lieutenant Colonel Arthur E. Sutherland, Jr., performed the hazardous journey to Bordeaux. After preliminary negotiation he arranged a meeting at a château near the village of St. Vivien on the afternoon of September 24. A week previously, negotiations had been undertaken by French patriots to obtain the surrender of this force, and the German officer in command at that time had indicated willingness to capitulate. In Colonel Sutherland's negotiations, however, a new commander appeared, an ardent Nazi replacement for the one who had been willing to surrender. The new commander stated that he was under orders to hold his position to the last. He unqualifiedly and definitely refused to entertain any suggestion of surrender. The prospect of another bloodless victory faded, and negotations were finally abandoned. The German force remained, and control of the port of Bordeaux was denied the Allies until the very end of hostilities.

With Brest reduced, General Elster's ragged forces interned, and final disposition of the forces made for the protection of the south flank, Ninth Army's work on the Brittany Peninsula was all but finished. Civil Affairs Detachments were dispatched to render assistance to French Government officials in the re-establishment of their communities after the years of German occupation. Critical items such as food and soap were distributed to the civil population, as well as Diesel oil to operate small power plants in an effort to restore some of the normal life of the communities. Prompt action was necessary in several instances to prevent the spread of sporadic outbreaks of typhoid, paratyphoid, and diphtheria. There were also several cases of anthrax discovered in humans and animals in the Brest area. Medical supplies were made available to the French public-health officials, who carried out group immunization, isolation, and hospitalization under supervision of Ninth Army. Rehabilitation of public utilities, restoration of a free press and radio, and assistance in the re-establishment of local government were welcomed by the French officials who bore the great responsibility of restoring liberated France.

On September 24, 12th Army Group issued a letter of instructions which included orders to Ninth Army to move the VIII Corps to positions in Belgium–Luxembourg between the first and Third Armies generally along the Siegfried Line. Army Headquarters was to be moved to the new area when necessity demanded it. The 29th Division was assigned to the First Army and was to be dispatched prior to the movement of other VIII Corps troops in order to bolster the American penetration of the German frontier north of Aachen. It will be recalled that in its initial instructions of September 5, 12th Army Group had directed that Ninth Army "prepare for further action to the east and on the right (south) flank of Third Army." Now the mission was changed to direct the Army's planning efforts to the area between St. Vith on the north and Metz on the south between First and Third Armies. (*Map No. 3.*)

The first great problem was the movement of troops to the new zone of action. When Brest fell on September 18, there were some 80,000 United States troops in the Brittany Peninsula. The movement of some of these already had been accomplished and the remainder now must be dispatched. In addition to the VIII Corps troops in the Brittany Peninsula, a concentration of service troops had been established in the Fontainebleau Forest south of

Paris, and sixteen battalions of reinforcing artillery and tank destroyer units had been concentrated on the site of the French artillery range at Coëtquidan, southwest of Rennes. These troops, too, were to be moved northeast. Complicating the movement problem, particularly in the case of heavy artillery, was the lack of rail facilities and tank transporters. It was imperative that one of these two means be used to transport the heavy tractor prime movers or a prohibitive wear of the tracks of the vehicles would be incurred. Some full-track prime movers already sent over the roads had had practically one hundred percent track failures. Some units with this particular equipment had to be left behind for several weeks before they could join the Army in its new area.

Another problem requiring special measures was the large stock of ammunition left over from the battle of Brest. It will be recalled that less than a month earlier the lack of sufficient ammunition had held up the attack against Brest. Once the flow of ammunition began, it could not be cut off quickly and easily, and as a result nearly 25,000 tons remained in the Brittany area. By utilizing provisional truck companies formed from artillery units, and by increasing the organic ammunition load of each artillery organization, some 12,000 tons were taken by Ninth Army to its new area of operation. In addition, several thousand troops and some 2,500 tons of miscellaneous supplies and equipment were moved by provisional truck companies. Two to three round trips of 1,000 to 1,200 miles were required to complete the movements. Unit maintenance facilities were unable to keep abreast of maintenance services required for such continous operations over such great distances. Ordnance maintenance companies took over the maintenance job, and 600 trucks were serviced in three days, so that the units from which the provisional truck companies were formed could be able to move promptly when needed to the Army's new combat area.

The 29th Infantry Division began moving to First Army on September 24. VIII Corps troops followed immediately, and on September 26, VIII Corps Headquarters initiated its movement to Bastogne, then just another town in southeastern Belgium but later to become the scene of one of the war's most heroic battles. On September 29, Ninth Army Headquarters began moving to its new command post at Arlon, Belgium.

Ninth Army's first chapter of battle experience was ended.

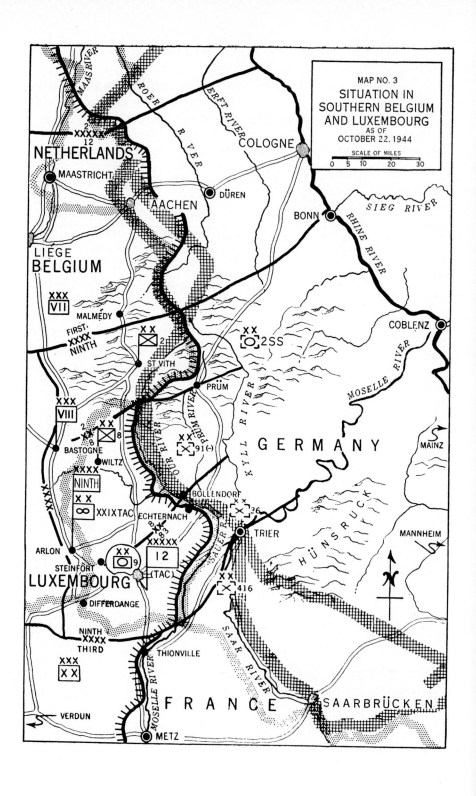

MAP NO. 3

SITUATION IN
SOUTHERN BELGIUM
AND LUXEMBOURG
AS OF
OCTOBER 22. 1944

SCALE OF MILES

0 5 10   20   30

CHAPTER 3
THE NOVEMBER OFFENSIVE

NINTH Army Headquarters opened in Arlon, Belgium, on October 2. (*Map No. 3.*) A location in the larger and more commodious city of Luxembourg had attracted the Army Commander, for he had served in the Grand Duchy during World War I, but Luxembourg was less suitably located for communications and travel in the new Army sector. Since the lateral roads through the city were not secure, on a front often held only by a thin line of patrols, all north and south movement had to be made over the road net centering on Arlon, some fifteen miles to the rear. Later, the Tactical Headquarters of 12th Army Group was established at Luxembourg.

The site of the new Army command post was l'Ecole Normale, a large building which had originally been a teachers' college, but which had been turned into a hospital by the Germans. It had been left indescribably dirty when they abandoned it in their hasty retreat; scattered debris and clogged-up plumbing presented a minor rehabilitation project for the headquarters personnel. Incessant rains, which mired the roads and parking places throughout the area, did nothing to decrease the difficulties of opening the new command post and of maintaining contact with elements still hundreds of miles to the rear. A considerable portion of the Army Headquarters was still functioning more than 400 miles away at Rennes. It had been necessary to leave staff personnel in Brittany to supervise the movement of the remaining units from that area to the east and to complete the execution of Ninth Army responsibilities there. For most of October the Army Headquarters carried on as a split entity. Before the month was out, portions of the Army were simultaneously operating in five different countries—France, Belgium, Luxembourg, Netherlands, and Germany.

These widespread operations brought obvious complications. In particular, communications between Arlon and Rennes were extremely difficult and never completely reliable, since the entire route of electrical communications was through 12th Army Group and Communications Zone areas and their efforts were directed to higher priority tasks. The Army furnished messenger service between the two echelons daily by arranging for couriers to meet in Paris, thus making a round trip each day. Communication difficulties at Arlon were further reduced by Ninth Army's initial tactical use of a new type of radio commonly known as VHF (Very High Frequency). This highly specialized radio, operating in conjunction with a regular wire-carrier system, was designed to transmit two telephone conversations and four teletype, messages simultaneously on one radio channel. Telephone calls were routed over the radio by the operators at the Army switchboard. The familiar warning of the operator, "This is a radio circuit; your conversation is subject to interception," became well known to Army and subordinate staff personnel. It was originally anticipated that VHF radio would be used only to supplement the normal wire lines. However, it proved so reliable and convenient that it was soon accepted as an independent means of communications in itself, and it became standard procedure to have parallel wire and VHF facilities available on every major communication link. The VHF radio link proved its worth in October at Arlon, when it provided for a considerable period the only means of communication over a vital line.

On October 4 the relief of First Army units by elements of VIII Corps having progressed satisfactorily, Ninth Army assumed responsibility for the sector generally between Bollendorf and St. Vith. (*Map No. 3.*) Initially in its new area Ninth Army was a very small army indeed. From the Brest operation it had brought its one Corps, the VIII, now reduced in size to two infantry divisions, the 2d and the 8th, with a correspondingly small number of supporting troops. The 94th Infantry Division, which was responsible for protecting 12th Army Group's south flank, remained under Army control until October 9, when it passed to direct control of the Army Group.

The Army's main mission now was to build up its forces in the Luxembourg–Southern Belgium area so that it could increase the frontage of its sector, thereby relieving both First and Third Armies of defensive responsibilities and permitting them to concentrate their forces on narrow fronts for offensive action. Ninth Army, too, was to build up an offensive striking force from units arriving at the beaches and ports of western France. The program of increasing the Army's strength began promptly. XIII Corps

Headquarters, by now in an assembly area in Normandy, was ordered to be prepared to move east on Army orders and progressively to relieve units of VIII Corps and Third Army as far south as Metz as soon as additional divisions and the supplies to maintain them could be furnished. Advance parties of this corps moved from Normandy to the new front and began reconnaissance to carry out the orders.

III Corps continued its mission of receiving troops arriving on the Continent from the United Kingdom and from the United States, and the XVI Corps, most recently arrived, under command of Major General John B. Anderson, was alerted to be prepared to take over the mission of III Corps. By October 10 the exchange had been effected and III Corps was then transferred to Third Army. XVI Corps Headquarters remained on the Normandy Peninsula to execute the troop-processing mission until November 30, when it moved to Tongres, Belgium, and the Communications Zone assumed responsibility for the reception of troops.

On October 12 the 83d Infantry Division, formerly holding the line of the Loire River and subsequently under Third Army command, came back to Ninth Army when the boundary between the two armies was moved south to include the area currently occupied by the division. The 9th Armored Division, as yet uncommitted in combat, began moving from Normandy to just north of the city of Luxembourg. A portion of the division was to take its place in the line under command of VIII Corps, and the remainder was to constitute a previously unavailable mobile reserve to counter any German attack in the thinly held sector, where, in fact, the Germans did later launch their Ardennes counteroffensive. By the time the Army relinquished this front, late in October, it had three infantry divisions in the line over a ninety-mile front, with elements of one armored division backing them up and the remainder of the armored division en route.

The concentration, build-up, and operation of these forces were greatly handicapped by the factor that was adversely affecting all Allied forces on the Western Front—the extreme shortage of transportation facilities and, hence, of supplies. The railroads of France, severely damaged at critical points by the retreating German forces, remained largely inoperative despite almost superhuman engineer efforts to repair them. Destroyed bridges created the principal bottlenecks, but in many cases marshalling yards and switching and railroad signal facilities were so severely damaged as to prohibit operation. Added to these was the extreme scarcity of all types of rolling stock.

The only recourse was to use truck transportation, and as a result the trucks themselves soon became scarce. The Red Ball Express program and the part it played in delivering supplies to the advancing armies has already been described, but there was a penalty to be paid for the advantage thus gained. The wear and tear on trucks was extremely high. Ninth Army, operating in the center of the front, had but five truck companies assigned, a total of some 250 trucks. Of these almost fifty per cent were in such condition from hard usage that they had to be declared inoperative upon assignment, in order to permit maintenance personnel to restore them. In one instance, for example, a single truck company coming under Ninth Army control had but eleven serviceable trucks out of its normal strength of fifty. Spare parts, tires, and tubes became scarce items and they, too, had to be transported from the shores of western France to the Army area. Again Ninth Army, as it had in Brittany, formed provisional truck companies utilizing the trucks of army and corps troops awaiting operational assignment. The employment of these provisional truck companies greatly increased truck wear, and it was necessary to assign five ordnance automotive maintenance companies to the full-time job of repairing and maintaining the provisional truck companies at a time when all maintenance facilities were already badly strained.

While the use of provisional truck companies was of invaluable assistance, still there were not enough trucks and the demand far exceeded the supply. As it became apparent that truck transportation never would be adequate and that priorities for the use of trucks must be established, an organization was set up, as a part of Army Headquarters, to exercise centralized direction and control of the dispatch and movement of every truck assigned to the Army. It was the beginning of a winter during which trucks were to become the most important single item of equipment on the Continent, and it was only by making decisions as to their use and exercising close control at Army Headquarters that the proper balance between troop and supply requirements could be attained.

Back at Rennes, one of the more difficult situations facing the headquarters personnel was the rehabilitation of the artillery used in the reduction of Brest. The heavy bombardment carried on there had resulted in considerable wear of artillery tubes, particularly in the heavy-caliber weapons. The weapons in general needed a thorough going-over, and the supply of tracks for the self-propelled guns and full-track prime movers was critically short. The Army secured a calibration team and calibrated all the heavy artillery. An ordnance medium maintenance company was assigned the full-time task of overhauling all weapons. Track and other necessary parts were available only at the port of Cherbourg and were held on priority for First and Third Armies. Nearly two weeks and several thousand jeep miles were consumed before this priority bottleneck was broken and the needed supplies were obtained.

Acting to solve the critical over-all problem of transportation facilities and to insure that each of the armies received supplies in keeping with its size and mission, 12th Army Group now instituted a policy allocating maximum tonnages per day for each army. Each army bid for tonnages which it estimated necessary to meet its needs for an ensuing period. Upon considering all these requests, the Army Group established the total to be delivered to each army daily. Ninth Army's allocation at this time was thus determined to be 350 tons per division per day. This figure put the Army on a starvation diet for supplies and left it impossible to build up the necessary stocks for any offensive action. Although an immediate build-up of supplies was not anticipated, plans were made for a supply concentration in the Arlon–Bastogne–Steinfort area in the event the Army should be given an offensive mission and a corresponding increase in tonnage allocations.

With only a defensive mission to accomplish at the time, ammunition was strictly rationed to insure that expenditures were held to an absolute minimum until repair of rail facilities and higher tonnage allocations permitted a larger flow of supplies. Fortunately, enemy artillery fire received during the period was very light, the only notable exception being intermittent harassing fires from heavy field guns and railway guns. Artillery missions, particularly counterbattery, could therefore be held to a minimum without jeopardizing the lives and operations of our troops.

The supply of food and types of rations fluctuated greatly during this period, chiefly because of the rail transportation diffi-

LEK RIVER

WAAL RIVER

MAAS RIVER

ARNHEM

NIJMEGEN

EMMERICH

CLEVE

REES

NIERS RIVER

XANTEN

RHEIN

GELD

NETHERLANDS

MAAS RIVER

EINDHOVEN

VENLO

DI
'UER

KREFEL

ANTWERP

ROERMOND

MÜNCHEN-
GLADBACH

ROER RIVER

DEMER RIVER

SENNE RIVER

LOUVAIN

MAASTRICHT

WÜRM RIVER

INDE RIVER

JÜL

BRUSSELS

AACHEN

LIÉGE

BELGIUM

MEUSE RIVER

MONSCHA

SAMBRE RIVER

ST VITH

MAP NO 4

THE RHINELAND

AND ADJACENT REGIONS

SCALE OF MILES

0   5   10   15   20   25

BASTOGNE

LUXEM-

BOURG

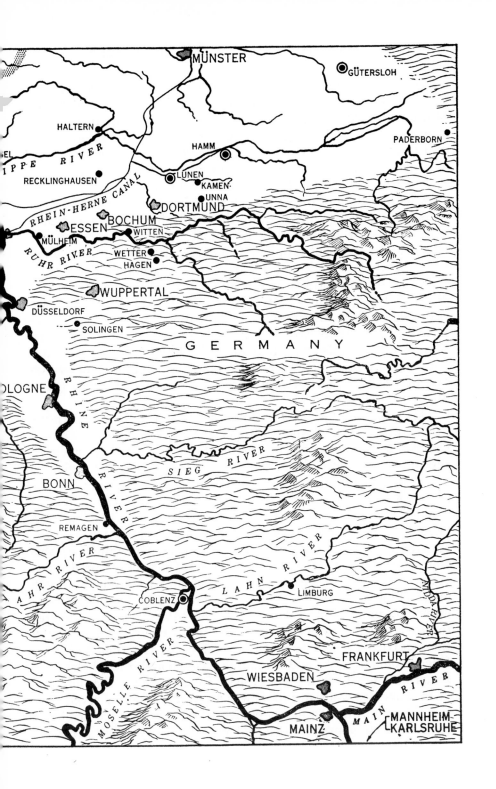

lines reported that their mission was to harass lines of communication and that they were supplied by parachute. The possibility of paratroop action was always present, constituting more of an annoyance, perhaps, than an actual tactical threat.

The nuisance value of parachutists is well illustrated by an incident which occured on October 17. Late in the evening of that day 12th Army Group informed Ninth Army Headquarters that reliable sources of information indicated that German parachutists were dropping in the vicinity of Differdange, a small town about twelve miles southeast of Arlon and about the same distance southwest of the city of Luxembourg, the location of the Tactical Headquarters of 12th Army Group. Of more importance, perhaps, was the fact that Differdange was also the site of a steel plant, which at that time the Communications Zone was bending every effort to put into operation to produce steel I-beams used in bridge construction. The 2d and 5th Ranger Battalions, veterans of the D-day landings in Normandy and of the Brest campaign, were alerted in a nearby area where they had been reorganizing, re-equipping, and retraining after their rigorous campaigns. The 83d Division, in whose area the alleged drops had occurred, was also alerted. Precautionary measures continued through the night, but with the dawn and the receipt of negative reports from reconnaissance agencies investigating the incident, it was concluded that the false report had begun with a farmer's discovery that a few head of his cattle had been butchered, and that this incident had been absurdly magnified and aggravated by the difficulties of foreign languages and by the imagination of the worried populace.

The period at Arlon was one of concentrated planning. 12th Army Group's instructions contained in Letter of Instructions No. 9 of September 24 had read in part as follows: "Move the VIII Corps to occupy the front progressively between Bollendorf and the present north boundary of V Corps as vacated by elements of First Army. Corps troops committed to action will be kept to a minimum until the present supply situation is improved. As additional divisions become available, the Ninth Army front is to be extended southward to include Metz, relieving Third Army units in that zone."

Definite planning had to be accomplished, then, to provide for taking over the sector to the south. In addition, General Simpson

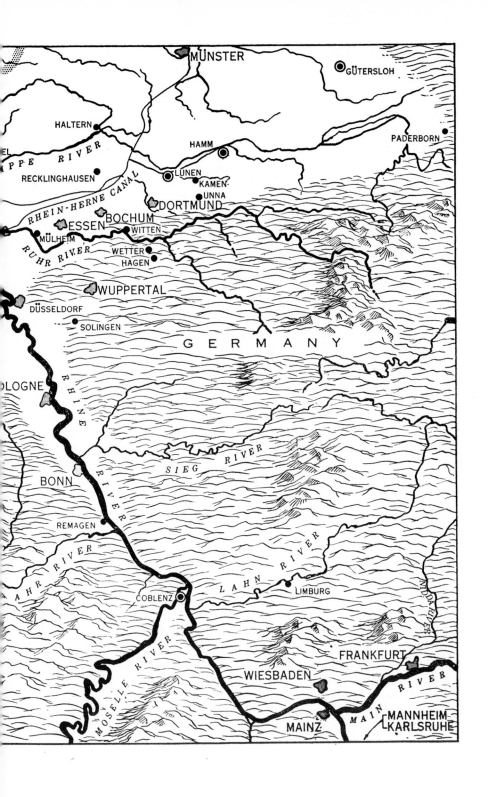

culties. Army stock piles became as low as one day's supply, in contrast to the five days' which it was desirable to maintain. However, in addition to the one day's supply maintained in the Army depot, the troops always had one additional ration in the unit kitchens. At one time Army-baked bread achieved the status of a delicacy, and the coarse Belgian bread enjoyed a brisk illicit trade with individuals whenever it was found.

In its instructions of September 24, 12th Army Group had directed that Ninth Army contain the enemy forces along its front. This containing mission was, of course, made necessary by the temporary shortage of supplies. Concurrently, however, all armies were directed to endeavor to keep the situation fluid on their fronts at all times and to use every opportunity to kill Germans. Ninth Army operations between October 4 and October 22 were governed by these instructions. For the most part, German forces facing Ninth Army troops appeared content to offer stubborn resistance to patrols and minor offensive activities along their defensive positions, which were, with the exception of a small stretch east of St. Vith, an integral part of the Siegfried Line. (*Map No. 3.*)

This was Ninth Army's first contact with the famed defensive barrier protecting Germany proper from invasion from western Europe. It was a system of fortifications organized in strength and in depth in accordance with the importance of the region to be protected and the suitability of the terrain for operations by armored forces. Concealment of the works had been carefully planned from the beginning, and wherever possible earth had been piled around and on top of the fortifications. Four years of inactivity and the growth of grass and foliage had improved this concealment. The line consisted chiefly of a zone of small concrete forts sited to support each other and to produce closely interlocking areas of fire. The forts were usually completely connected by underground communication cables. These were later to prove valuable to our own combat units when they penetrated the Siegfried Line. The works of early construction had reinforced concrete walls and roofs five feet thick and loopholes with armorplate nearly four inches thick. In later works, the thickness of the concrete walls and roofs was increased to nearly seven feet, and the armorplate to nearly eight inches. The average height of the forts from foundation to roof was twenty feet, and about six feet of this was below ground level. In addition to the forts, which were designed to protect the weapons mounted within them and the crews serving these weapons, there were a number of other shelters designed for the protection of headquarters, reserve troops, and such supplies as ammunition. Extensive antitank obstacles consisted of concrete dragons' teeth, curved steel rails, and ditches or escarpments which ran along the forward edges of the positions. Mines were laid to strengthen the antitank obstacles, and in addition minefields were laid in front of the obstacles to canalize attacks on the stronger defenses. The Siegfried Line was a formidable obstacle, not only in front of the Ninth Army but all along the Western Front.

The caliber of the troops manning these defensive positions was far inferior to that of the works they occupied. The high casualties inflicted upon the German Army since the landings in Normandy often forced the German High Command to a policy of utilizing small infantry combat groups ranging in strength from 150 to 500 men in lieu of maintaining the integrity of organized units. Each of these battle groups operated in a specific zone under the command, usually, of a division headquarters whose troops had been depleted and which now provided the command element for an assigned area. Though the mission of these combat groups was ordinarily an infantry mission, the group often included personnel from many arms of the service and in various degrees of health and strength. Air force, artillery, antiaircraft, and other personnel were included in their numbers, while some were convalescents with previous battle experience, recent inductees, or merely members of the local home-guard forces. Comparatively low quality troops were used to man the fortresses, where mobility was of slight importance, while the troops of higher quality were withheld to restore lost positions by counterattacking.

In general, the Army's operations in the Luxembourg–Southern Belgium area, as well as the operations of the opposing German forces, consisted of intense patrolling and small-scale raids supported by limited mortar and artillery fire. No appreciable advance was effected anywhere in the zone, and the several small German counterattacks launched during the period were easily repulsed, usually by artillery fire alone. Enemy air activity was light and sporadic. Some German soldiers captured behind the lines reported that their mission was to harass lines of communication and that they were supplied by parachute. The possibility of paratroop action was always present, constituting more of an annoyance, perhaps, than an actual tactical threat.

The nuisance value of parachutists is well illustrated by an incident which occured on October 17. Late in the evening of that day 12th Army Group informed Ninth Army Headquarters that reliable sources of information indicated that German parachutists were dropping in the vicinity of Differdange, a small town about twelve miles southeast of Arlon and about the same distance southwest of the city of Luxembourg, the location of the Tactical Headquarters of 12th Army Group. Of more importance, perhaps, was the fact that Differdange was also the site of a steel plant, which at that time the Communications Zone was bending every effort to put into operation to produce steel I-beams used in bridge construction. The 2d and 5th Ranger Battalions, veterans of the D-day landings in Normandy and of the Brest campaign, were alerted in a nearby area where they had been reorganizing, re-equipping, and retraining after their rigorous campaigns. The 83d Division, in whose area the alleged drops had occurred, was also alerted. Precautionary measures continued through the night, but with the dawn and the receipt of negative reports from reconnaissance agencies investigating the incident, it was concluded that the false report had begun with a farmer's discovery that a few head of his cattle had been butchered, and that this incident had been absurdly magnified and aggravated by the difficulties of foreign languages and by the imagination of the worried populace.

The period at Arlon was one of concentrated planning. 12th Army Group's instructions contained in Letter of Instructions No. 9 of September 24 had read in part as follows: "Move the VIII Corps to occupy the front progressively between Bollendorf and the present north boundary of V Corps as vacated by elements of First Army. Corps troops committed to action will be kept to a minimum until the present supply situation is improved. As additional divisions become available, the Ninth Army front is to be extended southward to include Metz, relieving Third Army units in that zone."

Definite planning had to be accomplished, then, to provide for taking over the sector to the south. In addition, General Simpson immediately initiated planning to cover the possibilities of a thrust east to secure a bridgehead over the Rhine River in conjunction with an attack to take Metz or as a single operation while containing and by-passing Metz. Terrain studies were prepared covering the entire area along the west bank of the Rhine from Mannheim to Cologne. Estimates of enemy strength and enemy reactions to possible attacks in the Ninth Army zone of action were prepared, and the Army Commander devoted considerable time to a study of possible offensives to be undertaken.

Four possibilities were developed and studied in detail. (*Map No. 3.*) First, an attack launched generally from the vicinity of Prüm, taking advantage of the gap already created in the Siegfried Line and driving along the rugged high ground almost directly eastward to Coblenz. Second, an attack launched from the junction of the Moselle and the Sauer Rivers northeastward along the valley of the Moselle to Coblenz. A third possibility considered was the exploitation of the Metz Gap, famous gateway to Germany. This could have been accomplished, after reduction or encirclement of the fortress of Metz, by a drive to the northeast, south of the rugged Hunsbruck Mountains and Forest, to seize a bridgehead in the Mainz–Wiesbaden area. Finally, consideration was given to an attack to the northeast from the St. Vith–Prüm area across the Rhine somewhere in the vicinity of Bonn, followed by a drive to the southeast along the far side of the Rhine.

The scene of planning interest shifted abruptly and dramatically on October 10. Although written instructions had not yet been issued, definite word was received from 12th Army Group that Ninth Army would take over a zone north of the Aachen area (*Map No. 3*), in the northernmost part of the 12th Army Group, adjacent to the British 21 Army Group commanded by Field Marshal Sir Bernard L. Montgomery. In the broad offensive scheme now beginning to develop, Ninth Army would be built up in the new area to drive east to the Rhine and thence north in conjunction with a drive by 21 Army Group east and south. Planning for future operations which, until October 10 had been directed toward crossings of the Rhine between Mainz and Bonn, was now quickly turned to the new Army zone of action in the north. By October 13, under the direction of the Assistant Chief of Staff, G-3, Colonel Armistead D. Mead, Jr., plans had been developed to the point where General Simpson gave them his personal attention and study. It is interesting to note that of the plans considered in detail by the Army Commander at this time, those covering an advance to the Rhine and the encirclement of the Ruhr industrial area beyond the Rhine included the almost exact strategic maneuvers which four to five months later were so successfully utilized. (*Map No. 4.*)

One plan provided for an attack through the existing gap in the Siegfried Line at Aachen, with the axis of attack east from the Aachen area to the Rhine River at Cologne. It was then contemplated that the Rhine would be crossed north of Cologne and the Ruhr enveloped from the south. The second plan, which was substantially the one finally carried out, also exploited the existing gap in the defenses at Aachen, but provided for an armored drive northeast to the west bank of the Rhine in the vicinity of Wesel. This would position Ninth Army to cross the Rhine north of the Ruhr industrial area and to advance over the north German plain, enveloping the Ruhr from the north. Perhaps the success of the execution of these operations was due in substantial part to the early conception of sound plans and to the education of the Army and subordinate staffs in the over-all battle planning.

In the regrouping to place Ninth Army in its new zone of action north of Aachen, the shortage of transportation then available to American forces in Europe dictated that there be a minimum of physical shifting of troops. Therefore it was decided that the procedure of wholesale trading of units by two armies should be used to accomplish the regrouping. Generally speaking, the VIII Corps, with the divisions and supporting troops then assigned to it, would pass to control of First Army, while the XIX Corps, with its divisions and supporting troops already engaged in the Aachen area, would come under the command of Ninth Army. Like units of both army and corps troops would be made the subject of "paper transfers." For instance, artillery was exchanged on a caliber-for-caliber basis. This policy was modified in certain instances to retain old, well established command relations. Similar arrangements were reached on supplies. Stocks were generally left in place until such adjustments as were necessary were made on paper or by adjusting future deliveries. It was further decided that the personnel of Ninth Army Headquarters remaining in Brittany should now move direct to the city of Maastricht in the Netherlands, the site selected for the new command post of the

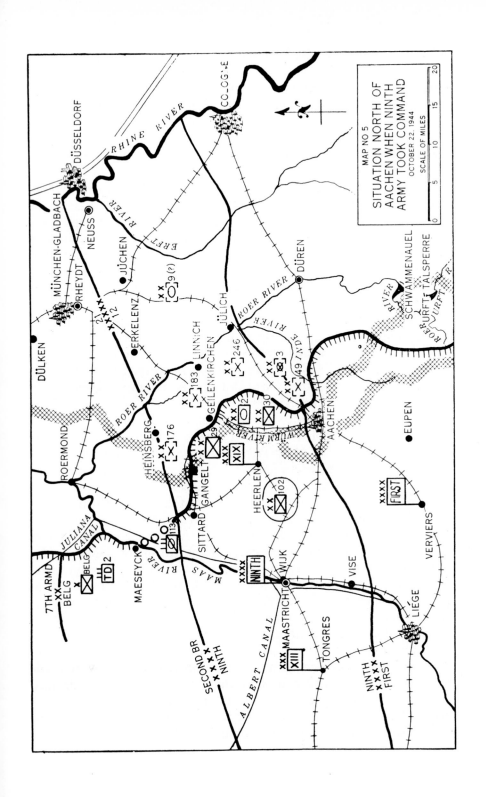

MAP NO 5

SITUATION NORTH OF
AACHEN WHEN NINTH
ARMY TOOK COMMAND

OCTOBER 22, 1944

SCALE OF MILES

0   5   10   15   20

Army. XIII Corps Headquarters was diverted, too, and directed to move to the vicinity of Tongres, Belgium (*Map No. 5*).

At this time, in view of the ever-present and continuing difficulties inherent in truck transportation for long-distance delivery of supplies, it was decided that in the Ninth Army area a systematic rehabilitation of railroads would be initiated and that in all future operations a high priority would be placed on rail reconnaissance in forward areas. The repair and rehabilitation of selected lines were emphasized. The Advance Section of Communications Zone, the agency charged with the delivery of supplies to armies and with the construction, maintenance, and operation of the railroads, wholeheartedly concurred in this decision and cooperated with and strongly supported Ninth Army's program of maximum supply by rail.

At noon on October 22 the Army closed its command post at Arlon and opened in Maastricht. Simultaneously, command of the VIII Corps passed to First Army, and Ninth Army took command of the XIX Corps in the area north of Aachen. In Maastricht the forward echelon of the Army Headquarters occupied the *Tappan Kazerne*, an army post which formerly housed elements of the Netherlands Army, and a neighboring Catholic school building, both on the outskirts of the city and west of the Maas River which divides Maastricht from the adjoining companion city of Wijk. East of the river, and actually closer to the front lines, the rear echelon of the Army Headquarters was established in Ambachts School in Wijk. Little was it thought at that time that the Army Headquarters was to be in the Maastricht area for nearly five months, the longest period in any one location during its entire history. Maastricht, with its quaint, cobblestone streets, narrow and irregular, with its broad river and numerous canals, its many churches, its wrecked bridges, and its friendly, clean, God-fearing people, was to become a familiar home for the men of the Ninth.

With the opening of the command post in Maastricht, the Army signal center reached normal size for the first time. The switchboard was enlarged to provide six operator positions, and the teletype room began its first use of automatic tape transmission. From this time on, the necessary equipment was generally available, and the signal center operated on the same scale as those of the other armies on the Continent.

Issued on October 21, 12th Army Group's Letter of Instruction No. 10 recorded the first written instructions for Ninth Army in its new zone of action. (*Map No. 5*.) There were three important elements in the Army's new mission. First, it was to "continue the present action of the XIX Corps in coordination with First Army effort. XIX Corps' cavalry now outside the Army Group boundary, will remain in position." This was merely an order directing that until the build-up for the contemplated attack could be completed, present positions were to be held and action already initiated was to be continued. This was particularly applicable to the battle for Aachen, in which XIX Corps and VII Corps were cooperating. As a matter of fact, Aachen surrendered on the afternoon of October 21, the very date the order was published.

The significance of the instructions to continue operations of XIX Corps' cavalry in a zone outside of the Army Group boundary lay in the fact that this cavalry was operating in the Maeseyck area, north of Ninth Army's northern boundary, as the link between the Ninth Army and British Second Army, commanded by Lieutenant General Sir Miles C. Dempsey. Since British Second Army did not have available any unit to replace it, it was deemed advisable to retain the cavalry in place. This cavalry actually comprised a small task force consisting of the 113th Cavalry Group, with two cavalry squadrons, a light tank battalion, a combat engineer company, and a tank destroyer company attached. Its mission was to defend the Army north flank from Gangelt to Maeseyck, a front of 21,000 yards, which was a staggering distance for a unit of this size. Skillfully utilizing its strength and maintaining alert patrols, it was able to accomplish successfully a mission that might well have been assigned to a much larger force, and thus contributed to the strengthening of the Army forces farther to the south and east.

The second major element in the Army's new mission was to "attack in zone to the Rhine in close conjunction with First Army, protecting its left flank." The date for this attack was set as November 5, with a proviso that it be made not more than two days prior to the attack of the British Second Army from the Nijmegen bridgehead area southward between the Rhine and the Maas. This date was changed, on November 4, to November 10.

In general, the key to the situation as far as timing was concerned, was the current British attack to free the port of Antwerp. This mission had priority over all other operations in Europe, since the securing of the harbor facilities of Antwerp was of paramount importance if the campaign into Germany was to be continued throughout the winter. Once the Antwerp approaches had been cleared, the British forces engaged there could be transferred to the northeast and the coordinated attack of all three American armies, plus the British army, could be launched. American aid in the Antwerp battle was furnished in the form of the recently arrived 104th Infantry Division, commanded by Major General Terry de la M. Allen, which, although assigned to Ninth Army, was diverted to the Antwerp area and placed under British control for commitment. Thus Ninth Army played a part even in the Antwerp struggle, for it furnished personnel reinforcements and logistical support to the 104th Division during the fight. Supplying and maintaining this division, 100 miles away, before the main Army supply and maintenance facilities had been established, presented another unusual problem not found in the book, the kind of problem that Army supply personnel were beginning to regard as commonplace.

The third major element in the Army's new instructions had an important bearing not only on the coming attack, but also on the planning for future operations. (*Map No. 4.*) Army Group directed that "after the attack of the First Army has reached the Rhine, Ninth Army will attack northward between the Rhine and the Meuse [Maas] Rivers and gain contact with [later modified to read 'in conjunction with'] British Second Army. It will then take over the area west of the Rhine to Rees, inclusive. New inter-Group boundary will be announced later." Since First Army was directed to attack eastward to seize Cologne and Bonn, this meant that Ninth Army must attack eastward until the Rhine had been reached, in order to protect the north flank of First Army, then turn its attack sharply to the north and advance to meet the British and thereby clear all enemy resistance from the area west of the lower Rhine. It is interesting to note that Ninth Army's occupancy of the west bank of the Rhine was laid down at this time as extending as far north as Rees. In effect, this assigned for the time being, Rhine River crossing sites to Ninth Army considerably farther north than later developments permitted. A seemingly unimportant point, but it had a considerable influence on all future planning conducted by the Army for several months.

In the Army's new zone of action (*Map No. 5*) the XIX Corps, commanded by Major General Raymond S. McLain, occupied a 25-mile front extending north from Aachen to the vicinity of Geilenkirchen, then northwest to Maeseyck on the Maas River. The XIX Corps Artillery, commanded by Brigadier General George D. Shea, comprised one field artillery observation battalion, three group headquarters, and thirteen artillery battalions. The Corps was completely committed to action and for the first time held the entire Army front with its two infantry divisions, one armored division, and supporting troops.

Major General Leland S. Hobbs' 30th Infantry Division was on the right (south), Major General Ernest N. Harmon's 2d Armored Division was in the center, and Major General Charles H. Gerhardt's 29th Infantry Division, formerly under Ninth Army at Brest, was on the left (north). Extending the Army left flank to the northwest was the 113th Cavalry Group, Reinforced, whose mission has already been discussed. Farther to the north was the 7th Armored Division, commanded by Major General Lindsay McD. Silvester, assigned to Ninth Army, but attached temporarily for operations to British Second Army. Like the 104th Infantry Division under the British, the 7th Armored Division was furnished personnel reinforcements and logistical support by Ninth Army. Likewise operating under the British and under the 7th Armored Division, with a mission similar to that of the 113th Cavalry Group, was a Belgian brigade headquarters and another small U. S. task force of XIX Corps troops under the 2nd Tank Destroyer Group. XIII Corps Headquarters, not yet operational, was located in the Tongres area about ten miles southwest of Maastricht. East of Maastricht the 102d Infantry Division, commanded by Brigadier General Frank A. Keating, was assembling as it moved up from Normandy.

Positions of the XIX Corps when the Army took over command included an 11-mile front inside the Siegfried Line north of Aachen, where penetrations had been effected to a depth of some six miles. With the fall of Aachen on October 21 and the contemplated coordinated attack due to be launched early in November, no sizable offensive action was planned for the immediate future. Instead, the time prior to the attack would be spent in

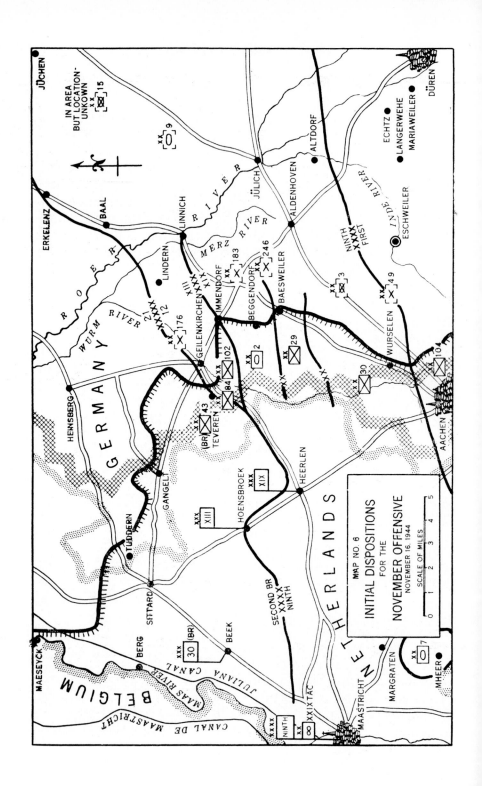

MAP NO. 6

INITIAL DISPOSITIONS
FOR THE
NOVEMBER OFFENSIVE
NOVEMBER 16, 1944

SCALE OF MILES
0   1   2   3   4   5

planning, in building up supplies, and in giving as much rest as possible to the veterans who had been fighting continuously from Normandy to the German borders, and who were definitely in need of at least a few days' rest. With this in mind and also with the intention of providing some battle experience to fresh units, the infantry regiments of the 102d Infantry Division were made available to General McLain to permit a rotation of front-line troops of the 29th and 30th Infantry Divisions and the 2d Armored Division. Consequently, on the 27th of October, the three regiments of the 102d went into the line across the XIX Corps front, each replacing a regiment in one of the front-line divisions.

Opposite Ninth Army forces were the major elements of five German divisions. (*Map No. 5*). From north to south across the front, these were the 176th Infantry, the 183d Infantry, the 246th Infantry, the 3d Panzergrenadier, and the 49th Infantry Divisions. In addition, it was believed that there was at least one armored division in immediate local reserve. With the fall of Aachen the enemy adopted an attitude of passive defense. He was continually active in improving his defensive positions and in making local readjustments in troop dispositions, but he showed little offensive spirit, even foregoing his usual counterattacks. However, to the north of Ninth Army and west of the Maas River in the sector of the British Second Army and of the American 7th Armored Division the German launched a limited offensive, probably with the twofold purpose of relieving the pressure on his forces in the western Netherlands and thus delaying the opening of the Scheldt Estuary and consequent freeing of the port of Antwerp, and also with the intention of delaying or forcing abandonment of an offensive in the American sector which he undoubtedly knew was being prepared. That German intelligence was cognizant of Allied regrouping was proved when thousands of German leaflets announcing the arrival of the Ninth Army was dropped in the city of Maastricht even before the Army command post had been opened.

In view of the German salient on the thinly held Army north flank from the Geilenkirchen area to Maeseyck and the road net favorable to a possible German attack in the general directions Heinsberg–Sittard or Heinsberg–Gangelt (*Map No. 6*), the Army Commander located a small reserve in the area south of Sittard to be quickly available to counter any possible enemy thrusts against this flank. From October 30 to November 9, when the British XXX Corps concentrated in the area prior to taking over a portion of the sector from the Army, one battalion of armored infantry from the 2d Armored Division and one to two battalions of infantry from, at various times, the 29th and 30th Infantry Division, constituted this reserve.

Logistic difficulties continued to be critical factors as the Army moved to concentrate troops in the new area and to build up supplies for the offensive. The shortage of certain items of supply became more acute daily. Estimates of the quantities of critical items available for shipment to the Army could not be obtained. Army liaison officers were maintained at Paris and at Cherbourg to expedite the shipment of especially needed items by rail or by loading to capacity the replacement cargo vehicles allocated for delivery to the Army. In fact, although motor transportation remained short throughout this period, much-needed supplies often had to be moved from Communications Zone depots to Army depots by using Army vehicles, in some instances involving trips as far back as Paris.

The tonnages which were delivered by Communications Zone were in accordance with allocations, but as yet the intermediate depot system in the Communications Zone had not been developed to the point which enabled the Communications Zone to ship balanced levels of supplies as requested by the Army. Such available items as gasoline, food, and miscellaneous supplies were shipped in excess of amounts requested as substitutes for scarce items. A natural result was a comparative over-supply of items available in the Communications Zone and an increasing shortage of other items critically needed. Tonnage figures of supplies delivered were equal to those requested, but the contents of the deliveries were often a surprise. As an example, two carloads of unwanted anvils were received in lieu of badly needed items of engineer supply. The over-supply of gasoline brought obvious disadvantages. It arrived in the Army area in bulk in tank cars and had to be decanted into five-gallon cans before being issued to the using units. The number of such cans and the decanting facilities available to the Army were inadequate to handle the quantities of bulk gasoline received; consequently, tank cars, at a premium throughout the Theater of Operations, were left standing idle, and the railroad sidings at the decanting points were seriously congested. As the Communications Zone supply system was further developed these conditions were of course corrected, and balanced supplies were soon being delivered.

The item of field artillery ammunition remained a critical one during the entire period, as it was in general throughout the war. The Army Commander himself gave detailed personal attention to this problem, and by setting up a program of severely rationed allocations he was able to build up a reserve for the coming attack. This procedure was to be a normal one throughout the winter. 12th Army Group exercised control of the allocation of ammunition to the various armies. Based upon the anticipated activity factor for each army and upon the ammunition available, the Army Group furnished each ten days a statement of the ammunition allocated and physically available for delivery from the Communications Zone to Army depots. The ammunition thus made available was the object of the most detailed and thorough study by the Army Artillery Officer, Colonel Laurence H. Hanley, in connection with the operations planned or under consideration by the Army. As a result of this study, a program was drawn up, in coordination with the appropriate special and general staff sections, for the allocation of ammunition to the various corps and the Army field artillery brigade for the ensuing period. Each ammunition allocation received the personal approval of the Army Commander. During relatively quiet times, when no offensive action was contemplated, ammunition expenditures were cut to the very bone so that stocks could be built up to permit effective expenditures during offensive operations. It was necessary to continue this system until shortly after the Army crossed the Rhine, when the rapidity of the action and the relative decrease of hostile resistance made the necessity for ammunition rationing a thing of the past.

The city of Maastricht was the keypoint of Ninth Army's new supply area. It was the hub in the road net providing ingress and egress for the multitude of depots which stocked the various items of supply. Consequently the road net, and particularly the bridges, in the Maastricht area presented a highly complicated problem in engineering and traffic control, a problem whose solution was imperative if the contemplated offensives were to be successful. Maastricht is in reality an island formed by the Maas River on the east and the Albert Canal on the west. (*Map*

No. 5). To this island there were but three means of access: the two bridges over the Maas River and the one over the Albert Canal. The bridge situation was aggravated during the latter part of October when the temporary pile bridge across the Maas began to settle because of scouring around the piles, making restriction of traffic necessary during the period of repair. To alleviate this situation a 25-ton ponton bridge was constructed across the river at Maastricht. Further, the Advance Section of the Communications Zone was requested to rehabilitate the Wilhelmina Bridge across the river at Maastricht, to bridge the Albert Canal at Maastricht, and to construct a bridge over the Maas River at Visé, about eight miles south of Maastricht. The Visé bridge, a Class 40 structure,[1] provided considerable relief after its completion on the 5th of December. The later extension of British Second Army's south flank south of Maeseyck and east of the Maas threw additional burdens on the Maastricht bridges, for their troops had to be supplied over these routes until bridges of their own could be constructed.

The bottleneck effect of the limited number of crossings of the Maas River and the Albert Canal brought about the decision to place the majority of the Army supply depots east of the Maas, so that in case of damage to the vital Maastricht bridges, ample supplies would be available east of the waterways. However, in locations east of the Maas, the road net (*Map No. 6*), which fanned out from the Maastricht area, forced the headquarters and supply and maintenance installations to be concentrated in a relatively small zone. Suitable depot sites were very limited. Since the water level was just below the surface of the ground, depots and maintenance shops had to seek hard standing or else find themselves buried in the mud. A rigid Army policy of insisting on hard standings for all major supply installations paid large dividends throughout the winter. In the absence of other suitable sites, the road shoulders immediately adjacent to hard-surfaced roads were used, providing an added advantage of making installations easier to guard. The road systems in the Netherlands and Germany were admirably suited to this solution.

---

[1]The numerical value of the load classification given to a bridge may normally be considered to be the load-carrying capacity of that bridge in tons. In general, Class 40 structures will carry all division loads, while Class 70 structures are required to handle the heavier loads of corps and army.

All main roads were flanked on both sides by wide shoulders which had been built to accommodate bicycle and pedestrian traffic, and receiving trucks could be loaded from supplies stacked on the shoulders without getting off the hard surfaces. It was an ideal arrangement for rations and gasoline, and worked especially well in the case of ammunition where a multitude of different fuzes, propelling charges, and shell sizes were involved, and dispersion was imperative. In some instances ammunition supply points stretched along the roads for distances as great as twenty miles. Road-side depots saved incalculable time and labor in the movement and storage of supplies and proved so effective that they were continued even after the countryside was dry.

Maintenance installations likewise were set up on hard standings as near to hard-surfaced roads as facilities would permit. Mines, factories, school yards, and village public squares were used. A paint factory, for example, became the main ordnance depot, and the streets and side roads in the vicinity were used for vehicle storage. This was quite a contrast to the conditions encountered later when the installations were moved into the industrial area of Germany, where suitable facilities were available in large numbers.

On November 4 Ninth Army issued its orders for the coming offensive. (*Map No. 6.*) The XIX Corps was directed to continue its current containing mission, to regroup its forces in preparation for the attack to the east, and upon order to advance to the Rhine in its current zone, making its main effort on its right and protecting the north flank of First Army. The XIX Corps was also to protect the north flank of Ninth Army from Immendorf eastward. Upon reaching the Rhine it was to reduce all enemy resistance in its area. XIII Corps, using initially the 102d Infantry Division and the 113th Cavalry Group, Reinforced, was directed to assume control of a zone on the Army north flank from the vicinity of Immendorf to Maeseyck on or about November 7, and to contain the enemy in this zone until relieved by elements of the British Second Army on or about November 15. After relief by the British, XIII Corps was directed to be prepared for further operations to the east on the left of XIX Corps.

With its highest priority mission that of protecting the left flank of First Army, which was making the main effort of the

12th Army Group in the direction of Cologne, considerable coordination between Ninth Army and First Army was required, as
well as similar and more detailed coordination between XIX Corps
and VII Corps, First Army's left flank unit. Consequently,
numerous conferences were held to effect complete understanding
of plans, particularly those relating to boundaries, time of attack,
estimated timetables of advance, and the air effort to be made in
cooperation with ground operations. With a heavy bombing
attack scheduled to precede the jumpoff, timing for the initiation
of the offensive had to be planned with the weather as a primary
consideration. The final attack date was set as November 10 or as
soon thereafter as weather would permit close air support, but in
any event not later than November 16. Elaborate plans for the
final decision as to the hour and day of attack had to be prepared;
these included designation of the commander who would make
the decision under any given set of circumstances, the time by
which the decision must be reached, and the methods by which
all forces, both ground and air, were to be notified.

The XXIX Tactical Air Command, Ninth Army's cooperating
air echelon, had moved its headquarters from Arlon to Maastricht
coincident with the move of the Army headquarters. Much in
the same way as Ninth Army and First Army had traded troops,
so XXIX Tactical Air Command and IX Tactical Air Command,
the air unit cooperating with First Army, performed a similar
operation, and XXIX Tactical Air Command was now composed
of the 36th, 48th, 373d, and 404th Fighter-Bomber Groups, and
the 363d Tactical Reconnaissance Group. This was the XXIX
Tactical Air Command's first actual operation in close combat cooperation with Ninth Army, for during the brief period in the
Luxembourg–Southern Belgium area, where higher headquarters
desired that the front be kept as quiet as possible, it had confined
its efforts to longer range missions deep behind the German lines.
To insure complete exchange of information and the close coordination of air and ground operations, Ninth Army and XXIX
Tactical Air Command adopted measures which had already
proved successful in other air-ground operations on the Continent. Small parties of Air Forces personnel, known as air-
ground cooperation parties, were attached to headquarters of
corps, divisions, and in certain cases combat commands and regiments. These parties were equipped with special radio sets for

direct contact with cooperating aircraft. Under ideal conditions, voice radio contact was maintained between the ground elements and the cooperating aircraft during the entire time they were airborne on their missions. The air units—flights, squadrons, or groups—were passed from one ground cooperation party to another—corps to division to combat command or regiment—until they were guided to their targets or had accomplished their mission.

At corps and divisions, the officer in charge of the air-ground cooperation party advised the commanding general and his staff on the capabilities and limitations of the cooperating air arm and on air matters in general. Each corps artillery headquarters and the headquarters of the 34th Field Artillery Brigade (Army Artillery) were provided with a special radio set, manned by Air Forces personnel, to provide communications between ground and air in the adjustment of artillery fire by high-performance aircraft. These same headquarters were likewise provided with high-powered radio sets to operate in a net, under the control of the Army Artillery Officer and included a radio set at the Army Photo Interpretation Detachment, to insure the rapid dissemination to artillery units of the interpreted results of air photographs of enemy installations. The Army Photo Interpretation Detachment itself, comprising a group of specialists in the study and interpretation of air photographs, was located in close proximity to the Air Forces photo reproduction unit so that it could have immediate access to the results of aerial photographic missions.

To complete the air-ground picture and further to insure smooth operations between air and ground units, small parties of ground forces personnel, known as ground liaison officer teams, were attached to Air Forces groups. The duties of these teams were to brief the Air Forces personnel on ground tactics, to keep the air units abreast of the current ground situation, and to maintrain up-to-the-minute bomb lines. In addition to these detailed measures for air-ground coordination in lower units, the command post of the Tactical Air Command was habitually located in the immediate vicinity of the Army command post, and the two commanding generals and their staffs were in intimate daily contact.

For the first half of November the power of the XXIX Tactical Air Command was directed at disrupting and destroying the

German supply and transportation system on the front of the Ninth Army and in harassing and inflicting casualties upon the Germans by attacking the many small fortified towns which they were using as strongpoints in their complex and powerful defense system. Marshalling yards, supply depots, and critical rail choke points were attacked continually. Fortified villages were attacked as often as reconnaissance indicated activity within them. The dive bombers carrying on this program used incendiary bombs and Napalm (jellied gasoline), as well as general purpose HE bombs.

XXIX Tactical Air Command's staff, meanwhile, directed the bulk of its efforts in coordinating with Ninth Army, First Army, and IX Tactical Air Command the plan for the air support to be given the offensive later in the month. An elaborate and detailed plan called Operation Q was developed. This operation was a joint effort of both Tactical Air Commands in the zones of both armies. It was designed to execute the mission of neutralizing prepared positions, destroying enemy personnel, and disrupting communications and supply in the enemy area over which Ninth and First Armies were to operate. Included in the plan was consideration of such factors as the weather, the weight of effort to be used, air-ground coordination, safety precautions, and the marking of friendly front lines and communications. Finally, three separate and distinct plans were completed, since it could not definitely be foretold what strength of air forces would be made available at the time of the attack. One plan included the use of the heavy bombers of the American Eighth Air Force and the British Royal Air Force Bomber Command, the medium bombers of the IX Bombardment Division of the American Ninth Air Force, and, of course, the fighter-bombers of the IX and XXIX Tactical Air Commands. The second plan included only the medium bombers in addition to the normal fighter-bomber support, and the third plan was based on the eventuality that only fighter-bombers would be available for the attack.

Weather, of course, was the determining factor as to what air forces would be available and consequently as to which plan would finally be put into operation. The heavy bombers were based in the United Kingdom and, though weather might well permit operations of fighter-bombers based comparatively close to the front lines, it might well prevent the operation of the heavies. On the other hand, weather which might prevent operations of the close-based fighter-bombers might permit take off and return by the medium and heavies, and through bombing by instruments rather than by visual methods, their targets could be attacked. It was necessarily a complicated plan because of the characteristics of airplanes and their sensitivity to weather.

Final plans were approved by the Ninth Air Force on November 7. In general, as the basis of all three plans (*Map No. 6*), the Eighth Air Force heavies would attack the Eschweiler and Langerwehe areas in the south, the R.A.F. Bomber Command heavies would attack the Düren and Jülich areas farther east, and in addition, the towns of Heinsberg, Erkelenz, and Baal on the north. The medium bombers of the IX Bombardment Division would attack towns on a wide arc spread from northeast to southeast in front of the attacking ground forces—Jüchen, Linnich, Aldenhoven, Echtz, and Mariaweiler. The fighter-bombers would provide the close-in support, mostly on call from ground troops.

The net result, if favorable weather permitted the employment of all types of planes, would be a heavy bombing of the strongly defended areas in front of the attacking forces, supplemented by pinpoint attacks on selected communication centers, and by direct close-in support by the fighter-bombers for the attacking ground troops. The details of the plans for the air strikes in the zones of First and Ninth Armies differed in that First Army, based on the success of the St. Lô breakthrough, desired an area "carpet" bombing by the mediums and heavies in the zone of its attack. Ninth Army, on the other hand, specified that the air effort in its zones be 'target" bombing on keypoints, communications and road centers, fortified towns, and other known enemy installations. The plans provided flexibility in case either the heavies or the mediums were unable to participate, for in that case the fighter-bombers would attack the more important of the targets scheduled for the heavier bombers. Plans also provided detailed time schedules designed both for the safety of the ground troops and to eliminate interference of the various echelons of airplanes with one another. To illustrate the complicated arrangements necessary to stage such a supporting effort by air power, because of the uncertainty imposed by weather, the following summary of the decisions as to the establishment of D-day is given:

If November 10 is suitable for visual bombing by Ninth Air Force, and weather forecasts indicate that November 11 will be suitable for fighter-bombers, then D-day will be November 11 and the Eighth Air Force will attack under provisions of the first plan on November 10.

If weather on November 11 and 12 is suitable for Eighth Air Force participation, this organization will notify the Commanding General, First Army, by 10 o'clock the night before, and the following day will be D-day.

From November 13 to 16 the decision for the naming of D-day will rest with the Commanding General, First Army. Weather permitting, maximum air cooperation will be the deciding factor. The Eighth Air Force will notify First Army each evening by 10 o'clock if weather conditions will permit the Eighth Air Force to attack on the following day.

D-day will be no later than November 16, regardless of air cooperation or lack of same.

Previous incidents of the bombing of friendly troops led to the use of precautionary measures to assure the safety of the ground troops. Included in Ninth Army's forces was the 30th Infantry Division, which had suffered heavy casualties during the carpet bombing which preceded the breakthrough at St. Lô. Its presence was an added reminder of the necessity for careful planning in the staging of a heavy, close-in bombing effort. Important safety measures included the marking of targets by artillery-fired colored smoke shells and the use of cerise and yellow marking panels placed parallel to the forward lines of the infantry units, approximately 500 yards apart along the entire Army front.

XIII Corps became operational on November 8, taking over the responsibility of the XIX Corps for the sector northwest from Immendorf to Maeseyck. (*Map No. 6.*) Under its command, from north to south, were the 113th Cavalry Group, Reinforced, and the 102d Infantry Division, released by XIX Corps after about two weeks' duty of providing rotation of battle-weary units. Also under command of the XIII Corps but not committed for action were the 84th Division, under command of Brigadier General Alexander R. Bolling, newly arrived in the European Theater and as yet uncommitted in combat, and the 7th Armored Division, under command of Brigadier General Robert W. Hasbrouck, recently returned to Ninth Army control from British Second Army where it had borne the brunt of a German attack in the swampy area southwest of Venlo.

On November 9 the British XXX Corps, commanded by Lieutenant General B. G. Horrocks, with the British 43d Infantry

Division, concentrated in the rear of the XIII Corps sector prepared to move forward and relieve the XIII Corps in the northern portion of the sector. This relief was accomplished on November 12 when the XXX Corps, under British Second Army, assumed responsibility for the front from the vicinity of Teveren northwest to Maeseyck. At the same time Ninth Army temporarily turned over the operational control of the 84th Infantry Division to XXX Corps to provide sufficient forces to that Corps to stage an attack on the town of Geilenkirchen in coordination with the First Army-Ninth Army attack.

Geilenkirchen had been a thorn in the side of the Allies ever since the first penetration of the Siegfried Line had been effected south of it. It was a strongly fortified anchor of the Siegfried Line and a highly important road and rail center for movements both forward and to the rear. Considerable study had been devoted to the question of the method and timing best suited to reducing this strongpoint. The narrow funnel between Aachen and Geilenkirchen through which Ninth Army was forced to launch its attack and support the build-up of forces to carry it on beyond the Roer River brought about the decision that Geilenkirchen should be reduced very shortly after the initial assault eastward. Since Geilenkirchen lay astride the 21 Army Group-12th Army Group boundary, an element of surprise would be introduced against the Germans by a strong attack with a single force along the boundary, thus employing, in reverse, the Germans' own long-time tactics—so well exemplifiied in their World War I offensive of March, 1918—of striking at the boundaries between national forces. Then, too, Geilenkirchen could best be reduced by a double envelopment from the west and south of the city, and XXX Corps was taking over the area west of it. Furthermore, the British had ample ammunition to permit artillery support on a far more lavish scale than American supply permitted. All these factors caused the Army Commander to decide that the entire responsibility for the Geilenkirchen action should be given to XXX Corps. The 84th Division, then, was to receive its baptism of fire, like the 104th Division, under British command and was soon to become, along with Ninth Army, familiar with British nomenclature and terms. When "the AGRA was going to sweeten it up a bit," all soon learned that the Army Group of Royal Artillery would reinforce the artillery firing.

Enemy patrolling, light artillery fire, and minor air activities continued, as well as a few small-scale unsuccessful attacks. In general, Ninth Army intelligence activities under Colonel Charles P. Bixel, Assistant Chief of Staff, G-2, determined that the German command knew quite well that an attack was impending and that it would be directed eastward, but was uncertain as to its exact timing. In contact with our forward elements (*Map No. 6*) were the same enemy divisions that had been in the line when we initially took over this front—in order from north to south, the 176th, 183d, and 246th Infantry, the 3d Panzergrenadier, and the 49th Infantry Divisions. One panzer division was known to be immediately available—the 9th Panzer Division close by to the north of the Army front, and the 15th Panzergrenadier Division was known to be in the vicinity "on call." In addition, it was estimated that further enemy strength could be brought to bear in the form of additional infantry, panzer or panzergrenadier divisions.

The terrain over which the battle would initially be fought was flat, open ground stretching eastward to the Roer River. Level cultivated fields containing many ditches and low hedges were dotted with numerous compact villages spaced one to two miles apart. This was a mining area, too, and coal mines with their enormous slag piles and mine shafts, as well as numerous factories, coupled with densely populated areas where stone houses and buildings abounded, rounded out the general pattern of the landscape. It was appreciated, of course, that these built-up areas would be used by the Germans as strong defensive positions, since the villages were close enough to be mutually supporting. Buildings and houses which commanded good fields of fire and provided observation were reinforced by the defenders; in fact, many an innocent-looking house was merely the useful camouflage for a pillbox constructed within its walls. Machine guns, light artillery and even tanks were hidden in the buildings. Many houses had fortress-like cellars with twelve-inch concrete for roofs. The road net available, both to attacker and to defender, was adequate, with numerous narrow, surfaced secondary roads supporting the main highway net. However, in Ninth Army's area the heavy traffic demanded by the effort of supplying strong forces on a narrow front, and the unfavorable weather, created a terrific burden of road maintenance, both before and during the operation.

A factor which exerted influence upon planning and operations at this time and which later was to affect even more the life and history of Ninth Army was the system of dams south of Düren in the zone of the First Army. (*Map No. 5.*) These dams controlled the water level of the Roer River. By manipulating or demolishing them the enemy could make a crossing of the Roer impracticable, or if the crossing had already been made he could interrupt the supply of forces on the eastern bank for a considerable period of time. To strengthen First Army's main effort in the coming attack and to permit the taking of the dams, both the 99th Infantry Division, commanded by Major General Walter E. Lauer, newly arrived in the Theater, and the 104th Infantry Division, reverting from British control after its part in the successful campaign to free Antwerp, were passed from Ninth to First Army. The potential threat of the dams was so strong that shortly before the attack all Ninth Army units were instructed that, with the exception of light reconnaissance elements, they would not cross the Roer River without first obtaining express Army authority. The Ninth Army Engineer, Colonel Richard U. Nicholas, initiated special intelligence studies of the Roer dams. Data secured from the European Theater Headquarters and from the Army Photo Interpretation Detachment were augmented by captured German engineering drawings of the dams themselves and their effect as a barrier.

As D-day approached, bad weather came. The skies were leaden day after day, and intermittent rain fell, deteriorating roads, flooding the streams, and giving rise to grave doubts as to whether or not tracked vehicles could maneuver over the muddy plains that lay west of the Roer. Major General Harmon, whose 2d Armored Division tanks were a spearhead of the attack in the Army area, was especially concerned. In addition to the burden of considering whether or not the trafficability of the soil would permit the maneuvering of his tanks off the roads, he had the problem of commencing the movement of the tanks each night from concealed positions in the rear to the line of departure for the attack, since notification of whether or not the following day would be D-day could not reach him in time to permit completion of the movement by daylight without an early start. Just before D-day was finally decided upon, he personally mounted one of his tanks and maneuvered about in the fields east of the Wurm

River to see how the going was. The tank could make only two to three miles an hour in low-low gear. Still in doubt, General Harmon turned to the tank commander.

"Can we make it, sergeant?"

"Yes, sir," came the quick answer.

With characteristic faith in the GI, General Harmon was satisfied. If the sergeant and his tank could make it, the division could make it. He informed General Simpson that the mud, though providing a serious handicap, would not present an insurmountable obstacle to his attack.

From November 10 on, each day became a worried wait until the weather forecast permitted a decision on the following day's activities. Day by day went by and each one saw the postponement of D-day. Finally, with November 16, the day on which the attack was set to go, coming up, air support or not, the weather broke and the forecast gave indications that the air support plan, involving the heavy and medium bombers as well as the fighter-bombers, could be adopted. Orders were issued that the ground attack would jump off at 12:45 P.M., November 16.

Shortly before noon the Eighth Air Force, with 1,204 heavy bombers escorted by 485 fighter-bombers, dropped 3,679 tons of bombs in the Eschweiler area. (*Map No. 6.*) The RAF Bomber Command, with 1,188 four-engined Lancasters, dropped 5,640 tons on their targets, chiefly on Düren and Jülich. Medium bombers of the IX Bombardment Division executed heavy attacks on Linnich in Ninth Army's zone and on other town areas in First Army's zone. The center of Düren was destroyed and the remainder of the city was badly damaged. The marshalling yards north of the city were damaged and all rail lines leading into it were severed. The destruction inflicted upon Jülich was such that few buildings were left standing with walls above the first floor, and many of the city streets disappeared under piles of rubble or in gaping craters. In the Eschweiler-Langerwehe area, towns and villages were destroyed or badly damaged. The railroads were obliterated in many places, and numerous highways were rendered impassable. The air operation was executed as planned, with the exception of the attack on Aldenhoven. There, the hope that the ground troops could make an early and rapid advance to seize the town immediately after the jump-off occasioned a last-minute cancellation of the scheduled attack.

Although it was never possible to assess accurately the results of the heavy bombing efforts preceding the attack, subsequent investigation and intelligence reports indicated that considerable damage, particularly to communications, was inflicted, and that the psychological effect upon the defenders was probably higher than hoped for. In general, the bombing was accurate, and those towns selected as targets were either destroyed or heavily damaged. Casualties among enemy personnel probably fell short of expectations, but the explanation is to be found in the disposition of enemy troops in the open country surrounding the towns rather than in the towns themselves. A noncommissioned officer prisoner from a German infantry division reported that his men completely ignored all orders during the attack and were in a dazed condition for forty-five minutes after the bombing. Communications, in particular telephonic communications, were interfered with as far back as division headquarters, and the slow reaction of the enemy in moving his reserves was no doubt due, in part at least, to the effect of the bombing. A gratifying feature of the air attack was the absence of casualties to friendly troops. Proper selection of targets and safety precautions taken to prevent casualty-producing incidents were completely effective.

The artillery contributed to the success of the heavy bombing effort by executing a counter-flak program designed to reduce to a minimum the weight of enemy antiaircraft fire brought to bear on the planes taking part in the air strike. In addition, the artillery marked numerous targets for the Air Forces with colored smokes. Again, this type of operation required a mass of prior planning. Detailed information as to the paths of the planes, the times of their arrival, and the altitude at which they would fly was obtained from the air units participating. The artillery then developed a plan to suppress with artillery fire all enemy flak batteries within range of the bombers. A list of the locations of all German antiaircraft weapons was made and kept up to date. The information necessary to build up this list was obtained through photographic observers, location of enemy batteries by sound-and-flash battalions, and from statements made by prisoners of war. The success of the ground effort to assist the bombers is reflected in the following message issued by the IX Bombardment Division of the Ninth Air Force whose medium bombers participated in the air attack:

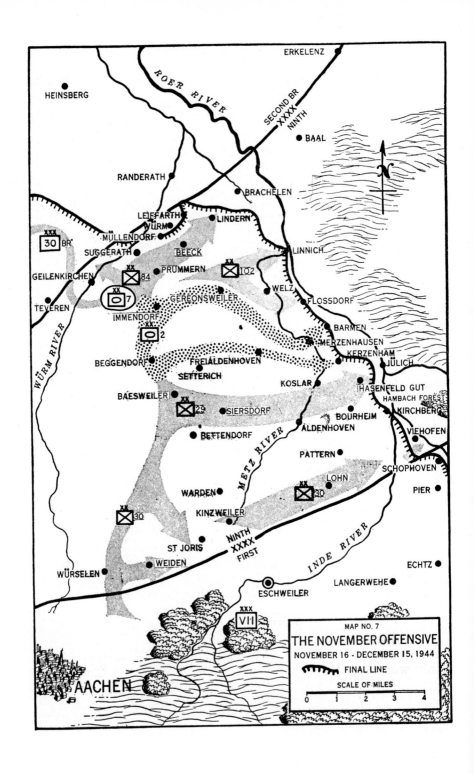

MAP NO. 7

THE NOVEMBER OFFENSIVE
NOVEMBER 16 - DECEMBER 15, 1944

FINAL LINE

SCALE OF MILES

0 1 2 3 4

It is believed that the 12.5% flak battle damage sustained by IX Bombardment Division aircraft which participated in Operation Q would have been substantially greater if the counter-flak artillery fire had not been used. This statement is based on the heavy antiaircraft defenses at target and on the cloud condition at target. At least 40% battle damage was anticipated, if targets were attacked without counter-battery fire. Please notify artillery units concerned.

At 12:45 P.M., on November 16 the initial echelons of XIX Corps' attacking troops left their line of departure and struck eastward. (*Map No. 7.*) From south to north elements of the 30th and 29th Infantry Divisions and the 2d Armored Division, without benefit of the usual artillery preparation, advanced rapidly in the face of surprisingly weak resistance. The surprise gained by launching the attack at midday and by foregoing an artillery preparation, up to that time an almost certain indication of an American attack, contributed to the success of the first day's operation. Gains of one-half to two miles were recorded by nightfall, and seven small German towns were captured. As the Germans recovered balance, however, the opposition stiffened and before the day was over all forces were heavily engaged. German resistance became particularly strong in the many small towns. In addition to the activity of the XIX Corps, the XIII Corps' 102d Division moved out to conform to the advance of the 2d Armored Division near Immendorf, in order to maintain contact and prevent exposing the armored division's north flank.

On November 17 the 2d Armored Division, its tanks battling both the mud and a full-scale German counterattack in the vicinity of Gereonsweiler, was able to inch forward only a half mile. Enemy tactics in this engagement were characteristic of those he employed generally throughout the European campaign. Bringing up reinforcements comprising approximately forty-five Mark V (Panther) and Mark VI (Tiger) tanks of the 9th Panzer Division, veterans of the Russian front, and of the 15th Panzergrenadier Division, incorporating elements of the once renowned Afrika Korps, he threw this weight, supported by infantry, against the 2d Armored Division. The heavily armored Tiger tanks were able to deliver damaging fire upon the American Sherman tanks from a range of 3,000 yards or more, and at this range even the 90mm projectile of the new American tank destroyer would ricochet off the front of the Tiger. These new tank destroyers, only recently received by Ninth Army, and still few in number, were getting their first full-scale battle test. Fighting furiously, the 2d Armored Division beat off four distinct counterattacks, including two strong enemy efforts to regain the town of Immendorf, and kept its advance going, though slowly. The 29th and 30th Infantry Divisions also met stiff opposition.

November 18 repeated the story of the 17th, although German air activity became comparatively heavy. All three divisions pushed slowly eastward, making gains of up to a mile against the bitter, fanatical opposition of the German forces defending each of the numerous small towns and communities. The 29th Division continued its advance, securing several small road centers. The 30th Division succeeded in clearing Würselen, a suburban area lying northeast of Aachen, fighting its way through one of the most heavily mined areas experienced in the war up to that time. Other populated areas to the east, including Weiden, Warden, Bettendorf, Siersdorf, and the major portion of Setterich, were cleared against strong resistance based particularly on the defensive strength of the pillboxes, concrete emplacements, and fortified houses which abounded in the area, supported by innumerable small-scale local counterattacks.

Within this southern section of Ninth Army's zone, particularly in the path of the 30th Infantry Division, large concentrations of both antitank and antipersonnel mines were encountered. Approximately thirty percent were the new-type antipersonnel Schü mines, small nonmetallic mines constructed with a wooden case and detonated by any light pressure placed on the hinged lid. Glass Topf mines, too, were discovered in this area for the first time. These large antitank mines likewise contained no metal. Neither of the new mines could be detected by the standard mine detector then in use. Prodding was resorted to, and the relatively new nonmetallic mine detector was pressed into service, but it proved too sensitive and slow in operation to be of much use during an advance. Long-handled pitchforks proved the most effective means of prodding for the Schü mines.

On November 19 the 30th Division broke through on the south flank to advance two miles and clear five towns. However, its advance east of St. Jöris and Kinzweiler was prevented by heavy German fire coming from the town of Eschweiler in the First Army zone of action. Until the left flank elements of First Army could clear Eschweiler, the 30th Division would have to stand fast. The advance of the 29th Division in the center continued slowly, with a maximum advance of one and one-half miles. Farther north, though, the town of Geilenkirchen fell, in an action initiated the previous day by the British XXX Corps, with the American 84th Infantry Division making the main effort. The town of Prummern had been secured on the 18th, and now on the 19th the 84th Division drove all the way through Geilenkir-.chen to capture Süggerath, a mile and a half to the northeast. The Germans were definitely sensitive to the advance on the north flank, for here, too, they counterattacked with infantry supported by some fifteen to twenty tanks just north of Prummern. The action was repulsed by the 84th Division. This division was off to a good start in its first battle, and General Horrocks, commanding the XXX Corps, complimented it highly on the skill with which it conducted its first engagement. International amity was further increased when the British, during the cold wet weather, issued to the 84th Division the standard rum ration provided for British troops.

The initial rapid success in the Geilenkirchen area was due in part, no doubt, to the large quantities of artillery ammunition expended there. In the reduction of Geilenkirchen the American artillery units which supported the 84th Division fired nearly twice the quantity of light and medium artillery ammunition expended by like units of the XIX Corps in the initial attack phase. In addition, British divisional artillery ammunition expenditures were more that twice those of American divisional artillery. Of course, ammunition to provide a similar scale of artillery activity over the entire Army front simply was not available.

In the operations of the 84th Division around Geilenkirchen, the XXX Corps introduced Ninth Army troops to their first use of antiaircraft searchlights to produce artificial moonlight or "movement light." The principle of artificial moonlight is the reflection of powerful searchlight beams off low cloud banks into the enemy positions. A dark night with low clouds gives the best operating conditions. The searchlights are emplaced in defilade 4000 to 6000 yards behind the front lines and 2000 to 4000 yards apart. The lights face the front lines and are elevated to about twenty degrees above the horizontal. This elevation leaves a dark band between the lights and the front lines and gives maximum illumination in the area of the enemy front lines. The light is directed into the eyes of the enemy and tends to screen our own troops. Enemy personnel and installations are illuminated from the front, and any movements are easily detected. The light intensity is about equal to that of a full moon on a clear night and is sufficient to permit attacking troops to pick the easiest route of approach and to avoid obstacles which would otherwise greatly hinder their progress.

The first reaction of troops on experiencing this illumination was to make them very reluctant to move, for they felt exposed and naked. However, after a little experience, this feeling was outweighed by the advantages of artificial moonlight, and it became in great demand by front-line troops to assist them in movement, in the relief of units, and in the detection of enemy movements. In the initial phase of the attack on Geilenkirchen, the night was too clear to reflect the beams, and the artificial moonlight was not satisfactory. Later in the same operation, however, the effectiveness of the illumination improved greatly.

By November 19, the fourth day of the offensive, the pattern of the fighting had been quite well established. It was found to conform, too, to the action taking place in the First Army zone. The Germans were making use of every defensive trick known to them, defending every strongpoint and every village, counterattacking viciously every advance, and showing no signs of either weakness or an intention to withdraw. The character of the enemy's fixed defensive works obviated extensive maneuver by the attacking forces. The enemy, knowing how the attack must come, had only to block it head-on and inflict the maximum casualties and delay.

On November 20 German tanks reappeared in numbers and continued the tank-versus-tank battle with the 2d Armored Division, which had begun on November 17. In conjunction with the reappearance of his tanks, the German stepped up his usually weak air effort on November 21, when forty-five enemy aircraft performed bombing and strafing missions, night and day, in the XIX Corps area. The tank fighting in which the 2d Armored Division was now engaged comprised what the Germans chose to call "the greatest tank battle of the Western Front." Between sixty and eighty Tiger and Panther tanks were thrown against the 2d Armored Division, which fought the more heavily armored

German forces with every weapon available, including its tank destroyers, its artillery, its infantry, and its supporting fighter-bombers, as well as its own tanks. The fighting was extremely bitter and the casualties high, but the 2d Armored Division pushed slowly on and by the 21st not only had taken Freialdenhoven and Gereonsweiler but also had gained the high ground north of Gereonsweiler, the key terrain west of the Roer River. In the planning stages of the operation, the Army Commander had often stressed the importance of this high ground. Its value was proved by the advantage it afforded General Harmon's attacking forces; once they had gained it they were never driven from it. In the center of the zone the 29th Division continued its advance against the same bitter resistance, gaining about two miles on November 20 and slightly more on the 21st. By the 22d, however, it was stopped, fighting all day in Bourheim, two miles southwest of Jülich, with no advance.

By the 20th, the VII Corps, on Ninth Army's right flank, had punched through the resistance south of the inter-Army boundary. On November 21 the 30th Division made gains of three miles to the east and established contact with VII Corps troops on its south flank. On the 22d, however, it ran into extremely heavy resistance upon pushing into the small village of Lohn, located near the inter-Army boundary. Here, German fire from the adjacent, mutually-supporting town of Pützlohn in the First Army zone made it impossible for the division to move supporting weapons forward, and shortly before dark the infantry elements were forced to withdraw from the town. On the next day, however, the 30th Division was back in the battle, and it again entered Lohn, this time to stay. An easier victory also was accomplished by the 30th Division on this date after executing a brilliant maneuver and taking advantage of a ruse to gain its objective. During the night of the 22d-23d, the Division moved one regiment of infantry north into the town of Aldenhoven in the 29th Division zone of action. Then, while the attack at Lohn was going on, occupying the entire attention of the German forces in that area, the regiment moved out quickly from Aldenhoven and attacked southeast toward Pattern. They captured Pattern with only light casualties before the defenders were even aware of their danger. Two Tiger tanks were knocked out at a range of but sixty yards.

Meanwhile, in the British zone of action to the north, the resistance had stiffened after the initial successes at Geilenkirchen. On November 21 the 84th Division, attempting to capture the small towns of Beeck, Würm, and Müllendorf, encountered intense fire from pillboxes, heavy artillery, mortars, and antitank weapons and was able to advance only 300 yards during the day. The following day, infantry elements succeeded in entering Beeck, but were promptly driven out by a German counterattack, and the attack on Würm made no progress. In this situation at 6:00 o'clock on the night of the 22d, the 84th Division reverted to the control of XIII Corps after its initial five days of battle action under British XXX Corps. At this time, too, the 34th Field Artillery Brigade became operational directly under the Army with the mission of supporting the entire Army attack. Under the unit's command were two 240mm howitzer battalions and one 8-inch gun battalion. These were the "heavies" of the Army, and they proved useful despite the deplorable lack of sufficient ammunition to make them truly effective. With observation provided by fighter-type aircraft of the XXIX Tactical Air Command, they destroyed two important enemy bridges over the Roer River, one with the phenomenally small expenditure of only nine rounds, the other with but twenty-two rounds.

All across the front, night after night, the Germans staged sharp counterattacks. Although usually successful in repelling these threats, Ninth Army forces suffered casualties and disruption of plans which added to the delay in the advance. A series of counterattacks, staged against the 2d Armored Division in their position on the high ground north of Gereonsweiler, were all successfully repulsed. Merzenhausen, reached on the 22d by the 2d Armored Division, was found to be vigorously defended by German tanks and infantry. A German counterattack from Bourheim at daylight on the 22d, directed against the 29th Division, revealed the presence of a new German unit, the 340th Infantry Division, thrown in to halt the progress in the center of the line where the 29th was approaching the Roer River. This turn of events had its effect, and on November 23 the 29th and the 2d Armored were held fast.

For three days, from November 24 through the 26th, a virtual stalemate existed all across the front, although the 29th Division, after three days of bitter fighting, cleared the town of Bourheim on the 24th and held it against a strong coordinated counterattack on the 26th. This counterattack was the fourteenth major effort on the part of the enemy to stop the Army's advance since the jump-off on November 16. At Koslar, two miles north of Bourheim, two companies of infantry of the 29th Division were cut off for three days. At Merzenhausen, still farther to the north, the 2d Armored Division fought back and forth through the town, at times occupying it jointly with the enemy. On the 24th the 10th SS Panzer Division was identified, revealing the presence of the second reserve armored division to be thrown into the battle.

On November 27 the tactical picture brightened as Ninth Army launched attacks all along the front which were to break the back of coordinated German resistance west of the Roer. The 30th Division, on the right, went for Altdorf, a mile and a half away, and in the face of extremely heavy small-arms, mortar, and artillery fire, cleared the town by the 28th and closed up to the Inde River throughout its zone of action. The attackers caught an entire company of enemy infantry attempting to withdraw here, and virtually annihilated it. At the end of the day Ninth Army forces held the west end of the damaged bridge over the Inde River at Altdorf, and German forces defended the east end.

The 29th Division, in the center, pushed out on the 27th with two infantry battalions to relieve the two companies cut off in Koslar. Reaching the town by nightfall, it found a fierce battle raging. The relieving forces lent their assistance in clearing the town, and Kirchberg as well, on the following day. In addition, south of the Aldenhoven–Jülich road the 29th Division closed up to the Roer River and found that the railroad bridge at Jülich had been destroyed by the Germans. Farther north on November 27 the 2d Armored Division fought back into Merzenhausen and established a firm hold on the town, captured two more objectives near Barmen, and beat off a tank-supported infantry attack launched from the Flossdorf area. This attack, launched in the early evening, cost the enemy high casualties when he ran into heavy artillery fire. On the 28th the 2d Armored Division took Barmen, the last town west of the Roer in its zone of action. On November 29, then, the German resistance remaining west of the Roer and Inde Rivers in the XIX Corps zone was confined to two small pockets in the zone of action of the 29th Division, one at Hasenfeld Gut and one in the Jülich Sportsplatz.

The scene of action now shifted to the north, where the XIII Corps on November 29 began its attack to clear its zone west of the Roer River. With the 102d Division on the right and the 84th on the left, the XIII Corps drove northeast with its main objective the securing of the crossing sites at Linnich and the expansion and protection of the north flank of the Army. Brigadier General Roland P. Shugg's XIII Corps Artillery, comprising at this time one observation battalion and nine artillery battalions under three group headquarters, supported the Corps attack. The 7th Armored Division, although not committed to action as a unit, likewise supported the attack with its division artillery, and was kept close behind the infantry divisions, on an alert status, prepared to back up the attack should the opportunity present itself. The 102d Division captured Weltz on November 30 and entered into a close-range, all-out battle for Flossdorf.

By December 1 two of the 102d's infantry regiments were stopped—one in front of Flossdorf, the other fighting for the high ground north of Linnich. Shortly before noon on that date, the division commander, General Keating, sensed an opportunity for his reserve regiment, the 406th, and ordered it into the battle between the two stalemated units. With a tank battalion attached, and strongly supported by dive-bombers and artillery, this regiment slipped into Linnich itself and by the end of the day controlled two-thirds of the town. The resistance from the surprised Germans was stubborn and they made good use of dug-in tanks, pillboxes, booby traps, and mines, but the town was progressively occupied. The 84th Division's battle for Lindern, Beeck, and Leiffarth was even more difficult. Pillboxes along the Wurm River, while sited toward the west, nevertheless proved to be of great advantage to the defenders, even though out-flanked by the maneuver of hitting them from the south. Frequently repeated in the fight in this area was the German habit of reoccupying during the night pillboxes from which they had been driven during the previous day's action. To combat this practice Ninth Army demolished all concrete pillboxes as quickly as possible after capture. Lindern was taken on November 30, but the fanatical defenders of Beeck and Leiffarth held out until December 2. This marked the limit of advance on the Army north flank for some time to come.

By December 2 the 29th Division had regrouped its forces and prepared its plans to reduce the two German strongpoints still holding out at Hasenfeld Gut and the Jülich Sportsplatz. Hasenfeld Gut, a group of stone farm buildings, afforded the enemy excellent defensive positions. The Sportsplatz, the athletic stadium of the town of Jülich, was even more formidable. A large, concrete structure with its entrance on the east side, away from the attackers, it was surrounded by a high wall and a water-filled moat. To the west of the stadium the ground which the attackers must approach was a barren plain some 800 yards broad, heavily mined and booby-trapped, and completely covered by German fire. The two strongpoints were well sited and their reduction was to prove costly and difficult. Heavy air and artillery support was delivered to assist the attacking infantry, but still the sieges went on. On December 6 fighter-bombers of the XXIX Tactical Air Command carried out an excellent strike on the Sportsplatz. The pilots dived daringly low in order to drop their bombs squarely on the target, but the ground troops following up the air effort were repulsed with heavy losses. Finally, on December 8, 29th Division infantrymen filtered into both strongpoints and on the following day these two costly objectives were taken.

The final advance to the Roer River was made on December 14, when the 30th Division crossed the Inde River and moved up to the Roer, occupying the small town of Viehofen without casualties. This action followed the capture of Schophoven and Pier just south of the inter-Army boundary by First Army's 104th Division, after an extremely bitter battle. Now Ninth Army's forces, after nearly a month-long campaign, were closed up to the Roer River and preparing for a crossing. The precluding factors were the Roer River dams, whose capture by First Army had been deemed necessary before launching the attack across the river.

While the operations in the battle area "up front" were continuing despite the difficulties imposed by terrain, weather, and strong enemy resistance, events behind the front were generating equally difficult conditions.

Excessive rains created discouraging conditions throughout the entire area. Beginning November 15 the Maas River began to rise to a ten-year record flood which reached its crest on November 29. The two-way temporary pile bridge at Maastricht was closed and, in fact, almost given up for lost. Eventually it was saved from extensive damage by the unique expedient of weighting down its deck with sandbags and by attaching anchor cables to the bridge. A Bailey bridge had been placed on the ruins of a partially demolished permanent bridge near the center of the town, and heavy vehicles untilized this structure during the flood. Light vehicles were passed over the 25-ton ponton bridge, which although reduced in capacity by the swift currents which reached a high of eleven feet per second, was never closed except to adjust for water level. During the period this bridge was lengthened from 470 feet to 670 feet to accommodate the increased width of the river resulting from the flood. It carried a daily average of 2,000 vehicles and essential civilian traffic consisting of wagons, carts, bicycles, livestock, and pedestrians, thereby relieving the strain of traffic on the Bailey bridge. Since British bridges downstream were rendered inoperative by the flood, the traffic required to support their XXX Corps east of the Maas was necessarily added to the heavy burden already carried. To control the overload of traffic on the Maastricht bridges, strict traffic control was enforced twenty-four hours a day. As they approached the access roads leading to the bridges, vehicles were classified and were directed to the appropriate bridge. Both bridges were necessarily operated as alternating one-way bridges, and, as a result, there was constant congestion on the access roads on both sides of the river. So many British vehicles were involved that military police were furnished by the XXX Corps to augment the American forces and to assist in the direction of British traffic.

Traffic difficulties were considerably reduced, however, and maximum use of roads and bridges was insured by the Army policy of keeping the "light line" well forward, generally on or in advance of corps rear boundaries. Behind the light line all traffic was permitted to operate with normal headlights and driving lights, taking full advantage of the relative inactivity of German aircraft at night. Many potential traffic accidents from blackout driving were thus obviated, and all night movements, particularly those of heavy supply trucks and large supply convoys, were greatly facilitated.

Throughout the Army area, roads deteriorated seriously under the combination of foul weather conditions and heavy traffic. Increased road maintenance measures and road-saving traffic control were put into effect. To assist the troops in their efforts to stop the disintegration of road surfaces, the Army established a plant at Maastricht to make asphaltic premix. This material was made available to engineer units for patching ravelled pavement edges and potholes. Efforts were made, but with little success, to obtain asphaltic emulsion for use in patching during periods of inclement weather. Great difficulty was encountered throughout the area by vehicles carrying mud onto the hard-surfaced highways from the dirt roads and fields in which they had been operating or bivouacked. Mud soon caused a slippery coating on the highways. In addition, it was picked up by passing or leading vehicles and thrown against the windshields of trailing or passed vehicles, temporarily blinding the drivers, These two effects resulted in many accidents and traffic difficulties. Ordnance maintenance companies stationed heavy wreckers at critical points, and ordnance road patrols covered all main routes to repair breakdowns and recover wrecks. To combat the mud problem an excessive number of engineer troops had to be employed, and a comprehensive mud-control program was inaugurated which required all troops, both combat and service, to keep the hard-surfaced roads adjacent to their bivouacs and other installations continually serviced and free from mud. The rigid Army policy of placing all supplies on hard standing or on road shoulders adjacent to hard-surfaced roads proved a tremendous aid in mud control, since it permitted the great numbers of supply trucks to operate habitually on hard-surfaced roads and prevented their carrying mud onto the roads. By all these measures, control of the mud problem was finally successfully gained. It became apparent, however, that many roads would be lost to effective use through sheer physical wear and tear of heavy traffic, and emphasis was therefore maintained on rail rehabilitation.

The narrow front on which the Army was operating placed a premium on space of all types. Adequate storage facilities and issuing points for supplies were not always available. The country had been bitterly fought over; few buildings were standing which could be employed as supply points or service installations. The need for shelters and space for adequate clearing stations, field and evacuation hospitals, and storage installations necessitated constant reconnaissance as the attack progressed. Even a minor change in a boundary caused extreme concern to the affected units. Every available space within their area was jam-packed with supplies or installations.

Expenditure of supplies naturally increased with the tempo of the offensive, particularly when an additional corps became operational; consequently the equipment shortage became more serious. For example, during the period between November 18 and 25, heavy battle losses resulted in a shortage, at one time, of 111 medium tanks, a shortage unmitigated by any hope of early replacement. These losses were especially serious. Owing to the critical over-all shortage of medium tanks, the number authorized the armored divisions by War Department tables of equipment had been arbitrarily reduced, with the result that the divisions already were operating with less than the number they had been trained to employ. In the 2d Armored Division, one of the two "heavy" armored divisions operating in the European Theater, the number of medium tanks authorized had been cut from 232 to 200; in the standard armored divisions the authorization had been cut from 168 to 150, and separate tank battalions had been cut from 54 to 50. The number of light tanks authorized had been similarly reduced.

Shortages occurred in a number of smaller items, and local manufacture produced gratifying results in many instances. For example, when a need arose for extended end-connectors for tank tracks, five-inch steel extensions were welded on the standard end-connectors to provide additional flotation on muddy soil. The extensions were supplied by local manufacture, and even though the product was inferior and required considerable maintenance, the problem was greatly alleviated for medium tanks. The devices did not prove satisfactory, however, for light tanks. Various other spare parts for vehicles and for mess equipment were also manufactured locally.

Captured materials and troop-produced items were added to the stocks to reduce shortages. Substantial quantities of engineer supplies were captured, particularly lumber, electrical supplies, hardware, and machinery. While the shortage of engineer troops prevented full exploitation of these materials, they were a valuable asset. To combat a lumber shortage, engineer combat units were diverted from their normal duties to logging and the operation of sawmills. During full-scale production, sawmills operated by the Army produced as much as 60,000 board feet per day.

The shortage of certain highly specialized units was a grave concern, particularly in Army troops. For example, the Army signal service was short a heavy construction battalion. This situation was aggravated by the necessity for maintaining normal operations and at the same time retraining signal construction units in the rehabilitation and maintenance of underground cables. The normal field communications over open wire lines and spiral-four cables had been superseded in the new area by the utilization of large existing commercial cables in a net that included Maastricht, Liège, Aachen, Heerlen, and Sittard. Ninety percent of the trunk telephone circuits of the Army net were now carried by cable, and the necessary personnel had to be trained in the highly specialized technique of handling such lines. Also lacking was a signal photographic company. In order to meet the many photographic requirements, general assignment photographic teams and a photographic laboratory team were furnished by 12th Army Group to provide coverage for the various corps and divisions. This system left much to be desired, since constant shifts in assignment were necessary to make maximum use of the means available, and commanders strenuously objected to having their photographers changed. Satisfactory service was obtained only by the later assignment of a photographic company.

Again, in the case of engineer troops, a topographic battalion was lacking, and the expedient of using a corps topographic company reinforced by an engineer map depot detachment had to be devised. This hybrid unit had to bear the load of the increased map production necessary for the attack to the Roer and also for the compilation of an emergency road map of Germany. In quartermaster troops only one depot company was available. It was therefore necessary to use a railhead company to operate the Army food depot and a gasoline supply company to operate the Army gasoline railhead, and to reinforce the available depot company with service company personnel in the operation of the quartermaster parts and equipment depot.

A shortage of military police units was somewhat relieved by the use of Netherlands and Belgian troops. During the first week in November, Ninth Army forces were augmented by a battalion of Fusiliers of the Belgian Army and three battalions of Storm Troops of the Netherlands Interior Forces. These were used as security police. Spread throughout the Army area, they were immediately placed on duty to assist in guarding wire communications, gasoline dumps, ordnance depots, and the Army prisoner-of-war inclosure. A special signal intelligence detachment also was formed from the Netherlands Interior Forces. This detachment, of some fifteen men, had as its principal duty collecting, interpreting, and making available to the Army all possible information concerning the German civil and military communication systems. Its work proved invaluable.

There were problems, too, in securing proper individual replacements—or reinforcements, as they were later called. Not only were these short in numbers at times, but also it was found that those furnished needed refresher training and combat orientation prior to assignment to combat units in the forward areas. In cooperation with the 18th Reinforcement Depot, which was the Theater Ground Force Reinforcement System agency for Ninth Army, the Assistant Chief of Staff, G-1, Colonel Daniel H. Hundley, established a program to give these men training. Each division furnished combat-experienced officers and noncommissioned officers to act as instructors. Combat demonstrations were presented, and the replacements were trained in day-to-day living under combat conditions, in the care and firing of all small arms, German as well as American, and in methods of detection of and protection against mines and booby traps. Discussion periods offered the men who were soon to get their first experience in actual battle an opportunity to find the answers to their down-to-earth questions. The confidence instilled in the newly arrived replacement was as valuable as the additional training in how to conduct himself on the battlefield. Coupled with subsequent special treatment upon arrival at the division to which assigned, this program had the effect of permitting the new man to adjust himself more quickly into the ranks with his veteran companions.

In view of the shortage of personnel reinforcements, close attention was given to the prompt return of casualties discharged from hospitals. Casualties returning to their units had often been unreasonably delayed and in some instances had been returned without proper clothing and equipment. Travel time from hospital to unit was reduced and unnecessary "waiting" eliminated. In addition, all hospitals and replacement installations in the Army area were authorized to stock small amounts of clothing, equipment, and ordnance material to insure that the returnee was properly equipped.

A Ninth Army cemetery was established at Margraten, in the

Netherlands about seven miles east of Maastricht, on November 10. The site of this cemetery was carefully chosen, both as to location and capacity, for it was to be used as the principal burial place for all Ninth Army dead, to avoid establishment of cemeteries on German soil at a later date. There was a strong feeling on the part of the soldier against burial on enemy soil, and the disadvantage of transporting the bodies over a great distance for burial was reduced in practice by the fact that later, after the Roer River was crossed, casualties became light. The perfection of a standing operating procedure for division, corps, and Army collecting points for the dead resulted in an almost perfect record in identification. Under the supervision of the Army Chaplain, Colonel W. Roy Bradley, chaplains of each faith were in constant attendance at the cemetery, as they were at all Army hospitals.

With Ninth Army troops operating in Germany proper, where nonfraternization orders prohibited any mingling with the population for diversion or recreation, it became imperative to establish rest centers in the Netherlands. During October and November a number of such centers were opened, with each division and corps organizing its own. Here men from the forward area enjoyed two- to three-day rest periods. Red Cross facilities were available, and motion pictures, United Service Organizations entertainment, and Special Service "live talent" shows were provided. Laundry and bath facilities, no minor items, were also to be found at these rest centers.

For the further comfort and well-being of the individual soldier, quartermaster fumigation and bath companies throughout the Army were stocked with sufficient clothing to effect a fresh change for front-line soldiers, in conjunction with a hot bath, when relieved for short periods of rest. The dirty clothing was then laundered, sized, repaired, and reissued to members of the next unit relieved. It mattered little to the front-line soldier whether the clothing was new or resulted in a tailored fit, as long as it was clean.

In the early autumn of 1944 the intensive program of soldier voting, begun while the Army Headquarters was still in England, drew to a close. Under the supervision of the Army Special Services Officer, Colonel Frederick J. de Rohan, by War Department direction an Army-wide campaign of information, visits, and inspections had been conducted to insure that each individual was informed of his voting rights, qualifications, and duties as a citizen.

The approach of winter brought certain special problems. With transportation scarce, supply agencies now must add huge quantities of sleeping bags, overshoes, additional blankets, and shelter tents to the heavy demands already required by the operating armies. In view of the prevailing rain, a shortage of overshoes in size 10 and larger presented difficulties, particularly in connection with the control of trench foot.

Front-line infantry units, because of the conditions under which combat forced them to live, were especially hard hit by the disabling and painful ailment of trench foot. The term "trench foot," a hold-over from World War I, designates a condition brought on by exposure to moisture and cold, in which the skin becomes discolored and tender, blisters may form, and gangrene and the loss of toes may result. The primary cause is reduced circulation of the blood in the feet. Forced inactivity in the foxholes and slit trenches of forward positions, in wet and cold and snow, were the major contributing factors. If not discovered and treated promptly, trench foot could cause permanent injury. Even light cases meant the loss of the man's fighting ability for some time. Hospital admissions illustrate the gravity of the situation. Admissions for trench foot constituted over seven percent of all admissions, both combat and non-combat, to Ninth Army hospitals in November. On one day, November 25, hospital admissions for trench foot were sixty-five percent as great as those for all combat wounded. That the answer to trench foot lay in prevention rather than cure was recognized in the early fall, and warning and preventive measures were published to the command. As winter came on these measures were increased, stressing the necessity for keeping the feet dry and warm, for insuring good circulation—by massage if necessary—and for changing into dry socks. Army supplied lower units with sufficient extra supplies to permit them to send up dry socks with the daily rations.

The supervision of the prevention of trench foot was stressed as a command function, and commanders realized its importance because the depletion of their units could be severe. As the condition became widely recognized and understood, the incidence of injury slowly decreased. Preventive measures brought results. In November, for example, in order to prevent glutting the Army evacuation hospitals with these cases, it was necessary to establish the policy of transferring them immediately to general hospitals in the Communications Zone. In contrast, soon after the turn of the year, although snow, cold, and forced inactivity continued, the number of cases had decreased sufficiently to permit the majority to be treated within the Army area at a provisional convalescent hospital, assuring a more rapid return to duty. Constant vigilance in prevention continued to be a necessity, however, and only with the advent of spring did trench foot cease to be a major problem.

Another medical situation that was given close and detailed attention was combat exhaustion, or battle neurosis. The stresses of war and, particularly, active combat in many instances produce what may roughly be called mental disturbances. In World War I these cases were ascribed to "shell shock" and were not very well understood. However, the importance of mental disease was recognized at the beginning of the mobilization for World War II, and efforts were made to minimize its occurence. As a part of their physical examination, inductees were subjected to a screening interview by a psychiatrist. In many instances a history of past mental disturbance or traits of character predisposing to such disturbance was disclosed, and the person was deferred. In addition, each training division was assigned a psychiatrist to assist unit commanders in handling the problem of personality readjustment, note early indications of mental disease in the command, and do what he could to treat the milder cases.

The mental disorders brought out in combat fell into two categories: First, there were cases arising from simple mental fatigue; that is, combat exhaustion. Second, there were the true psychiatric disorders, precipitated by experiences in combat. The psychiatric disorders constituted a minor group, but they necessitated extensive treatment and prolonged hospitalization. The combat exhaustion cases, however, if discovered early enough, were found to be amenable to treatment, and the majority of cases could be returned to duty. Treatment consisted chiefly in change of environment, rest, narcosis (suspended activity induced by drugs), feeding, and frequently psychoanalysis and proper evaluation and explanation of his condition to the patient. After recovery, if it were indicated, the soldier was reassigned to a position or unit more in keeping with his ability to withstand the ordeal of combat. This may have meant transfer from a rifle platoon to a company headquarters or even from a division to corps or army service troops.

In September neuropsychiatric casualties accounted for 5.8% of all admissions to division medical clearing stations. This figure rose to 9.8% in October and 10.5% in November. Of these an average of 40% were returned to duty.

In October these cases were being treated in three types of installations—division clearing stations, evacuation hospitals, and a small, under-staffed neuropsychiatric hospital. Early in November, a Combat Exhaustion Center, operated by one company— later two companies—of the 95th Medical Gas Treatment Battalion, was established in the Army area. All psychiatrists assigned to evacuation hospitals were placed on special duty at the center. A great deal of informative material on the diagnosis and treatment of mental cases was disseminated to all surgeons, and the following plan was adopted:

All true psychiatric cases would be evacuated immediately to general hospitals.

Mild cases of combat exhaustion would be treated in the division area. Here the treatment was simple, consisting of removal from actual contact with the enemy, plenty of hot food, and an opportunity for sleep. If the patient had not recovered within forty-eight hours, he was to be transferred to the Combat Exhaustion Center.

More severe cases would be transferred directly from the division to the Exhaustion Center. Here they would be given adequate nursing care and the greatest possible change in environment, and they would be assured sufficient rest by the administration of sleep-inducing drugs. In many instances it was possible to draw out from the patient, while in a partial state of narcosis, the facts immediately related to the onset of his symptoms. This was of great value in the readjustment of the soldier.

The merit of this system was borne out in the reduction of evacuations from the Army area. By December, seventy percent of the neuropsychiatric cases admitted to division medical clearing stations and Army hospitals were being returned to duty, in contrast to the forty percent returned before the establishment of the Combat Exhaustion Center.

When Ninth Army assumed responsibility for an area in Belgium, the southern Netherlands, and Germany, it began its first substantial participation in civil affairs and military government activities. The particularly important problems in this field which faced Colonel Carl A. Kraege, the Assistant Chief of Staff, G-5, were those of providing considerable amounts of supplies, particularly food, to the Belgian and Netherlands people and the rehabilitation of industrial installations which could contribute to the war effort. Enormous quantities of supplies of all types were brought into the Maastricht area and turned over to Netherlands authorities for distribution by them, under Army supervision, to the needy people. Clothing was scarce, and after a survey of requirements had been made by the Army staff, immediate steps were taken to procure the necessary items and make them available to the civil authorities.

At the time of their liberation, the people in this area of the southern Netherlands were existing on a very low caloric diet. In raising the diet from a near starvation level to the required minimum to sustain life, many obstacles were encountered. Civilian supplies had, of course, to compete with ammunition, army equipment, and army supplies in general for transportation. In addition, warehousing in the restricted Army area was an acute problem. Through strenuous efforts, however, sufficient supplies were built up, together with a reserve in small warehouses scattered throughout the city of Maastricht. The provision of this reserve was a wise measure, particularly in December when the German Ardennes counteroffensive increased the difficulty of obtaining shipments from the rear.

Closely connected with the civilian food supply situation were the conditions of agriculture and transportation. The Army arranged for the importation of seed—mainly potatoes and vegetables—and later gave impetus to a Victory Garden program which turned out very successfully. The general lack of fats in the civilian diet called for rehabilitation of the dairy industry. Surveys made by the Army showed, surprisingly, that the dairy industry had not been hurt as badly as the Netherlands authorities had thought. What was needed, first of all, was strong control of distribution by the civilian authorities. The transportation situation had, of course, a direct bearing on the distribution of food. The Army directed its efforts toward the coordination of existing facilities—road transportation, railroads, canals, barges —and such rehabilitation as could be affected, to expedite not only military but also civilian supply. Through the Advance Section of Communications Zone, which controlled the railroads, Ninth Army made arrangements for civilian transportation both of supplies and passengers. Passenger transportation was an item of greatest importance, of course, in labor and industrial problems.

This area of the Netherlands and Belgium is an important mining and industrial area. The Army encouraged the reactivation of industrial plants and compiled a comprehensive report of all major industries in the district. Many industries were given Army contracts, and for the first time in Ninth Army history the procurement of special or essential supplies from local civilian sources became possible and quite necessary. The administrative function of this procurement, complicated by the continually changing policies of the Netherlands and Belgian governments, proved to be a special problem. Individual supply services, as well as the Army general staff, were forced to give individual attention to every transaction by the Army with the governments concerned.

The rehabilitation of the mining industry was closely tied in with the question of food. The Germans had "babied" the Netherlands miners in order to increase production and had been amazingly successful. During the latter part of the German occupation, miners were given a ration of 4,200 calories per day, extra cigarettes, and even liquor. Ninth Army did not attempt to dictate to the Netherlands authorities how the important supplies should be distributed among various consumer groups, but owing to an agreement between Netherlands and Belgian authorities concerning exchange of coal (necessitated by the difference between the types of coal in the two nations) it was an accepted policy to give Netherlands miners the same rations as the Belgian miners. This fell far short of the German ration and caused considerable labor trouble. While this was essentially a matter for Netherlands authorities to handle, the need for coal by the Army and by industries holding Army contracts was acute, and consequently Army Headquarters watched the situation closely and constantly rendered aid and advice to the civil authorities.

Initially some German coal mines in the Aachen area were in our possession, and later, as the offensive progressed, more were overrun. Most of them were found in relatively good condition. Immediate steps were taken to get these mines in operation. Some of the surface structures had been destroyed and some flooding of the mine shafts had occurred, but the Germans, shrinking from a scorched-earth policy, generally left managerial and technical personnel to supervise the preservation of the properties. Two mines in the vicinity of Eschweiler were placed in production shortly after they had been captured, but not until about the first of the year were they able to produce any appreciable excess over their own requirements for pumping. It was, however, possible to supply Army units with some coal for space heating and for hot water. More mines were gradually opened in the face of many problems, of which labor was the most difficult. The Germans had evacuated all skilled miners, many of whom were Poles of long residence in the area. The remaining miners were of poor quality and extremely reluctant to work. Money was no inducement to them, since there was nothing they could spend it for. They desired to stay at home with the idea of protecting their property and families. Through constant effort the labor supply was gradually increased and some of the labor problems solved.

Apart from the need for coal for industry, a chief interest of the Army in the coal mines lay in the production of electricity from the large power plants in the mines. Some were in need of repair, and it was necessary for military government to organize civilian work crews for the repair of plants and transmission lines, obtaining assistance from Advance Section engineers when special equipment and technical experts were required.

There was particular activity in the rehabilitation of all electric power plants and transmission lines, which were of vital importance to the Army. Special engineer officers coordinated and facilitated this work and maintained close liaison with the First Army and with 21 Army Group because of the wide distribution and close integration of the electric power system. A striking example of this close integration was displayed in the Army's use, for a long period of time, of electric power which was being generated behind the enemy lines in territory held by the Germans. It was apparently not feasible for the Germans to interrupt the main power lines to prevent this.

A major engineering task was later undertaken in the rehabilitation of large parts of the distribution system of the Aachen Water District. Army military government engineers, in cooperation with their counterparts in First Army, organized the repair of the entire system, since the broken water mains constituted a serious danger to public health and hence to the occupying troops. Temporary repairs were successfully made.

Intimate contact was maintained between Army health authorities and civilian health agencies to protect the local population from epidemics which would have their inevitable effect on the Army. The incidence of communicable disease was carefully watched, and serums and antitoxins were provided, usually only with the greatest difficulty in view of the general shortage of these supplies. Drugs and medicines provided for public health, through Army assistance or cooperation, included diphtheria antitoxin, antiscabiotic drugs, insulin, and DDT for delousing and typhus control. In maintaining public health, the cooperation of the Netherlands Green Cross System was particularly helpful. Public health nurses were unselfish in their devotion to duty and frequently traveled long miles on foot, in shabby footwear, when shoe leather was worth its weight in gold.

With Army units stationed in Germany, in Belgium, and in the Netherlands, and with the necessity for frequent official visits into France, the varying currency needs for individuals had to be met, under the supervision of the Army Finance Officer, Colonel John L. Scott. Not only did troops have to be paid in the money of the country in which they were serving, but also rigorous restrictions were required on currency exchange to prevent black market operations in those currencies which were at a premium. The Army Inspector General's Section, under Colonel Perry L. Baldwin, prepared regulations to prevent individuals from benefiting by illegal currency operations and from transmitting, through postal and other financial channels, excessive sums of money which could not be properly accounted for.

Ninth Army's position in the Maastricht region brought its first major contact with flying bombs; the Army rear area was squarely in the path of the buzz bomb attack against the port of Antwerp. Launched from sites in the rugged terrain near the Rhine River south of Cologne, the V-1s traveled some 200 miles to their target, flying a generally northwest course that carried most of them over the area between Liège and Maastricht. Antwerp was the most remunerative target for flying bombs at that time, but the increasing effectiveness of the defenses around the city heightened the possibility of a shift in the German attack.

Antiaircraft guns were shooting down more than half of the bombs that approached Antwerp; some units destroyed as high as eighty percent of the targets they engaged. With a possible shift of German targets in mind, Colonel John G. Murphy, the Army Antiaircraft Officer, made plans to defend against any attack made in the Army area.

Normally the flying bomb was employed as a strategic weapon, since its inaccuracy robbed it of any tactical value. Troops and supplies were relatively safe from the weapon when they were dispersed. Communications and supply centers close to the front were usually too small to constitute profitable targets. However, the restricted rear area of the Army had forced such a high concentration of supplies and so complex a communications network that it did present a suitable target for a concentrated attack by flying bombs. Under the 55th Antiaircraft Brigade, the Army antiaircraft brigade commanded by Brigadier General Samuel L. McCroskey, a defense belt of eight heavy antiaircraft batteries was established southeast of Maastricht to meet the threat. By the middle of November the guttural burble of the buzz bombs could be heard day and night over the Ninth Army area. As many as a hundred a day were reported, with flashes of exploding bombs occuring more and more frequently. Army personnel became well conditioned to the sound of the V-1s. When the characteristic roar was heard overhead—well and good; that meant that the bomb was still flying, the motor had not yet cut off preparatory to the diving descent of the 1,000 pounds of high explosive. If the motor cut off, that was the time to take cover. Although many buzz bombs cut off over Maastricht and exploded nearby, none ever struck the city directly, in spite of the German radio announcement to the Netherlands people that they intended to destroy the city because of the headquarters and supply installations located there. Coupled with the flying bombs were numerous random explosions in the Maastricht area. These were attributed to various other long-range artillery-type weapons with which the Germans were known to be experimenting. Use of such weapons was confirmed from fragments of finned artillery projectiles which struck in the Army area.

Graphical analysis of the incidence of the flying bombs showed, however, that no target in the Ninth Army area was under a planned attack, and that Antwerp was still receiving the heaviest blows. The defense belt was maintained and all guns were ready to fire, but the command to fire was withheld because, until the Germans turned their attention to Ninth Army's area, it was better to accept the occasional crashes than to fire at the buzz bomb. Against a full-scale attack an antiaircraft defense belt could protect a target such as a city, a port, or any particular installation, but protection had a price. For every bomb that exploded in the air when fired on, three or four could be expected merely to turn off course and crash. The defense belt, therefore, was best established in an isolated area so that no damage would result to installations from the fall of bombs rendered erratic when hit. Since the crowded conditions of the Army rear area meant that almost any explosion would do some damage, the results did not justify taking the bombs under fire unless an attack on Maastricht and its vital bridges should be launched.

In December the flying bomb attack waned. Each succeeding day saw a smaller number of V-1s over the Ninth Army until on the 7th not a single one was reported. By the 12th the attack was resumed, but Maastricht was still not the target, and the scale of the attack was far below the November high. More bombs were being launched against Liège, and some of those directed at Antwerp now came from the north. Few now passed over the Army and, with the lessening possibility of a direct attack on Army installations, coupled with the increased demands for normal antiaircraft protection that accompanied the German counteroffensive in mid-December, the defense belt was abandoned. The era of Ninth Army's interest in and threats from the flying bomb was over.

When the final action of the November offensive had ground to a stop along the flood-threatened Roer River on December 14, Ninth Army had advanced from eight to twelve miles across an eleven-mile front since jumping off from its Wurm River line on November 16. In general, the advance had been a slow and costly affair. Ninth Army's casualties had been just over ten thousand —1,133 killed, 6,864 wounded, and 2,059 missing or captured. The cost to the enemy had been much higher. German prisoners taken totalled 8,321. Enemy dead were estimated at 6,250, of whom 1,265 were actually buried by Ninth Army. The German defense never cracked despite Allied air and artillery superiority. For example, XXIX Tactical Air Command alone had dropped

1,150 tons of bombs and 22,200 gallons of Napalm during November, with a loss of 18 fighter-bombers. XIX Corps alone expended 56,000 rounds of light artillery ammunition and 34,000 of medium during the first four days of its attack. Yet the Germans had defended their positions with dogged and thorough determination. The terrain over which the campaign took place was well suited to defense and had been well organized. During the weeks that preceded the offensive the Germans had worked feverishly to improve their positions. Community digging had produced many antitank ditches, tank traps, and dug-in shelters on the open ground. The villages had all been turned into strongpoints with houses prepared to shelter tanks, machine guns, and light artillery pieces. The roads and other avenues of approach had been heavily sown with mines. This was fighting in Germany itself and the defenders of the Reich were loath to give up even a yard of homeland soil. The Germans called this campaign "the most terrible and ferocious battle in the history of the whole war," and Ninth Army units participating heartily indorsed the description. Ninth Army lost 84 medium and 15 light tanks destroyed, while knocking out an estimated 110 German tanks, many of them the heavily armored Tigers and Panthers. Even after the attackers' main forces had reached the Roer, the defenders held out in small pockets to the end, although all hope of successful resistance was gone. The same type of dogged resistance marked the battle going on simultaneously on both flanks of Ninth Army, particularly in front of the main effort being staged by First Army on the south. The operation that had aimed at the capture of Cologne and the closing up to the Rhine was now stalled along the muddy western banks of the flood-threatened Roer.

CHAPTER 4
PREPARATION FOR "GRENADE"

O PERATION Grenade, the drive from the Roer River to the Rhine, was probably Ninth Armys most brilliant contribution to Allied victory in Europe. It proved to be the key which unlocked the door that permitted the surging Allied forces to break through north and south of the Ruhr and bring Germany to defeat in a rapid, overwhelming advance across Germany.

In a sense, Operation Grenade was a continuation of the November offensive which had been designed to drive straight to the east with the objective of capturing Cologne and uncovering the Rhine, both north and south of Cologne. Then, after regrouping, Ninth Army would turn north to outflank the Siegfried Line, destroy the enemy forces west of the Rhine, and secure the river crossing sites north of the Ruhr. First Army was to provide the weight in this attack, making its main effort along the axis Düren-Cologne. Ninth Army's role was to protect the left flank of 12th Army Group, of which it was then a part, and to assist the advance of First Army. But the hoped-for breakthrough never came. Three elements delayed the day of payoff: the bitter, all-out resistance of the enemy; the hovering presence of the Sixth SS Panzer Army; and the flood threat of the Roer River dams. The strong delaying action offered by the Germans slowed down the attack and denied the U.S. forces any opportunity to exploit their gap through the Siegfried Line. The dual threat of the Nazis' last large mobile reserve in the west, coupled with the flooding possibilities offered by manipulation of the Roer River dams, indicated that a piecemeal crossing of the Roer provided the least chance of success, since the bridgehead might be isolated and annihilated. General Bradley, with characteristic consideration for economy of the lives of his doughboys, would take no such chance. His only alternative was to push up to the Roer throughout his zone, meanwhile attacking to seize control of the dams. Should the attack for the dams fail, he could still plan to cross once he had closed up tightly to the Roer and grouped all of his forces for multiple, simultaneous crossings.

So in the early days of December, Ninth Army and the northern portion of First Army licked their wounds after three weeks of hard fighting and conducted the savage, time-consuming, "little" battles of the Jülich Sportsplatz, Hasenfeld Gut, Schophoven, and Pier. (*Map No. 7.*) As Ninth Army closed in its zone along the Roer River, the front-line divisions thinned out their forward elements, and the main portions of the divisions were pulled back to prepare for the next offensive operation. Similarly the principal elements of the 7th Armored Division were placed in assembly areas in the rear of the XIII Corps zone. These measures, designed to rest and refit the Army's forces for the next strike forward, were in fact soon to have quite a different result in that they facilitated the Army's prompt movement of troops to other places on the American front. Meanwhile, the southern wing of First Army prepared to launch an offensive to take the Schwammenauel and the Urfttalsperre Dams. (*Map No. 5.*) These two were the key dams of the Roer River system. Once they were captured, the flood threat would be a thing of the past.

Heavy air strikes against the dams had been initiated. They were carried out during the first two weeks of December, whenever weather permitted, as preparations were completed to take the dams by ground operations. On December 4 a force of heavy bombers of the RAF Bomber Command carried out an aerial attack attempting to blast breaches in the faces of the dams to empty them of their water and thus destroy, for months at least, their potential flooding value to the Germans. Hits were observed, but no noticeable breaches resulted. The effort was repeated in force on December 11 when 668 RAF Lancasters dropped several thousand tons of bombs, including some of their 12,000-pound blockbusters. Although both the massive earthen Schwammenauel Dam and the curved concrete Urfttalsperre Dam were hit several times, no apparent serious damage was inflicted. The effort was abandoned in favor of the surer, but more costly, attack by ground troops.

The ground attack toward the dams had progressed only a limited distance in three days when new events developed to force its abandonment, for the time being, and the devotion of all Allied attention on the Western Front to one spotlighted battle area.

The German counteroffensive in the Ardennes was on.

On the morning of December 16 the brilliant, if ill-fated, Ger-

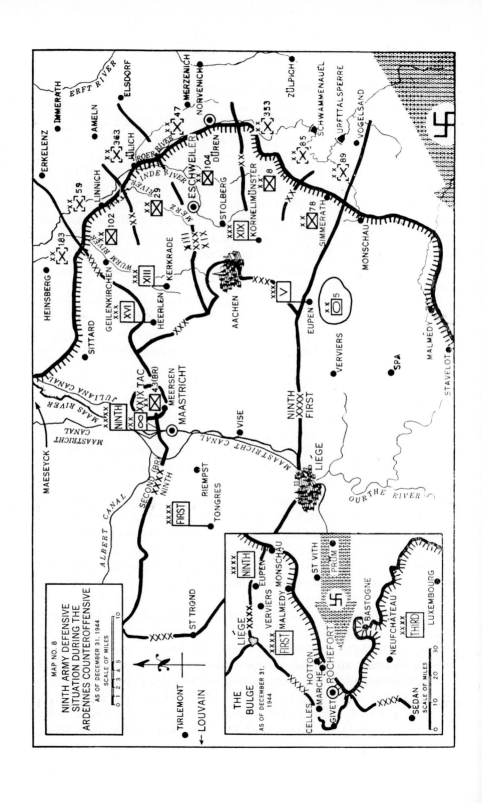

MAP NO. 8

NINTH ARMY DEFENSIVE
SITUATION DURING THE
ARDENNES COUNTEROFFENSIVE

AS OF DECEMBER 31, 1944

SCALE OF MILES
0 1 2 3 4 5   10

THE BULGE

AS OF DECEMBER 31, 1944

SCALE OF MILES
0   10   20   30

man plan to break through the forested plateaus of the Ardennes to reach the Maas, capture Liège and Maastricht, and strike northwest for Brussels and Antwerp, was revealed by its rapid, well executed overrunning of First Army's thinly held southern flank. All thoughts and plans of an Allied offensive to the Rhine had to be scrapped for the time being. The initiative had passed to the enemy. With his north flank secure behind the flood-threatened Roer, the Maas, and the Rhine, he had chosen a vulnerable Allied spot to make what was to be his last bid for victory. Flinging into the battle his carefully hoarded armor, he was striking deep toward the vital Allied supply lines in an effort to split the northern armies from the southern and render impossible for months to come a strong offensive action on the Western Front.

So Ninth Army turned its thoughts from an impending drive across the Cologne plain and devoted its energies to supplying reinforcements to First Army, that it might cope with this threatening surprise move. Divisions resting and refitting for the next Ninth Army offensive were available for immediate dispatch to assist First Army in the bulge now developing to the south. On December 17, the second day of the German attack, the 7th Armored and 30th Infantry Divisions were en route to the scene of the counteroffensive, going to the St. Vith and Malmédy areas, respectively. (Map No. 8.) Three days later, the 84th Infantry Division was en route to the south to the Hotton area. The following day the 2nd Armored Division also moved to First Army in the Celles area. On the same day, the 75th Infantry Division, commanded by Major General Fay B. Prickett, newly arrived from the port areas and assembled near Tongres, moved to First Army in the vicinity of Hotton. Ninth Army thus sent south, during the first week of the attack, a total of five divisions and supporting troops on a corresponding scale.

On December 20 Ninth Army passed from 12th Army Group to the operational control of 21 Army Group, and on December 22, the Army took over from First Army the front of the VII Corps to the south, extending from Simmerath north almost to Jülich, in order to permit Major General J. Lawton Collins, VII Corps Commander, to form a counterattacking force to blunt the spearhead of the German offensive. Within four more days, by December 26, Ninth Army had improved its defensive positions and regrouped forces, enabling it to send three more divisions to the fast-growing force which was to turn defeat into victory in the snow covered forests of the Ardennes. The 5th Armored Division, commanded by Major General Lunsford E. Oliver, and Major General Robert C. Macon's 83d Infantry Division, both of which had come under Ninth Army when it took over the VII Corps sector, were sent to First Army in the Eupen and Rochefort areas, respectively. The British 51st Highland Division, commanded by Major General J. G. Rennie, which had been brought into the Meersen area east of Maastricht on December 22 under operational control of Ninth Army for use as an Army reserve, also passed to First Army and moved to the Liège area. The force of the XXIX Tactical Air Command, too, was devoted to the battle of the Ardennes. Fighter-bomber support was yielded temporarily by Ninth Army, and what air reconnaissance and harassing of the enemy lines of communications was performed on the Army front was executed by planes of the British 83d and 84th Groups.

Since First Army was now fighting in a southerly rather than an easterly direction, Ninth Army's XVI Corps headquarters, which had moved up from Normandy late in November and was not yet operational, now vacated its command post location in Tongres, Belgium, and moved forward on December 22 to Heerlen to permit First Army's main headquarters to occupy the Tongres location. First Army's rear echelon headquarters moved to St. Trond.

When the regrouping of forces had been completed, Ninth Army held a defensive position from Simmerath to Linnich, a distance of forty miles, with five divisions under two corps, XIII and XIX. (*Map No. 8.*) Under XIX Corps on the right (south) were the divisions formerly under First Army in that sector— the 78th Infantry Division commanded by Major General Edwin P. Parker; the 8th Infantry Division, which had been under Ninth Army at Brest and in the Southern Belgium-Luxembourg area, now commanded by Brigadier General William G. Weaver; and Major General Terry de la M. Allen's 104th Infantry Division. In the XIII Corps sector were the 29th and 102d Infantry Divisions, which had fought in the November offensive under Ninth Army. There was no hope of an offensive for the time being. Ninth Army, back on a starvation diet of ammunition, must insure that no northern arm of a German pincers could ever strike in through the Aachen or Sittard areas to link up with the drive through the Ardennes.

In a Letter of Instructions dated December 19, the Army had set forth detailed directives for the organization of the ground and defined defensive lines to be prepared by the corps. Priority for work on various defensive positions was laid down and coordination between adjacent units provided. An engineer annex supplemented the general instructions with specific details in regard to mines, wire, and demolitions. Overlays showing the locations of vital highway and railroad structures were issued to corps, and priorities were established for the destruction of the installations if this should become necessary. In addition, the Army developed counterattack plans which included the use of the 5th Armored Division, which would be made available by 21 Army Group, if needed, and various British units whose operational control would be exercised from time to time during the ensuing month.

Initially, some difficulty was experienced in getting the front-line divisions, which had been attacking for so long, to occupy their positions in the necessary depth to insure an effective and flexible defense, but this situation was soon corrected. At the conferences held to coordinate the Army's new defensive plans, representatives of the British Second Army and of its corps and other units on the Army north flank were present, and complete information was exchanged to insure an effective tie-in of defensive measures between the two armies.

With the Army under the operational control of 21 Army Group, the headquarters took on an international aspect. The closest contact and liaison were maintained with the higher and adjacent British headquarters. Increased British liaison personnel were added to the various British, French, Belgian, and Netherlands personnel already associated with the headquarters. Field Marshal Montgomery, in his colorful beret, pullover sweater and corduroy trousers was a frequent visitor, as was Prince Bernhard of the Netherlands.

Ninth Army had no intention of withdrawing from its sector unless driven out. Nevertheless, the continued development of the powerful German drive to the south indicated the possibility of concurrent enemy drives against the Army from the south or north, or from both, probably with a view to capturing supplies in the Army area to permit continuation of the German offensive. Accordingly, plans were made for the evacuation or destruction of important supplies and installations should a withdrawal become necessary, but these plans were made known to lower echelons within the Army only to the minimum extent necessary to insure their implementation if the necessity arose. Where items were practically indestructible and the tonnages so high as to preclude evacuation, the destruction of certain key parts was planned. Bailey bridge materials, for instance, were to be rendered useless to the enemy by the evacuation of the small connecting parts of the steel bridges. Similar instructions were issued throughout the Army concerning the measures to be taken to prevent equipment and supplies falling into enemy hands if he penetrated the Army area. Commercial and military electrical communication installations were to be rendered inoperable by the removal of critical parts. Instructions were issued for the destruction of captured enemy ammunition on orders from Army, and of bulk explosives and certain American ammunition on orders from area defense commanders. The then new and highly secret VT proximity fuze for artillery shell was to receive first priority for destruction.

On Christmas Eve, with the progress of the German offensive lending some weight to the boast that the city of Maastricht would be leveled, preparations were initiated to develop sheltered space for the Army Headquarters, to permit operations to be continued undisturbed by heavy bombing or shelling. Basements and underground rooms were surveyed and sandbagged or shored. Complete accommodations for living and working under cover were soon available, if needed, including an emergency signal center and sufficient underground distribution cable to provide internal communication in the event a move became necessary.

The logistical power of Ninth Army, too, had to be diverted to First Army to meet the threat in the Ardennes. Four quartermaster truck companies were relieved from Ninth Army and sent to First Army. In addition, two similiar companies, attached to the 7th Armored Division, were left attached when that division went to First Army's command, resulting in a total transfer of six of Ninth Army's twenty-six quartermaster truck companies. Moreover, since First Army had urgent operational needs for its truck companies in displacing its supplies to the rear, Ninth Army furnished the transportation needed to motorize transferred infantry divisions for rapid movement to the battle area. Temporary loss of the use of this multitude of cargo trucks was aggravated by the inclination of the transported units to retain the transportation under their control after arrival in the First Army area. Only by the expedient of sending a Ninth Army officer with each convoy was it possible to recover the vehicles so dispatched within any reasonable length of time. Because of this policy and even more because of the remarkably high operating efficiency of the truck companies, Ninth Army managed to carry on its own tremendous movement of supplies occasioned by the German breakthrough.

This supply movement was twofold. First, those critical supplies whose capture was threatened by enemy action had to be moved to safer locations in the rear; and, second, the transition from an offensive to a defensive mission required the delivery to forward units of increased stocks of defensive supplies such as barbed wire and mines.

All the supply depots in the Ninth Army area had been located on the east side of the Maas River. This had been done purposely in order to reduce the traffic burden on the limited capacities of the Maas River bridges and also to insure, in case of destruction of the bridges by enemy air action, the uninterrupted flow of supplies to the troops in the forward areas. Now with the threat of the German counteroffensive, plans had to be perfected quickly to displace or destroy more than 100,000 tons of supplies and equipment should a withdrawal to the west bank of the Maas become necessary. Moreover, large quantities of supplies, located well forward, had been taken over in the old VII Corps sector of First Army. The port of Antwerp had been opened and supplies and equipment which had previously been very scarce were being released to the Army in large quantities. A reserve depot for ordnance parts and major items was established at St. Trond. Similarly, a reserve ammunition supply point, with a balanced stock of two units of fire, was established at Riempst, and a reserve depot for signal supplies was located at Louvain.

Levels of supplies in the forward part of the Army area were, of course, reduced by a program of temporarily stopping deliveries and permitting daily consumption from reserve supplies. Shipments of gasoline were discontinued, the unloading of signal supplies was halted, and certain of these supplies, including 1,000 reels of spiral-four telephone cable, 8,000 miles of field telephone wire, 100 radio sets, 3,000 flashlights, and 10,000 batteries, were furnished to First Army to support its operations. In the case of engineer supplies, only those items such as barrier and fortification materials, needed to improve defensive positions, were unloaded in the Army area. The remainder was kept loaded on freight cars for quick movement if an enemy breakthrough threatened. During the period, general fortification supplies became short, but never critically so. Mines, however, were so scarce that First Army was asked for a credit in that item as a means of establishing a reserve. Credit was granted, but the situation improved to such an extent that it never became necessary to use it.

In ammunition, only those items immediately required for accomplishment of Ninth Army's new defensive mission were brought into the area, and the remainder was made available to First Army. Artillery ammunition expenditures were severely restricted. To alleviate the ammunition shortage, one artillery battalion was issued German 105mm howitzers, and these were fired until all available ammunition of this type was exhausted. Two artillery battalions were issued British 25-pounders, for which ammunition was obtained from the British. In view of the restrictions on artillery ammunition special emphasis was placed on ammunition for and the use of the infantry 81mm mortar. Every effort was made to keep every weapon of the Army's reduced fire power firing. Ordnance contact parties visited combat units daily and checked all equipment available, to keep it in first-class condition and to prevent minor defects from becoming major ones.

Those momentous winter days were busy ones for both the front-line soldier and the services of supply. Every agency of the Army felt the emergency imposed by Germany's last great offensive action. Heavy troop movements and an unusual volume of relay and press traffic created an unusual demand for communications. Traffic through the Army signal center increased enormously. Teletypewriter traffic rose from a daily average of 30,000 groups to a peak of 79,000 groups. Security restrictions imposed on wire lines increased the daily number of groups handled in the code room from 6,000 to more than six times that figure. Personnel to operate signal installations had to be increased.

Cryptographic personnel alone was tripled. Close supervision of radio operation was demanded to insure the security of the many troop movements, and a heavy burden was imposed by the frequent and rapid changes in assignment of radio nets, call signs, and frequencies

Wire-line breaks, particularly those due to enemy bombing and to vehicular traffic, were more numerous, throwing an additional burden on radio facilities. The cables between Maastricht and Liège, in particular, were broken a number of times by flying bombs. Additional VHF radio link systems were procured, however, making the Army signal system more flexible in keeping with the tactical situation. Moreover, emergency communications were planned and installed to permit the headquarters to move to the rear if the situation required. The transfer of Ninth Army to the operational control of 21 Army Group required additional signal communications. The existing circuit between Maastricht and 21 Army Group at Brussels, one hundred miles away, was of poor talking quality, but by combined British-American effort three good telephone and two teletypewriter circuits were soon established.

The need for special winter clothing—shoepacs, the special cold-weather shoes; inner soles; ski and arctic socks; cotton field trousers and caps; and ponchos—had been forseen and requisitions had been placed. Now the snow and ice of winter had descended and these items were sorely needed by foxhole dwellers. Shipments were expected to arrive about the middle of January, but it was not until the latter part of January, and only in small lots, that this clothing was to begin to arrive. The bulk of this special clothing arrived too late for maximum utilization and later presented a special salvage problem.

The story of the procurement of white snow-suits designed to provide winter camouflage is an interesting one. When the heavy snowfalls in late December and early January created a demand for such equipment it was discovered that they were not in stock anywhere in Europe, and furthermore, that there was not sufficient white material available to make them. They must be improvised. So Military Government personnel, utilizing public address systems mounted on trucks, drove slowly through one after another of the larger German towns in the Ninth Army area calling upon the German civilians to bring to the trucks all suitable white cloth available in their homes. Tablecloths, bed sheets, and even underwear were collected. As each individual turned over the articles, he was given a receipt for later redemption by the German Government. When the campaign was completed, the Army had a total of 41,500 bed sheets. Cotton cloth, 32,000 linear feet of it, was purchased from Belgian sources, various other items collected in this odd operation were added, and a factory was established with Netherlands civilians as tailors. Seventy-five thousand snow-suits were in the hands of the troops before the end of the month.

The procurement of some 3,000 pitchforks for mine probing was accomplished by novel methods too. In the November offensive it had been discovered that the pitchfork was a highly useful tool for locating the wooden *Schü* mines so numerous throughout this area. Unavailability through routine supply channels could not be accepted as an excuse for not providing these tools to the troops. All the hardware stores of Belgium, the Netherlands and Germany within the Army area were visited, and a total of 3,000 such "mine detectors" was unearthed.

Spare parts for quartermaster general-purpose equipment— field ranges and gasoline lanterns—now became scarce. Contracts were let for manufacture of the most critically needed spare parts in Liège. An Army spare-parts depot was established to control the distribution of the limited stocks. This system of control and distribution was found to be most efficient and workable.

The cold, wet, winter weather seriously affected the maintenance of all types of equipment, particularly ordnance weapons and vehicles. Operation in the mud and snow caused brakes to wear out rapidly. While vehicles were standing, brake lining froze to brake drums and caused axle failures when the vehicles were moved. To increase tank mobility, the program for the manufacture of extended end-connectors for tracks was vastly expanded. Two hundred thousand extended end-connectors were manufactured and installed, using raw material and production facilities in Belgium and France. Tanks had additional difficulties in securing any footing at all on icy pavement using conventional rubber track, and it was necessary to weld cleats to each section of steel track. Mud clogged the exhaust pipes of general purpose vehicles, creating heavy demands for replacements for burned-out valves. In addition, maintenance suffered from icy, muddy working conditions and from the fact that all vehicles were heavily caked with mud all winter. Before any preventive maintenance services or repair work could be accomplished, this mud had to be removed. Ordnance set up wash racks throughout the Army area, located beside streams, lakes, or ponds, and using engineer pumps and hose. Power lubrication equipment was also provided, with ordnance personnel to supervise and aid in lubrication. All troops were encouraged to use these facilities and their location was published in administrative orders.

During the early part of December continuous freezing temperatures and light snows which packed under the weight of vehicles caused a thin layer of ice to form on all paved roads, creating a serious traffic hazard. The sand piles that had been placed along all the important roads throughout the area in anticipation of this condition proved of particular value, and all general engineer troops were chiefly occupied spreading this sand, concentrating their efforts on curves and on steep grades. Netherlands and Belgian civilians, too, were employed. Heavier snows brought increased difficulties. Maintenance of roads through the roadside ammunition supply points was particularly essential. In clearing one road, a large quantity of 240mm howitzer shells was covered up and the shoulders of the road had to be probed to locate them. Snow drifts covered up ammunition stacks and toppled over shells stacked on their bases. Crews were required to clear ammunition stacks of snow to minimize wetting if a thaw came. While the freezing weather continued, considerable study was given to the problem of road foundation failures in case of thaw, but despite extensive research no solution was found and the conclusion was reached that no over-all traffic control plan to protect the roads during the thaw period would be practicable.

During the latter part of December, Ninth Army, First Army, and Advance Section of Communications Zone, whose areas of operation had been affected by the German offensive, came to certain agreements to coordinate construction and maintenance of road and railroad nets. In the vicinity of Visé, Ninth Army troops constructed a Class 70 floating Bailey bridge across the Maas River and a similar connecting bridge over the Albert Canal. Advance Section agreed to complete the bridges over the Albert Canal west of Maastricht as rapidly as possible. These structures were examined at this time to see whether Bailey bridging could be employed to span the remaining gaps, but such an expedient was found to be impracticable. Advance Section ceased railroad work in the forward area of both armies to preclude possible capture of its heavy equipment, which could have been replaced only with great difficulty. With some of the troops thus released, Advance Section was able to relieve Ninth Army engineer troops of maintenance of three fixed bridges in Maastricht, the operation of the Maastricht asphaltic premix plant, the operation of a quarry near Visé, and various other continuing tasks.

The completion of the reconstruction of the Wilhelmina Bridge in Maastricht by the Advance Section and its opening to traffic on December 23 was a godsend to the Army traffic agencies, which were carrying the extremely heavy burden of troop and supply movements. As an example of the density of traffic movements, during the period December 17 to 27, eleven divisional motor movements and a correspondingly large number of supporting combat and service movements were staged through the Army area.

The Army began construction of a Class 40 Bailey bridge across the Albert Canal west of Maastricht on December 31, completing it nine days later. This was a unique structure consisting of two 150-foot triple-truss, double-story spans and one 120-foot double-truss, double-story span. The total length of the structure was 424 feet. Because of the extremely high banks of the canal, the bridge had to be supported on Bailey crib piers fifty feet high, and became the first bridge constructed under operational conditions using piers of this type. Owing to the unusual design, engineers from the headquarters of 21 Army Group and the European Theater of Operations visited the project at various times during construction. This bridge provided an additional lane of traffic across the Albert Canal for movements to the west, inasmuch as there existed in that vicinity only one two-way bridge across the canal from Maastricht, whereas four bridges over the Maas River at Maastricht provided a total of six traffic lanes from the east. Later, when the defeat of the German offensive in the Ardennes obviated the emergency need, this unique bridge was dismantled, but it had served its purpose of providing an additional traffic corridor.

German activity, both ground and air, threw into sharp focus the vital importance of the bridges across the Maas, and they were prepared for intentional destruction, if necessary. To avoid sympathetic detonations resulting from near misses of aerial attacks, demolition charges were stored at sufficient distance to avoid accidental destruction, yet near enough to permit rapid replacement and intentional demolition. In addition, detailed security measures were adopted for protection of the bridges. Twenty-four-hour guard was maintained, protective booms were constructed, and automatic weapons were sited to cover all bridge approaches. Flood lights were installed to illuminate the vicinity of the bridges. Protective barbed wire was erected around all piers and abutments to prevent enemy swimmers from placing explosive charges. In the past the Germans had made several attacks against the British bridges in the vicinity of Nijmegen farther to the north. Some of these attacks had been made by "gamma swimmers," in specially constructed protective rubber suits, who approached the bridges from upstream, guiding floating charges of explosives which they sank adjacent to the piers and then detonated. Other attacks had been made from the air or by using floating mines, some of which were built to resemble harmless floating logs.

To combat such attacks, Ninth Army guards were ordered to fire on all water-borne objects approaching the bridges. Residents along the river's edge, fearing ricocheting bullets, complained frequently, but the orders stood. On at least one occasion this vigilance was rewarded when a sentry on duty on the Bailey bridge over the Maas River at Visé fired eleven shots upon a small floating object resembling the top of a steel helmet which was barely awash and had bobbed under two upstream protective booms. On the eleventh shot, when the object was still 150 yards from the bridge, it exploded with force sufficient to spray the guard and to shake severely the houses along the river's edge.

Increased antiaircraft activity marked this period. The German air force was making a determined effort to interfere with the transfer of troops and supplies to the battle farther south by intensified attacks on bridges and roads, particularly when convoys could be discovered. In three days in mid-December the enemy sent more than four hundred aircraft over the Army area. On the nights of December 17 and 18 there was almost continuous aerial activity and the Maastricht sirens sounded "raid" and "all clear" alternately throughout the night. In one twenty-four-hour period, antiaircraft units in Ninth Army's zone fired in 126 separate engagements and claimed a total of 24 aircraft destroyed or probably destroyed. From this peak the comparatively heavy German air effort gradually decreased, until it flared up again on the first day of the New Year.

A brilliantly planned German air effort marked the advent of 1945. Starting about midnight, just as the New Year began, the enemy sent in a steady stream of single aircraft. These planes appeared to have no definite targets in Ninth Army area, although an attack on Maastricht, where an evacuation hospital was bombed, was undoubtedly an attempt to strike the nearby *Tappan Kazerne*, occupied by the special staff of the Army Headquarters. The chief mission of the planes attacking in the forward areas appeared to be the harassing and tiring of antiaircraft and defending air force personnel. This was coupled with an all-out, widespread destructive attack upon the principal Allied airfields in northern Europe. The main German air forces formed up over the airfields of the Rhine area in the early dawn of New Year's Day. Strict radio silence was observed, an excellent accomplishment in the assembling of such a large force of aircraft. Dropping down to tree-top level, and taking advantage of the terrain to mask their activity from radio-detecting devices, hundreds of planes approached the forward areas of the Army zone undetected until they were picked up visually by air guards. The German pilots, probably without experience or practice due to the lack of fuel for their training, were unable to weather the violent antiaircraft fire they met once they were detected. The majority of the planes in the Army area broke formation and scattered to attack targets of opportunity. The Army command post was strafed during the morning briefing of the staff.

Throughout the area it was a field day for antiaircraft gunners. A crew in the Hürtgen Forest brought down a German fighter with one round from a 40mm gun. At the height of the attack, five separate columns of smoke, each marking a destroyed German aircraft, could be seen from the command post of XIX Corps. In the furious one-hour battle, seventy of the two hundred German planes that attacked in the Ninth Army area were shot down. The German air effort was more successful against the rearward airdromes, particularly those of the British, whose large loss of planes made itself felt in the reduced air reconnaissance later available to Ninth Army.

All during these tense days of late December and early January the possibility of a strong German ground attack against the Army's thinly held forty-mile front was a matter of concern. (*Map No. 8.*) The left (northern) flank of the Army was particularly vulnerable, because of the road net favorable to the Germans for an attack from the Heinsberg area. Every available intelligence agency was used to the utmost in an effort to discover any signs of an enemy build-up on the Army front. Aerial reconnaissance was of greatest importance. With the forces of XXIX Tactical Air Command diverted to meet the German threat in the south, the Army had to rely principally on British aerial reconnaissance agencies, but late in December these were drastically reduced because of increased enemy activity in the British zone. The Army then became almost completely dependent, for daylight aerial reconnaissance, on such assistance as could be given by elements of IX Tactical Air Command, whose facilities were already strained to meet the requirements of First Army. However, the British agreed to, and frequently did, fly unscheduled tactical reconnaissance missions across the Ninth Army front and flank. Night photographic and night visual reconnaissance, which the British had been performing for several weeks over the Army front when planes were available and the weather permitted, was stepped up considerably during the early days of the Ardennes counteroffensive, but had to be reduced greatly after the first of the year because of severe plane losses inflicted by the enemy in his New Year's Day attack.

Ground patrolling and reconnaissance were intensified, and extensive use was made of agents behind the enemy line. Although several of our agents crossing or recrossing the front lines were killed by our own or by enemy troops, many returned successfully and brought back valuable information. All air and ground intelligence agencies, however, produced no evidence of a German build-up threatening the Army, and during the period of the Ardennes counteroffensive there was little change in the composition and location of enemy forces on the Army front.

The Germans were known to be parachuting or infiltrating saboteurs and agents behind the Allied lines in connection with their counteroffensive. Some of these captured in other areas had been found to be equipped with American uniforms complete in every detail and with perfect American indentification papers.

In Ninth Army areas forward and rear, as a part of general security measures under the Army Provost Marshal, Colonel Robert C. Andrews, all road patrols and traffic control points looked upon everyone with suspicion. Reliance was not placed on normal passwords and indentification papers. As a means of causing German agents to betray themselves, occupants of vehicles were required to answer a multitude of questions likely to be known only to Americans or to those from the particular section of the United States from which the individual said he. came. The asking of such questions as these came to be routine:

"What's Babe Ruth's first name?"

"What's a Model T?"

"Who is Connie Mack?"

"Who plays in the Rose Bowl this year?"

To a man from Indiana: "What is South Bend famous for?"

To a man from Brooklyn: "How did the Dodgers make out this year?"

All travelers on Ninth Army roads had to assure alert guards that they were, in fact, the persons they claimed to be.

Active measures for the defense of the Army sector were continually carried out. Towns were fortified as strongpoints, and communication trenches and field fortifications were set up, interlocking the towns in a defensive network with barbed wire, anti-tank ditches, and minefields. Extensive use was made of harassing programs designed to keep the enemy off balance, deceive him as to the Army's dispositions and intentions, interdict his movements, deprive him of rest, and at the same time conserve the Army's strength. All available weapons, including artillery and mortars, tank destroyer and tank guns, antiaircraft weapons, and machine guns firing at long range, were used to the limit of available ammunition in planned programs of suddenly concentrated fire on selected sensitive points. Combat patrols and night raids of up to company strength were aggressively employed. In addition to their normal activities these raiding parties often placed booby traps in enemy installations.

Occasionally, dummy tank concentrations were prepared to deceive enemy aircraft, and tanks were driven back and forth behind the lines at night to give the enemy the impression that armor was being massed on the front. Under the supervision of the Army Publicity and Psychological Warfare Officer, Colonel

Kern C. Crandall, psychological warfare was emphasized, and use was made of leaflets fired in artillery shells, and of loudspeakers.

The Germans, while not aggressive, were alert and reacted promptly with mortar and artillery fire to attempts by patrols or raiding parties to operate east of the Roer River. They, too, sent out patrols to obtain prisoners and information, but their main activity was intermittent harassing artillery and mortar fire.

Reverberations of the enemy counteroffensive to the south were felt in the Army casualty evacuation system. Of the average of 2,500 patients being admitted weekly to Army hospitals, approximately forty-five per cent were being evacuated to Communications Zone hospitals in the Liège area. However, in that area, during January, two general hospitals were bombed, one was isolated by enemy action, and a holding hospital at an air strip damaged. In addition, the increased demand for supplies, ammunition, and personnel in the reduction of the Ardennes salient so taxed the railroads that evacuation of casualties from the Liège area was greatly reduced. Thus there occurred not only a reduction of available bed space in the general hospitals, caused both by damage and by an influx of casualties from the Bulge, but also a delay in clearing these hospitals. The only solution was increased air evacuation, but during this period the weather was poor and few planes were able to fly.

Army hospitals, therefore, were forced to absorb the backlog and to operate with a high census and reduced empty bed space. Evacuations dropped to thirty-four per cent during late January. It was fortunate that Army casualties during the period were relatively light. The situation was relieved by improvement of the weather which permitted air evacuation and the eventual reestablishment of adequate general hospital facilities in Liège by Communications Zone.

The snow and cold emphasized the critical billeting situation with which the Army had to contend all winter, particularly until the attack across the Roer gained additional area for the housing of troops. Specific policies had been laid down to insure that units received fair and proper treatment in the distribution of shelter accommodations. As far as was consistent with the tactical situation, troops were provided quarters with the maximum protection from the weather, using vacant buildings and public structures whenever possible, and making every use of existing structures adaptable for quarters. In liberated territory the billeting of troops in homes with civil population was forbidden. Separate quarters for troops were obtained by using permanent barracks, hotels, private buildings and houses, and existing camps. Quarters were selected so as to minimize contact with the German population, to the extent of making exclusive use of complete areas or sections of towns, where practicable. Application of these principles and cooperation by adjacent and subordinate units enabled Ninth Army to increase its quartering capacity from approximately 160,000 in early December to nearly 320,000 early in March.

To increase further the comfort and welfare of the troops, shortages in quartermaster fumigation and bath units were relieved by the use of shower facilities in coal mining districts of the Netherlands and Germany. Thousands of men were bathed weekly by this expedient.

The inclement weather, coupled with the fact that many of the troops had been constantly in combat since the invasion of Europe, developed a serious requirement for welfare measures of all kinds. Leaves, furloughs, and passes were increased. Passes to Paris and Brussels were inaugurated, and the comforts and facilities of rest centers were enlarged. It was anticipated that when offensive operations were resumed, the advancing divisions would not be able to maintain conveniently their rest centers in the Netherlands and Belgium. Accordingly, plans were made to take over division and corps rest centers, as the Army moved forward, and to enlarge and expand them as permanent Army installations. In the meantime, all available recreational features were emphasized. The cooperation of the American Red Cross in providing Clubmobiles, the mobile doughnut-and-coffee units for frontline troops, and in establishing doughnut dugouts, lounges, reading and writing rooms, and other recreational facilities, was of great assistance.

As the Army carried out these various measures for the welfare of its troops and the defense of its sector, after the turn of the year it became more apparent daily that the bold last-ditch offensive effort of the German war machine was doomed to failure. Ninth Army could again turn attention to offensive planning. The threat of the Roer dams was still present. (*Map No. 8.*) The Army had always felt that the dams should be taken at the earliest moment by offensive ground action, and now initiated detailed planning to seize the dams when and if forces were made available. In addition to the troops with which the defensive mission was being carried out, it was estimated that three divisions and appropriate supporting troops would be needed to capture the dams or so to threaten them that the Germans would release their 100 million cubic meters of water and end, for a long period to come, the threat of untimely flooding of the Roer River. These plans, once made, were held in readiness should the mission be received and the forces made available.

The magnitude of the threat of the Roer Dams was evaluated early in January in Ninth Army Engineers Technical Notes No. 4, "Roer River System and Its Reservoirs," a detailed study of the physical characteristics of the Roer River and the seven dams located on it and its tributaries, together with the possible effects of the manipulation of the dams by the enemy. Important sources for much of the evaluation included a translation, secured from 12th Army Group, of a German study of the military effects possible from manipulation of the dams, and enemy documents, including detailed drawings of the dams themselves, captured by Ninth Army troops. The captured documents and detailed drawings were of particular value in computing the run-off to be expected under various conditions and, most important of all, in enabling the Army Engineer to arrive at an accurate advance estimate of when the river, if once flooded, would recede sufficiently for a crossing to be initiated.

The two principal dams, whose manipulation could affect the level of the Roer River on the Army front, were the Urfttalsperre (the upper dam), a concrete arch dam capable of impounding 45,500,000 cubic meters of water, and the Schwammenauel (the lower dam), an earth-filled dam with a capacity of 100,700,000 cubic meters. The upper dam's principal military value to the enemy was as a means of storing water by which he could increase at will the amount of water in the lower reservoir. Demolition of the upper dam would flood the river as far as the lower and empty its contents into that reservoir. It would take an estimated two months to discharge all the capacity of the upper reservoir through the existing outlet under the dam into the river leading to the lower reservoir, but there was a power tunnel from the upper structure through which a maximum of twenty-two cubic meters per second could be discharged into the river through a hydroelectric plant about two-thirds of a mile downstream from the lower dam, thus by-passing it. This flow could be increased to an estimated 52 cubic meters per second by the complete destruction of the penstocks at the point where they left the tunnel.

The lower dam was the key of the system. If it remained intact and contained no more than 60 million cubic meters, it would retain any flood released from the upper dam. Because of the nature of its construction, the demolition of the lower dam would become increasingly difficult to accomplish as the water level in the reservoir receded. Attempts to rupture the lower dam by aerial bombardment had already proven unsuccessful. It was not known whether the Germans had previously prepared the dam for demolition.

The enemy could obtain the most intense and sudden military effect by demolishing the lower dam when its level had been raised by the addition of the water from the upper reservoir. By so doing he would loose a catastrophic flood over the entire length of the Roer Valley, which would wash out all crossing means. Captured German evacuation orders anticipated a nine-foot rise downstream from Düren, with the flood wave reaching Jülich about three and one-half hours after the rupture of the dam. Width of the flooded area would vary between 1000 and 3000 yards. The flooded areas would drain off sufficiently to permit the supply of troops across the river within two to four days in the hilly country and within five to six days in the flat country.

As an alternative, the Germans could leave the dams intact and, by demolishing the outlets from the lower dam and the outlet from the upper dam through the power tunnel, could initially release a maximum of 202 cubic meters per second. This volume of water, added to the normal run-off, would result in a general three-foot rise in the river, a stream velocity in excess of ten feet per second, and a width of up to 1200 feet. The flood thus caused would be general and would endanger floating bridges. Unless added to by excessive rain or melting snow, the flood could be expected to last ten or twelve days before receding to the point where an assault crossing and installation of floating bridges would be feasible. Either of the alternative flooding possibilities open to the Germans constituted a formidable threat to offensive operations across the Roer.

Giving the first indications of post-Bulge planning, on January 4, 12th Army Group had issued a Letter of Instructions ordering an attack by First and Third Armies, upon their junction and upon the capture of St. Vith, directed from the Prüm–Monschau line to the vicinity of Bonn. (*Map No. 4.*) First Army was scheduled to return to the command of 12th Army Group upon junction with Third Army. Ninth Army was to continue to operate under 21 Army Group, although its specific mission had not yet been announced. General Simpson had discussed the situation briefly with both General Bradley of 12th Army Group and Field Marshal Montgomery of 21 Army Group, but other than an indication of a possible mission of seizing the Roer River dams, nothing specific had yet been worked out. General Simpson had no knowledge of what forces would be returned to his command, but he felt very strongly that in order to achieve the final destruction of the German armed forces, the Ruhr industrial area must be enveloped and the heart of Germany entered. He appreciated, too, that the shortest road to Berlin was across the plains of northern Germany. And finally, he was convinced that the most economical method of securing jumping-off points for these future operations was an attack north and northeast from his currently held positions, outflanking the Siegfried Line north of the Aachen gap (*Map No. 9*), and destroying all German resistance between the Rhine and the Maas.

Ninth Army's basic plan for such an operation was of long standing. Shortly after the Army had moved to the Maastricht area in late October General Simpson had presented the plan to General Bradley, who had recognized its merits. But the progress of the preparations for the November offensive with First Army making the main effort generally east, was such that the Ninth Army plan to strike northeast had not been put into effect at that time.

On January 12 Genèral Simpson reviewed his own situation as it affected and was affected by the whole of the Allied dispositions along the entire Western Front. It is interesting to note that at this time, of a total of 68 Allied infantry (excluding airborne) and armored divisions on the Western Front, 47 were American, 13 (including one Polish division) were British or Canadian, and 8 were French. General Simpson felt that Ninth Army was in the most suitable position to launch the telling blow and that, were he

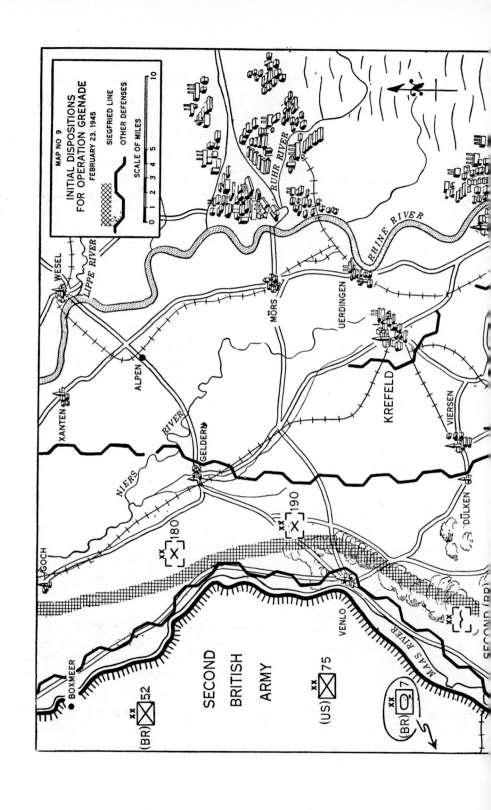

MAP NO 9

INITIAL DISPOSITIONS
FOR OPERATION GRENADE
FEBRUARY 23, 1945

Siegfried Line
Other Defenses

SCALE OF MILES
0 1 2 3 4 5   10

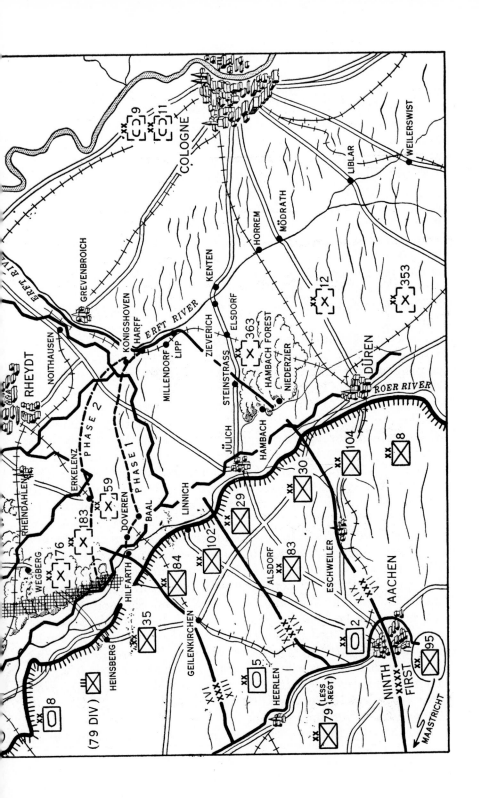

given a total of 12 divisions and the necessary supporting troops for three corps, he could launch a strong offensive to the northeast which would surely carry all the way to the Rhine. As viewed from the 12th Army Group point of view, this plan had one serious objection. It would necessitate the withdrawal of forces from the Prüm–Monschau front and their rapid concentration in Ninth Army's area in order quickly to take advantage of the disorganized German position in the west occasioned by his defeat in the Ardennes. It would mean shifting the main attack from Bonn to somewhere north of Cologne. Furthermore, it had to be decided whether First Army should take over the zone from Simmerath to Jülich, which it had relinquished to Ninth Army in mid-December, or whether Ninth Army's attack, if launched, should be staged from a broad front extending down through Düren.

The Army Commander, after carefully reviewing the situation existing on the Western Front in the middle of January, presented his proposal for a strong Ninth Army attack northeast to the Rhine to Field Marshal Montgomery. He pointed out the two chief advantages of making the main effort well to the north on the Western Front: namely, the shorter distance to the main objective—the Ruhr industrial area—and the shorter supply lines resulting from proximity to Antwerp—now operational and the main port on the Continent. Other advantages to which he called attention were the adequacy of the road net, both supporting and within the contemplated area of operations, the absence of thickly forested areas which had proved such an obstacle both southeast of Aachen and in the Ardennes, and, closely allied to this advantage, the opportunity for using large formations of armor. The Allied military superiority was greatest in four respects: in armor, in fighter-bombers, in comparatively abundant transportation, and in an adequate gasoline supply. General Simpson proposed that an attack be launched on the terrain best suited to exploit these items of Allied superiority. The argument that it would take time to shift American forces from the Ardennes to the Jülich-Linnich area was countered by pointing out that it would take the Germans longer to make a corresponding shift. The proposal was simple, carefully thought out, and promised results of tremendous importance.

Field Marshal Montgomery was quick to see the advantages of

the plan. A Ninth Army attack northeast to the Rhine fitted in naturally with a prospective attack of the First Canadian Army south between the Maas and the Rhine. Since the proposal to have Ninth Army make the main 'effort on the Western Front required major shifts of American troop units and logistical support, the Field Marshal submitted the plan to Supreme Allied Headquarters for approval. General Eisenhower made his decision promptly. The offensive operations of First and Third Armies were to be continued, but when they became unproductive of satisfactory results the main effort on the Western Front would be shifted north and Ninth Army would be strongly built up for offensive operations under 21 Army Group. Accordingly, on January 21 General Simpson received instructions from Field Marshal Montgomery of which the following are extracts:

> The enemy is in a bad way; he has had a tremendous battering and has lost heavily in men and equipment. On no account can we relax, or have a "stand still," in the winter months; it is vital that we keep going, so as not to allow him time to recover and so as to wear down his strength still further. There will be difficulties caused by mud, cold, lack of air support during periods of bad weather, and so on. But we must continue to fight the enemy hard during the winter months.
>
> The main objective of the Armies on the Western front is the Ruhr; if we can cut it off from the rest of Germany, the enemy capacity to continue the struggle must gradually peter out.
>
> A further, and very important, object of our operations must be to force mobile war on the Germans. We will therefore continue through the winter to conduct such operations as will:
>
>   *a.* Gain intermediary objectives toward the Ruhr.
>
>   *b.* Place us in a good jumping-off position for a mobile campaign in the spring.
>
>   *c.* Wear down the enemy's strength at a greater rate than our own.
>
> The first stage in carrying out this policy must be to close up to the line of the Rhine.

Intention [*Map No. 4*]

> To destroy all enemy in the area west of the Rhine from present forward positions south of Nijmegen as far south as the general line Jülich–Düsseldorf, as a preliminary to crossing the Rhine and engaging the enemy in mobile war to the north of the Ruhr.

Plan in Outline

> To carry out a converging attack with Canadian and Ninth Armies. Canadian Army to attack southeastwards with its left on the Rhine (Operation Veritable). Ninth Army to attack northeastwards with its right on the general line Jülich–Düsseldorf (Operation Grenade). Second

Army to hold in the center, and to cross the Maas in the Venlo area when ordered.

The operations of Ninth Army are to be supported by the left wing of 12th Army Group.

The future layout that we want to achieve is to face up to the Rhine from Düsseldorf northwards on a front of three armies: Ninth Army: Düsseldorf to Mors (exclusive); Second Army: Mors to Rees (inclusive); Canadian Army: Rees (exclusive) to Nijmegen.

As soon as operations elsewhere will allow, Ninth Army will be brought up to a strength of four corps and twelve divisions. Of this total, one corps of two infantry divisions will be allotted temporarily to the operational command of British Second Army.

At the same time, 12th Army Group is to extend its left flank northwards and take over the front of Ninth Army up to Jülich (exclusive.) [*Map No. 9.*] When this is completed, Ninth Army, consisting of three Corps and ten divisions, will be holding a front on the Roer River between Jülich (inclusive) and Roermond. From the right portion of this front a strong attack will be launched toward the Rhine, the right flank being on the general line of the road Jülich–Neuss. This is Operation Grenade.

Right flank protection is to be provided by the left wing of 12th Army Group as far as the bend in the Erft River at Harff, thereafter Ninth Army will protect its own right flank on the general line of the Erft River, which flows into the Rhine just south of Neuss. Left flank protection will be organized initially by Ninth Army. In the later stages of the offensive the left flank will become protected by the operations of the right flank of Second Army, operating on the axis of the road Venlo–Mors.

The target date for Operation Grenade cannot yet be fixed. Ninth Army will make all plans and preparations so that the operation can be launched at the earliest possible date after 15 February.

Once Veritable and Grenade are launched, the situation will call for continuous and sustained operations. Good man-management will be vital; every possible opportunity must be taken of pauses to rest units, even if only for short periods, and a good system of reliefs must be organized. Only in this way will we be able to keep up the momentum of the attack and thus force the battle to swing relentlessly our way.

These, then, were the orders for the contemplated operation.

The ensuing week, following the receipt of Field Marshal Montgomery's directive, was spent in intense preparation for the operation. Final designation of divisions and supporting troops for the operation had not yet been received, but the assumption was made that priority of forces and supplies would be given. The Army Commander and his staff were eagerly confident, convinced that the contemplated offensive held the promise of breaking the back of the German army on the Western Front.

As they did for every major action of the Army, the Army Commander and his staff followed certain definite and clearly formulated procedures in their own planning, in acquainting the several corps with the plans, and in coordinating the planning and actions of the corps. A complete formal estimate of the situation was prepared by the Army staff. After approval by the Army Commander, the final detailed plan was prepared and a planning directive was issued to the several corps. Each corps was required to present to the Army Commander its formal estimate of the situation and its plans based thereon. Final presentation was made in the presence of all corps commanders and key Army and corps staff officers. Thus each corps knew exactly what the others were to do, and why. The several plans were then "war gamed"—played out on the map—so that the development of the action could be thoroughly previewed and every possible contingency discussed in detail.

Time and again the Army staff had discussed details of terrain, enemy dispositions, enemy capabilities, and the enemy's defensive lines in the area north of Cologne and west of the Rhine. For the offensive in November a plan of attack had been developed to secure this same ground, and firsthand knowledge was available from that battle to answer many planning problems. Some of the factors remained constant; some were new. Here was the same terrain, the same road and rail net, the same mutually supporting fortified villages, the same large cities; but the enemy's defensive positions had been improved, even though his forces available to man them had been reduced. However, it was with respect to the dispositions and capabilities of Ninth Army, and of the forces flanking it, that the most substantial changes were found.

The first great point of difference was that in contrast to the November offensive, when First Army made the main effort and Ninth Army protected its left flank, now Ninth Army would provide the main assault while First Army protected its right flank and conformed to its advance. This meant, in effect, that Ninth Army could take the shorter route to the Rhine against lesser obstacles and attack northeast in the direction of Neuss, rather than striking east to support First Army's attack. Ninth Army, therefore, had much greater freedom of action and could plan its maneuver to the best advantage. It could carry this flexibility of planning right into the battle itself, changing direction as it saw fit to accomplish the destruction of the enemy.

The second point wherein the situation had changed to a major degree was on the Army's north flank. (*Map No. 8.*) In that area there was no longer the strong threat of a German counterattack designed to sever vulnerable supply lines. In mid-December British XII Corps, commanded by Lieutenant General Ritchie, had relieved British XXX Corps on the Army flank, taking over all troops in the sector formerly under XXX Corps. Jumping off on the morning of January 17 and proceeding cautiously and methodically, XII Corps carried out an operation designed to eliminate the so-called "Heinsberg Pocket." This area, lying southwest of the Roer River between Geilenkirchen and Maeseyck, was only some seventeen miles wide and five to ten miles deep. Yet it had always been a thorn in the side of the Allies, for it provided the Germans with a bridgehead over the Roer from which they could launch a drive to the vital supply center of Maastricht. Elimination of the pocket had been planned a month earlier, but execution was delayed when the battle of the Ardennes broke. Now, with the Ardennes fight on the upturn and with forces available to them, the British began the elimination of this sore spot. Major operations ended on January 26 after ten days' fighting. Adjacent Ninth Army forces, supported by dive bombers of the XXIX Tactical Air Command, which had returned to operation in cooperation with Ninth Army, closed up to the Roer River in their zone northeast of Geilenkirchen. By the successful completion of this operation, the west bank of the Roer north from Linnich to Roermond was cleared, with the exception of a few relatively unimportant pockets of resistance. The north flank threat was eliminated.

A third major factor in the changed situation was the Canadian First Army's attack down from the north which was planned even as the plans for Ninth Army's offensive were being completed. This attack would draw heavily on the German forces between the Rhine and the Maas. His scanty reserves would have to serve to plug the holes on two fronts in this limited battle area. Throughout the winter, 21 Army Group had studied the possibilities of driving southeast from Nijmegen (*Map No. 4.*) to outflank the Siegfried Line from its northern end and to eliminate German forces positioned between the Maas and the Rhine. Plans had been developed in detail and, had it not been for the battle of the Ardennes, the operation probably would have been launched early in January. Now, in the latter half of January, as the Ardennes situation eased and forces became available, concentration of units was begun for Operation Veritable, the code name given to this drive southeast along the lower Rhine. Canadian First Army, with practically all of the forces of 21 Army Group under its command, was to execute the operation. Troops from British XII Corps, upon completing reduction of the Heinsberg Pocket, were to be hurried to the north for an early February attack whose objective would be the line Geldern–Xanten. Ninth Army could thus count on a southward drive by the British to meet the Army attack to the northeast.

As the situation later developed, the Canadian Army's attack on February 8, after a good start which was launched with a terrific artillery preparation from 1,500 guns, bogged down because of the extremely poor road net supporting it. Flooding of the lower plains between the two rivers reached alarming proportions, and at times major units had to be supplied by amphibious vehicles. However, the advance progressed despite all the difficulties, and by February 12, Cleve, the northern hinge of the Siegfried Line, had been secured. From then on until the final junction with Ninth Army nearly a month later, Canadian First Army's action was a slow, methodical, punching ahead, meanwhile laboriously building bridges and roads in the rear, and fighting the elements and the terrain, which proved to be as great an enemy as the paratroopers who provided the bulk of the opposition.

The final element bearing on Ninth Army's plans for the coming offensive—the taking of the Roer River dams (*Map No. 8*) —was decided late in January when the 12th Army Group Commander, who had recognized since early fall the necessity of eliminating this threat, ordered that First Army launch an attack to seize them. The attack was to jump off on January 30, with strong forces of First Army's V Corps composed of the 2d and 9th Infantry Divisions, the 78th Infantry Division, which would pass from Ninth to First Army, and such elements of the 7th Armored Division as could operate in the forbidding tank country leading to the dams.

On January 28 all major points in the Ninth Army plan for Grenade had been decided, and on that date the final Army planning directive was issued to the XIII, XVI and XIX Corps. Excerpts from this directive follow. (*Map No. 9.*)

> First U.S. Army and Third U.S. Army will continue operations eastward pursuing the withdrawal of German forces in the Ardennes area. When these operations become unproductive of satisfactory results, and upon order of the Supreme Allied Commander, the main effort on the western front will be shifted north. 21 Army Group will then advance to the Rhine River in zone and prepare to cross in strength.
>
> First Canadian Army is preparing to attack southeast from the Nijmegen area, with the objective of clearing the area between the Rhine and the Maas as far south as the general line Xanten-Geldern. Target date for this operation ("Veritable") is 8 February.
>
> Second British Army will hold the line of the Maas from Roermond to Boxmeer and will later cross the Maas in the Venlo area upon order of Commander-in-Chief, 21 Army Group. It will assist the attacks of Ninth U.S. Army and First Canadian Army with all possible means.
>
> Ninth U.S. Army will relieve elements of Second British Army along the Roer River southeast of Roermond as soon as forces are available. Subsequently Ninth U.S. Army will attack northeast from the Jülich–Linnich base to destroy the enemy in zone and to seize the west bank of the Rhine between Neuss (inclusive) and Mors (exclusive). Target date for this operation ("Grenade") is indefinite, but plans will be completed and preparations made to initiate the attack at the earliest possible date after 15 February. The exact time cannot be set until reliable information as to availability of divisions, supporting troops, and supplies is provided.

*   *   *   *

> 12th Army Group will attack on its left to protect the right flank of Ninth U.S. Army as far east as Harff.
>
> Tactical Air Command will operate in cooperation with Ninth U.S. Army. Medium and heavy bomber effort is anticipated. Initially this effort will likely be proportioned to Ninth U.S. Army and First U.S. Army on the right flank in approximate ratio of two to one.
>
> Operation Grenade will be executed in accordance with one of two general plans. Plan I will require a rapid advance, including maximum exploitation by armored units. The conditions favoring such an operation are firm (dry or frozen) ground, a general deterioration of enemy forces opposing our advance, and the advance eastward beyond the Erft River of First U.S. Army units on our right flank. The existence of all three of these conditions will not necessarily be required for staging the rapid advance. Plan II will call for a slower, more methodical advance made necessary by wet, muddy ground, very strong enemy resistance, and threatened flanks.
>
> If the violence of our attack should cause disruption of the enemy resistance each Corps will be prepared to conduct relentless pursuit in zone, and phases will be abandoned in favor of taking full advantage of our opportunity.

Once the attack is launched, it will continue until final objectives are secured. In order to maintain the impetus, units will be rotated and briefly rested insofar as operations permit, so that leading echelons will be revitalized and the forward momentum insured.

After giving detailed phase lines for both plans the directive continued:

Measures to insure the secrecy of concentration of additional troops involved in the operation will be included in plans. Contact with the enemy prior to the attack will be maintained substantially stable, so that no indications of build-up for an attack will be apparent.

* * * *

The intention of British Second Army of crossing the Maas in the Venlo area had long been included in the plans for an Allied offensive in this area. As it developed later, an assault crossing was never made here, but it must be given some attention because of the effect it had on the plans. Venlo was a key communications center whose importance could not be underestimated. In order to insure an early opening of the supply routes to provide for a build-up for crossing the Rhine, it was essential to accept no delay effected by a last-ditch enemy stand in and around Venlo. Therefore, British Second Army was assigned the mission of preparing the Venlo assault. That it was never executed was due chiefly to two reasons: first, the forces necessary, an estimated minimum of one corps of two divisions, which had to be American forces since all units of British Second Army available for offensive action had been turned over to Canadian First Army, were never provided; and, second, the rapid advance of XVI Corps in Operation Grenade, outflanking Venlo on the east, eliminated any necessity of taking it from the west.

After considerable discussion and consideration, the Army Group boundary was set. Initially, it extended from just south of Jülich to the Erft River bend at Harff, and then along the Erft River to the Rhine. This left Ninth Army a very narrow base from which to launch an attack. The whole initial crossing zone of the Army was less than seven miles wide. A considerable portion of this stretch was unsuitable for assault crossing of the Roer, particularly with the existing conditions of current, river banks, and approaches. The initial boundary included all of the Hambach Forest to VII Corps under First Army. This forest had long been considered a serious threat, since it provided excellent concealed assembly areas for German reserves very close to the crossing sites. In order to insure rapid and thorough clearing out of the forest, it was highly desirable that it be included entirely to one unit. However, in spite of this, as the more detailed planning progressed, it was necessary to drop the boundary four miles south and to include the western portion of the Hambach Forest to Ninth Army in order to permit a Ninth Army division to cross south of Jülich. Another boundary question arose in the case of Aachen. Both Ninth and First Armies felt the absolute necessity of having Aachen included in their zones, since Aachen was the hub of the road and civil communications nets and the terminus of the operating railroad net. General Bradley, to whom the task of arbitrating this problem fell, neatly solved it by violating a time-honored principle of setting boundaries, drawing a line through the center of Aachen, and giving the northern half of the city to Ninth Army, the southern to First Army.

Initially the target date for Operation Grenade was set as February 15. Army gave corps until February 10 to complete their plans and preliminary preparations. As it developed, the target date was subsequently advanced to February 10, and plans and preparations had to be speeded up accordingly. With the Canadian First Army's attack already underway on February 8, the sooner Grenade could be launched, the more could be gained by the double attack on the enemy.

In contrast with the November offensive, this operation was not to be immediately preceded by a heavy daylight bombing effort. Two major considerations caused this decision. First, such a bombing would require that the attack be launched in the daylight, say about noon, as it was in the November offensive, in order to enable the bombers to leave their bases in the daylight and complete the journey to the target. Ground troops very strongly desired to make their assault crossings of the Roer under the cover of darkness, even at the expense of foregoing the assistance of heavy bombers. Second, to permit heavy bombing on the east bank of the river close enough to knock out enemy forward installations would require a withdrawal, for the safety of the ground troops, of as much as 3000 yards to the west. This was undesirable, for the approaches to the river offered little concealment and the assaulting echelons would be exposed to heavy enemy fire as they advanced in daylight to form for the crossing. Therefore, instead of an initial bombing of key features immediately in front of the assault, the assistance of the heavy and medium bombers was to be employed in knocking out communications immediately in rear of the battlefield and in isolating the battlefield.

Under the direction of Brigadier General James E. Moore, the Army Chief of Staff, two general schemes of maneuver were set up by the staff; one to be employed in event the action progressed favorably, permitting a rapid advance; the other in event poor trafficability, strong enemy reaction, or an exposed right flank required that the advance be more slow and methodical. General Simpson felt that if Ninth Army could achieve a degree of surprise by turning its attack to the north abruptly after crossing the Roer (Map No. 9) and with reasonably good luck in weather and footing for vehicles, it might be able to thrust northeast along the narrow corridor between München-Gladbach and the Erft River, then extend the penetration between München-Gladbach and Neuss to outflank the enemy defenses and wreak havoc in his rear areas. On the other hand, should the fight be bitter in its initial stages, and should First Army be held up in the Hambach Forest, or should rain and thaw deny Ninth Army the opportunity to exploit its advantage in armor, it might well have to clean out the forested bulge east of Roermond in order to provide a wider base from which to support a drawn-out ammunition-consuming battle.

In either event, with fast going or slow, an initial bridgehead was essential. This bridgehead must insure the use of both Linnich and Jülich since the road net through these two centers was necessary to support an operation of such magnitude. Therefore, the first objective was the seizure and consolidation of the Jülich-Linnich bridgehead. The dominant terrain feature east of the Roer was an oval plateau which had been dubbed "the Linnich-Harff Plateau." During the months of planning Ninth Army staff officers had developed map knowledge of this small piece of terrain equal to their well remembered familiarity with "Little Round Top" and "Cemetery Ridge" of Gettysburg fame. Phase I of the operation, for either a slow or a rapid advance, was the seizure of this plateau. Once it was taken, the remainder of the attack was all downhill.

At the same time, and as part of Phase I, the right flank of Ninth Army must close to the Erft River and make contact with the left flank of First Army in the vicinity of Elsdorf, an important communications center just east of the Hambach Forest and some three miles short of the Erft. If this division crossing in the Jülich area progressed rapidly, it would drive straight east to accomplish this mission. If, on the other hand, the division crossing south of Jülich were able to clear the western half of the Hambach Forest rapidly enough, it could turn east at Steinstrass to make contact at Elsdorf. It was considered wiser in planning to hold these two possibilities equally open to adoption.

Phase II was an enlargement of the bridgehead seized in Phase I. That Phase II might well be an indistinguishable outgrowth of Phase I was recognized from the very beginning. However, if the going proved to be slow, a wider base of operations was essential before the Army was committed to any bold penetration. The Phase II line would bring both flanks to rest on river barriers and give maximum protection to vulnerable dispositions to meet a counterattack. Should such a counterattack be forthcoming, it was estimated that this was approximately the time and place at which it would come.

Considerable study was given to the initial role to be played by XVI Corps, commanded by Major General John B. Anderson. Although not yet operational, the corps headquarters had participated in the planning for the coming attack, and when troops became available the corps would take over the sector of British XII Corps in the Heinsberg area on the north. XVI Corps would then hold by far the widest zone, extending from north of Linnich, down the Roer to its junction with the Maas at Roermond. Moreover, in this zone the enemy held all the advantages. He had extremely fine observation overlooking the Roer and the southwest approaches to it. He had excellent wooded assembly areas, well traversed by roads, behind him; in these he could mass considerable reserve strength with little risk that its presence would be detected by the Allies. And finally, particularly in the southeastern portion of the zone, he had a strong segment of the Siegfried Line, with innumerable concrete pillboxes. So it was decided that XVI Corps should confine its initial effort to wiping out the last enemy pockets of resistance on the near side of the river and to demonstrating strongly in order to deceive the enemy temporarily as to the location of the actual crossing farther upstream. Then, when XIII Corps had secured the area north-west of Hilfarth by attacking along the Baal-Doveren axis, XVI Corps could make unopposed crossings at Hilfarth and proceed with its attack to roll up the Siegfried defenses from the south and east.

After having turned north, secured its flanks, and gained a base for further operations, the Army would have a choice of pushing its attack in one of two directions. By that time, too, it would be known whether a fast or slow plan was favored by existing conditions. If the stage were set for a rapid advance, it was intended, first, to envelop and reduce the München-Gladbach area from the south and east and, second, to drive north with the right flank on the Rhine up to Mörs, while at the same time western elements were clearing out the pocket south of Venlo. It had always been estimated that the two areas where the enemy could hole up and resist to the bitter end were München-Gladbach and the Siegfried Line with its surrounding forested area south from Venlo to Heinsberg. The great hope, then, was that a thrust could be made to Neuss, then north along the Rhine, providing the twofold advantage of by-passing the strongest resistance initially and of trapping German forces in the pocket. The risk that had to be calculated in this plan was that of pushing a sizable force through the gap between München-Gladbach and Grevenbroich, where it would be vulnerable to counterattack from both sides and possible isolation. Only if the conditions set up for the rapid advance existed—that is, good footing, a deteriorated enemy, and strong right flank protection provided by First Army forces— could the chance be taken and this bold action initiated.

The basic difference in the plan for carrying out the operation should a slow advance be forced upon the Army was that after securing the enlarged base of operations the main effort was to be made on the left flank, with XIII and XVI Corps cooperating to reduce the Siegfried Line and to clear the area west of the line Harff–Dulken–Venlo. The purpose here was to open supply routes, particularly those from Heinsberg and Roermond, in order to build up in the forward area supply levels necessary to carry on a slow supply-consuming battle. Of course this meant that the closure to the Rhine would be made in an easterly rather than a northerly direction and that any hope of trapping substanial German forces must be abandoned. Even in the planning stage, however, it was realized that the best features of both the slow and the rapid plans might well be combined and carried out simultaneously. The chief difficulty in all the planning was a dependable estimate of how strongly the Germans would resist the attack.

A minimum of one division was to be held in Army reserve. In the campaigns of France and Germany every commander on the Western Front had decried his lack of a reserve, but seldom was able to correct the deficiency. From the very beginning of the planning for this operation, the Army Commander was adamant on the question of reserve. He was going to have one. He did. The reserve, never less than one infantry division, was held out for a twofold purpose. First, of course, it was the force with which prompt exploitation could be made of any breakthrough achieved. Second, it provided a means by which a tired division might be relieved, the tired division taking the fresh one's place in Army reserve and the impetus of the attack maintained.

By February 1, when the Army finally received a definite approval to execute the offensive, corps and division plans were well along. Change of target date, therefore, from February 15 to the 10th, caused no great concern. On February 6 a final Army Letter of Instructions for the attack was issued. It confirmed fragmentary orders already issued, and confirmed or modified the basic instructions given in the planning directive of January 28. With the thirteen-day delay eventually imposed, an amendment to these instructions had to be issued on February 22. Certain portions of the letter of instructions, as amended, are quoted below:

> The enemy expects an attack from the west in the Aachen area. It is believed that he suspects the general locale, but not the direction; further, that he is fairly well aware of the Ninth U.S. Army's general strength and disposition.
> The enemy's tactical doctrine is to defend his front lines with infantry, and to hold armored units in mobile and strategic reserve. In attempting to frustrate a crossing of the Roer River, however, he may place his armored units well forward.
> All evidence points to the enemy having recently augmented his front line elements with relatively limited forces. He continues to strengthen his defensive installations in depth.
> The First Canadian Army's attack has encountered three armored units

(15th Panzer Grenadier, 116th Panzer, and elements of Panzer Lehr Divisions), probably under the XLVII Panzer Corps. The 7th Para Division, groups from three others (2d, 6th, and 8th), two infantry divisions (84th and 180th), and a group from the 346th Infantry Division, are also committed. Additional units will probably be drawn in.

An attack now by Ninth U.S. Army can expect to meet, initially, and in addition to the troops now in the line, two weak infantry divisions and one, possibly two, armored divisions. With elements of Panzer Lehr Division identified further to the north there is some reason to believe that either the 9th or the 11th Panzer Division, possibly both, are now available to the enemy in the Koln [Cologne] area. The 3d Panzer Grenadier Division, . . . [in the First Army area], shows evidence of attempting to disengage there; it could be recommitted against "Grenade" within three days following disengagement. It is estimated that two additional, weak infantry divisions can be made available within a week, from disengaged troops further south. While believed to the east of the Rhine, the 10th SS Panzer Division is not definitely located and the possibility of its sudden appearance cannot be disregarded.

It is considered that a quick breakthrough of the enemy's Roer River line, followed by the vigorous exploitation of every enemy weakness, could enable the Ninth U. S. Army to accomplish its mission with rapidity.

The probability that the Roer River dams may be in enemy hands at the time of crossing the Roer River requires strong initial build-up east of the Roer River to insure self-sufficiency of the bridgehead during the possible flood period. Flooding can be expected to innundate all of the Roer River valley and to interrupt traffic for 5 or 6 days.

* * * *

At this time it must be noted that the possibility of the Roer River dams remaining in enemy hands at the time of the river crossing, was fully foreseen. It was this threat, particularly, which caused the Army to prescribe that there be four divisions crossing simultaneously on the narrow front. If a sufficient build-up could be gained quickly on the far side of the river, the bridgehead could be retained against counterattacks throughout the flood period and then the attack continued once the flood had receded. In order to insure that the bridgehead could be maintained even with the supply lines cut behind it, Army had issued instructions on February 5 to the several corps, calling upon them for their detailed plans to cope with such a situation. Attention was directed to certain factors, including the following: establishment of a flood-warning system by Army; emergency air drop of supplies to be set up by Army; retrieving of bridge equipage after flood warning and before flood crest; repair of crossing equipment, bridges, and approaches after a flash flood; stockpiling bridge equipage and supplies above expected high-water levels; stockpiling food, fuel, and ammunition at a minimum of three days of supply east of the river. Corps were also informed of the availability of certain amphibious vehicles and landing craft in Army supply. Plans called for by these instructions were submitted and reviewed by the Army staff prior to the target date. Later, of course, enemy action preceding the crossing obviated the necessity of carrying out all of the plans made, but many of the situations considered became actualities, and the precautions taken contributed to the over-all success of the operation.

The emergency air supply planning referred to above was developed with the assistance of CATOR (Combined Air Transport Operations Room). The C-47, the great cargo aircraft adopted from the commercial airlines and employed so extensively in the war, was used in this plan. The ship has a load capacity of two and one-half tons. A total of ·500 of them was loaded and held in readiness. Of these, 100 were concentrated at an airfield at Liège while the remaining 400 were distributed on other fields on the Continent to take off at call. The supplies so loaded were sufficient to support one division for one day. To assist in putting the plan into execution, a liaison officer from CATOR, whose headquarters was in Paris, was dispatched to the Army and remained at its headquarters before and during the operation until it was finally determined that the air lift would not be needed. In addition, CATOR also brought forward pathfinder teams from airborne units stationed in the United Kingdom, and these teams later crossed the Roer with the assault troops with the mission of locating and properly marking suitable dropping zones for the airborne supplies should any be needed.

In keeping with its three major missions—maintaining air superiority, isolating the battlefield, and attacking targets in close cooperation with the ground forces—XXIX Tactical Air Command kept pace with the Army throughout the planning stage. General Nugent estimated that the German air force was capable of putting into the air on the northern portion of the Western Front no more than 300 single-engine fighters, 75 jet aircraft, 70 night bombers, and 350 night fighters. Against this force he could count on 300 fighter-bombers from his XXIX Tactical Air Force, an undetermined number of reinforcing fighter-bombers from IX Tactical Air Command if the situation demanded, 600 medium bombers on call from the IX Bombardment Division of the Ninth Air Force, and some 2,400 heavy bombers of the Eighth Air Force and the RAF Bomber Command based in the United Kingdom.

The maintenance of air superiority was a problem of comparatively little concern. German airfields within range of Ninth Army's battlefield were not too numerous, and by periodically attacking them and by diverting fighter-bombers, whenever required, for interception purposes, the Tactical Air Command felt fully confident of preventing the German air force from interfering to any appreciable degree with the progress of the ground forces' operations. Likewise, the question of providing close support to the attacking elements, once the operation commenced, was well answered by the fact that the close cooperation between ground troops and air forces had already been quite satisfactorily developed and practiced by Ninth Army and XXIX Tactical Air Command units.

The most difficult problem was isolation of the battlefield. Obviously the most effective way to isolate the prospective battle area was to destroy all the Rhine River bridges, from Wesel to as far south as Bonn, by medium and heavy bomber effort. Ninth Army had requested such an effort in November without results and now urgently repeated the request. After careful consideration the Air Forces announced that they did not have the strength to carry out such an undertaking in any reasonable length of time, considering the number of bridges, their extremely rugged structure which made them almost invulnerable to air attack, and the limitations imposed by the weather, which during this period of the year severely reduced the number of operational flying days. It was determined, then, that the XXIX Tactical Air Command fighter-bombers should carry on an extensive program of battlefield isolation west of the Rhine commencing on February 1st and continuing until D-day.

Tactical reconnaissance and photo reconnaissance activity was increased to absolute capacity. During the month of February a total of 42,234 photo prints was delivered to the artillery of the Ninth Army alone, and more than 500,000 prints were delivered to corps and divisions. Some divisions requested and received as many as 450 prints of each particular photo.

Large shipments of artillery ammunition were now arriving by rail, and on several days the tonnage received was between four and five thousand tons. These shipments, together with restrictions on expenditures, had developed a build-up of nearly 45,000 tons. Consequently it was determined that ammunition was available for a strongly desired artillery preparation. The allocation of ammunition for the entire attack was a compromise between what the artillery wanted and what the supply agencies calculated they could deliver. In effect, it was the maximum which could be obtained and delivered to the guns. The allocation for XIII Corps, XIX Corps, and 34th Field Artillery Brigade was approximately as follows:

Day	Units of Fire
1st	3
2d	2
3d	1
4th	1
5th	1
Thereafter	½ per day

For XVI Corps it was:

Day	Units of Fire
1st	1
2d	1
3d	1
4th	½
5th	½
Thereafter	¼ per day

To insure full and continuous ammunition supply for the two corps making the assault crossings, special measures were taken in accordance with the preference of the corps. XIII Corps was provided with a mobile reserve of ammunition for establishment east of the Roer of a corps ammunition supply point, later to be taken over by Army. In XIX Corps, Army was to establish a special ammunition depot across the Roer immediately after the crossing.

In addition to securing an ample supply of ammunition, a supply of the newly developed VT proximity fuzes for artillery shell was obtained. An outstanding American technical development of the war, this fuze, embodying in effect a small radio in the nose of the projectile, assured a devastating burst of high-explosive shell in the air just above a ground target. A program of demonstrations had already been given to instruct troops in its use and to dispel any fear of premature bursts. This program proved of great value, for the troops accepted the fuze enthusiastically and were alert to take advantage of its great possibilities.

While the subsequent postponement of Operation Grenade gained some thirteen days for preparation, the bulk of this time was valuable more for training, for subordinate unit preparations, and for increasing supply stocks than it was for Army planning. Basically there were few changes or modifications of the over-all Army plan. It became definitely known that British Second Army would stage no attack across the Maas from the Venlo area and therefore that Ninth Army's contact as it pushed north would be with Canadian First Army rather than British Second Army. This same decision, together with the ultimate availability of additional divisions gave Ninth Army, finally, a total of twelve divisions rather than ten, the figure upon which the initial planning was based. In consequence one additional division was attached to XIX Corps, giving it three infantry and one armored division. XIX Corps was weighted in this fashion because all the signs pointed to the probability of a rapidly moving attack in its zone. The remaining additional division was placed under the operational control of British Second Army to assist in holding its line along the Maas.

Concentration of the forces which were to take part in the offensive began on January 27, nearly a week before final confirmation had been received of the intention to carry out the operation. However, the organization and disposition of troops could not be delayed if it were to be completed by jump-off time, for on January 27 only two of the twelve divisions which were ultimately to play a part in the action were under Ninth Army command and in approximate positions for the assault. It was realized, too, that the massing of the troops, plus the tremendous build-up of supplies, was going to tax to the utmost the capacity of the rail and road net, particularly in light of the rapid deterioration of the roads because of thaw and rain.

The thaw, accompanied by warm rains, came early in February

just when troop movements were at their heaviest. Many of the main supply routes began to show serious disintegration within a very short time. Since it was imperative to keep supplies and troops moving, and yet necessary to protect the road system as much as possible, traffic was routed over alternate routes, and many roads whose pavement edges and shoulders showed promise of failure were made one-way. In some instances, troop movements were allowed over sections of roads with the full realization that the road would thereby be so badly damaged that complete reconstruction would be required. On such roads, engineer troops stood by to assist the convoys by spreading rock, gravel, or rubble where needed and by pulling stalled vehicles through with tractors. Ordnance road patrols were increasingly active in their efforts to keep routes free of wrecks and breakdowns. Occasionally, where delay could be accepted, troop movements were deliberately postponed or columns actually halted along a road to permit completion of temporary repairs. The situation became so serious that it was necessary to deny a request of British Second Army to move elements of two armored divisions over Ninth Army roads and across the Maas River at Maastricht. They were asked instead to postpone these troop movements until the road situation improved or until suitable bridges existed across the river farther to the north. Engineer work, other than road maintenance, was reduced to a minimum to increase the number of troops and amount of equipment available for road work. Netherlands civilians were employed and the Belgian Highway Department cooperated by undertaking maintenance or repair of certain sections of road. Non-engineer troops were pressed into service. With this extreme, all-out effort the necessary troop movements and supply deliveries were accomplished, but it was not until the end of February that traffic was again moving without restriction over the Ninth Army road net.

An alarming situation arose early in February when another flood similar to that of November occurred on the Maas River. The Maastricht pile bridge was closed to traffic and again saved by anchoring it and weighting down the deck with sandbags. The British floating Bailey bridges over the river in the vicinity of Berg (*Map No. 6*) and Maeseyck were also closed. At Maeseyck, a pile bridge under construction by Ninth Army suffered the worst damage. The center line of this new bridge had been located downstream from the wreckage of the former fixed bridge because the floating Bailey was occupying the only suitable site upstream. When the river flooded it washed the wreckage of the former fixed bridge downstream into the partially constructed bridge and the bridge building equipment. Two cranes which were being utilized for driving piles were sunk when the barges on which they were mounted capsized. Fortunately the flood was of a short duration and all the bridges were reopened shortly after the attack jumped off. The construction of the pile bridge at Maeseyck, however, was delayed for several weeks.

On January 27 the 5th Armored Division, commanded by Major General Lunsford E. Oliver, passed from control of First Army to Ninth Army and began its movement to the Aachen area, although one combat command of this division was earmarked to assist the attack of the 78th Division in conjunction with First Army's battle for the Roer dams. On February 1, after a long trek from Seventh Army, the 35th Infantry Division, commanded by Major General Paul W. Baade, began to arrive in the Army area. This unit was destined to replace British troops in the Heinsberg area as Ninth Army took over from British Second Army the front northwest to Roermond (*Map No. 9*), a preliminary move to the launching of the attack. On the next day, February 2, the 8th Armored Division, commanded by Brigadier General John M. Devine, was transferred to Ninth Army, from Third Army, where it had only recently received a brief initiation to battle. It, too, was to be committed to replace the British on the Army north flank. These reliefs had been completed by February 6, and on that date XVI Corps became operational, with the 35th Infantry and 8th Armored Divisions, and the British 7th Armored Division attached for operations only, taking over the zone from north of Linnich to Roermond from British XII Corps. While it had been intended that all enemy resistance on the near side of the Roer River in this area be eliminated by the British, the XII Corps, striving to meet a regrouping schedule for another operation turned over responsibility with several pockets of resistance remaining.

On February 3 the 30th, 83d, and 84th Infantry Divisions, and the 2d Armored Division, now commanded by Brigadier General Isaac D. White, were returned to Ninth Army from First Army. On the same date, the 95th Infantry Division, commanded by Major General Harry L. Twaddle, passed to Ninth Army control from Third Army. All began their movement to the scene of action without delay, and by February 7 they had closed in the Ninth Army area. The remaining two divisions, the 75th Infantry, commanded by Major General Ray E. Porter, and the 79th Infantry, commanded by Major General Ira T. Wyche, were not assigned to Ninth Army until February 17 and did not complete closing into the Army area until February 18. Both of these divisions came from far-off 6th Army Group and had been fighting in the battles of the Saar and the Colmar pocket. It was a troop movement problem of considerable magnitude to assemble these ten divisions, to say nothing of all the supporting troops, in the limited zone of action of Ninth Army in time to be disposed correctly for the battle.

One additional complication added to the difficulties attendant in the concentration. First the 95th Infantry Division, and later the 75th Infantry Division, were moved to the area of VIII Corps of British Second Army, holding the west bank of the Maas from Roermond north to Boxmeer. British Second Army had been called upon to furnish additional troops to keep the Canadian First Army attack going, since the terrible terrain and weather conditions and the strong resistance from enemy paratroop elements had worn down the assault echelons of that Army at a faster rate than was anticipated. Hence Ninth Army was required to supply forces to British Second Army to hold their line along the Maas. This task was performed by the 95th Division from February 13 to 22, and by the 75th Infantry Division from February 22 until the advance of Ninth Army northward east of the Maas eliminated the enemy and the further necessity of such defensive operations. Since, in the initial stages of its attack, Ninth Army did not have maneuver room to employ all twelve divisions, the weakening of its strength by furnishing troops to British Second Army in no way affected the operation.

In the concentration of troops for the impending battle, the Army took elaborate steps to conceal from the enemy the strength of the concentration and the identity of the units concerned. The orthodox methods, including a maximum of troop movement during darkness, invocation of radio silence, the removal or concealment of shoulder patches, vehicle bumper markings, and the like, the location of unit concentration areas well to the rear, the restriction of circulation of newly concentrated personnel, particularly to avoid their presence in large towns, and the limitation of artillery registration to a necessary minimum, all were employed. In addition such unusual measures were resorted to as assigning temporary telephone code names and omitting all information regarding the newly concentrated units from normal situation reports. This latter scheme, however, aggravated by the extended delay prior to the jump-off, offered such obstacles to the flow of information that the measures were relaxed, since security value was outweighed by the confusion caused.

Signal agencies played a major part in concealment plan. On February 3 it was noted that radio traffic, which had never exceeded 6,000 groups per day, had soared to 12,000 groups per day. If allowed to continue to climb, German monitors could have deduced the time of the expected jump-off by interpretation of the activity evidenced by increased radio traffic. It was necessary immediately to control the radio traffic level, but this could not be effected suddenly without permitting its implication to be obvious. Traffic levels of previous days were studied and a decline in traffic produced so as to indicate a normal decrease in activity. The excess radio traffic was diverted to other means of communication, particularly telephone, although this meant that the telephone service must struggle under the greatest load it had ever carried. Before the jump-off Army Headquarters telephone centrals on one occasion handled a record load of 20,000 calls in one day.

Radio traffic was expedited by a system, perfected after many experiments by Army radio personnel, which permitted remote operation of radio sets up to a distance of thirty miles. Using this system, the Army signal service located its transmitters from one to three miles from the Army Headquarters and remotely controlled them from a radio receiving center in the vicinity of the Army Headquarters message center.

While it was appreciated that the enemy secured considerable information regarding the build-up for the attack, particularly by means of his active air reconnaissance, nevertheless it was quite well established that he did not succeed in gaining the Army's complete order of battle, even though subsequent postponement of the attack gave him thirteen additional days in which to build up his intelligence picture of the operation. Had the assault been made earlier, as intended, it is quite probable that the element of surprise would have been very high, since movement of men and supplies to the Army following the Ardennes battle had been so rapid and so well executed that the Germans could not have picked up more than a portion of it.

On February 7 General Simpson called his corps commanders together for a final coordinating conference. General McLain of the XIX on the right, General Gillem of XIII in the center, and General Anderson of XVI on the left—all were ready and anxious for the battle to commence. At this meeting, which was to be the last discussion of plans before the attack, the coming operation was "war-gamed." The Army Commander discussed detailed refinements of the plans and alternative measures which might have to be taken in event certain situations developed. Particularly he stressed the possibility of either XIII or XIX Corps being required to use the bridgehead of the other, should one bridgehead be held up, in order to pass attacking forces into the battle to assist the blocked units. Further he cautioned against mixing units. "Keep your battlefield orderly!" he said, "Keep units intact!" Details of coordination between corps along the boundary separating their zones were discussed, and arrangements were made for positive, reciprocal assistance. Employment of the Army reserve was outlined. All corps commanders saw where they could make good use of the Army reserve division at some stage of the operation. It was made clear, however, that when the Army reserve was passed to a corps, it could expect to release another division to Army control. Since VII Corps of First Army was now assigned the mission of protecting Ninth Army's right flank, not only to the Erft, as originally planned, but all the way to the Rhine, the chances were good that XIX Corps would probably push through east of München-Gladbach whether the going was fast or slow. Every possible turn of events was examined. The planning stage was over; the fate of the operation was now in the hands of the men who were to do the fighting. H-hour and D-day were set for 5:30 A. M., February 10.

CHAPTER 5

FROM THE ROER TO THE RHINE

O N the south flank in the meantime, through the early days of February, First Army had driven the stubbornly resisting Germans through the mined and booby-trapped forests, through the snow-filled ravines and gullies, along the deep-rutted dirt roads and trails that led to the Schwammenauel and Urfttalsperre reservoirs (*Map No. 8*), which controlled the waters of the Roer River. The attack was pushed relentlessly. Gradually, fighting for every yard, the Germans were thrust back until on February 9 they were forced to play their trump card. At this time with the hot breath of the attackers on their necks, and appreciating that they could no longer retain control of the 111 million cubic meters of water which had given them protection for the past two months, the Germans cleverly blew open the discharge valves on the large lower dam. At the point where the penstock from the upper reservoir emerged from the hillside downstream from the lower dam, they likewise destroyed the discharge valves, thus permitting water from the upper reservoir to drain into the river below the lower. By these measures the Germans accomplished the maximum long-term discharge and created for the longest possible period a water barrier to separate them from the poised forces of Ninth Army and First Army's VII Corps.

Before the discharge valves were blown, the Urfttalsperre Dam, upstream, had filled to its capacity of 45,500,000 cubic meters and was discharging over its spillway. The Schwammenauel Dam contained 65,500,000 cubic meters, about two-thirds of its capacity. The Roer River watershed was covered with snow to a depth of some three feet. Downstream from the dams the Roer already was crowding its banks, with the current at certain points reaching the very high velocity of nine feet per second, the very maximum for installing and maintaining floating stream-crossing equipage. Even before the water behind the dams was loosed, the river crossing promised to be such a difficult and precarious one that, on the afternoon of February 9 General Simpson had already postponed the attack for twenty-four hours in the hope that control of the reservoir waters would be firmly in our hands before the crossing was made.

Within a few hours after the destruction of the discharge valves, the river rose approximately five feet and attained a width, dependent on the terrain through which it coursed, of from 400 to 1200 yards. The velocity increased to an estimated average of ten and one-half feet per second. This was no flash flood but a long-term condition which the Army Engineer forecast would maintain from fourteen to seventeen days. The water stored by the two reservoirs, reinforced by the substantial run-off of abnormal rain and snow, was a weapon of great value and was extremely well employed by the German command.

At last the threat had become an actuality. Once expended, though, it could never be used again. So, although it was a bitter disappointment for Ninth Army to have to face the loss of some two weeks of precious time, nevertheless there was solace in the knowledge that once the Army crossed the river, it need never again fear the severing of its supply lines by a man-made flood. While there was to be a loss of time, it would not be a total loss. Troops were immediately turned to increased training efforts, rehearsing on the streams west of the Roer the detailed teamwork they were to exercise in the actual crossing.

The build-up of supplies, particularly ammunition, was enhanced by the delay in jump-off. If there had ever been any doubt as to the adequacy of the logistical support for the operation, it was now dispelled. During the week ending February 10, 32,924 tons of supplies had been brought into the Army area by rail. During the week ending February 17, 44,555 tons were brought in. This welcome increase taxed the transportation facilities of the Army to the maximum, and prompt off-loading and transportation from railheads to supply points could not have been accomplished had not an additional ten truck companies been assigned by 12th Army Group to augment the twenty-seven already assigned to the Army, and had not three companies temporarily attached to First Army now been returned. At the same time transportation requirements were reduced through an extremely efficient recovery system. Every piece of ordnance equipment that was damaged beyond repair was systematically stripped of all serviceable or repairable components. Approximately thirty per cent of all automotive parts required for Operation Grenade was furnished from recoveries made at ordnance collecting points. Transportation could thus be released from hauling parts and be increased accordingly for other uses, particularly for ammunition transport. During the "extra days" large quantities of engineer and signal equipment were released and shipped to the Army. Tanks and other ordnance equipment, which had been critically short for so long, now arrived at a rate which permitted not only filling existing shortages but also establishing a substantial Army reserve.

All agencies were able to utilize the additional time prior to the jump-off to good advantage. The Army signal service prepared additional circuits in cables running to Heerlen, Geilenkirchen, and Sittard. Forty circuits were completed right up to the Roer River edge at Linnich. With the assistance of the detachment of Netherlands signal intelligence personnel attached to the Army, considerable information was gathered regarding existing cables and telephone and telegraph facilities beyond the Roer. Engineering training and experiments in matters pertaining to river-crossing operations continued. New ordnance matériel had permitted the supplying of better types of equipment to many units, and these were able to complete their conversion and training. Nine tank destroyer battalions had been converted completely with better weapons, including six battalions receiving the M36, 90mm self-propelled gun. One light tank battalion had been completely re-equipped with the new M24 light tank carrying a 75mm gun. Armored divisions and cavalry reconnaissance units had likewise been issued the new light tank, greatly improving their fire power.

While the swollen Roer could hold earth-bound ground forces of the Army successfully, it was no barrier to the XXIX Tactical Air Command, whose tactical and photo reconnaissance planes and fighter-bombers roamed the skies between the Roer and the Rhine, charting the defenses of the enemy forces, isolating the battlefield, and wreaking damage on the hostile troops' transportation and communications facilities. Utilizing those seven days of the period between February 9 and 21 when weather permitted operations, XXIX Tactical Air Command, now five fighter-bomber groups strong, unleashed an all-out effort directed on the road and rail bridges beginning at Neuss and southwest to Noithausen, Lippe, and Zieverich. (Map No. 9.) The bridges were substantially damaged, but generally speaking, the results were disappointing. Of more tactical import was a widespread rail-cutting attack completed for the most part on two days, February 16 and 21. On February 21 alone, the rail lines were cut in 109 places. These attacks were reinforced by the bombing of marshalling yards and communication centers south of Neuss and west of Cologne, at Grevenbroich, Königshoven, Kenten, Horrem, Modrath, Liblar, and Weilerswist, and produced excellent results, contributing heavily to the difficulties the enemy experienced in his attempts to reinforce and supply his units in the battle area for the impending operation. He was further harassed by attacks on his communication centers at Jülich and, southeast and northeast thereof, at Niederzier, Hambach, and Millendorf. In addition, all available aircraft of the XXIX Tactical Air Command took part on February 22 in a general attack of some 8,000 to 9,000 Allied airplanes directed against rail and water transportation targets throughout Germany. Approximately 8,500 tons of bombs were dropped on some 200 targets, for the most part on rail bridges and marshalling yards. Whereas the accurate accomplishments of such an effort are difficult to assess, it can be reasonably concluded that this extremely heavy attack contributed materially to the weakening of the enemy and consequently to the success of the ground forces' progress.

The delayed date of attack enabled Army intelligence agencies further to establish the order of battle of the German forces on the front and to estimate with greater accuracy the reserves he might bring against the attack. Operation Veritable on the north had drawn all, or substantial elements of, the following German divisions:

> 84th Infantry Division
> 180th Infantry Division
> 346th Infantry Division
> 15th Panzergrenadier Division
> 2d Parachute Division
> 6th Parachute Division
> 8th Parachute Division
> 116th Panzer Division

Prior to Ninth Army's jump-off it was estimated that the following German units held the line opposite the Army, from north to south:

Elements of 8th Parachute Division
176th Infantry Division
183d Volksgrenadier Division
59th Infantry Division
Elements of 363d Volksgrenadier Division

In addition, it was estimated that the Germans had one static defense division occupying positions along the Erft River, that they had either or both the 9th and 11th Panzer Division in the Cologne area, and that they could disengage one or two weak infantry divisions from the south to employ against the impending Ninth Army attack.

When the original D-day of February 10 had to be abandoned, February 17 was selected for consideration as the earliest date upon which there was any hope of launching the attack. The Army Engineer charted the action of the river day by day, utilizing the data which observers stationed on the west bank were securing every few hours. Particularly valuable were the observations of those unnamed heroes who crept out under heavy enemy fire in vicinity of the dams to record their readings. These observations were reinforced by successive air photographs of the reservoirs, and by interpretations by the Army Photo Interpretation Detachment to show the water level remaining behind the dams. Daily the Engineer advised the Army Commander of river conditions. Unseasonable rains and the run-off of the melting snow blanketing the watershed kept the water level behind the dams high despite the discharge. February 17 came and went with the river conditions too forbidding for a crossing attempt, but the Army Engineer on this date gave a long-range prediction of February 24 for the recession of the flood.

On the afternoon of February 21 General Simpson again considered in detail the very complicated question of the best date to make the crossing. He weighed the calculations of the Engineer, who predicted that by midnight of February 22-23 the river would have receded enough, and its velocity decreased enough, to permit the initiation of a successful, if difficult, crossing. By February 24, the exact hour unpredictable though probably about noon, the final emptying of the lower dams was calculated to produce a sudden drop of the river and the complete recession of the flood. Then the weather predictions were considered. Fair weather had held for several days and had vastly improved the footing for tanks. The weather forecast promised a continuation of this favorable weather for two or three days. Beyond that the forecaster could make no confident prediction. The Army Commander also considered the element of surprise. If he waited for the river's complete return to normal on February 24, he probably would sacrifice all surprise of timing. Conversely, if he launched his attack at an earlier date he might well catch the Germans still comparatively unprepared and laboring under a false sense of security behind a still formidable water barrier. Finally, he concluded that the advantage of surprise and the promised good weather outweighed the difficulties of crossing the still swollen but falling stream. General Simpson determined that the hour of attack would be 3:30 A.M. on February 23. Immediately the order went out to the troops. The pent-up energy of the preceding weeks was now converted into feverish, yet quiet, last-minute preparations.

Look now at the picture backstage just before the curtain rises. (*Map No. 9.*) From just north of Düren to the confluence of the Roer and the Maas, at Roermond, the now powerful Ninth Army was disposed in depth behind a narrow 30-mile front. On the right (south) flanked by First Army's VII Corps, was the battlewise XIX Corps of Major General Raymond S. McLain. The hedgerow fighting in Normandy, the race across France, Belgium, and the Netherlands, the breaching of the Siegfried Line, and the participation in the capture of Aachen were already accomplished history of this corps. It had two divisions poised behind the rushing waters, sharing almost equally an eight-mile front along the Roer. On the south, the 30th Division, returned from its heroic month's labors in the Ardennes, was back, substantially in its old position, ready to take up where it left off in mid-December. It had shifted south a bit in order to gain the use of crossing sites which had been spurned two months before. Now these sites were necessary in order that a strong, rapid build-up might be achieved. On the north of the 30th Division, opposite Jülich, was the 29th Infantry Division. Across this four-mile front where many had fought and died in late November and early December, the men of the division occupied the ground that had been their home for three long winter months. Eight miles back, in the vicinity of Alsdorf, General McLain placed his 83d Division, closely backing up his two assaulting echelons. Almost another eight miles to the rear, positioned to take advantage of the road net fanning out from Aachen, was his armor, the 2d Armored Division. The right, then, was strongly disposed in depth yet pushed up as close as the zone and the dictates of security would permit. Three infantry divisions and an old-type heavy armored division, all at full strength and fully equipped, were waiting for the signal to be off to the Rhine.

Major General Alvan C. Gillem's XIII Corps, in the center, occupied a somewhat narrower zone of about six and one-half miles. It had the November offensive behind it, and three months' familiarity with the terrain it was occupying. This corps was disposed, like XIX Corps on its right, with its infantry up and its armor back. The men of the 102d Infantry Division held Linnich and the area to the south. They quickly populated this slender, three-mile zone. To their north, stretching for nearly four miles, but with the bulk of its forces in the southern portion, was the 84th Infantry Division. Back some fifteen miles, in the vicinity of Heerlen, the 5th Armored Division made ready and waited.

Brigadier General John F. Uncles' 34th Field Artillery Brigade, comprising three battalions of 240mm howitzers and one battalion of 8-inch guns, was directly under Army control, and was positioned generally astride the XIX-XIII Corps boundary so that its long-range heavy weapons could support both of these corps.

On the left, occupying a good half of the entire Army front and looking forward confidently to its first offensive action, was Major General John B. Anderson's XVI Corps. Spaced almost evenly across the front from right to left were the 35th Infantry, 79th Infantry, and the 8th Armored Divisions. The 79th, however, had only one regiment of infantry committed, the remainder of this division being in corps reserve and limited to action on express Army order. The division, less one regiment in the line, was concentrated some seven miles northwest of Aachen. In the Army Letter of Instructions of February 6 this restricted employment had been applied to the 8th Armored Division, but the subsequent release from XVI Corps of the British 7th Armored Division to go north to assist in the Canadian Army attack, the arrival of the 79th Infantry Division, and the estimate that infantry, rather than armor, would more likely be committed in the initial stages of the battle, caused this minor shift in dispositions.

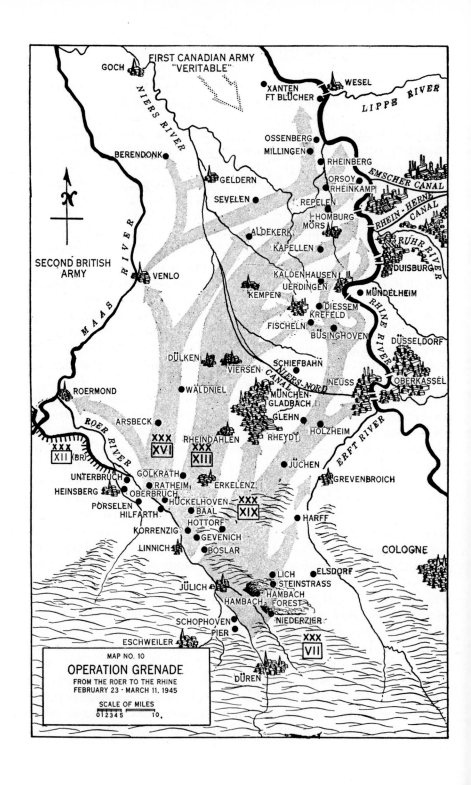

MAP NO. 10

OPERATION GRENADE

FROM THE ROER TO THE RHINE
FEBRUARY 23 - MARCH 11, 1945

SCALE OF MILES
0 1 2 3 4 5   10.

The 75th Infantry Division was "on loan" to British Second Army and lost to Ninth Army's immediate use. However, west of the Maas, ten to fifteen miles south of Maastricht, was the Army reserve, the 95th Infantry Division, ready to move on six hours' notice. This unit was held back both to deny the enemy knowledge of its presence in the battle area and to reduce the load on the already heavily burdened road net.

The dispositions were complete; all hands awaited H-hour.

Beginning at 2:45 in the morning of February 23 there thundered a 45-minute artillery preparation, during which over a thousand guns of Ninth Army, plus those of First Army on the south and British Second Army on the north, shook the earth and illuminated the sky from south of Düren north to Roermond and on to Venlo. Then the doughboys of the 30th, 29th, 102d and 84th Divisions lowered their assault boats into the violent, still flooded Roer and loosed the offensive juggernaut that was to crunch continuously and relentlessly across German soil for two months, finally to bring Germany to her knees, a hopelessly defeated enemy. The furious, shattering artillery effort smothered the zones of XIII and XIX Corps with an average of nearly two and a half projectiles per yard of front. It was designed to disrupt the enemy's communications, paralyze his traffic, and silence his artillery. It was further intended to aid in concealing the location of the main effort of the attack by covering the noise of men and equipment moving up to the crossing sites.

Fighting the river as well as the enemy gave the assaulting elements a difficult first day. Bridging operations were begun almost immediately, yet because of that very fact their vulnerability was increased, and bridges were lost to enemy action as well as to difficult river conditions. However, pushing on even after darkness fell on the first day, the 30th Division on the right had advanced better than two miles beyond the river by midnight, to occupy Hambach and Niederzier, two small road centers at the edge of the Hambach Forest. (*Map No. 10.*) The crossing sites in this division's zone were particularly bad, the condition of the exit roads giving the greatest trouble. Bad luck contributed, too, to what might be considered a rather slow beginning. For instance, upon completing one bridge there was discovered at the exit point on the far bank a 500-pound unexploded bomb which had been dropped there by an Allied aircraft sometime in the past. By rare, unfavorable coindence, it lay exactly in the spot chosen for a bridge. Undoubtedly, though, the very choice of such an uninviting crossing zone as was used by this division contributed materially to the surprise gained in this area. As the historic day came to a close, two foot bridges were in operation and two treadway bridges were under construction in the 30th Division's zone.

The 29th Division, too, had its share of difficulties. On one occasion mines on the west bank of the river which had escaped detection in preliminary reconnaissance destroyed a number of amphibious craft and forced abandonment of the crossing site. Twice bridges almost completed were lost to enemy artillery fire and the swirling waters of the Roer. However, when the day ended, the infantry of the 29th had taken Jülich, the key communications center immediately east of the river and the symbol of German defense of the Roer River line. Only the Citadel, a moated fort, remained in German hands, to be taken the following day with the aid of tank-borne flame throwers. In the division zone two foot bridges had been successfully completed and maintained, one heavy ponton bridge was in operation, and a treadway bridge and an infantry support bridge were under construction.

In the XIII Corps zone the 102d Division had crossed in extremely good order and pushed east on a broad front for two miles. The corps bridging operations in this division zone had produced two foot bridges, an infantry support bridge, and a treadway bridge, all completed and in use by the end of the day. Two more treadway bridges were under construction. Every infantry battalion of this division had gained the far side of the river in the very first day of the attack. Farther north the 84th Division, limited to a single crossing site, determined to make the most of its opportunity. Leading with but one battalion, due to the lack of "elbow room," it quickly reduced Korrenzig, built up its forces rapidly and slashed northward along the main Linnich–München-Gladbach highway for a distance of four miles to seize the important communications center of Baal. This advance was the most spectacular development of the day and set the pattern for the type of quick unexpected jabs at the enemy that were to be continued all through the operation.

Nor was XVI Corps idle as the great offensive got under way. In addition to staging its demonstration, the corps advanced all along the right and center óf its line. Several pockets of enemy resistance were eliminated, notably those at Porselen, Oberbruch, and Unterbruch.

By the end of the first day, success of the offensive had been practically assured. The only really burning question, that of how much interference the Roer River would impose upon the operation, had been answered, and it was now known that not only could infantry be crossed in assault boats and other craft but also bridges could be built rapidly and maintained so that tank destroyer and artillery support could be crossed into the bridgehead. Twenty-eight battalions of infantry were east of the Roer, and seven Class 40 bridges were either completed or so well along that, barring unforeseen circumstances, they could be counted on for use on the following day. It had not been done easily, but it had been done. Enemy action had been only light to moderate; surprise gained by the crossing before flood recession had been expensive in bridging equipment, but it had been economical in the lives of men. Ninth Army losses were 92 killed, 61 missing, 913 wounded. More than 1,100 prisoners had been taken, and an estimated total of more than 400 enemy killed.

Too much cannot be said for the gallantry, stamina, and courage of the individual soldier. In the cold and the dark—wet, sometimes half-drowned—always exposed to every hazard of enemy action—still he pressed forward to insure the success of the crossings and the expansion of the bridgeheads. These were men of highly trained and well equipped units, skillfully directed and supported. The Army planned and "supplied" their effort, the several corps directed and coordinated it, but the divisions and the supporting troops "fought" it, principally through the endeavor of thoroughly trained and battle-tested junior officers and men. Many of the units, too, had just returned from the successful and hard-fought Battle of the Bulge. There was certainly present an element of retaliation against the Germans for their initial successes and the damage done there. In the battles to be fought, almost without let-up, all the way from the Roer deep into the heart of Germany, the American soldier was to prove himself a better soldier than the German.

Under the over-all supervision of the Army Chemical Officer, Colonel Harold Walmsley, the use of screening smoke played an important part in the crossing of the Roer. The plans had included the employment of both mechanical and chemical smoke generators to deny the enemy observation of troop-ferrying operations and bridging activities. In the 30th Division zone from Pier to Schophoven, protection was provided against direct and aerial observation, chiefly to permit an early start in the construction of the two heavy bridges. The screen was started at 6:30 A.M., but a south wind, unexpected by weather forecasts, required a movement of the generator and a delay in effective screening until 8:00 o'clock. This screen was originally planned to be maintained for twelve hours but was actually maintained continously for thirty-three hours. The 30th Division credited the smoke cover with substantial contribution to the completion of the northernmost bridge five hours ahead of schedule and without a single casualty. Farther to the south the smoke screen was less effective, but even there it contributed to the success of the operation.

In the 29th Division zone a similar smoke-screening program was planned. The screening was begun at 3:50 A.M. and continued until 5:15 A.M., but at that time it was discontinued because of interference with the observation of artillery fire. The subsequent destruction of a treadway bridge in this area by German artillery fire might have been avoided had the continuation of the smoke screen been feasible.

The enemy order of battle proved no surprise. Identified on the first day of the operation were the 59th and 176th Infantry Divisions and the 183d and 363d Volksgrenadier Divisions—all units whose presence in front of Ninth Army had long been appreciated. In addition, the usual hodgepodge of miscellaneous units was contacted.

XXIX Tactical Air Command, flying a greater number of sorties than it had ever before accomplished in a single day, provided close support to the attacking columns. Fighter-bombers took the place of those tank destroyers and tanks which remained as yet on the west bank of the river. At Baal, for instance, northeast of Linnich, when an armored counterattack threatened the spearhead of the 84th Division, Thunderbolts went into action and claimed the destruction of three tanks and the damage of as many more. In an excellent strike against a motor transport depot, three squadrons of fighter-bombers claimed destruction or damage of large numbers of vehicles.

When darkness fell, the German air force began its attack on the bridges, strafing and bombing with single planes, and succeeded in destroying two Class 40 bridges. Counterattacks by ground forces began, too, but they were local and were contained in every case by the forces in the vicinity. The strongest of these efforts took place in the vicinity of Baal and in the Boslar-Gevenich sector east of Linnich.

On the south flank in First Army, experiencing similar difficulties but accomplishing similar progress, VII Corps' 8th and 104th Infantry Divisions kept pace in the attack. This was important, for it was highly desirable that Ninth Army's right wing be free to continue the attack through the Hambach Forest, undeterred by any threat which might cause it to turn attention southward.

Grenade's second day, February 24, was particularly a build-up day during which the infantry forces in the bridgehead were increased to 38 battalions, and supporting troops to the extent of 3 tank destroyer battalions, 4 tank battalions, and 8 field artillery battalions crossed the river and went into action. This was made possible by the completion of a total of 7 Class 40 bridges in addition to 12 lighter bridges. But the main build-up was in supplies. Initial crossings had been made, of course, with only those supplies that the attacking echelons could carry. Now it was imperative to get the unit trains across and to build up supplies to support further operations, particularly those which might be necessary to reduce major counterattacks. By the end of the second day, when a considerable quantity of supplies had been put into the bridgehead and a large number of tactical bridges completed, the German's capability of isolating Ninth Army forces on the east bank of the Roer and annihilating them was a thing of the past.

Two outstanding tactical developments took place on the second day of the attack; one was the good progress of the 30th Division, on the right, which carried it almost completely through that portion of the Hambach Forest which lay within Ninth Army's zone; the other was the surge to the north by XIII Corps, with both the 84th and 102d Infantry Divisions making remarkable progress. The rapid clearance of the Hambach Forest eliminated the long-dreaded counterattack on Jülich from this ideal forming-up area. It also indicated that the eastern portion of the Forest, lying in First Army's zone, might likewise be cleared quickly and permit VII Corps to keep pace with Ninth Army's advance, thereby realizing one of the prerequisites to the adoption of the plan based on a rapid advance. XIII Corps' substantial progress was significant in the indication it gave of weakening German resistance, the advantage it gained by occupying the western end of the Linnich–Harff Plateau, and the promise that subsequent northwesterly progress would afford XVI Corps an early opportunity to get a toe-hold in its future zone of advance.

The Army Commander was now watching the battle very closely for indications of the tempo it was to take. He had two spots to watch particularly. On the boundary between XIX and XIII Corps, the rapid progress of XIII Corps to the northeast had created the danger of its right flank being unprotected. This possibility had been forseen long before, even in the early planning stages of the operation, but now it was a reality. General McLain had committed a regimental combat team of the 83d Division in this area, attaching it to the 29th Division. This was done not only to increase the strength of his attack but also to facilitate rapid, progressive entry of the 83d Division into the fight. Now he pushed this unit into the attack in order to close up on his left flank. General Gillem likewise took action to offset the danger by ordering elements of the 5th Armored Division up to his right flank.

The other point calling for the Army Commander's special attention was the impending large-scale commitment of XVI Corps. The plans had called for XIII Corps securing the Huckelhoven–Ratheim–Golkrath triangle northwest of Baal in order to permit XVI Corps to make an unopposed crossing of the river and occupy a line of departure from which to launch its attack to the north. However, being loath to slow down in any way the northward impetus of the 84th Division, the Army Commander now considered the possibility of the XVI Corps going across at Hilfarth on its own. So on February 24 he directed that XVI Corps feel out, during the night of February 25-26, the enemy defenses at Hilfarth, and, if practicable, seize a bridgehead with a small force.

It was on the second day of the battle that the German air force staged its greatest effort of the entire operation. Making 38 raids with a total of 97 aircraft of all descriptions, the Luftwaffe struck time after time to destroy the bridges now spanning the Roer. For the first time jet-propelled aircraft appeared against ground targets. The enemy paid for his effort with a loss of 18 planes destroyed by antiaircraft artillery alone. The bridges were un-damaged. The 405th Fighter-Bomber Group, unable to prevent morning attacks because of the weather, braved a 1500-foot ceiling to maintain constant vigil over the bridge sites for the remainder of the day.

On this date, too, the first knowledge of the location of the German reserve armor came to light when infantry elements of the 9th Panzer Division were contacted in the vicinity of Ham-bach. This was hardly a surprise, for this unit had been estimated to be somewhere near Cologne or west thereof. However, no con-centration of armor was met anywhere along the front, all Ger-man effort in this respect being confined to small movements of tanks or assault guns.

The third day of the operation, February 25, saw a general advance of two or three miles all along the XIX and XIII Corps fronts. By now the XIII Corps salient, some six miles wide and about three and one-half miles deep, was aimed directly at Erkel-enz, the first large road center in the path of the advance. The progress followed the pattern of the preceding day. The enemy put up a stiff fight in each of the small towns which dotted the plain between the Roer and the Erft. The reduction of these cen-ters of resistance was accomplished with great skill and ability; rapid movement to the outskirts of the town, then the deployment and coordinated attack of it, finally the mop-up, the reorganiza-tion, and the advance to the next town—this was the oft repeated story in the XIII Corps advance. Making an effort to stem the tide, the enemy shifted elements of the 176th Infantry Division to the south and committed, piecemeal again, infantry elements of the 11th Panzer Division. On the south flank, XIX Corps had definitely turned the direction of its attack to the north, with its progress following, generally speaking, the same pattern as XIII Corps. At Steinstrass, at the north edge of the Hambach Forest, sharp, heavy fighting occurred when elements of the 9th Panzer Division, now definitely established west of the Erft River astride the inter-Army Group boundary, fought to delay the advance of the 30th Division. By mid-afternoon, however, this resistance had been stifled and Steinstrass seized, and by midnight the night-fighting 30th had gone on to take Lich, just north of Steinstrass. On the other side of the XIII Corps salient, XVI Corps jumped off at 8:00 P.M. in its attack to feel out enemy strength in Hilfarth. Mines here were very numerous and well covered by fire. The 35th Division had to pay a heavy price for its first bridge site over the Roer.

At the bridge site in Linnich the protecting antiaircraft artillerymen, with skill and a dash of luck, provided a remarkable example of marksmanship when a Messerschmitt 262, a jet-propelled plane, glided in and released two bombs in an effort to destroy the bridge. The 40mm guns opened fire, destroying the plane and hitting one of the bombs, exploding it in mid-air. The bridge was not damaged.

Perhaps the most important development at this time was the movement of armor. The Nazis' defenses were beginning to give way, and it was time that armored units be brought forward and pushed for a breakthrough. Ninth Army armor began to roll on February 25 as Combat Command B of the 5th Armored Division initiated its movement to Hottorf, northeast of Linnich, to get in place for the projected encirclement of Erkelenz. In the First Army zone, on the night of February 25-26, VII Corps' 3d Armored Division moved up to Düren, from whence it was to launch an attack for Elsdorf and a junction with XIX Corps on the Erft. On February 26 Combat Command B of the 2d Armored Division moved southeast of Jülich, whence it was to be committed on the same day in Steinstrass under the 30th Division.

While XIX and XIII Corps laid plans to continue to drive straight ahead, XVI Corps moved elements of the 35th Division, positioning them for action on February 26, a maneuver in which the forces attacking across the Roer at Hilfarth would be assisted by other 35th Division forces passing through the zone of the 84th Division and cutting northwest to take Huckelhoven. This change in the original plan, wherein XIII Corps was to seize this area, would permit XIII Corps to keep all of its resources directed to the north.

There was no doubt now that Ninth Army, with problems of supply and traffic well in hand, was firmly established on the broad plain east of the Roer and was headed for the Rhine. For the time being the Army could but watch for signs of a hole in the enemy's line and pray that the weather, which had been good so far but which now threatened to change, would not deny the opportunity for the quick armored thrust which was planned. Rain fell on February 26 but it was light, and while it grounded the Thunderbolts and the Mustangs of the XXIX Tactical Air Command, in general it had little effect on the course of the ground attack.

XIII Corps, in pushing its salient even farther north, made an overwhelming assualt on Erkelenz, a key locality in the German defense system, and seized the town despite the fact that the German 338th Infantry Division was newly committed in its defense. This marked the first occasion during the offensive that Ninth Army had run into a major enemy unit brought into the area from elsewhere on the Western Front. The 338th Infantry Division was en route from the Colmar Pocket, far to the south, to Geldern, to back up the heavily engaged forces fighting it out with the Canadian First Army on the water-logged plain north of Geldern, when it was shunted to the Ninth Army front. It was an ill-conceived commitment, however, for it came to the defense of Erkelenz bit by bit and saved neither Erkelenz nor its own fighting strength. Again elements of 11th Panzer Division tried to block the advance, and prisoners taken from this unit supplied the information that it was their commander's intention to hold south of the line München-Gladbach-Grevenbroich. With its positions now secure, and with powerful resources still uncommitted, Ninth Army welcomed any intention of the enemy to stand and fight. It could only mean his destruction—*west* of the Rhine.

Again the tempo stepped up slowly across the front. Gains of up to three miles were general. However, in the limited zone across the Roer where the XVI Corps was fighting for room enough to initiate a full-fledged attack, elements of its 35th Division ran into hard fighting around Huckelhoven. Nevertheless, on this day, the fourth of the operation, there was satisfaction that all three corps now were committed, at least in part, across the river. From here on they could fight for maneuver room and expand their zones as they would. The spectacular action of the 26th occurred not in Ninth Army's zone but in the area of General Collins' VII Corps where his 3d Armored Division broke away for ten miles northeast from Düren to reach Elsdorf. This action served to settle once and for all any concern for the security of the right flank. Strong forces were now keeping pace on the south, and the 9th Panzer Division, punished by both armies, was scarcely a formidable foe any longer.

Even while these operations were setting the stage for developments of the succeeding days, General Simpson and General McLain were conferring, plotting the breakthrough toward Neuss. The big question was the order of commitment of the 83d Infantry Division and the 2d Armored Division. Already one regimental combat team of the 83d was operating under command of the 29th Division in the left of the XIX Corps zone, and on the right of the corps zone one combat command of the 2d Armored Division was fighting with the 30th Infantry Division. More troops could now be moved up to carry on the attack. It must be one division or the other. There was not sufficient capacity over the Roer bridges and on the roads leading therefrom to permit simultaneous movement of the remainder of both divisions. The core of the problem was the belt of German defenses, particularly trenches and antitank ditches, which stretched southeast from Rheydt to Grevenbroich on the Erft River. Could the armor get through these defenses or must infantry lead the way? The 30th Division would be pulled east up against the Erft River as the action developed, to guard the eastern flank, and the 29th would thrust north toward Rheydt and München-Gladbach, making a hole for the force chosen to plunge through to Neuss.

There was a strong argument for spearheading this force with the 83d Infantry Division, since it was acknowledged that if the defenses were strongly held the infantry division would be the most suitable force to cope with them. On the other hand, should the defenses prove reasonably soft, it was the armor that was best suited to punch through and exploit the golden opportunity offered. Because of the road space required by the heavy-type armored division, a decision to move the 2d Armored first meant a two-day delay before the infantry division could be moved and committed. If the infantry division were moved first, however, and then the armored division were found to be needed, only one day's delay would be introduced. The decision could not be postponed; it had to be made then. After a careful consideration of all the factors, General Simpson determined to take the risk and decided in favor of the armor. Orders were therefore issued to concentrate the entire 2d Armored Division east of the Roer in position for a drive through to Neuss.

The 2d Armored Division's entry into the battle is excellently described by *Time* correspondent Sidney Olson:

From the air in a Piper Cub the tank drive was a thing of sheerest military beauty. First came a long row of throbbing tanks moving like heavy dark beetles over the green cabbage fields of Germany in a wide swath—many tanks in a single row abreast. Then a suitable distance behind, came another great echelon of tanks even broader, out of which groups would wheel from their brown mud tracks in green fields to encircle and smash fire at some stubborn strongpoint. Behind this came miles of trucks full of troops, maneuvering perfectly to mop up by-passed tough spots. Then came the field artillery to pound hard knots into submission . . .

And always overhead swung and looped the Thunderbolts keeping the tanks under absolute safety umbrellas and from time to time diving to knock out trouble points beyond the front . . .

This was one of the War's grandest single pictures of united and perfectly functioning military machines in a supreme moment of pure fighting motion.

The phase lines set up in the planning were not permitted to hamper the operations of any unit so long as flanks could be kept secure. Penetrations were encouraged. Thus XIII Corps kept pushing on without waiting for XIX Corps to complete its wheeling around on the outside of the circle. A change of direction of attack from east to north was now virtually completed. On several occasions already, in local actions, this change of direction had paid dividends. Ninth Army forces time and again drove north to bag surprised Germans who were facing to the west even as they were overrun.

In front of XIII Corps, the crushing of the German forces continued. Near Waldniel a replacement pool of some 15 officers and 100 enlisted men was taken intact. Nearby, an artillery battalion was captured, complete with its commander and all of its guns. More important, near Rheindahlen, west of Rheydt, the taking of prisoners of Panzer Lehr Division gave concrete evidence of the mutual effect of Ninth Army and Canadian First Army efforts, for Panzer Lehr had been struggling in the north to stave off the advance of the Canadians. Now it was appearing in the south, prepared, its captured, defiant personnel contented, to defend the stronghold of München-Gladbach. The protectors of the Ruhr were hard pressed. The reserves for the one battle must be withdrawn from the other. The movement of Panzer Lehr Division down from the north had been traced with keen interest at Army headquarters. If the Germans had chosen to commit the division farther south, along the Rheydt–Grevenbroich defense line, its heavily gunned tanks in dug-in positions might have delayed the anticipated breakthrough toward Neuss. Its commitment in the München-Gladbach area was welcome news.

XIII Corps worked its 5th Armored Division into position on its right and gave orders to carry the attack as far as it could go. XVI Corps, too, initiated its armored move, directing one combat command of the 8th Armored Division to cross behind the front left to right, pass through the bridgehead at Hilfarth, and attack to the north. The roar of the tank treads was increasing in volume. Elements of three armored divisions were moving into the battle. Time was growing short for the German cause west of the Rhine; the juggernaut was gathering speed.

The sixth day of the operation, the last day of February, may well be considered the "breakthrough" day. Though it is very difficult, in any operation, to put the finger on the exact moment and the exact place where the tide of battle turns, nevertheless the action of XIX Corps' 2d Armored Division, with the 331st Regimental Combat Team of the 83d Division attached, in driving eight miles to the northeast on the Army right flank to carry its forward elements within seven miles of the Rhine, definitely determined that the back of German resistance along the approaches to the Ruhr was broken and that soon the Nazi high command would find its forces in the west divided.

The enemy was not unappreciative of the threat to his cause. Along the Rheydt–Grevenbroich defense line he contested hotly, with particularly savage fighting in the vicinity of Jüchen where, with antitank guns, tanks, and dug-in infantry, he temporarily checked the advance of the armor. But he was doomed. In its fighting from the Roer to the Rhine the 2d Armored Division was to kill more Germans than in any other battle from Sicily through the advance into Germany and the fighting in the Bulge. By nightfall on the last day of February the defenses guarding the corridor to Neuss had been overwhelmed, and the 2d Armored Division was heading for the Rhine.

Less spectacular, perhaps, but equally important was the continous advance of the 29th Division toward München-Gladbach. An advance of five miles there straightened out the battle line, for although XIII Corps continued its progress to the north, the sharp salient which it had formed by its rapid progress ever since crossing the Roer was now almost a straight line with only a shallow dip where the line met the densely populated area of München-Gladbach. Panzer Lehr Division provided the resistance to the 29th Division's advance, but it was not a strong effort by that once formidable organization. For the most part, its tankers were forced to fight as infantrymen because there was no gasoline for their tanks. On one occasion an entire company was captured—the confused Germans thinking they were "in the reserve area."

The weather, which had for two days practically eliminated air support, now broke clear again, and all across the front fighter-bombers joined in the field day. Four hundred and nine successful sorties were flown, and destruction or damage of sixteen tanks was claimed, together with remunerative attacks on many other targets. At one point, in a woods west of München-Gladbach, fighter pilots themselves picked up a slugging match between Shermans and Tigers and swooped down into the battle to damage six of the Tigers. XIII Corps' prisoner-of-war count ran high on this last day of February as the enemy forces on its front fought sharp delaying actions to cover what appeared to be a general withdrawal. Now the enemy must think of extracting his remaining odds and ends from the Siegfried defenses south of Venlo, for XIII Corps' northward advance was making these positions precarious. Tactical reconnaissance pilots reported the rearward movement of the *Ersatz* battalions which only recently had replaced the 8th Parachute Division in the Roermond area when that unit moved north to contest the advance of the Canadian First Army. As February came to a close, the German Army of the Rhineland had only one course of action, retreat across the Rhine.

What troops the Germans had occupying the once vaunted Siegfried Line must have been intent on their efforts to avoid the avalanche flowing in on them, for XVI Corps armor and infantry both struck out from their limited bridgehead across the Roer and against very light resistance fanned out to seize important road junctions such as Arsbeck. On their right flank the armor might have broken away on a substantial thrust toward Venlo, but disappointingly it became snarled and beset with traffic difficulties engendered by the demolition by the retreating Germans of a few well chosen bridges. The breakaway in this area must wait.

If the last day of February was the turning of the tide, the first day of March jumped forward in the most spectacular advance of the operation. Perhaps the outstanding event occurred when XVI Corps sent a motorized task force, including the 320th Infantry Regiment of the 35th Division, and the 784th Tank Battalion, north all the way to Venlo. Stopping only occasionally to eliminate light resistance, the task force rolled down the road into the very city itself. Venlo, bastion of the Siegfried Line and impregnable Maas fortress, had been taken from the rear without a fight. Cavalry patrols entered Roermond, too, to find it unoccupied but highly mined.

XIII Corps, after six days of steady advance to the north, added another seven miles to its progress by now turning northeast toward Krefeld and the Rhine. The astounding surprise of the operation occurred in the XIX Corps zone when one infantry regiment, the 29th Division's 175th, cleared the great city of München-Gladbach in a single day. This German city of 170,000 people was the largest captured by Allied forces up to this time in the war. Located twelve miles from the Rhine and twenty miles from the Maas, it was a potential fortress denying the approaches to the Ruhr. Hitler's threat that every great German city would be defended to the last, as was Aachen, gave rise to conjecture as to the manner in which the enemy would fit München-Gladbach into his defensive plan. Ninth Army had spent many an hour planning the envelopment, the reduction, if necesary the siege, of München-Gladbach. Now in one day one regiment of United States infantry solved the problem!

On the right flank, as the 2d Armored Division turned north from Glehn toward Krefeld and Uerdingen, the 83d Division picked up the attack on Neuss and drove into the outskirts of the city itself. The bend in the Erft had been passed and the Army south flank was exposed for some thirteen miles, until First Army units could come forward on the other side of the river. Elements of the 30th Division pushed up around the corner as far as Grevenbroich, and the 83d Division took on the mission of flank protection from there on, in addition to its attack on Neuss. The Niers Canal northwest of München-Gladbach and the Nord Canal between München-Gladbach and Neuss both proved to be substantial water barriers, but the delay they occasioned was only temporary.

The advance on this first day of March was so rapid that aircraft of the XXIX Tactical Air Command could find few remunerative ground targets. However, the Luftwaffe chose this date for another flare of activity, and our fighter pilots searching the skies deep into Germany, as well as over the battle area, fought engagements with an estimated 110 enemy aircraft. Twelve German planes were claimed destroyed, two probably destroyed, and seventeen damaged, for a loss of seven XXIX Tactical Air Command planes.

March 1 also saw the Army shifting forces, regrouping, and introducing fresh units into the battle in order to maintain the intense pace of the operation. The 75th Infantry Division, less one regimental combat team, was released from the operational control of British Second Army, since hostile forces had been practically eliminated from the east bank of the Maas. This division was now attached to XVI Corps, and simultaneously the 79th Infantry Division, which could have been committed *in toto* only on Army order, was detached from the corps This gave XVI Corps two complete infantry divisions and an armored division with which to continue its drive to the Rhine. The 79th Infantry Division in turn was attached to XIII Corps. This division, uncommitted in the operation except for one regiment which had initially held a portion of the line, would be available if needed for continuation of the XIII Corps attack. Then the reserve division, the 95th Infantry, was attached to XIX Corps, again with the intention of providing fresh troops to maintain the pressure until every last German west of the Rhine had been wiped out. The 29th Infantry Division, which was now pinched out as a result of the northward advance of the 2d Armored Division, was ordered to assemble in the vicinity of München-Gladbach and pass to Army reserve.

The battle itself was won; now the pursuit and the mopping-up remained. The objectives from here on were to inflict the maximum punishment on German forces attempting to withdraw across the Rhine and by bold, rapid pursuit to seize intact, if possible, at least one of the eight Rhine bridges in Ninth Army's zone—three in the Neuss–Düsseldorf area, one at Uerdingen, and four from Duisburg north. Both General Eisenhower and General Bradley visited Ninth Army on March 1 and 2. In discussions and observations of the rapid progress of the Army toward the

Rhine, the Supreme Commander evidenced to General Simpson and General Bradley his intense interest in the Ninth Army plans for seizing a Rhine bridge. The battle for the bridges began in earnest with the first closing to the Rhine on March 2.

On the morning of that day, infantry elements of XIX Corps' 83d Infantry Division reached the Rhine just south of Neuss, while later in the day tankers of the 2d Armored Division closed up to the river north of Neuss. The Rhine had been reached at last. As our troops gazed at the historic river toward which Allied forces had been fighting for so many months, any possible mental hazard presented by the name of the great waterway was dissipated. Though the Rhine was a formidable barrier, it was just another river and could be successfully hurdled any time the powers that be gave the command. Marking the historic occasion, the first radio-photograph transmitted directly from the Army area to the United States was dispatched at this time, culminating the highly successful efforts of Army photographic units throughout the attack and indicative of the rapid transmission of news and photographs to the waiting population back home. This picture showed troops of the Ninth Army on the Rhine River for the first time.

Neuss itself was almost completely cleared during the day. The Germans withdrew in orderly fashion, however, and demolished all three of the Neuss–Düsseldorf bridges. Of the eight Rhine bridges in the Army zone, three were down, five to go. But before the Neuss–Düsseldorf bridges were destroyed, an attempt to seize by ruse, one of them located at Obercassel, a suburb of Düsseldorf, provided one of the remarkable stories of the war. An 83d Division task force, composed of units from the 330th Infantry Regiment, the 736th Tank Battalion, and the 643d Tank Destroyer Battalion, staged a play for high stakes that almost paid off. Moving by night and disguising their tanks to resemble German tanks, with accompanying infantry walking beside and behind the tanks to make themselves as inconspicuous as possible and with German-speaking Americans mounted on the fronts of the tanks to do any talking required, this task force passed through the enemy lines some ten miles to Obercassel. They passed German outposts with a few German words interspersed with many "Heil Hitlers." They went unchallenged past German soldiers, some carrying the German equivalent of bazookas, which they never fired. At one time a German foot column was marching down one side of a road while the task force moved along the other side of the same road! Obercassel was reached without a shot being fired.

As dawn came, a German soldier on a bicycle in a passing column apparently identified the nature of the task force. When challenged he refused to halt, instead increasing his speed to get away. There was no recourse but to shoot. The shot that ended the bicyclist's life also ended the ruse of the task force. Its identity known, it turned its fire power on the German column, wiping it out. The Obercassel town siren blew to give warning, and although the task force drove quickly to the bridge and even got tanks on it, the bridge was blown before it could be captured.

The 2d Armored Division maintained its drive to the northeast in a series of sharp local fights. Towns and roads were defended more vigorously, for the German forces were becoming hemmed in ever more tightly. At Schiefbahm, northeast of München-Gladbach, elements of Panzer Lehr Division made a determined counterattack in an effort to reach the Rhine. It was repulsed only after hard fighting. Scattered bits of the 7th and 8th Parachute Divisions appeared, too, attempting to bolster the defense of the retreat routes. And on the southern flank, three miles northeast of Grevenbroich, the long-expected counterattack against the Neuss spearhead finally was launched. German infantry, reinforced by tanks, hit hard here and reached almost to the Jülich–Neuss highway before they were turned back. Fighter-bombers contributed to the ultimate blunting of this attack as part of a record-breaking effort of 624 sorties staged by the XXIX Tactical Air Command. This effort, in addition to giving considerable close support of the ground troops, aimed particularly at the German rail system. Thirty-three locomotives were claimed destroyed during the day, and rail lines cut in seventy-two places.

On March 2, too, XIII Corps moved into Krefeld with elements of the 102d and 84th Infantry Divisions and the 5th Armored Division. A captured map had revealed a German plan to defend strongly along a line generally through Krefeld and west to Kempen, to enable their forces to the northeast to make orderly withdrawals across the Rhine. To prevent this maneuver, the Army determined to strike in force with both XIII Corps and

XIX Corps. The unexpectedly rapid advance to the north of the 2d Armored Division found this element of the XIX Corps already threatening to slice between Krefeld and the Rhine. At the same time elements of all three divisions of the XIII Corps were driving into the city from the southwest, the west, and the northwest. The boundary between the two corps was immediately moved to the north so as to enable XIX Corps to continue its drive north. This boundary change occasioned a necessary shift of the weight of XIII Corps to the north with a resultant temporary slowing down of its advance. However, it prevented pinching out the XIX Corps against the Rhine and therefore allowed the continual application of the full weight of the Army in the drive to cut off German crossing sites and pocket the enemy west of the Rhine.

The over-all offensive, which through its first week pivoted on Linnich and wheeled about counterclockwise from the east to the north, now operated with its field reversed, the pivot at Neuss, the sweep clockwise, and the direction shifting from north to east again. On the outside of the circle during the second day of March, the XVI Corps task force from the 35th Division, which the previous day had pounded all the way to Venlo, now cleared the city and rolled another fourteen miles to the northeast to enter Sevelen. The 8th Armored Division, too, shaking the bad luck which had dogged it in the form of poor roads and demolished bridges, now swung to the northeast to a point five miles northwest of Kempen. Although initial plans and directives for the operation had limited Ninth Army's northern advance to the general line Venlo–Mörs, conditions had now changed. Cancellation of the British Second Army attack across the Maas to the Rhine from the Venlo area, the comparatively slow progress of the Canadian First Army due to poor road conditions and bitter enemy resistance, the rapid progress of Ninth Army's vigorous attack, and the development of more definite plans for the prospective Rhine River crossings all contributed to the necessity of redefining the zones of action for elements of 21 Army Group. This was done on March 1, when 21 Army Group set a boundary between Ninth Army and Canadian First Army which ran generally from Venlo to Rheinberg. On March 2, then, Ninth Army issued the third and last Letter of Instructions for Operation Grenade, embodying the verbal orders which the Army Commander had issued during the preceding few days and laying particular emphasis on the last stage of the operation, the desperate attempt to secure intact at least one bridge over the Rhine. The following are excerpts from these instructions:

> The enemy forces opposing the Ninth U.S. Army are weak. They display signs of disintegration. There are no major reinforcements in sight.
>
> The Ninth U.S. Army has penetrated the enemy's Düsseldorf bridgehead position. His bridgeheads immediately to the north obviously center about Duisburg and Wesel, respectively. These are believed to have standing garrisons of Replacement and Flak units, whose value is negligible unless reinforced with field forces.
>
> There are virtually no field works south of the Ruhr, west of the Rhine, though it is possible that along the waterfronts of the larger towns, docks and houses have been prepared for defense.
>
> The enemy undoubtedly will attempt strongly to defend the entrances to the Ruhr. On the basis of captured documents and aerial reconnaissance it is estimated that the enemy's bridgehead defense of the Ruhr will follow the general line: Orsoy–Rheinkamp–immediately east of Mörs–Kaldenhausen–Diessem–Bosinghoven . . . [thence generally east to the Rhine].
>
> It is considered that the continued vigorous advance of the Ninth U.S. Army will prevent the enemy's orderly withdrawal of field forces into his bridgehead positions. In this case the enemy will be unable properly to consolidate and defend such positions, in order later to escape east of the Rhine.
>
> Ninth U.S. Army will:
>
> (1) Continue its attack to the north and northeast to eliminate enemy resistance in the area between the Rhine and Maas Rivers from Neuss (inclusive) to Rheinberg (inclusive).
>
> (2) Seize intact bridges over the Rhine River wherever possible.
>
> (3) Be prepared to extend zone of action to the north to assist advance of First Canadian Army.
>
> (4) Be prepared to establish bridgeheads east of the Rhine if the situation permits, and exploit such bridgeheads to advance to the east.
>
> All units will continue to maintain the present momentum of the attack in order to retain the initiative which is now firmly in our hands.

On March 3 the battle for the Rhine bridges continued unabated. The Germans were fighting desperately to extricate as many troops as possible for the struggle they knew must come shortly with an all-out Allied effort to cross the Rhine. Elements of 15th Panzergrenadier Division, 190th Infantry Division, and 406th zBV (Special Operations) Division, the latter a hodgepodge of units under one command, all yielded prisoners as they fought delaying actions to permit their withdrawal by ferry and other river craft or over the diminishing number of bridges still standing over the Rhine. The use of river barges in ferrying operations offered new opportunities to the fighter-bomber pilots, who claimed twenty-nine such craft destroyed and nine damaged, in addition to the day's claims of large numbers of locomotives and freight cars destroyed or damaged. The first of the Rhine bridges to be reached had been the Neuss–Düsseldorf bridges, whose shattered, twisted spans had been discovered the previous day, March 2, by the 83d Infantry Division. Now, farther to the north, just south of Uerdingen, the 2d Armored Division made a supreme effort to seize the highway bridge, and actually had armored elements on the western end of the bridge when it was blown by the Germans. It was a bitter disappointment to see this opportunity lost at the very last moment, but German demolition preparations had been thorough and efficient. Four bridges were now down, four to go.

To the north of Krefeld, XIII Corps' 84th Division, fighting its ninth consecutive day of intense all-out battle, lunged forward another nine to ten miles, with corps cavalry covering its advance and elements of the 5th Armored Division, which had been pinched out in front of Krefeld, protecting its left flank after a rapid and well executed movement to get into position on the north. Farther north in the XVI Corps zone, the day was marked by the long-sought junction with the Canadians when elements of XVI Corps cavalry, operating north of the Army boundary, made contact, first in the little village of Berendonk, and later at Geldern.

Now the battlefield was becoming too limited to accommodate the full strength of Ninth Army's power. The 29th Infantry Division, in Army reserve, sat quietly occupying München-Gladbach. The 30th Infantry Division held the right flank along the Erft River to the vicinity of Holzheim, but the advance of the First Army had excluded it from further battle role. Clearing Neuss and the area to the northeast left the 83d Division with no further enemy forces to fight west of the Rhine. Thus in XIX Corps only the 2d Armored and elements of the 95th Division which had been brought up to assist in clearing the Uerdingen area were still actively operating. In the XIII Corps the 102d Division, upon clearing Krefeld, was pinched out and left to garrison the city, at the same time reverting to corps reserve to be recommitted only on Army order. Hence, with the 79th Division assembled in Erkelenz and uncommitted to action, XIII Corps likewise had only two divisions, the 84th Infantry and 5th Armored, actively engaged. In XVI Corps, the 75th Division was now concentrating east of the Maas, but its journey was a long one, since heavy bridging at Venlo was still not completed. With the 8th Armored Division assembling in corps reserve after capturing Aldekirk, XVI Corps was fighting only one division, the 35th. On the ninth day of battle, then, so rapidly and so successfully had the action developed that seven of the Army's twelve divisions were relegated to nonoffensive roles.

On March 4 important action was limited to the clearing of Mörs, the entry into the outskirts of Homberg, and the capture of Repelen. Soupy weather kept aircraft grounded as the tedious house-to-house fighting progressed. All manner of German units took part in this stubborn defense, with elements of 15th Panzergrenadier Division providing the core of the resistance. Fighting in the area around Uerdingen continued. In the northern section of the town the 2d Armored Division countered a night attack staged by a regiment of infantry, while in the southern part the 95th Division fought all day against the die-hard fanatics of the 8th Parachute Division. German resistance had stiffened in the limited area still occupied by enemy troops west of the Rhine, and constricted room for maneuver against this resistance made it increasingly difficult to wipe out what remained. In football terms, Ninth Army was in the shadow of the goal post, and picking up yardage was a slow and difficult task.

However, late this day and well into the next, General Simpson spent many hours considering a plan of action to make a surprise crossing of the Rhine in the area north of Düsseldorf, including the Mündelheim bend opposite Uerdingen. For the preceding three days the Army Commander had had his staff devoting considerable time to plans for exploiting the seizure intact of any one of the bridges that crossed the Rhine in the Army zone. On March 4, with the possible opportunities already reduced from eight to four by successful enemy demolition action, the whole question of an early surprise crossing of the Rhine was brought into sharp relief when General McLain of XIX Corps presented a plan for forcing a crossing in his zone, securing a bridgehead, and driving to the east to envelop the Ruhr from the south. He requested authority to embark on this operation within two to three days. March 4 and 5 were devoted to a detailed study of the possibilities offered by this plan and to the consideration of the risks involved and the effect on future operations.

Two basic plans were finally evolved, both based on the seizure of an initial bridgehead between Düsseldorf and Mündelheim. In either case, the ultimate objective set up was the capture of Hamm, the rail center at the northeastern corner of the Ruhr industrial area. (*Map No. 4.*) Hamm was selected because it was considered the key outlet through which poured the products of industry from the Ruhr to the Wehrmacht. One plan visualized a drive by one corps along the axis Düsseldorf–Wetter–Unna–Hamm, while a second corps cleared and expanded the bridgehead north to the Ruhr River. A second plan envisaged striking north from the initial bridgehead, crossing the Ruhr River, and then turning east to drive on Hamm. As this operation progressed it would avoid Essen on the east and clear the east bank of the Rhine on the west in order to permit progressive bridging by additional forces and the eventual commitment of all three corps of Ninth Army. General Simpson decided to present the details of both these plans to Field Marshal Montgomery with his recommendation that a surprise crossing of the river be executed either by assault or by capitalizing on the capture of a bridge, and further, if a surprise crossing were made by either method that the plan to drive north, then east along the northern face of the built-up Ruhr area be adopted.

Owing to his desire to assault across the Rhine on a broad front simultaneously with both British and American forces, the plans for which had been in development for months and the preparations for which were even then rapidly reaching completion, Field Marshal Montgomery made the decision to withhold any early crossing of the Rhine and to continue with plans for the execution of Operation Plunder, as the coordinated assault crossing of the Rhine between Rheinberg and Emmerich was known. So the course of history as it might have developed had Ninth Army leaped the Rhine early in March will never be known. Of one point Ninth Army men are certain—it could have been done, and done successfully.

March 5 saw the completion of Operation Grenade as it was

originally planned. (*Map No. 10.*) The Rhine was uncovered from Düsseldorf to Mörs and the original mission was accomplished. The violent, short-lived battle for the bridges was also finished. By nightfall the four spans from Duisburg north, standing when dawn broke, had all been destroyed by the Germans. The great structures bridging the Rhine in Ninth Army's zone were but twisted masses of wreckage washed by the water of Germany's greatest river. Though the struggle to eliminate the last vestige of resistance west of the Rhine was to continue for another six days, eleven days of continous, brilliantly executed battle had brought an end to the labors of both XIX and XIII Corps. On this rainy Monday their forces reduced the last stronghold in Uerdingen, cleared Homberg, and overran Orsoy, where the frantic Germans abandoned vast quantities of supplies as they crowded aboard east-bound ferries. Two corps were now closed against the river, and the long-range guns of the Army could reach deep into the heart of the Ruhr as far as Essen.

In the XVI Corps zone on the north flank, elements of the 35th Infantry Division and 8th Armored Division now teamed to strike forward and enter Rheinberg, a village three miles west of the Rhine which was later to leave its imprint in history when it lent its name to the crossing site for the Ninth Army's plunge across the last major barrier guarding the Reich. Resistance was stiffening, however, in this northern corner of the Army front as German paratroopers threw a ring in front of Wesel, chosen as the escape outlet for all that was left of the German army which had attempted to stem the advance of both the Canadian Army and Ninth Army in the Rhineland.

The story of the next six days is the story of the elimination of that pocket. XVI Corps' task was an extremely difficult one primarily because of restricted maneuver room. Limited by the Rhine River on its right and the Canadian First Army closing in toward the same objective on its left, the corps was forced to fight a battle to clear a triangle whose base was only some five miles wide and whose apex, eight miles from the base, was old Fort Blücher, standing guard on the west bank approaches to Wesel, the road and rail center on the east bank of the Rhine just north of the Lippe River. The boundary between Canadian First Army and Ninth Army was successively changed to include more territory to the north to Ninth Army. Coordination with another army along the constantly changing boundary, and attempts by the strategic air forces based in the far-off United Kingdom to destroy the Wesel crossings by heavy bombing, gave birth to problems which added to the delay inherent in ferreting out resistance bent on covering the final escape routes. During March 6, 7, 8, and 9 elements of the corps cavalry and of the 35th Infantry, the 8th Armored, and the 75th Infantry Divisions battled mile by mile to clear Rheinberg, Millingen and finally Ossenberg, where the Germans made a strongpoint of every house. The German 190th Infantry Division, the 116th Panzer Division, and 2d, 7th, and 8th Parachute Divisions, all took part in an extremely well executed retrograde movement, a type of operations at which the Germans had become masters. Rain and dense clouds persisted all through this period, keeping XXIX Tactical Air Command planes on the ground, although upon request of the 35th Division, twelve pilots of the 366th Fighter-Bomber Group staged a daring mission on March 6 to effect the silencing of thirteen gun positions in and around Ossenberg with their bombs, rockets, and machine guns, giving valuable assistance to the reduction of this enemy strongpoint. On March 10, finally, enemy resistance was crushed, although his withdrawal was made in good order. Night fell on March 10 with leading Ninth Army elements only 100 yards from Fort Blücher. When, early on the morning of March 11, the last small group of weary Germans was cleaned out of the old fortress, the offensive was completely ended.

Enormous quantities of supplies were involved in supporting the Army's winter operations and the drive from the Roer to the Rhine. For example, for the period December 10, 1944, to March 11, 1945, 26,494,933 rations (77,514 tons), 20,806,185 gallons of gasoline (74,657 tons) and 833,505 gallons of Diesel oil (3,-236 tons) were issued to troops of the Army. The supply of the vast quantity of gasoline was greatly facilitated by the installation of a pipeline from Antwerp, initially to Maastricht by the Advance Section, Communications Zone. This pipe line consisted of one 6-inch and two 4-inch pipes with an input capacity of 2,815 tons per day, and capable of delivering 1,035,920 gallons per day. However, sufficient tank cars and trucks were not available to transport that amount from the tank farms to the decanting area, and there was a shortage of personnel to accomplish the decanting of the gasoline into five-gallon containers for delivery to the troops. Accordingly, approximately eighty-five per cent of the Army's gasoline was furnished by the pipeline, and the remaining fifteen per cent of the gasoline, and all allied products, were shipped by rail and truck from a Communications Zone depot at Liège, where decanting was accomplished prior to shipment. By February 1 the pipeline was in operation to Maastricht, where a tank farm, for storing the gasoline, and a decanting area had been established. When the early thaw came, however, the decanting station at Maastricht could not sustain the heavy traffic, and in view of the coming operations a forward decanting area was established at Lutterade, east of Maastricht. Gasoline was then transported by tank-truck from the Maastricht tank farm to the decanting station at Lutterade; truck and rail transportation were used from that point forward. With the crossing of the Roer and the rapid advance of the Army to the Rhine, a still more advanced storage and decanting area was established near Wegberg, west of Rheydt (*Map No. 9.*) and sufficient stocks were built up there so that the principal gasoline supplies to forward troops could be made without crossing the Roer River bridges. When the Army reached the Rhine, a new terminus was selected for the pipeline at Alpen, southwest of Wesel, and construction was begun on a new tank farm there.

As Operation Grenade was coming to a close, the Army command post moved forward sixty miles from its winter quarters in Maastricht. The forward echelon opened in München-Gladbach on March 10, using the slightly damaged local courthouse and neighboring buildings for shelter. The rear echelon, "Conquer Rear," established itself in the adjoining city of Rheydt on March 20. This movement established the headquarters in the largest city the Army had taken up to that time.

As the activities and responsibilities of the Army had expanded, the size of the headquarters and the numbers of personnel associated with it had naturally increased. The complexity and size of the headquarters of a modern field army exemplify the diversity of modern warfare. Included among the various relatively small but highly important elements necessary for an Army to perform its own housekeeping and to execute its strategic, tactical, territorial, and military government and civil affairs functions were the following: postal units, machine records units, weather detachments, engineer utilities detachments, technical intelligence teams of the various services, war crimes investigation teams, ordnance bomb-disposal squads, military police criminal investigation detachments, detachments of mobile radio broadcasting companies, traffic regulating groups, Office of Strategic Services detachments, and civil censorship, counterintelligence and document detachments. In addition, sizable units of signal, transportation, military police, antiaircraft, and cavalry troops were required to enable the headquarters to communicate, and to move and protect itself, under the supervision of Colonel James A. Warren, Jr., Headquarters Commandant and Commanding Officer of Special Troops.

Liaison personnel from Allied forces and cooperating services swelled the totals. The diversity of the uniforms made the headquarters area a colorful spectacle. U. S. and Royal Navy, British Army, Royal Air Force, Canadian, French, Belgian, Netherlands, UNRRA (United Nations Relief and Rehabilitation Administration) and American Red Cross personnel, war correspondents of many Allied nationalities—all were closely associated with the Army in the performance of its manifold functions.

As the Army closed along the Rhine, the plans which had been worked out before the beginning of the offensive for the establishment of a widespread system of Army rest centers in the larger towns of the Netherlands were now put into effect. The Army took over corps and division rest centers and enlarged them as permanent establishments which were available to all troops of the Army on pass quota basis. In the towns of Maastricht, Heerlen, Sittard, Valkenburg, Kerkrade, Treebeck and later Eisden, large facilities were established where troops could be sent for several days of needed rest, recreation, and entertainment. These proved invaluable morale factors, and as the Army advanced still deeper into Germany, the program was further expanded. At its height, under the supervision of Lieutenant Colonel George W. Bailey, Jr., who had formerly been senior liaison officer for the headquarters, the Army system of rest centers accommodated 5,000 individuals on a "hotel service" basis. Every facility was provided for the entertainment, convenience, and comfort of the individual soldier—hotel rooms with beds and linen, individually served meals, recreational rooms established by the American Red Cross, and a wide variety of other features for leisure hours, including moving pictures and special services entertainments under the supervision of Lieutenant Colonel Kenneth K. Kelly, who had succeeded Colonel De Rohan as Army Special Services Officer. More than 120,000 individuals were accomodated by the rest centers during the Army's operational period in Europe.

As the might of Ninth Army rolled across the plains to the Rhine, it left in its wake uncounted multitudes whose individuals included homeless German civilians, Allied displaced persons, Allied prisoners of war, and the bewildered, ineffective Volkssturm, the hastily formed home guard of Germany. Never before had the Army been faced with the responsibility of sorting out and dealing with such heterogeneous masses of humanity. Many of these people wandered about at will until Army agencies could bring order out of chaos. Initially they interfered with tactical operations by cluttering the roads, slowing down traffic, hampering counterintelligence activities, and clogging the prisoner-of-war evacuation channels into which they were often erroneously directed. Military Government detachments of corps and divisions, augmented by such spare detachments as the Army could furnish, acted quickly to alleviate the situation. Coordinating with the other Army agencies concerned, they established policies which not only solved the problem west of the Rhine but stood in good stead later when the same problem, greatly magnified, was met east of the Rhine. Among the guiding principles developed were the following:

Only high civil functionaries and persons whose services were of particular use to the enemy or its government or those leaders who incited the people to resistance were confined.

All German citizens, displaced persons, and inmates of concentration camps were ordered to "stand fast" in order to reduce to a minimum the movement of the populace.

No civilians were to be accepted in prisoner-of-war channels unless a properly executed arrest certificate accompanied the individual.

All members of the Volkssturm were to be disarmed and disbanded in place and returned to civilian occupation. As an exception, individuals who actively resisted disarmament might, at the discretion of the troop commander concerned, be treated as prisoners of war.

Upon arriving in a newly captured town, the Military Government Officer immediately posted the proclamations and ordinances of the Supreme Allied Commander in order to inform the populace of the restrictions under which it was to live from then on. He discharged whatever Nazi Party personnel remained in the local government and appointed a *Bürgermeister* to supervise the carrying out of orders by the citizens. The *Bürgermeister* was charged with the care, feeding, and housing of all displaced persons in the area. The unburied dead were interred and the work of clearing the debris initiated. A police force was established, the rationing system restored, the schools suspended, and civilian courts established to assist military courts. Utilities were repaired to provide light and water to the advancing Army and to the civil populace. Curfew and circulation restrictions were placed in effect, and all German firearms were confiscated. These were only the immediate local steps taken to re-establish law and order under Allied control. Then began the long term, over-all program of the Allied Powers.

Prior to the crossing of the Roer River, Military Government activities in Germany had been of a minor nature. Only four cities with a population of 5,000 or greater had been occupied, and the smaller towns had generally been demolished to such an extent that the normal community life had stopped. However, this situation changed considerably once the Roer was crossed. It was estimated that in the Army area between the Roer and Rhine Rivers the civil population was over 500,000, and approximately 273,000 of these were within five miles of the Rhine. More than forty Military Government detachments were deployed by the Army in this area by March 15, and by the 23d of the month fifty-eight detachments were operating.

In anticipation of the many problems confronting small units in occupied enemy territory—problems which were sure to increase as the Army advanced farther into Germany—a pocket-size booklet entitled *Guide to Occupation of German Communities by Small-Unit Commanders* had been published and distributed throughout the Army long before the Roer was crossed. This booklet consolidated in one convenient reference all the information the unit leader needed for guidance in occupying German communities—what to do about property, billets, the local officials and police, nonfraternization, and similar problems. It provided a practical guide which was of assistance in the conduct of occupation before Military Government proper took over.

With the crossing of the Roer, the civilian food problem increased sharply, and the experience gained in the smaller area west of the river stood the Army in good stead. The relatively large civilian population between the Roer and the Rhine stood perilously close to starvation, principally for lack of distribution control, before the Army food experts got busy. Swift measures to reclaim the original food control and distribution system before it disintegrated, and to facilitate its operation, were very successful. All food stocks discovered were quickly rationed. This food was used not only to sustain the German civil population but also to take care of the displaced persons, whose feeding was made a responsibility of the local German government. In an effort to prevent starvation in the coming winter, strong measures were taken to get as much land as possible under cultivation. To permit full use of daylight hours for tilling the fields, farmers were generally relieved from circulation restrictions and curfew regulations. Unemployed city labor was directed to the rural regions to reinforce the struggling farmers.

With the uncovering of some fairly large cities which had been badly battered, serious sanitary problems from damaged water and sewer systems were encountered. A modern community is utterly dependent upon the smooth functioning of its sanitary facilities, and its population has not acquired the partial immunity of people who habitually live under more antiquated sanitary conditions. It was essential, therefore, that minimum standards of sanitation be re-established in these large cities, a task of great magnitude and seriousness. Military Government officers showed great ingenuity in quickly organizing German agencies, experts, and private organizations to effect temporary but adequate repairs to water and sewer systems.

Medical measures to prevent epidemics were undertaken immediately. With the discovery of more than 180 typhus cases, most of them displaced persons, in the Army area west of the Rhine, an energetic program for the discovery and isolation of typhus fever cases and the further prevention of the disease was carried out. Mass disinfection with DDT powder was ordered for all displaced persons. About 10,000 displaced persons were evacuated to the Netherlands, Belgium, and France, and over 15,000 were cared for in sixteen camps established in the area.

When General Eisenhower had visited his front-line troops during the early winter months he had said, "I promise you we will fight on without let-up all through the winter. We shall give the Germans no rest. We shall destroy their armies west of the Rhine!" As the winter faded and signs of spring appeared along the Western Front, Ninth Army, in a sustained drive of fifty miles had in seventeen days, with less than 7,300 casualties, captured a total of nearly 30,000 enemy soldiers, killed an estimated total of about 6,000 more, overrun the rich Rhineland plain, and added the might of its heavy artillery to the power of the strategic Air Forces in the interdiction of the Ruhr, the industrial heart of Germany. More than that, it had opened the flood gate of offensive operations which, before this one operation was completed, had already seen the reduction of Cologne and the seizure of the bridgehead across the Rhine at Remagen by First Army, and the initiation of the drive to Coblenz by Third Army. As the drive from the Roer to the Rhine came to a close, the Allied Armies took their places in the positions from which they were to spring for the heart of Germany and in conjunction with the forces of Soviet Russia accomplish victory in Europe. Operation Grenade was the overture which General Simpson and his men played to open history's greatest military symphony.

CHAPTER 6
CROSSING THE RHINE

THE Rhine was the last great barrier protecting the heart of the German homeland against invasion from the west. Since the time of Caesar it had been the historic dividing line, the do-or-die line where Germans stood fast to translate into action the resolute theme of *The Watch on the Rhine*. The classic river of medieval song, mythology, and fable, it had always held a peculiar fascination for the German mind. In modern times, the interplay of geography, natural resources, and productive developments had placed, just beyond the river, the great industrial area of the Ruhr. The crossing of the Rhine in great strength and the separation of the massive Ruhr industrial powerhouse from the remainder of the Reich would wrench out the vital organs of Germany's war-making capacity.

By March 11, when Ninth Army completed closing up to the Rhine, the Canadian First Army and British Second Army had also completed the clearing of all Germans west of the Rhine in their zones north of Wesel and at once started preparations to cross the river. (*Map No. 4.*) On March 7 the U. S. First Army, immediately to the south, had seized the railroad bridge at Remagen and was widening its bridgehead east of the Rhine while continuing to eliminate the last enemy resistance in its zone west of the river. Farther to the south, Third Army was engaged in crossing the Moselle River and closing up to the Rhine near Coblenz, preparatory to crossing that river. At the extreme southern end of the Allied lines, Seventh Army and the French First Army had reached the Rhine at Colmar and Strasbourg, whereupon they proceeded to reduce the Siegfried Line defenses along the German border near Saarbrücken and Pirmasens, preparatory to their own Rhine crossing.

Like the invasion assault across the English Channel, the plans and preparations for crossing the Rhine consumed much more time than the actual execution of the attack. Giving priority, of course, to other and more immediate needs for planning and supervising current operations, Ninth Army planning for the Rhine crossing was carried on, almost continously, for six and one-half months. The assembling of river-crossing equipment extended over five months, and there were engineer troops training specifically for the task of getting the Army across the Rhine most of the time during that same period. The divisions and supporting troops finally scheduled to make the assault crossing trained and rehearsed their part for two weeks. By way of contrast to all these plans and preparations it was only eight days, from the time the first thunderous artillery firing began to soften up the defenses on the east bank of the river for the attacking infantry, until the bridgehead, as originally prescribed in the attack order, was secured. Within nine days of the assault crossing, all three corps had their combat echelons east of the river.

The general location of proposed crossing sites changed greatly as Ninth Army Rhine planning progressed. While still in Brittany, when 12th Army Group had directed that the Army be prepared for a move to the east to take over a zone of action on the southern end of the front, planning was concentrated on the possible bridgehead areas around Wiesbaden, Mannheim, and Karlsruhe. (*Map No. 4.*) Then, with the move to Luxembourg completed and the Army committed in the center of the line, the stretch between Coblenz and Bonn came under consideration. Finally, when Ninth Army assumed its permanent position on the American north flank, it was the crossing sites stretching north from the Ruhr River that occupied its attention.

In mid-October at Arlon, upon receipt of the first intimation that the Army was to move north, planning efforts were directed toward a crossing of the Rhine in the north with the encirclement of the Ruhr as the ultimate objective. Tentative studies were accomplished to include the possibilities of crossing the river south of the Ruhr in the vicinity of Düsseldorf and enveloping the industrial area from the south; of crossing opposite the Lippe River and enveloping the Ruhr from the north; and of combining the action of these two to effect a double envelopment. These studies were merely preliminary, serving generally to acquaint the staff with the magnitude of the operation and the type of terrain upon which it would have to be executed. Their great value lay in the engendering of staff-thinking along such lines as the number and types of troops required, comparative advantages and disadvantages of the rather restricted number of crossing sites available, and, above all, the requirements in special equipment necessary to effect what was foreseen as the greatest river-crossing operation in history. The Army conducted these initial planning studies "on its own." There were no directives from higher headquarters to serve as a guide or to direct the efforts toward any particular crossing areas. Cooperation in providing information such as river conditions, general map coverage, and characteristics of newly developed amphibious and other stream-crossing vehicles and equipment was supplied by Theater and 12th Army Group Headquarters, but in those early days such information was meager. There were many battles yet to be fought and won before the Rhine was reached, and the demands of "first things first" tended to relegate Rhine River crossing problems to the background.

But even as the November offensive got underway, specific details were being accomplished. In the absence of any delimiting instructions from higher headquarters, the whole length of the Rhine from Cologne to Nijmegen was considered for possible crossing operations. Although no definite conclusions were reached, it soon became quite clear that a southern envelopment of the Ruhr industrial area offered little promise because of the obstacle formed by the Ruhr River on the southern edge of the heart of the industrial area which could be flooded by manipulation of dams, and because of the unfavorable terrain and road net to the east. Therefore, from then on slight consideration was given to any crossing south of the confluence of the Ruhr and the Rhine River except as a feint or as a limited objective crossing. Map studies, together with information of river conditions, indicated that the most suitable crossing sites north of the Ruhr River (*Map No. 4*) were probably those at Rheinberg, Xanten, Rees, and Emmerich, with a favorable demonstration or feint site on the south near Uerdingen.

A military geography study published by Ninth Army on December 25 included the following description of the Rhine in the area from Rheinberg to Rees. Here, in the lower reaches of the Rhine, the river flows through a broad flat valley, in contrast to the rugged, mountainous regions of the upper Rhine.

The Rhine varies from about 900 to 1500 feet in width, and maximum depth at low water is everywhere in excess of 10 feet. The river bottom is of sand and gravel. Banks are normally of sand and gravel and in many places are protected by stone revetments or by groins projecting into the river. The river is bordered by two continuous systems of dikes constructed of local earth and sometimes revetted. The summer dikes, so-called because they normally contain the summer high water but are topped by the higher winter floods, lie close to the river banks and vary in height from 0 to 10 feet. The winter dikes, designed to contain the highest flood of record, lie at a distance up to 2 miles back of the summer dikes. They usually stand from 12 to 15 feet above the surrounding terrain. The surface velocity of the river averages about 5 feet per second, increasing to 8 feet per second at highest navigable water.

Assuming, for its own planning purposes, that it would have access to whatever crossing sites it chose without interference from other forces, Ninth Army developed a number of preliminary outline plans in an effort to arrive at certain more or less definite conclusions upon which to base further detailed study. Various combinations of Ninth Army organization were set up and examined, as was the effect of concurrent operations by British Second Army, Canadian First Army, and airborne forces. It was recognized at an early date that should Ninth Army force a crossing north of the Ruhr it would part company, so to speak, with First Army, and operate with an open right flank for some time to come, probably until the encirclement of the Ruhr was completed.

With the projected November offensive and the accompanying hope that Ninth Army might well reach the Rhine before many weeks had passed, the month of November saw the Rhine River crossing planning accelerated. The halt on the Roer in the face of the flood threat, and the turn of events to the south, resulted in a lull, and it was not until the middle of January that the assault across the Rhine again took prominence in planning activities. By November 17, however, thought had crystalized to the extent that the Army Commander directed preparation of a detailed study of the engineer considerations and requirements inherent in the Rhine operations. At this time he specified the area between Cologne and Emmerich for further study and thereby delineated the limits of detailed planning.

By then a general basic plan of maneuver had been developed which was to provide a standard of comparison and the framework for all future work on the project. Using as a troop basis a standard organization of three corps totaling nine infantry and three armored divisions, together with appropriate supporting troops, the following general scheme (*Map No. 4*) was devised: on the south flank facing the Ruhr and holding the line of the river north from a junction with First Army south of Düsseldorf, a single corps, to be composed probably of two infantry divisions, would maintain a defensive position and concurrently stage a demonstration in the Uerdingen area. In the center, with boundaries generally along the Rhein–Herne Canal and the Lippe River, a second corps of three infantry divisions, utilizing the Rheinberg crossing sites, would assault and bridge the river and carry out a limited penetration north of the industrial area sufficient to seal off the Ruhr proper and provide security for the bridges. On the left flank, north of the Lippe River, utilizing generally the crossing sites at Xanten and Rees, a strong corps of three infantry and two armored divisions would make the main effort, a wide envelopment of the Ruhr, after first seizing the all-important communications center of Wesel. The remaining one infantry and one armored division were to be in Army reserve.

This plan contemplated simultaneous offensive action on the part of British Second Army on Ninth Army's left flank and left the Emmerich site, as well as any other sites farther to the north which might prove suitable, to that Army. This was but a broad outline plan based only on preliminary study of the meager information on hand. It is noteworthy that the basic principles and the general scheme of maneuver arrived at so early stood up with so little change in the later intensive detailed studies.

The Army Engineer, realizing the magnitude of his task, had initiated work on the Rhine River problem at a very early date. On October 18 he attended a conference at the city of Luxembourg with the Chief Engineer of the European Theater of Operations and the engineers of all American army groups and armies then operational. Preliminary decisions were made at that time to permit initiation of the assembly of the staggering stocks of river-crossing equipment which would be required. As soon as the Army move to the Maastricht area was completed, requisitions were prepared and submitted for the supplies and equipment required for the Rhine crossing and a special section of the main Army Engineer depot was reserved for such supplies.

At the same time, certain other steps were taken in connection with the planning and training for the Rhine River assault. An engineer combat group was established at Visé, Belgium, on the Maas River, as a Ninth Army agency for training in connection with Rhine River crossing problems. It established and operated

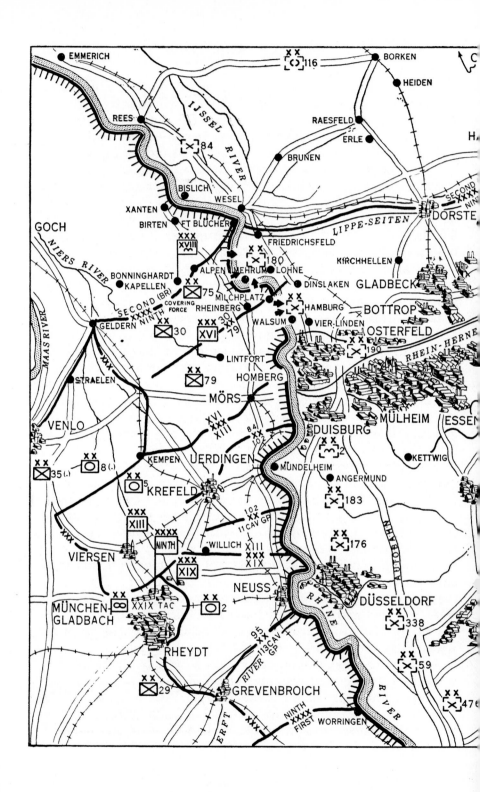

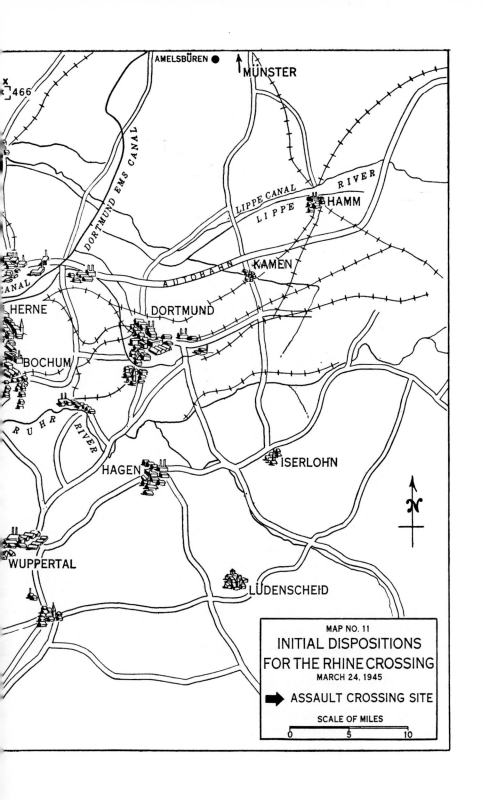

AMELSBÜREN ●

↑ MÜNSTER

☒ 466

DORTMUND EMS CANAL

LIPPE CANAL

LIPPE RIVER

HAMM

CANAL

AUTOBAHN

KAMEN

HERNE

DORTMUND

BOCHUM

RUHR RIVER

HAGEN

ISERLOHN

N

WUPPERTAL

LÜDENSCHEID

MAP NO. 11

INITIAL DISPOSITIONS
FOR THE RHINE CROSSING
MARCH 24, 1945

➡ ASSAULT CROSSING SITE

SCALE OF MILES

0   5   10

schools which trained engineer units of the Army in all types of floating bridging, ferrying, construction of protective booms, bridge maintenance, and the operation of stormboats, outboard motors, and assault boats. Particular emphasis was placed on training in the construction of floating Bailey bridges, since few engineer units had had experience in this particular type of work. The same group also was assigned the mission of assisting signal construction troops to train in laying cables and field wire across the Maas River.

On November 15 there was attached to the group a Navy detachment called Navy LCVP Unit Number 3. This unit was equipped with 24 LCVPs (Landing Craft, Vehicle and Personnel), and 24 LCMs (Landing Craft Medium), all-purpose cargo craft, with the necessary operating and maintenance personnel. Experiments were begun immediately on the methods of transporting LCVPs and LCMs overland, launching them into the water, and operating them in swift river currents. Later, a detachment of the 329th Transportation Corps Harbor Craft Company was attached to the group and conducted schools to train engineers in the operation of Seamules, 38-foot tugs powered by two 143-horsepower engines and capable of being disassembled into four sections of approximately equal size for transportation overland.

On November 24, the Army Engineer assembled the corps engineers and the commanders and staffs of all major Army engineer units and directed them to initiate their Rhine River planning. At this time operational plans had not developed to the point where it could be said which corps or how many corps would make assault crossings, but the general mission was outlined and sufficient detail furnished to enable consideration of the problems involved. All information gathered up to this date as to the characteristics and capabilities of various river-crossing means was presented, together with a preliminary engineer intelligence study on the Rhine River, and an estimate of the type and quantities of troops, equipment, and supplies which might be expected to be available.

Except for a meeting on December 6 with representatives of Major General Matthew B. Ridgway's XVIII Airborne Corps, little planning was accomplished on the Rhine River project from the first of December until the middle of January. The XVIII

Airborne Corps was developing plans for airborne operations in support of one or more armies when the time came for crossing all along the front. The interchange of ideas regarding the coordination of airborne and ground forces in a joint effort north of the Ruhr was very beneficial. However, shortly after this meeting, XVIII Airborne Corps was called upon to perform a ground mission under First Army in the battle of the Ardennes and was so completely occupied with this duty that temporarily it had no time for further planning. Ninth Army's attention, and indeed the attention of all the Allied headquarters in Europe, was devoted entirely to the blunting of the surprise German thrust, and it was not until mid-January that the Rhine crossing project again began to receive substantial consideration.

On January 12 the Army published Engineer Technical Notes Number 3, *Rhine River Study, Cologne to Emmerich,* presenting available engineer data pertaining to the planning and execution by subordinate units of an opposed crossing. A general description of the Rhine River Plain was given, including the possibilities for cross-country movement, the river-flooding capabilities of the enemy, and details of the dikes, both summer and winter. Considerable information was given relative to the characteristics of the river itself. Additional studies in greater detail, notably with regard to cross-country movement, dikes, flooding and approach roads were then in progress and were published as completed. From then on Rhine River information was issued as it became available, and the Army staff and subordinate units were provided with the technical engineer data necessary to prepare the details of operational plans.

On January 19, 21 Army Group entered into the Rhine River crossing planning when it held a meeting of the Chiefs of Staff and technical representatives of Ninth Army, British Second Army, and Canadian First Army. Much of the discussion at this conference was technical and dealt with special equipment. No actual decisions were reached, but much valuable information was interchanged with reference to the capabilities and available numbers of a great many items of equipment, most of them of an amphibious nature.

In the discussion of the tactical and logistical aspects of the operation it became clear that there was a difference of opinion between Ninth Army and British Second Army as to which Rhine crossing sites would be available to each Army. It will be remembered that Ninth Army had included in its preliminary studies the use of sites as far north as Rees, inclusive, but British Second Army, which had also initiated preliminary studies, was considering sites down to and including the Rheinberg area. It was pointed out by General Moore, Ninth Army Chief of Staff, that the Wesel bridges, together with the roads and area west thereof, were the minimum required for the support of American operations east of the Rhine and, therefore, the crossing sites in that vicinity should be allotted to Ninth Army. The British Second Army felt that the Wesel crossings would be required by them, at least initially, but acknowledged that the bridges would have to be constructed by Ninth Army engineers. Obviously, before much more planning could logically and reasonably be accomplished, some preliminary assignment of zones of action would have to be made.

The answer came in Field Marshal Montgomery's directive of January 21, dealing chiefly with instructions for the operations carrying the 21 Army Group forces up to the Rhine. This has already been referred to and quoted in part in the preceding chapter. In addition, however, this document included certain orders and information which directly affected the planning and execution of the Rhine River assault. The Field Marshal said, in part:

> When the opportune moment arrives, the Allied armies will cross the Rhine in strength north of the Ruhr and in such other places as may be ordered by the Supreme Allied Commander.
> The future layout that we want to achieve is to face up to the Rhine from Düsseldorf northward on a front of three armies: Ninth Army: Düsseldorf to exclusive Mors; Second Army: Mors to inclusive Rees; Canadian Army: exclusive Rees to Nijmegen. [Map No. 4.]
> The three selected crossing places over the Rhine north of the Ruhr are as follows and will be known by these names: Rheinberg crossing, Xanten crossing, Rees crossing.
> All plans will be made for crossing the Rhine in the Emmerich area as we require the road center in that place. From a study of the problem it appears likely that it may not be possible to cross in the Emmerich area in the face of opposition until the right or eastern bank of the river has been secured by troops put across at Rees. This may prove to be not the case.
> At a time to be notified later, one American corps of two infantry divisions will be allotted to Second Army.
> Second Army will be prepared, in due course and when ordered, to force

the crossings of the Rhine at Rheinberg, Xanten and Rees. The Rheinberg crossing will be carried out by the American corps.

Ninth Army was flabbergasted! The instructions of the Field Marshal left General Simpson's command with no part to play in the assault across the Rhine. True, one American corps of two divisions was to engage in the crossing, but it was to be placed under the command of British Second Army. A host of confusing questions immediately arose in the minds of Ninth Army's staff. Who would furnish supplies and evacuation for the American corps? Who would build the many necessary bridges for whose construction the British did not have sufficient equipment and personnel? What disposition would be made of the tremendous stocks of bridging and special equipment already being accumulated in Ninth Army's area? What mission would be given the strong Ninth Army of twelve divisions and ample supporting troops which would have completed a drive up to the Rhine and be far in excess of the forces required merely to hold the river line? It was a directive which made completely uncertain Ninth Army's role once the Rhine had been reached.

Other conferences with the British further developed the points of difference. The paucity of British bridging and stream-crossing equipment required that American engineer troops and facilities be used at certain sites contemplated for British crossings. More important, the combined divisions of the non-American elements of 21 Army Group appeared adequate only to securing a limited number of initial bridgeheads east of the Rhine and required, morover, the addition of the American corps to encompass all the proposed crossing sites. And, finally, the British lacked sufficient divisions to insure the breakout from the initial bridgeheads and the drive on into Germany. The exploitation of the value of the bridgeheads would have to be accomplished by other forces—by passing Ninth Army through British Second Army, a dubious procedure from a supply and logistical viewpoint.

Ninth Army and British Second Army, adjacent armies since October, had long engaged in mutual exchange of information and conclusions reached in preliminary studies of Rhine crossing problems. They had discussed the advantages and disadvantages of various crossing sites, possible objectives and missions on the far side, and the road net, troop assembly areas, and supply routes required on the near side. Late in January, about a week after the 21 Army Group instructions of January 21 had been issued, and despite the fact that Ninth Army was apparently to have no part in the crossing, they again entered somewhat lengthy discussions of their mutual problems. Perhaps the outstanding result of these discussions was a tentative agreement regarding the apportioning of crossing sites and the assigning of zones of action before the operation. The two army planning staffs agreed upon a scheme to divide the Xanten site, providing room for a two-corps American effort north and south of Wesel at the expense of reducing the frontage of Second Army's two-corps effort from Xanten north to Emmerich exclusive. The net result of this plan, should it be approved, would be to provide a simultaneous, three-army crossing of the Rhine with Ninth Army on the south, British Second Army in the center, and Canadian First Army on the north.

The proposal, when submitted to 21 Army Group, was disapproved and the Xanten and Rees sites were reserved exclusively for the use of British Second Army. However, the point of the plan was not lost, for the instructions assigning the Rheinberg crossing site to British Second Army, to be exploited by using an American corps, were rescinded, and on February 4 new instructions issued directing that Ninth Army make a one-corps crossing of the Rhine in the vicinity of Rheinberg, concurrently with the British Second Army attack on its left. In addition, the intention was expressed of assigning the Wesel crossings and the route east therefrom to Ninth Army's use once the bridgehead had been secured. Three additional divisions were to be brought from the Mediterranean to strengthen the British forces.

The outline of the operation to hurdle the Rhine was now becoming more clearly defined. The former "possibilities" were being confirmed as "directives." The strength and the composition of the airborne forces was still undecided, but their mission of seizing areas northeast of Wesel and attacking the city from the rear was settled. By early February a target date of March 15 was set for Operation Plunder, the code name given to the entire operation. Ninth Army's portion, the Rheinberg assault, was called Operation Flashpoint.

The over-all picture for the crossing, then, as set down by 21 Army Group visualized Ninth Army, on the right, holding the

Rhine River line from about Düsseldorf north to Duisburg with one corps while attacking in a narrow zone between the northern edge of the Ruhr industrial area and the Lippe River with a second corps. Its third corps was to be assembled for commitment north of the Lippe River to the east, as soon as the Wesel bridgehead had been established, the Wesel bridges constructed, and the routes through the town opened up. On Ninth Army's north flank, British Second Army would attack with two corps abreast, one at Xanten, the other at Rees, with a third corps in reserve for entry into the bridgehead as soon as possible. A fourth corps, the U. S. XVIII Airborne Corps, having either two or three divisions under its command initially, would conduct an airborne operation in support of British Second Army's attack, later withdrawing as a headquarters, turning over its American units to Ninth Army and its British units to British Second Army. Farther north, Canadian First Army would operate in the Emmerich area with its assault echelon initially under the command of British Second Army. The logistical support of American airborne units committed would be a function of Ninth Army.

A multitude of supply problems was completely unanswered early in February. Chief among these was the assignment of supply routes and areas suitable for the establishment of supply depots between the Maas and the Rhine. Many of these problems remained unsolved because the enemy still occupied the areas under consideration, but many more stemmed from the fact that the zone between the Maas and the Rhine was extremely narrow for a supply area, considering the tremendous magnitude of the operation. Extensive bridging would have to be done over the Maas, particularly in the British sector, to permit bringing up supplies. Furthermore, the establishment of supply depots was greatly complicated by the rains and flooding which made much of the available area unsuitable for use. The town of Venlo, Netherlands, communications center on the Maas River, and the Venlo–Geldern–Wesel road, the main west-east route in the area, were to be the subject of discussion and difficulty for many weeks to come.

On February 21, 21 Army Group issued a final directive generally confirming a number of points already discussed and finally defining the zones of operation of the various armies through the phase of securing the bridgehead. A provisional target date was established as March 31, but it was also laid down that the Rhine crossings would not take place until the entire area west of the Rhine north of Düsseldorf was cleared. For planning purposes a boundary was established between Ninth Army and British Second Army along the Venlo–Geldern–Wesel road. Because of the large bridging program to be executed at Wesel by Ninth Army, this road was assigned to the Army, but the Venlo bridge to be built by Ninth Army engineers was assigned to British Second Army, which also received "running rights" for concurrent use of the Venlo–Geldern portion of the road. Ninth Army was directed to extend its initial bridgehead, after assaulting in the Rheinberg area, to the south and east sufficiently to insure maintenance of its own forces south of Wesel and to insure the security of the bridges to be built at Wesel. Certain responsibilities for bridge construction were established. Ninth Army was made responsible, naturally, for all bridging in its own Rheinberg area. In addition it was assigned the mission of installing at Wesel one Class 40 floating bridge, one Class 70 raft ferry, and one semipermanent, one-way Class 70/two-way Class 40 bridge. Later on, it was decided that Ninth Army would install at Wesel an additional Class 40 floating bridge and also one Class 36 floating bridge, making a total of four bridges—three floating and one semipermanent fixed—built by the Army in the British zone at Wesel. Also, arrangements were concluded whereby American engineers of Communications Zone would construct a railroad bridge at that site. Finally, Ninth Army was to construct a semipermanent one-way Class 70/two-way Class 40 bridge at Venlo.

The definite decision on the Venlo bridge question was a welcome one, for it had been debated for months. As far as could be foreseen, this bridge was always to remain an exclusively British one. Hence, it was rather unusual that American troops and materials should be used in its construction. However, with the demands being made on the limited British engineer troops available, both in executing the attack between the Maas and the Rhine and in preparing for the Rhine crossing, it was imperative that American resources be used or the bridge would not be built. Its construction was assigned to the engineer group already scheduled to construct the fixed bridge over the Rhine River at Wesel, thus providing experience for this unit. The structure at Venlo was 950 feet long and built on timber piles. It was of unusual construction in that the deck was approximately 50 feet above the river bottom because the British wanted it seated one foot above the all-time high flood of 1926, and the axis of the bridge was at an angle rather than perpendicular to the river due to British insistence that a curved approached be avoided. Started on March 10, it was completed on March 23, nine days ahead of schedule.

At British request, Ninth Army also lent engineer assistance to them by assuming, late in February, the maintenance of roads and bridges in the rear portions of the British Second Army area. This assistance was continued until early April. A liaison officer from Ninth Army Headquarters was stationed at British Second Army Headquarters to relay British requests for work to the Ninth Army Engineer, who then issued instructions for its accomplishment.

In anticipation of the directive of February 21 from 21 Army Group, on February 19 General Simpson assigned to General Anderson's XVI Corps the task of preparing a detailed plan for the one-corps assault on the Rhine River. He did this with the caution that he had not as yet selected the corps which would actually perform the operation. His choice of the XVI Corps to do the planning was based chiefly on the fact that XVI Corps had less to do, initially at least, in the assault across the Roer and the advance to the Rhine which would be taking place concurrently with the planning of the Rhine crossing, and also because it was quite likely that the action of closing up to the Rhine would put XVI Corps in proper position for the assault and would therefore obviate any necessity of regrouping forces before launching the attack. A planning directive was issued to XVI Corps, excerpts from which follow (*Map No. 11*):

> Boundary between Ninth Army and Second British Army: road Venlo–Geldern–Fort Blücher (all inclusive Ninth Army)–then along the line of the Lippe River (exclusive Ninth Army). (Running rights on Venlo–Geldern road to Second British Army.)
>
> An airborne effort of one corps of three divisions will support the operation of the Second British Army. The area of employment will be determined. It will probably be employed in the vicinity of Wesel.
>
> XVI Corps will complete plans for crossing the Rhine in the Rheinberg area, then assist in securing the Wesel bridgehead. The Corps to execute the operation will be designated at a later date.
>
> Troops: Two infantry divisions
>   One armored division
>   Supporting troops.

Mission: (*a*) Force a crossing of the Rhine in the vicinity of Rhein-berg and establish initial bridgehead.

(*b*) Expand bridgehead to the general line Walsum–(A4030) [three miles northwest of Bottrop]—Kirchhellen–(A4440) [just west of Dorsten].

(*c*) Assist in the reduction of Wesel by supporting fires and by seizing the routes leading into Wesel from the south and southeast. Be prepared to seize intact any crossings over the Lippe River Canal.

Corps plan will include the composition of the assault waves, types of craft to be used, loadings, formations for crossing, and H-hour. A proposed Corps troop list will be included in the plan.

In addition, a list of special equipment available to the corps was provided, and an engineer annex was appended to the planning directive, setting forth engineer details such as the availability of maps, models, and engineer river-crossing equipment, and special data such as the manner of engineer supply and handling of traffic. Areas to be reserved for the construction of Army bridges were specified.

This planning directive, issued on February 19, was expanded and modified continuously between that time and the time of launching the attack more than a month later. Army and corps staff officers worked together continuously throughout the period and with the staffs of 21 Army Group, British Second Army, and First Allied Airborne Army as well. British Second Army held a series of three elaborate planning conferences on February 27, March 9, and March 19 at which certain information was exchanged between the staffs of all participating corps and higher echelons.

In early March, with the rapid progress of Ninth Army's advance to the Rhine, planning and preparing for Operation Plunder and for Operation Flashpoint were accelerated. By March 6 the proposed assault date had been advanced a week to March 24. Decision was made to limit the strength of the airborne operation to two divisions, the U. S. 17th Airborne, commanded by Major General William M. Miley, and the British 6th Airborne. The XVI Corps plans for its crossing included the use of two divisions in the assaulting echelon, and the 30th Infantry Division and the 79th Infantry Division were designated for this role. These two assault divisions were now withdrawn from the forward area and assembled at Echt, east of Maeseyck, on the Maas River for special training in river-crossing operations. The 30th moved back on March

6, the 79th on March 8. Here, working together with the 1153d and 1148th Engineer Combat Groups of the XVI Corps, the groups designated for their close engineer support, they practiced, in daylight and in darkness.

A company of DD Tanks from the 736th Tank Battalion was attached to XVI Corps at this time. These special amphibious tanks had been issued to the company in lieu of its normal equipment, and it had already had more than two weeks of strenuous training in their operation and maintenance. They consisted of standard Sherman tanks whose hulls had been waterproofed underneath and which were fitted with special canvas walls which provided enough displacement to float the vehicle. They were not in operating condition when received from the British, who had developed the device, and American ordnance troops were completely unfamiliar with the amphibious features. No spare parts, manuals, or drawings were received with the tanks, although some spare parts were finally secured through the British War Office in London. It had required two months of combined effort on the part of Army ordnance and the Army Armored Section, under Colonel Claude A. Black, together with on-the-spot improvisation and development, to place the equipment in operating condition.

Another tank battalion, the 747th, was assigned the job of operating LVTs, the amphibious cargo and personnel carriers sometimes called "Alligators." These, too, required a great amount of maintenance work before they could be used, since all had seen use in previous operations. The Theater stock of parts for the vehicles was negligible, and parts had to be obtained principally by cannibalization. The tank crews received intensive training in the operation of LVTs to provide ferry service for personnel and supplies during the Rhine crossing. A tribute to the thoroughness of their training is the record they established during the actual crossing operations, when out of the more than 120 employed, only one LVT was lost to enemy action, although more than 1,000 round trips were made ferrying assault troops.

Other special training was carried on. For instance, when a shortage of operators for motor-driven assault boats was discovered, the entire Army was canvassed for personnel with experience in the operation of outboard motors, and the 284 men so discovered were attached to XVI Corps and given special training in assault boat operation. The importance of the training and rehearsing carried out, chiefly on the Maas River, should not be overlooked. Problems and difficulties discovered and the measures taken to overcome them contributed greatly to the smoothness of the actual operation later on. As an illustration, it was discovered that an LCM would not carry a standard medium tank. It had been planned to use a number of these craft for ferrying the tanks. Theoretically, according to the measurements involved, the tank would fit on board the LCM. However, actual tests conducted in training on the Maas by the 743d Tank Battalion revealed that the clearance and freeboard were too small in practice to accommodate the operations of driving the tank on and off the craft. As a result, light tanks were substituted for medium tanks on the LCMs, and reinforced Bailey rafts, powered by five outboard motors, were used to transport the medium tanks across the river.

It was decided that the casualties in the assaulting corps could be reduced and the chances of a rapid expansion of the bridgehead could be enhanced if a demonstration succeeded in deceiving the enemy as to the location of the crossing effort. Assistance was enlisted from the 23d Headquarters Special Troops, equipped with a wide variety of special effects including inflated rubber tanks, vehicles, and artillery cannon, and appropriate sound tracks to convey noises of movement and action. It was hoped that the enemy would believe that Ninth Army's main effort would be launched in the vicinity of Uerdingen. Action taken to confirm this belief in the enemy's mind is summarized below.

Concentration of major troop units and equipage for Operation Flashpoint was accomplished with a view toward deceiving the enemy as to the actual Rhine River crossing area, strength of the crossing forces, and time of crossing.

A simulated build-up of forces was conducted in a general area west of Düsseldorf and the Erft River (*Map No. 11*) to indicate an assault crossing in the Düsseldorf–Uerdingen zone.

XIII Corps was charged with the mission of conducting a demonstration in the Düsseldorf–Uerdingen zone. No unit was to cross the Rhine River. It was of utmost importance that XIII Corps continue this deception even after Flashpoint began so as to immobilize enemy troops on the east bank of the Rhine River.

Air reconnaissance in the XIII Corps zone was on the same scale as that in the zone of the XVI Corps.

Radio silence was immediately effected in all units not in contact with the enemy and remained in effect until lifted by Army Headquarters. Prior to Operation Grenade, the positions of two divisions were disclosed by enemy interception of individual tank-to-tank radio sets. It was imperative that each individual concerned be impressed with the importance of complete radio silence.

Special attention was given to the complete concealment of artillery weapons and ammunition, and of engineer supplies in the zone of XVI Corps.

Upon displacement of artillery in the zone of XIII and XIX Corps the previous positions were made to retain their normal appearance. Movement of artillery units to new positions was made at night.

Dummy engineer parks were created in the zone of XIII Corps.

Engineer preparations, including the building of approach roads to the crossing sites, in the zone of XIII Corps were equal to or greater than those in the zone of XVI Corps.

Equipment and engineer camouflage personnel were made available to corps.

Patrolling was more intensive (approximately one-half greater) in the zone of XIII Corps than that in XVI Corps. The XVI Corps G-2 kept the XIII Corps G-2 informed of the number of patrols dispatched by XVI Corps.

Training of the 30th Infantry Division and the 79th Infantry Division took place on the Maas River under XVI Corps. Upon completing this training and prior to movement to their assembly areas, vehicle markings and shoulder patches were removed and not replaced until H minus 12 hours. Movement to the assembly areas was at night. No unit identifications were used on road signs or at assembly areas, including code names customarily used. Movement of individuals and vehicles in the assembly areas was held to an absolute minimum and maximum camouflage discipline was imposed. Vehicular movement was limited to that necessary for supply and evacuation. There were no passes or recreational trips permitted for troops in assembly areas.

XIX Corps conducted river-crossing training on the Erft River and Canal, and later moved one division to the Maas River training area when the 30th and 79th Infantry Divisions moved therefrom.

The information necessary to the execution of the deception was disseminated to the minimum number of subordinate commanders and staff officers to enable adequate implementation. A list of these individuals was maintained at each corps headquarters.

A great deal of work was required to execute the deception. In addition to widespread general camouflage activity, two major special projects were carried out in connection with bridging equipment. First all material in the five forward bridge parks was camouflaged to conceal its identity from air or ground observation, and a substantial portion of it was completely concealed to deny the enemy information as to the quantity being stored. Traffic to the parks was carefully controlled. Only trucks being loaded or unloaded were permitted inside the parks, and those trucks awaiting entry were kept dispersed under cover. These measures were so successful that, although various towns, including some of those at which parks were located, were subjected to enemy strafing attacks, none of this effort was directed at the parks. The second bridging deception measure was the construction of a large dummy bridge park in a woods west of Krefeld. All civilians were ostentatiously excluded from the dummy area. A factory was set up in Krefeld, shrouded in complete secrecy, for the construction of dummy assault boats, pontons, and covered frames representing piles of material. About seven days after the first material was hauled into the real bridge parks a treadway bridge company, with some added equipment, drove into the dummy bridge park area in daylight and began unloading. That night the company reloaded its equipment and moved back to the rear. At the same time, dummy material from the factory at Krefeld was brought into the dummy park area and substituted for the real material moved. This operation was continued on succeeding days with the dummy material being supplemented by a certain amount of real material. The dummy park was scattered over a much greater area than was the case in actual parks, and the piles were more dispersed and were kept in woods partially under trees to indicate that an effort at concealment was being made. So realistic was this dummy engineer park that it received enemy air attacks. Further to carry out the deception, approach roads to favorable bridge sites in the Krefeld area were constructed on a scale comparable to the construction accomplished preparatory to the real crossing farther north. To add to the realism of the deceit, the work was done at night using bull-dozers and tankdozers.

Upon the departure of the 79th and 30th Infantry divisions from the Echt training area, the 83d Infantry Division moved back to the vicinity, another move designed to confuse the enemy. Throughout the entire Ninth Army zone, intense efforts were made to maintain an equal scale of activity. On the north where XVI Corps was conducting its actual preparations, every means was used to conceal as much as possible such activity, while throughout the southern portion of the sector, XIII and XIX Corps units faked action of increasing intensity. When XIX Corps artillery units, which were to support the assault crossing, moved into their new positions in the XVI Corps area during the hours of darkness on the nights of March 17, 18, 19, they used routes well to the west to decrease the chance of enemy detection, and they left their evacuated positions in such a condition as to denote continued occupancy. Dummy guns were installed and personnel detachments were provided to continue a minimum of activity and retain the "lived in" appearance of the positions. In their new locality they camouflaged their installations, maintained radio silence, and limited the flights of their artillery observation planes.

To avoid disclosing the Army's intentions by the build-up of hospitals and the density of ambulances in the zone of XVI Corps, all red cross markings were covered on hospital tentage, move-ment of ambulances was limited to infiltration, and ambulances not on the roads were kept under cover and their red crosses hidden. To support the deception of a major effort on the south, a medical clearing company with additional tentage was set up in the area opposite Duisburg, and ambulance traffic to and from the dummy installation was maintained.

In the end, all the labor and time expended in the planned effort were well worth while, for the enemy's conception of Ninth Army's order of battle was discovered to be confused to the extent that neither of the assaulting divisions was properly located. Even as late as April 1 he expected a crossing of the Rhine in the vicinity of Uerdingen, and held major elements of three divisions —the 2d Parachute and the 176th and the 183d Infantry—in the Düsseldorf–Uerdingen area to repel a possible crossing. It was only when XVI Corps was fighting in the Ruhr itself that the

Germans began to shift their forces from possible southern crossing sites.

The logistical picture in Ninth Army prior to the attack across
the Rhine was brighter than it had been for any previous operation. The roads in the area east and north of München-Gladbach,
overrun in early March, were discovered to be in excellent condition, far superior to the roads west of the Roer. Hard standings
for supplies and suitable shelter for storage and maintenance installations were comparatively numerous. Hospitals, benefiting
from the low casualty rate in the advance from the Roer to the
Rhine, had ample room and were well located. A centrally located enemy cemetery had been established in the forward area,
permitting an estimated twenty per cent saving in transportation
of enemy dead. There was not even a critical shortage of any
major item of equipment or supply. Two-and-one-half ton trucks
and spare parts of all types were none too plentiful, but they
were adequate for the projected operation. Bridging, initially earmarked for the Rhine crossing, and organic equipment of engineer
bridge units, had become temporarily depleted because of the
unusual flood stage of the Roer when that river was crossed, and
it had been necessary to expedite to the utmost the recovery and
repair of bridging and further shipments from Communications
Zone, but these efforts had been substantially completed. Considerable quantities of captured German equipment had been put
into service. Thousands of feet of cable, tons of I-beams and
H-beams, paint, fortifications materials, building materials, and
signal equipment were utilized. Procurement by purchasing and
contracting officers also yielded needed items. For instance, 1200-
pound anchors were purchased from Belgian and Netherlands
barge owners and used to fill shortages of Rhine River requirements. Again, just before the Rhine crossing, twelve miles of
steel cable urgently required in the building of tactical bridges
were secured from factories in Brussels and Antwerp. In order to
meet the unusual demands for fixed bridges, it was necessary to
design and contract for the manufacture of pile-driving attach-
ments and hammers.

Engineer maintenance activities during the latter part of this
period were particularly heavy. The modification of treadway
bridges, the manufacture of hundreds of nailing strips for fixed
bridges, and the repair of equipage damaged during the Roer

crossing, all placed demands on maintenance units far in excess of normal. Confiscated enemy machine tools and equipment were used to augment the usual maintenance means.

The great logistical problem facing the Army was that of building up more than 138,000 tons of supplies close behind the new battlefront, including the movement of over 117,000 tons from the long-established depots in the Maastricht area. This build-up was accomplished during the period from March 4 to 24. It included 6,830 tons of food (more than 3,000,000 rations), 19,000 tons (4,650,000 gallons) of gasoline, 42,000 tons of ammunition, and 70,627 tons of other supplies and equipment.

Tonnage allocations by services were forgotten during this period, and shipment from Communications Zone depots was on an "availability" basis. Trucks were used to expedite delivery of last-minute shortages of small component parts of bridging.

The task of evacuating the depots and dumps in the old area reached its peak on March 12 when 1,529 trucks were dispatched carrying a total of 7,645 tons. Army quartermaster truck companies were reinforced by five companies dispatched from the Advance Section, Communications Zone, three of which were equipped with ten-ton trucks, and by three provisional companies formed from Army antiaircraft artillery units. In addition to the hundreds of trucks used to transport the stock piles which had been built up during the previous month, considerable special equipment was utilized. Approximately 70 heavy ponton truck-tractors, most of the tank transporters available to the Army, and 6 special trains were employed. For loading and unloading river-crossing equipment, 65 cranes varying in size from twelve- to forty-tons capacity were used.

Securing the various items of equipment unavailable in normal supply channels but vital to the success of the projected operation provided various problems, many difficult, all interesting. For instance, in the cutting of approximately 2,000 bridge piles and 10,000,000 board feet of lumber, Army engineers initially suffered many broken saw blades when their saws encountered shell fragments imbedded in the logs they were cutting. To screen out these steel-laden logs and eliminate the mounting heap of broken saw blades, the engineers hit upon the device of using mine detectors to discover and avoid the undesirable logs. Another instrument, a special electromagnet, was developed and mounted on trailers to "sweep" hard-surfaced roads of sharp shell fragments and thus prevent countless punctures in critically short tires.

At the last minute it was discovered that the netting for use in the antisubmarine booms at the Rhine bridge sites had been shipped incomplete. It was necessary to improvise floats using 55-gallon steel drums. Since sufficient drums were not available from normal supply sources and the time element was exceedingly short, engineer and quartermaster units were instructed to report all captured enemy stocks of the item to Army. Through the action of both services, the required number of drums was delivered to Army depots in sufficient time.

Rehabilitation of the railroad net east of the Roer River by Advance Section of Communications Zone progressed extremely rapidly. As in all previous situations, the Army itself laid great stress on pushing rail lines to the utmost, since rail transportation was such a vital supply advantage. Army personnel, together with Advance Section personnel, reconnoitered rail lines almost into the front lines as tactical operations progressed. Rail reconnaissance personnel were frequently under enemy small-arms fire. As a result of this intensive reconnaissance, and of the rapid reconstruction in its wake, the first train of supplies arrived in München-Gladbach on the morning of March 12. By the end of the month railheads were in operation at Rheydt, München-Gladbach, Viersen, Willich, and Kempen. (Map No. 11.)

A large portion of the mass supply movement consisted of engineer equipment, particularly stream-crossing equipment. Some 14,000 long tons were transported from the main Army depot at Maastricht to the five bridge parks in the XVI Corps area. These bridge parks were established behind the assault crossing sites, well forward but outside the range of all but the heaviest enemy artillery. Extreme difficulty was experienced, particularly on highways, in moving such heavy equipment as Seamules, LCVPs, and LCMs. The LCMs, for example, were 50 feet long, over 14 feet wide, and capable of carrying 60 men with equipment or 60,000 pounds of cargo. They required 16-foot vertical clearance, even after 19 inches had been cut off of the operator's armored tower, and were so wide that they forced most roads on which they were moved to become, temporarily, one-way routes. Then, after their movement to the forward assembly areas had been successfully accomplished, the cut-off armor had to be welded back into place on the operator's tower. In the complicated handling of all this heavy special equipment, ordnance tank transporters were used to good advantage, all during the training period, in the build-up of equipment, and in delivering it to the river's edge.

To permit the handling of the vast quantities of engineer material, the Army's levels of other classes of supplies were reduced. However, two and one-half units of fire of artillery ammunition were dumped at all artillery positions, and all units to participate in the assault crossings were issued four days' supply of operational rations and gasoline to be carried over the river in unit trains.

Preparations for the crossing required displacing 42,000 tons of ammunition in the Army ammunition depot to a point seventy-five miles forward. For this purpose, two ammunition companies and a mobile labor detachment were borrowed from Communications Zone to supplement the ten ammunition companies and two quartermaster service companies available to the Army. Two hundred and fifty trucks from quartermaster truck companies, provisional truck companies from the several corps, and 150 ten-ton tractor trailers loaned by Communications Zone were employed on ammunition movements. Rail transportation was used to the maximum extent as it became available. The bulk of the enemy ammunition which had been overrun presented too much of a transportation problem to be moved forward at this time, but a small amount of it was used for harassing fires. As the Rhine crossing approached, the usual increased burden of issues for the artillery preparation fell on the ammunition depot. Also it became necessary to install an ammunition supply point at Bonninghardt in the British area to support the American elements of the airborne drop and to assign an ammunition company in support of that operation.

Although the initial supply of the airborne divisions participating in the zone of the British Second Army was to be furnished by air drop under the control of First Allied Airborne Army, the responsibility for the supply and evacuation of the American 17th Airborne Division was to revert to Ninth Army as soon as contact was established between the ground assault troops and the airborne troops. Consequently, provisions were made for the maintenance of this division on a scale of 270 tons per day. A depot maintaining a three-day level of supply was established on the west bank of the Rhine, in the British zone near Kapellen exclusively to carry out this mission. It was stocked with food, gasoline, ammunition, and special items of signal and engineer equipment. An augmented company of DUKWs—the amphibious 2½-ton trucks which had proved so useful in ship-to-shore movements in the initial invasion of the Continent—was provided at the depot to transport supplies to the airborne division and to evacuate casualties on the return trip.

As it was expected that a large number of patients would be received from the 17th Airborne Division as soon as ground contact was made with the airborne forces, it was decided that the normal medical support afforded a division would be inadequate. After conferences with British Second Army, British XII Corps, and XVIII Airborne Corps, a special medical task force was formed, consisting of a battalion headquarters, one platoon of a field hospital, one platoon of a clearing company, a collecting company reinforced by an ambulance platoon, and an evacuation hospital. The clearing platoon, reinforced by collecting company personnel, was to establish a holding unit near Bislich, across the Rhine from Xanten, from which casualties were to be loaded initially on the DUKWs making the return trip. The remainder of the collecting company was to operate a loading point west of the river near Birten, where patients were to be transferred from DUKWs to ambulances and evacuated by road from this point to a hospital. Casualties requiring immediate surgical attention were to be taken directly to the field hospital at Kapellen, the others to the evacuation hospital further to the rear at Geldern. Both hospitals were augmented with teams of an auxiliary surgical group. The battalion headquarters, in addition to coordinating all phases of evacuation, was made responsible for handling and forwarding medical supplies to the division in the initial phases. To care for patients needing operative treatment prior to the link-up of the division with the overland echelon of the airborne forces, volunteer teams of an auxiliary surgical group were to go in by air with the division medical company.

During the entire period of preparation for the river crossing careful maintenance of roads was, of course, imperative to insure successful movement of the tremendous traffic load. The Venlo–Wesel road, the main artery, was improved. All portable bridges on the route were replaced with Class 70 timber bridges with the exception of one bridge around which a Class 70 by-pass was provided. The route subsequently received such an enormous amount of traffic that the surface of it was completely worn off from Venlo to Geldern, and as there was no premix plant available in the area, engineer troops were kept continously engaged in repairing the road with gravel and crushed rock.

Closer to the front, in the zone behind the crossing site, XVI Corps initiated an intensive program of road construction and improvement. Roads up to the winter dikes were both surfaced and widened to permit two-way traffic. Since most of this area was under enemy observation and within artillery range, the work was carried on principally during the hours of darkness. As a precaution and with the bitter lessons learned on the Roer in mind, all the proposed bridge-building sites and approaches thereto on the west bank were carefully cleared of mines. Also as the result of experience on the Roer, a plan was drawn up providing for notification to all downstream units of any derelict equipment lost or sighted at one bridge which might endanger bridges further down the river. A program was worked out for recovering and collecting assault boats and bridging equipment.

Anticipating the bottleneck at the Rhine River bridges in the movement of supplies, all divisions making the crossing were issued excess ordnance equipment and supplies to the fullest extent of their carrying capacity. Even additional cargo trucks were issued for this purpose. This excess equipment was to be absorbed in the initial battle losses. Armored divisions carried 6 to 12 excess tanks.

On March 9 First Army's 9th Armored Division accomplished the astounding and unexpected feat of seizing intact but wired for demolition the bridge across the Rhine at the town of Remagen south of Bonn. A bridgehead was established immediately and held in spite of severe German reaction. Undoubtedly the result of this bold stroke was an easing of the enemy opposition later encountered in the assault across the Rhine north of the Ruhr, and ultimately it facilitated a double envelopment rather than a single envelopment of the industrial heart of Germany. The plans for the Rhine crossing in the north went on unaffected, however, by the earlier crossing already completed farther south.

On March 9 Field Marshal Montgomery issued his "Orders for the Battle of the Rhine," and Ninth Army had the final and definite instructions for the role it was to play in the assault.

(*Map No. 11.*)   The mission laid down by 21 Army Group, composed of Ninth Army, British Second Army and Canadian First Army, was "to cross the Rhine north of the Ruhr and secure a firm bridgehead with the view to developing operations, isolate the Ruhr and to penetrate deeper into Germany." The plan was to cross the Rhine on the front of two armies between Rheinberg and Rees with Ninth Army on the right and British Second Army on the left, with the initial mission of capturing Wesel, the critical communications center in the area, and then expanding the initial bridgehead far enough south to insure the security of Wesel from enemy ground action, far enough north to permit bridging at Emmerich and the use of that road center, and far enough eastward to secure a strong bridgehead for further offensive operations. The bridgehead to be gained in the first phase was defined as the general line Duisburg–Bottrop–Dorsten thence north and west to the Rhine west of Emmerich. Ninth Army's part in the operation was to cross the Rhine south of Wesel, protect the right flank of 21 Army Group, and develop a bridgehead south of the Lippe sufficient to insure the security of Wesel and the use of Dorsten. Decision as to the exact delineation of the bridgehead was left to the Ninth Army Commander. British Second Army, assisted by an airborne effort on the part of the XVIII Airborne Corps, was to capture Wesel and secure that portion of the bridgehead north of the Lippe River. Canadian First Army was to insure the security of the port of Antwerp by holding securely the line of the Rhine and the Maas from Emmerich westward to the sea and was to make preparations for entering the bridgehead on the north flank when so ordered. In the second phase of operations Ninth Army, while holding the southern portion of its bridgehead securely, was to pass a corps through the right flank of British Second Army and secure the line Hamm–Münster. British Second Army was to advance to the north and northeast of Münster while the Canadian Army was to outflank the Ijssel River defenses north of Emmerich from the east, and capture key communication centers to open up the supply route north through Arnhem. (*Map No. 4.*)

On March 13 and 19, final instructions were issued by Ninth Army. Extracts from these instructions are reproduced below:

The enemy anticipates that the Allies will attack across the Rhine, north and south of the Ruhr. He estimates that airborne troops will be employed in connection therewith.

As yet there is no evidence of the installation of underwater obstacles, nor the existence of other defensive measures of special nature. His known defenses in the area are not formidable. Recent field fortifications in rear areas, prepared by civilian labor, often fail to take best advantage of the terrain.

All indications point to the concentration of artillery against the most feasible crossing sites, and the employment of the limited air force in desperation attacks on bridges.

The Ninth Army may expect to encounter some major elements of the elite German Parachute Corps. These troops, plus available armored elements, are expected to form the backbone of the enemy's defense. The forces for the defense of the Ruhr can come principally from withdrawals from North Holland, the rebuilding of divisions evacuated from the "Colmar Pocket" and other fronts, and the consolidation of units salvaged from west of the Rhine during recent operations. Its strength cannot be accurately estimated at this time, because of the constant shifting of enemy troops over the entire Western Front. Considering the enemy's over-all commitments, his shortage of manpower, and his tremendous need to maintain his depleted communication facilities, it is currently estimated that he can make approximately 70,000 men available for combat, between Emmerich and Düsseldorf, by the end of March 1945. This force is deemed insufficient to man the enemy's current defenses in depth or to construct extensive new ones.

While there are many indications that the majority of German soldiers and civilians realize that Germany cannot win, the enemy, from habit and training, continues to fight well. He has had the shock of one crossing of the Rhine. An additional crossing is certain to have an adverse effect upon morale. It is not believed that this will be sufficient to cause a sudden collapse, or extensive mass surrender. It is expected to reduce the tenacity of "last ditch stands."

The enemy undoubtedly will attempt to frustrate the river crossings, if able accurately to determine their location. Lacking this knowledge, it is anticipated that he will hold the river line thinly, concentrating his mobile troops to the rear with a view of frustrating the establishment of a bridgehead through counterattack. He may be expected to employ static units, including antiaircraft elements, to establish centers of resistance as he did at the Roer.

There is no evidence of secret weapons which could prevent the operation; however, he is likely to employ "human torpedoes" and floating mines constantly against bridges.

The enemy is capable of resorting to chemical warfare. He may do so in a last desperate effort to stave off immediate defeat.

It is considered that a surprise crossing, prosecuted rapidly and vigorously, will gain initial success. Thereafter, the limited mobile enemy forces may be expected to counterattack with skill and vigor. After they are engaged and fixed, a rapid build-up by Ninth Army should enable it to break up the hostile defenses and make extensive gains with relative ease.

21 Army Group will cross the Rhine River north of the Ruhr industrial area, and secure a firm bridgehead in order to develop operations to isolate the Ruhr and to penetrate deeper into Germany (Operation Plunder; target date, 24 March).

In Phase I crossings will be accomplished between Rheinberg and Rees, both inclusive, and an initial bridgehead established which secures Wesel and Emmerich. [Map No. 11.] The general line of the bridgehead will be Duisburg–Bottrop–Borken . . . [thence north and west to the Rhine west of Emmerich].

In Phase II the initial bridgehead will be extended to the east and north to the general line: Hamm–Münster . . . [and correspondingly to the east and north in the British and Canadian zones].

12th Army Group, with First U. S. Army on the left, will complete the elimination of all enemy resistance west of the Rhine and north of the Moselle, and will expand its presently held bridgehead in the vicinity of Remagen.

*   *   *   *

Second British Army will:
Upon establishing its right Corps along the general line of the railway between Dorsten and Borken, allow elements of Ninth U. S. Army to pass through and to assume responsibility for the area south of the road Wesel–Brunen–Raesfeld–Heiden (all inclusive to Ninth U. S. Army).

NOTE: XVIII U. S. A/B Corps, with 6th British A/B Division and 17th U. S. A/B Division attached, under operational command of Second British Army, will accomplish an airborne assault (Operation Varsity) . . . 17th U. S. A/B Division will pass to Ninth U. S. Army command as early as practicable for employment in a holding role on the Army south flank.

Ninth U. S. Army will:
Assault across the Rhine River in the vicinity of Rheinberg and secure that portion of the initial Army Group bridgehead within its zone.

Protect the right flank of 21 Army Group.

Hold the west bank of the Rhine River from the bridgehead area south to Worrigen (exclusive) with the minimum forces necessary to effect absolute security.

Retain one Corps of three infantry and one armored divisions in reserve, prepared to pass through the right Corps of Second British Army and advance to the general line: Hamm (inclusive)–Münster (inclusive), with its right flank established along the Lippe River from the vicinity of Dorsten to the east.

Assume command of 17th U. S. A/B Division when released by Second British Army and employ it in a holding role along the Army right flank.

Be prepared to employ remaining available forces to augment the attack on the line: Hamm–Münster, and to deepen the penetration into Germany.

XIX CORPS:

Troops 29th Infantry Division
83d Infantry Division
95th Infantry Division
2d Armored Division
Supporting troops

Mission

Be prepared to turn over present zone to XIII Corps on Army order.

Be prepared to move into bridgehead secured by Second British Army, to pass through . . . along the general line: Dorsten–Borken, and to advance in zone, making main effort on right, between Lippe River and the general line: Raesfeld–Heiden . . . Coesfeld–Münster (inclusive) to seize the line: Hamm–Münster.

Be prepared to take command of 17th A/B Division in place and to employ it in a holding role along the Lippe River east of Dorsten.

XIII CORPS:

Troops 84th Infantry Division
102d Infantry Division
5th Armored Division
Supporting troops

Mission

Assist river crossing of XVI Corps by fire from west bank of the Rhine, by demonstration in zone, and by destruction of all craft operating against bridges downstream.

Contain the enemy east of the Rhine in present zone, and be prepared to extend to the south of Worringen (exclusive), relieving elements of XIX Corps, upon Army order. Hold river line with minimum forces necessary for absolute security and maintain remaining forces in reserve.

Be prepared to operate east of the Rhine, taking over that portion of the XIX Corps zone lying generally north of the line: Heiden–Amelsburen.

XVI CORPS:

Troops 30th Infantry Division
35th Infantry Division
75th Infantry Division
79th Infantry Division
8th Armored Division (Operational control only)
Supporting troops

Mission

Assault across the Rhine River in zone, D-day, H-hour (to be announced) and secure initial bridgehead.

Expand initial bridgehead rapidly in order to permit bridging at Wesel at earliest possible time.

Establish contact with elements of Second British Army on left flank as early as possible and maintain this contact during advance to the east.

Seize intact, wherever possible, bridges over the Lippe River and the Lippe–Seiten Canal. Coordinate holding of any bridgeheads secured with elements of Second British Army.

Advance to the general line: Confluence of the Ruhr and Rhine Rivers–

along the Ruhr River and Rhein-Herne Canal to Osterfeld–Bottrop–Gladbeck–Marl–then north to Lippe River. Establish a strong defensive position on this line and prevent enemy ground action from interfering with use of the Wesel bridges.

Upon establishing final defensive position be prepared, on Army order, to release 30th Infantry Division and/or 8th Armored Division.

ARTILLERY:

34th FA Brigade is attached to XVI Corps for operations only. It will cross the Rhine River on Army order.

40th FA Group (with 547th, 548th, and 549th FA Bns attached) is attached XII British Corps for operations from positions west of Rhine River only.

XIX Corps Artillery with attached battalions . . . is attached XVI Corps for operations from position west of the Rhine River only.

The counterbattery policy prior to the preparation will be a silent one, except that counterbattery may be fired on guns and mortars which are effectively active.

XIII Corps will emplace one battalion of tank destroyers in zone of XVI Corps upon request of XVI Corps. The mission of this unit will be direct fire on floating objects which might endanger bridges downstream. It will replace the XVI Corps tank destroyer battalion originally performing this mission when the latter is withdrawn for commitment east of the Rhine. Details will be arranged by direct contact between Corps.

ENGINEERS:

Army will

At a time to be agreed upon with XVI Corps:

Take over, operate, and maintain bridges, booms, and ferries previously installed by Corps.

Construct and maintain two Class 40 floating Bailey bridges across the Rhine River in the vicinity of Rheinberg.

Provide the following crossings at Wesel as soon as enemy ground opposition has been eliminated thereat:

One (1) Class 70 ferry.

One (1) Class 40 treadway bridge.

One (1) Class 40, float reinforced, heavy ponton bridge.

One (1) Class 40, floating Bailey bridge.

One (1) Class 70 fixed bridge over the Rhine River, with a similar, connecting bridge over the Lippe River.

Assist . . . in clearing routes through Wesel.

Install necessary antidebris, antimine, and antisubmarine booms not previously constructed by XVI Corps.

Maximum use of lifesaving devices and means will be made by troops engaged in river-crossing operations.

Vehicles marked "PRIORITY—BRIDGE CONSTRUCTION" will be given priority on roads and bridges.

Lights may be used at night on bridge construction, at bridge parks, and to illuminate the river to detect floating objects. Their use will be coordinated with the AAAIS [Antiaircraft Artillery Intelligence Service] so that lights can be extinguished upon approach of enemy aircraft.

AAA:

Army will furnish AA protection and artificial moonlight at the Wesel crossing sites.

AA protection and artificial moonlight at the Rheinberg crossing site will be furnished initially by XVI Corps; later, this responsibility will be taken over by Army.

AA units will be on the alert to take under fire floating objects or craft directed at the bridges on the Rhine River but only as a secondary mission.

Extreme care will be exercised to conceal our intentions from the enemy, particularly as regards our crossing areas and time of crossing.

Troops will be instructed in the necessity of preserving captured supplies and installations, especially those providing fuel and power.

Troops will be instructed that when gliders are overrun they will be protected from unnecessary damage.

Area of grid square (A1333) [north of Bonninghardt] is the dropping area for towing cables used in Operation Varsity. This area will be cleared of troops until troop carriers have left the area.

In brief, General Simpson had decided that the XVI Corps would carry out the assault crossing while XIX Corps assembled to cross into the bridgehead at the earliest possible date and XIII Corps held the line of the Rhine until U. S. Fifteenth Army under command of Lieutenant General Leonard T. Gerow, which was now designated to take over progressively the area west of the Rhine from Ninth, could assume responsibility for its new zone. General Anderson's XVI Corps had developed a plan of crossing with two divisions simultaneously, the 30th Division on the north crossing in the Mehrum area and the 79th Division on the south crossing from the vicinity of Milchplatz. (*Map No. 11.*) In the 30th Division zone the first two waves were to cross over in storm boats and the third and fourth waves in double assault boats. Succeeding crossings would be made by LVTs, LCVPs, and such storm boats and assault boats as were still operative. In the zone of the 79th Division, the first wave of the assault would consist of 28 double assault boats and 2 storm boats per assaulting battalion. The second wave would comprise 21 storm boats and 11 double assault boats per battalion. Second-wave boats, plus those of the first wave still in operation, would return from the far shore to form the third wave. In both zones LCMs, LCVPs and DUKWs were to be utilized to take over the supporting weapons and supplies to the far shore. Tanks and tank destroyers were to be ferried across, except DD tanks, which of course would cross under their own power.

The 75th Division was to continue to hold the river line throughout the corps zone even as the attack jumped off, permitting the assault echelons of the other two divisions to pass through it. In addition, it would stage a demonstration in the south of the corps zone to deceive the enemy, and with its artillery, reinforced by the attachment of four light battalions, interdict the routes leading north from the Ruhr to prevent local German reserves from reaching the battlefield. Both the 75th and the 35th Divisions would be committed east of the river as the bridgehead expanded. The 8th Armored Division was to be held in reserve until the progress of the battle on the far shore gave indication as to where it could best be employed.

With only one corps conducting the attack, not only could it be weighted very strongly in artillery but also, until the battle moved out of range and until the other corps were committed, it could be supported by the bulk of all artillery available to the Army. The 34th Field Artillery Brigade and the XIX Corps Artillery were put under the XVI Corps Artillery, so that for the attack the XVI Corps had 34 nondivisional artillery battalions of all calibers, which, together with its 19 battalions of divisional artillery, gave the corps a total of 53 battalions of field artillery—division, corps, and army. In addition, antiaircraft, tank, and tank destroyer guns were to be employed extensively in a field artillery role.

To control and coordinate the tremendous concentration of artillery fire power, Brigadier General Charles C. Brown, the XVI Corps Artillery commander, used his own corps artillery headquarters and headquarters battery as the planning, supervising, and directing agency. Directly under him he had Brigadier General John F. Uncles' 34th Field Artillery Brigade with 13 battalions of medium, heavy, and super-heavy artillery under four groups, and Brigadier General George D. Shea's XIX Corps Artillery headquarters with 11 battalions under three groups. Both the XIX Corps Artillery and the 34th Field Artillery Brigade had general support missions, with one field artillery group from each reinforcing the fires of the assaulting divisions. Brigadier General Roland P. Shugg's XIII Corps Artillery and the 84th Infantry Division Artillery, adjacent to XVI Corps, were to participate in the artillery preparation and support the crossing with scheduled fires on call from XVI Corps.

XVI Corps reinforced the assaulting divisions themselves very heavily in attached artillery. To the 30th Infantry Division were attached 3 battalions of nondivisional artillery and the artillery of the 35th Infantry Division, making a total of 11 field artillery battalions directly under division control. To the 79th Infantry Division were likewise attached 3 nondivisional artillery battalions and the artillery of the 8th Armored Division, giving the 79th Division a total of 10 battalions.

In preparing the over-all plan of artillery fires for the crossing, the XVI Corps Artillery, using every available intelligence source, and thoroughly evaluating the evidence on each, obtained "shooting locations" on some 989 targets for the artillery preparation and the initial phases of the attack. These included 54 definitely located and 68 tentatively located enemy batteries, 43 enemy observation posts, 52 command posts, 36 depots or dumps, 24 assembly areas, 454 critical points or areas for interdictory fires, and 258 miscellaneous type targets.

The corps artillery fire plan comprised scheduled fires to be delivered from 1:00 o'clock until 10:00 o'clock on the morning of D-day, when they would be superseded by requests for fire or by observed fires. The fire plan was divided into three general periods—an extremely heavy one-hour preparation preceding the assault shortly after midnight; a three-hour period of heavy scheduled fires to be delivered in support of the advancing divisions during the hours of darkness; and last, fires to be delivered either on schedule or on call after daylight. The preparation itself was broken down into fifteen-minute phases: the first to be on enemy batteries; the second on communication centers; the third, a return to the enemy batteries; and the fourth, on the east-bank targets most desired by the divisions. During the first and second hours after H-hour (the time for the divisions to cross), at least fifteen minutes were scheduled for a return to the more important enemy batteries; any active battery was to be silenced immediately. After H-hour, the scheduled fires were to be lifted beyond the east bank sufficiently to permit assaulting troops to advance. The scheduled fires for each successive hour were similarly lifted to allow a margin of safety for troops advancing in the dark. To insure flexibility and to permit any needed changes in scheduled fires or the firing of additional missions on call, close contact was maintained between the assaulting divisions and the fire direction centers of the XVI Corps Artillery, XIX Corps Artillery, and the 34th Field Artillery Brigade.

Increased shipments and the continued application of the strict Army ammunition rationing program made relatively large quantities of artillery ammunition available to support the river crossing and the expansion of the bridgehead. For the period March 10 to March 23, daily ammunition expenditures were curtailed to approximately one-tenth of a unit of fire for each artillery piece. However, for the five days beginning March 24, the day of the crossing, the ammunition allocation was on a much larger scale than the Army had ever before been able to support. It provided an average of one unit of fire in all calibers for the divisional artillery with XIX Corps; four units of fire for XIII Corps; eight units of fire for the artillery with XVI Corps; and nine units for the heavy Army artillery of the 34th Field Artillery Brigade attached to XVI Corps.

XXIX Tactical Air Command developed plans in furtherance of its fourfold mission: namely, preventing the German air force from interfering with the preparation and conduct of the Army's assault crossing; impeding the enemy's effort to move ground forces and equipment into positions which would interfere with the Army's operations; assisting the landing operations of the XVIII Airborne Corps by intercepting enemy aircraft attempting to engage troop carriers and by attacking flak installations which would be capable of bringing effective fire to bear on the transport planes and, finally, assisting the advance of the Army by closely coordinated air attacks on the immediate front of the attacking ground troops.

Daily surveillance was maintained over all enemy airfields from which it was considered attacks might be launched to interfere with the impending crossings. Any activity on one of these fields which offered the least suggestion of offensive operations on the part of the German air force brought immediate and devastating attacks by XXIX Tactical Air Command fighter-bombers. This program kept the skies comparatively cleared of German aircraft, though small flights, operating without a set schedule or a definite pattern maintained reconnaissance in an effort to learn preparations for the crossing, or slipped through for isolated strafing attacks. Occasionally larger numbers of enemy fighters put in their appearance, as on March 11 when approximately twenty such craft operated over the XVI Corps zone in small flights making quick strafing passes at troops and vehicles. The Allied heavy and medium bomber effort included a comprehensive program of devastation of airfields deep in Germany but within striking distance of the proposed bridgehead and battle area. These were to be attacked any time they were reportd active.

The road and rail net was so intensive in the contemplated area of operations that it was thought impossible to hope for entire isolation of the battlefield. However, such targets as supply and communications centers, rail and highway bridges, and main rail lines were selected and submitted for attack by our heavy and medium bombers. Since a successful road interdiction program was unlikely, it was decided to neutralize the German motor transport system by conducting armed reconnaissance over the most important routes. Interdiction of the important waterways was undertaken by the heavy bombers, and a rail interdiction program, to be accomplished by destruction of bridges and rail lines at important choke points, was assigned to the XXIX TAC.

To assist the airborne effort, XXIX Tactical Air Command provided planes for flak-suppression missions and for top cover missions to protect the troop carrier planes during the actual air drop. To provide close cooperation for the ground forces the unusual scheme was adopted of actually assigning a particular fighter-bomber group the mission of operating with a designated infantry division. The 373d Fighter-Bomber Group was named to work with the 79th Division and the 366th Fighter-Bomber Group with the 30th Division. In addition, armed reconnaissances were to be flown over the area east of the Rhine between Wesel and Cologne and as deep as Dortmund.

During the few weeks preceding the attack across the Rhine the German air force conducted a special offensive against Ninth Army's artillery observation planes. Swooping down on the slow-moving, unarmed, unprotected Cubs, they made numerous strikes in the short period of their concentration on this type of target. Since the fighter-bombers of the XXIX Tactical Air Command could not be detailed to afford protection, because of the higher priority of the missions they were engaged in, a plan was evolved wherein the artillery was advised of missions planned by the fighter-bombers and consequently could take advantage of the protecting presence of a Thunderbolt in case the artillery observation mission could be timed for concurrent execution. The "eyes of the artillery," which had proved to be worth their weight in gold for the observation and adjustment of artillery fire, did not suffer heavily from the German air efforts against them, although casualties were higher than they had ever been. During the month of March, some 19 of the Army's force of 300 artillery observation planes were lost, with 8 of them destroyed by enemy air action.

Reduction of the town of Wesel was a problem widely discussed in the planning phase of the operation. In the first place, a very heavy bombing attack was to be staged against the town, probably shortly before midnight preceding the ground attack, and this was to be followed closely by a sneak attack of a brigade of British Commandos. It was expected that these special troops would actually get in the town under cover of darkness and be able to hold out there until joined by elements of the 17th Airborne Division striking southwest from their dropping zones northeast of Wesel. Wesel was the key to all future operations to the east, since it was the hub of the road and rail net. In order to permit early bridging and particularly the initiation of work on the fixed bridges, both road and rail, so that routes could be opened deeper into Germany, the enemy must not be allowed to hole up in Wesel and carry out a die-hard delaying action.

Among the preparations necessary prior to the attack date was the evacuation of civilians from the area along the western bank of the river, both to prevent them from interfering with the operation and to reduce the possibility of agents gaining information of the attack. A mass evacuation of civilians was effected for several miles back from the river in the British Second Army area, and this program was extended south into Ninth Army's area. In the Mörs–Homberg area alone over 35,000 persons were moved out of their homes.

Another unusual scheme was that of an extensive smoke screen all along the front. This screen became necessary initially when British Second Army units discovered that one of their large bridge parks was located within range of observed enemy artillery fire. It was too late to change its location, there was insufficient time to bring in the supplies only at night, and the only alternative, if the supplies were to be delivered to the park, was to cover the activity with smoke. Covering this one area, though, meant giving away the location of the river crossing unless similar smokings were established elsewhere to deceive the enemy. Consequently, beginning ten days prior to the attack a smoke screen approximately twenty miles long was maintained over the front of British Second Army and Ninth Army's XVI Corps whenever conditions of visibility demanded it. This necessitated a smoke control center, which was established at XVI Corps Headquarters and consisted of the Chemical Officer, XVI Corps, and the staff of the chemical battalion responsible for furnishing the smoke screen. To transport the huge quantities of fog oil and smoke pots required for this operation, trucks available from Army were augmented by additional vehicles from chemical units until such time as they were needed by those units to begin hauling mortar ammunition with which to support the crossing. The smoke-control center was maintained until the bridgehead was gained and expanded to the point where smoke covering of the river was no longer necessary.

By mid-March it was apparent that the proposed assault date of March 24 could be met. The airborne operation, and to a lesser extent the heavy bombing of Wesel on the night before D-day, injected complications into the final choosing of the date of attack. Weather, of course, would be the determining factor, although, should a protracted period of bad weather set in, the ground forces were prepared to launch the assault independent of the airborne effort and the support of airpower. Field Marshal Montgomery, at his headquarters near Straelen, half-way between Venlo and Geldern, was to receive each day at 4:00 P.M., commencing on March 23, the weather reports and the estimate of the First Allied Airborne Army as to whether or not weather would permit air operations the following day at 10:00 A.M., the dropping hour of the first airborne elements. Not later than 5:00 o'clock, then, he would announce his decision as to whether or not the following day was to be D-day, and this decision would be communicated promptly to the armies under his command.

Other problems were injected into the operation by the supporting airborne action. To provide for the safe outward and homeward journeys of the huge flights of troop-carrier aircraft and their accompanying fighters it was necessary to establish a corridor free from antiaircraft fire and to insure that even those planes which might be disabled or off course would not be misidentified and fired upon in the heat of battle. Precautions in this respect went so far as to prohibit all firing on any type of twin-engine aircraft whatsoever during the day of the air drop. The artillery, too, in addition to planning its counter-flak program, was to insure that necessary safety measures were taken to prevent artillery from firing into dropping or landing zones of the airborne units and to continue support of the attacking ground forces while still not endangering troop carrier planes coming in at low altitudes with troops or cargo. The use of screening smoke for aerial bombardment or artillery shelling was restricted to that which was absolutely certain of dissipating before it drifted to the dropping zones and landing zones with the attendant danger of obscuring them from the view of the incoming paratroopers and glider-borne troops.

The German antiaircraft defenses northeast of Wesel were particularly heavy, since the Germans appreciated that this naturally suitable spot might well be chosen by the airborne forces of whose probable employment they were well aware. A very heavy counter-flak program was therefore included in the artillery planning for the operation. The Air Forces, too, contributed to the program of flak suppression. Medium bombers of the American IX Bombardment Division and British Second Tactical Air Force dropped 800 tons of bombs on twenty-three known enemy antiaircraft positions, and the 406th Fighter-Bomber Group of the XXIX Tactical Air Command, at a cost of four fighter-bombers, flew low over the enemy antiaircraft position area between 9:00 A.M. and 1:00 P.M. on March 24, claiming the neutralization of 36 light and heavy flak positions.

Ninth Army provided a group headquarters, four field artillery battalions, and a tank destroyer battalion to the British Second Army for the purpose of increasing the support for the airborne Corps. In addition, it provided the personnel and equipment for six artillery radio teams whose mission was the coordination of the artillery support provided the airborne troops from the artillery on the near bank of the Rhine. These teams were trained in British methods of requesting and adjusting fire and were then employed to "translate" the American-phrased requests into British artillery action.

The prompt establishment of telephone communications across the Rhine promised some difficulty unless existing German cables could be used. Several lengths of 15-pair submarine cable were built on special order by a factory in Belgium. The cable was wound on reels capable of being transported by trucks to the river's edge, where the cable could be unwound as one end was pulled across the river by a power boat. In addition, cables were improvised by combining five spiral-four cables into one large conduit which could be played out from a reel mounted on a boat as the craft moved across the river. Finally, a German cable, carrying 103 pairs and running from München-Gladbach through Krefeld and Rheinberg and under the Rhine to Friedrichsfeld, was reconditioned and tested as far as the river's edge. Wire crews were stationed in the forward area prepared to cross the river at the first opportunity to locate and recondition this cable on the far side. If it could be put in service without delay, the greatest signal problem would be solved. As it developed, this large cable was good under the river, and after two days of strenuous activity to repair the bomb and shell damage and the breaks intentionally accomplished by the retreating Germans, the circuits were put in order and made available to corps for communications with their divisions on the far shore.

The program of mapping and related activities was an enormous one. By the time the operation was launched, approximately 800,000 maps of all types and scales were issued from the Army map depot. Three-color maps of a scale of 1:25,000 and four-color maps of a scale of 1:50,000 were reproduced early in the planning phase. Later, overprints showing enemy defenses, 1:25,-000 scale, were issued in large numbers. From 12th Army Group a series of maps covering the Rhine of a scale of 1:12,500 was obtained. Two copies of an actual model of the Rhine and adjacent territory in Ninth Army area, of a horizontal scale of 1:12,500 and a vertical scale of 1:3572, were secured. One of these was retained by Army and the other issued to XVI Corps. The models were of inestimable value in planning. Prior to the crossing, survey detachments of topographical units located benchmarks at strategic points along the banks from which engineer units were able to establish the predetermined elevation of the bridge seats. On March 11 a study was completed showing the monthly ten-year high- and low-water levels at Wesel and Orsoy, providing information for establishing the height of bank seats for floating Bailey bridges and the selection of locations for supply dumps near the river. As the attack date grew near, Rhine

River gauge observations, from stations which had been established along the river, were reported at eight-hour intervals on a 24-hour basis over special telephone circuits to the Army Engineer. Also, a river stage prediction service, which had been set up by European Theater of Operations, furnished accurate forecasts of the river stage to be expected during each succeeding forty-eight hours and indicated in general terms a forecast for a week or ten days. It was also prepared to give ample notification of dangerous quantities of debris.

Ninth Army intelligence agencies, active for months in securing all possible data for the Rhine River crossing, had intensified their efforts progressively as the Army advance pushed up to the Rhine. The Army was extremely anxious, of course, to know what forces would oppose it on the east bank of the Rhine and where and how strong their main defenses would be. Under Colonel Harold D. Kehm, who had become the Army Assistant Chief of Staff, G-2, in early March, every intelligence-gathering source was used, including aerial reconnaissance and photography, patrolling, radio intercepts, agents, and prisoners of war. Particularly valuable was the activity of the Army radio intelligence company, which devoted its whole attention to the location and identification of German units opposite Ninth Army east of the Rhine. A new direction finder, the SCR-291, was put to use with good results. Once the enemy forces had broken contact and were thrown to the far side of the river, information was much more difficult to obtain, and any indication of the speed and strength of his reorganization for the defense of the far shore was extremely important. Aerial reconnaissance showed that the fixed defenses east of the Rhine were not adequately prepared but that the Germans were making desperate efforts to supplement these defense systems by intensive digging of field fortifications. With the experience gained from a study of similar projects which the Germans had attempted between the Roer and the Rhine, it was not difficult to estimate rather accurately how long it would take the enemy to develop these hasty defensive measures to a really useful degree. It was apparent that he would not have time to do an adequate job.

Some 43,000 aerial photographs, including about 13,000 obliques, were made and distributed to Ninth Army artillery units in preparation for the crossing. During the week im-

mediately preceding the assault, a total of 37 photographic reconnaissance missions and 56 tactical reconnaissance missions
was flown and interpreted, showing little in the way of movement or regrouping of German artillery to meet the attack, but
establishing the two principal areas in which German artillery
was concentrated. In the area Löhne–Dinslaken–Vier-Linden
there were an estimated 7 light field artillery batteries and 10
dual-purpose antiaircraft artillery batteries. In the area beginning
southwest of Mülheim and extending west of Kettwig thence to
the southeast of Angermund there were an estimated 8 light field
artillery batteries and 10 dual-purpose antiaircraft artillery batteries. The remainder of the enemy's artillery, mainly heavy antiaircraft guns, appeared to be scattered and dispersed behind these
two areas. There was some evidence also of the presence of two
lines of artillery and antiaircraft positions running perpendicular
to the Rhine, one following the Lippe Canal and the other just
north of the Ruhr. Static antiaircraft artillery gun positions appeared to be augmented by mobile units.

Patrols were used extensively to seek out information on the
east bank of the Rhine and were coordinated across the entire
Army front, and with the British on the left flank as well, in
order to prevent excessive activity from indicating the crossing
sites to the enemy. Far-shore landing conditions for special craft
and other technical data were the object of patrols, as well as the
strength and dispositions of the enemy. On one occasion the reported presence of oil along the east bank of the Rhine opposite
the XVI Corps zone aroused concern in that it might indicate an
intended use of toxic gases or the establishment of a barrier of
fire, to be ignited when the assault troops began their crossing.
Investigation by a patrol disclosed that the oil was harmless and
had been spread by accidental damage to oil drums in the hasty
retreat of the Germans across the river.

Ground-defense installations along both the Lippe River and
the canals running east and northeast from the Rhine indicated
the Germans' intention to defend the Ruhr against an attack
from the north. There was no distinct natural or artificial line
of defense running generally north and south until the relatively
high ground between Borken and Haltern, some fifteen or twenty
miles east of the Rhine, was reached. However, in the area between the Lippe River and the Ruhr, which was to be Ninth

Army's initial zone of action there were discovered concrete emplacements of various types which would impede the advance of tanks. As to enemy troops, there were estimated to be the following divisions or substantial elements thereof, in order from south to north (*Map No. 11*): 59th, 338th, 176th and 183d Infantry; 2d Parachute; 190th Infantry; Division Hamburg (a hastily formed special unit) and 180th Infantry. In the British zone adjacent to Ninth Army were the 84th Infantry, the 116th Panzer, and the 466th Infantry, the last two being held mobile in the rear. In addition, there were many small units and Volkssturm troops whose usefulness was estimated as being rather doubtful.

It was expected that the attack across the Rhine would produce the strongest enemy air reaction yet encountered by Ninth Army. This estimate was strengthened when the German air force reacted to First Army's seizure of the Remagen bridge with strong defensive action.

The Allied air forces' program of isolating the battlefield had begun during the last week of February, and it continued beyond the D-day for the Rhine crossing. The series of attacks was carried out against important bridges and viaducts all the way from Bremen on the North Sea to Coblenz on the Rhine. In forty attacks, using more than 1,800 heavy and medium bombers, the air forces claimed destruction or crippling damage to sixteen of these bridges and viaducts. This program, it was estimated, not only hampered the vital economic traffic from the Ruhr to the rest of Germany, but it also interfered with any large scale movement of reinforcements or supplies to the Rhine front.

On March 21 and 22, in execution of the program of neutralizing the German air force, heavy attacks were delivered on ten airfields in the area immediately north of the prospective crossing operation. The Eighth Air Force, employing 1,200 heavy bombers, inflicted considerable damage on the runways and on the installations surrounding the fields. The escorting fighters joined in strafing enemy aircraft caught on the ground, and as a result the totals of destroyed aircraft mounted to 52 in the air and 116 on the ground. The attacks were continued on the morning of March 24 when some 1,430 aircraft delivered 4,105 tons of bombs on sixteen operational enemy airfields. These strong neutralizing attacks had their effect, for the Luftwaffe provided little opposition to the airborne operation.

The goal of all the months of planning and preparation was now drawing close. March 23 brought a weather forecast of favorable conditions for the following day and with it the decision that made March 24 the day of attack. Starting at 8:30 P.M. on March 23, units and equipment were checked, final details adjusted, and the engineers and infantry, with their storm boats and assault boats, assembled behind the summer dikes on the west bank of the Rhine ready to go. At 10:00 P.M. the British 1st Commando Brigade inaugurated the crossing when it moved quietly over and took up positions about 1,000 yards outside of Wesel. At 10:40 P.M. heavy bombers of the RAF Bomber Command filled the skies above the ill-fated town; fifteen minutes later Wesel was a mass of burning, smoking ruins as the Commandos moved in under the cover of darkness to begin its seizure.

At 1:00 o'clock on the morning of the 24th some 40,000 artillerymen touched off the spark of Ninth Army's attack when they opened a terrific, hour-long softening up of German positions opposite XVI Corps. For sixty minutes 2,070 guns averaged better than 1,000 rounds a minute in delivering a stunning attack on the German defenders, their communications facilities, and their defensive positions. In the preparation firing alone, 65,200 rounds —1,820 tons—of artillery ammunition struck the German defenses. From the beginning of the preparation to four hours after the launching of the crossings, 131,450 rounds—nearly 4,000 tons—were fired. An indication of the effect of the heavy artillery support given to the assault divisions is contained in a report of interrogation of prisoners taken on March 24:

> The first few hundred prisoners reached the Army cage within six hours after capture, many still being in a stunned or dazed condition from the artillery pounding to which they had been subjected. "Hellish"—"terrifying" was all some of them could say at first. One officer prisoner of war apologized for his seemingly incoherent answers, saying his head still felt thick and numb from the recent ordeal. Others who had recuperated from the first shock expressed professional admiration for the barrage, using such terms as *"prima"* (first class) and *"kolossal."* Artillery officers in particular attributed their plight to the destruction of communications facilities by our artillery fire. They sent runner after runner to make contact with the infantry and with their headquarters, but runners did not return and no radios were available. Some artillery officers stated they kept waiting for their own infantry to fall back, thereby giving a warning of the approach of our forces, but suddenly they found themselves flanked and captured by U.S. troops without even seeing their own infantry.

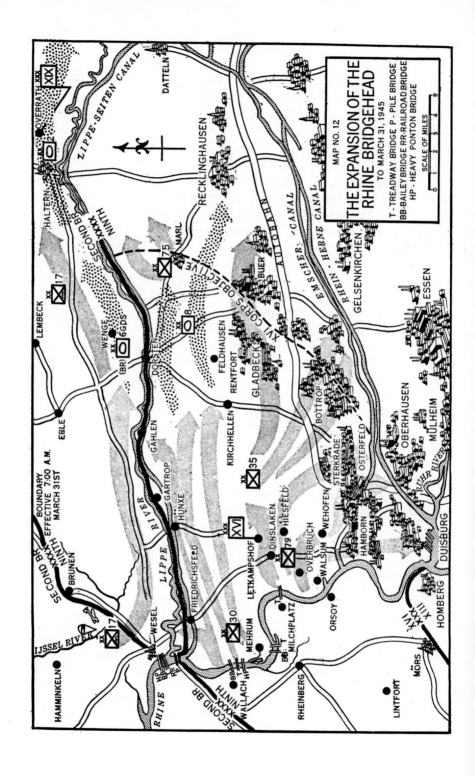

THE EXPANSION OF THE RHINE BRIDGEHEAD

TO MARCH 31, 1945

T - TREADWAY BRIDGE P - PILE BRIDGE
BB-BAILEY BRIDGE RR-RAILROAD BRIDGE
HP - HEAVY PONTON BRIDGE

MAP NO. 12

SCALE OF MILES

0 1 2 3 4 5

As the artillery preparation was completed, the first wave of the 30th Division infantrymen, three battalions abreast, left the west bank of the Rhine and headed across the 1200-foot barrier. (*Map No. 12.*) The outboard motors of their assault boats, usually cranky and uncertain in the cold hours of early morning, turned over without difficulty thanks to the precaution of putting them to bed the night before with chemical heating pads diverted from medical to engineer supply channels. With the first waves guided to their landing area by the red ribbon of machine gun tracer ammunition, the leading echelons of the three attacking infantry regiments established themselves on the far shore with little difficulty. South of the 30th Division, the 79th Division, with two battalions in assault, crossed the river at 3:00 o'clock in similar fashion, and its two assaulting regiments soon had elements firmly established on the far shore. Enemy fire from the east bank was relatively ineffectual, coming mostly from small arms and machine guns, and there were few casualties in the initial crossings. Within the first few hours the forward lines of German resistance were overrun.

The operation, as expected, became almost immediately more of an engineer construction task than a military tactical maneuver. With the first waves firmly ashore and blinking lights marking the boundaries of the following echelons, engineer troops initiated the back-breaking work of getting up the heavy ferrying equipment and then the bridging materials.

As the first major engineer job on the west bank, the winter dike, rising to a height of twelve to fifteen feet throughout the XVI Corps zone, had to be breached and roads constructed across the flood plain to the bridge and ferry sites. In the 30th Division zone, bulldozers were employed to breach the dike, and road construction was quickly completed, using prefabricated road material which had been previously loaded on all available trucks. In the 79th Division zone, cratering charges, which had been placed in the dikes prior to the assault, were set off shortly after the crossing of the infantry assault battalions, and the breaches thus formed were used for the access roads. A total of some 7.000 feet of road between the winter dike and the near shore was built immediately and thereafter constantly improved. Approach construction on the near side was much less difficult than on the far shore, where the approach roads were much poorer, and lack of heavy equipment, initially, made hand labor necessary for much of the work.

Troops poured across the river even as the engineers labored to get the approaches in shape. A company of tanks got across to lend support, and the "swimming" DD tanks crossed under their own power in the darkness. Using LVTs, which required no special river entrances or exits, the forces on the far shore were built up rapidly as the leading elements were taking their first objectives. In the first twenty-four hours, in the 79th Division area alone, LVTs completed 107 round trips. The handy DUKW also accomplished wonderful work, serving as a cargo and personnel carrier and as a general utility boat for bridge construction. The heavier and more awkward LCMs, LCVPs and Seamules were more difficult to handle, presenting many problems both in transportation and in launching. An unexpected low water level precluded their planned launching in the Alter Rhein, a small stream flowing north of Rheinberg into the Rhine, and it became necessary to develop suitable launching sites along the river and then to transport these craft forward over the congested road net to the sites. However, the lessons gained in the experimental and training period now stood in good stead, and the huge craft were lifted by cranes into the river, or their transporters were backed into the swift current and the craft floated off. The Navy personnel operating this equipment kept them going from the time of launching until the bridges were constructed, often operating under heavy enemy small-arms and artillery fire, with a loss of but one LCM and two LCVPs during the entire action. The LCVPs were to prove themselves by far the most useful of the heavy craft. They ferried personnel and light equipment and were used as power units for propelling rafts in the construction of bridges. The LCMs, on the other hand, were not to prove as valuable as anticipated. Used to transport tanks, tank destroyers, and heavy equipment, they were difficult to launch and in case of motor failure easily got out of control.

By noon on March 24 two Bailey rafts and several treadway rafts were in operation in the 30th Division zone. They were used to take tanks across the river during daylight hours until noon of the next day. In the zone of the 79th Division, where completion of the first bridge was delayed by enemy fire, even greater dependence had to be placed on ferries. Five Bailey rafts, the first one completed about 11:00 o'clock in the morning, were constructed and used for the first three days. By the end of the first day, as an example of the development of ferrying facilities, one medium tank was being ferried across in the corps zone every ten minutes.

Promptly at 10:00 o'clock on the morning of March 24 a great armada of troop-carrier planes appeared in the skies north of Wesel for the air drop in the zone of British Second Army. For 212 minutes aircraft passed in a continous stream, crossing the Rhine from the west, dropping their loads of fighting men and equipment, then turning right and left to clear the battle area quickly. A total of 14,365 troops, 109 tons of ammunition, 695 vehicles, and 113 artillery pieces dropped from the skies east of the Rhine in the initial lift, followed almost immediately by 582 tons of supplies brought in and dropped by 240 four-engined Liberators. The airborne forces met determined resistance from small arms, mortars, antiaircraft and other artillery everywhere they landed, but this resistance did not prevent them from rapidly consolidating and moving on to their objectives on schedule.

General Eisenhower and General Simpson watched the airborne assault from a church tower at the 30th Division command post in Alpen. The Supreme Allied Commander had come to the front the night before, and with General Simpson had spent the night at General Anderson's XVI Corps command post in Lintfort. There, from another churchtower, they observed the man-made thunder and lightning of the artillery firing beginning at 1:00 A.M., and early on the morning of the attack they began visits to the two assaulting divisions.

By the end of the first day there was little doubt as to the complete success of the assault across the Rhine. A bridgehead on the east bank was established between nine and ten miles wide and of a depth varying from three miles on the south to six miles on the north. Troops and supplies were building up rapidly in the bridgehead and bridge construction was far ahead of schedule. Due in large measure to the overwhelming artillery preparation and supporting fires delivered during the attack, our casualties had been remarkably light—41 killed, 450 wounded, and 7 missing. Some 2,100 Germans had been taken prisoner. A wounded soldier being evacuated back across the Rhine a few hours after the assault crossing, when asked how the fight was going, replied with enthusiasm, "We caught 'em with their pants down, and are kicking —— out of 'em!"

In the bridgehead the 79th Division on the south had advanced two to three miles against artillery, mortar, and small-arms fire. (*Map No. 12.*) It had overrun the small towns of Walsum and and Overbruch and the major town of Dinslaken. All nine infantry battalions of the division were on the east side of the river, plus a tank battalion and a tank destroyer battalion furnishing close support. On the north, the 30th Division met lighter resistance and by nightfall had progressed as far as six miles east of the river. Six small towns had been cleared and the division had pushed north across the Lippe Canal to reach the Lippe River just south of Wesel. The 30th Division also had all, nine of its infantry battalions on the far shore, as well as two tank battalions, one tank destroyer battalion, and two light field artillery battalions.

In the area of British Second Army, the Commandos were engaged in clearing the town of Wesel, and other British forces were expanding local bridgeheads in the face of somewhat stiffer opposition than that facing Ninth Army, due to a large extent to the presence of determined paratroopers in their zone of advance. The airborne drop, with the 17th Airborne Division and the British 6th Airborne Division, had been completed successfully and by dark they were on their initial objectives. The 17th Airborne Division was holding positions along the Ijssel River and was in contact with ground troops of the British Second Army. North of them the British 6th Airborne Division had captured five bridges intact over the Ijssel River, had reduced the town of Hamminkeln, and had also made contact with British Second Army ground troops. Supplies, special signal equipment, and heavy engineer equipment for the 17th Airborne Division had started across the river with the overland echelon at 5:00 P.M. on March 24. By daylight the next day supplies were being transported across the river by DUKWs in quantities more than sufficient to support the division's operations.

Although it had not been intended to start construction of the Rhine bridges until the bridgehead had been expanded far enough to eliminate observed enemy fire on the bridge sites, the light enemy resistance encountered and the availability of smoke for the concealment of sites permitted a change in plan whereby the construction of the bridges began on the first day of the attack, in some cases while the enemy still had observation. In the 79th Division zone, even though a bridge site at Milchplatz had been chosen in preference to two better sites located farther south but more exposed to enemy fire, construction of a 1260-foot tread-way bridge was considerably hampered by enemy artillery fire. Work began at 8:00 o'clock on the morning of the 24th. In addition to the interference from artillery fire, this bridge suffered damage from three runaway LCMs which broke loose and hit it after some 720 feet had been constructed. This accident cost 480 feet of bridging and forced the engineers to start again at the 240-foot mark. The desirability of locating ferry sites downstream from tactical bridges had been recognized, of course, and this was done whenever possible. However, often the only ferry site not requiring extensive preparation was immediately upstream from a tactical bridge. To reduce the danger to the bridges downstream, each ferry was equipped with two anchors which were to be cast in the event of power failure. In spite of these measures, discouraging accidents such as that of the Milchplatz bridge occurred. This bridge ultimately reached completion late in the afternoon of the third day, March 26.

Bridging in the 30th Infantry Division zone progressed with less difficulty, due primarily to its "inside" location, less exposed to enemy action. At 6:00 o'clock on the morning of March 24, only four hours after the initial assault wave had embarked, work was begun on a float-reinforced, 25-ton ponton bridge, some 1150 feet in length, at Wallach. It was completed at 1:00 A.M. on March 25, although its use was delayed by the necessity for road work on the far approach. Eventually, considerable improvement of the approach roads had to be made after traffic had started using the route, because the lack of road-building equipment and the unexpectedly early completion of the bridge had resulted in hasty preparation of the approaches. At 6:30 on the morning of March 24 the 1110-foot treadway bridge at Mehrum was started. Construction was delayed by artillery fire, which knocked out 144 feet of the bridge. Then at 10:00 o'clock the next morning a Seamule drifted against it, destroying the alignment and restricting traffic until 5:00 o'clock in the afternoon, when the errant Seamule was finally removed. Also started at 6:30 in the morning of the first day was the 1150-foot treadway bridge at Wallach, which was constructed with remarkable speed. Until 8:15 in the morning all the treadway rafts, later to be incorporated into this bridge, were used as ferries. Then, at 8:30, far-shore ground reconnaissance indicated desirability of shifting the site of the bridge 100 yards to take maximum advantage of the existing far-shore road net. Despite these delays the bridge was the first one completed and was opened to traffic at 4:00 o'clock in the afternoon of March 24. Later it, too, was damaged when a Bailey raft loaded with a tank got out of control and floated into the bridge. The bridge was repaired and put into operation for keeps by 2:00 o'clock on the morning of the 25th.

For protection against debris, floating mines, barges, explosives-filled motor boats, submarines, and enemy swimmers, booms were constructed across the river both above and below the bridges. Antitank guns and self-propelled tank destroyers were dug into the dikes all along the corps front in position to fire upon objects and craft approaching the bridges. An engineer river patrol, consisting of two Seamules, operated continuously above the bridges. The missions of the patrol were to intercept any derelict barges or other large floating objects and either beach or anchor them, and to prevent enemy swimmers from reaching the bridges. During the early stages of the operations each boat detonated a small explosive charge in the water every five minutes during the hours of darkness to discourage attacks by enemy swimmers.

To provide antiaircraft protection for the crossing sites, all Army antiaircraft units, except those still needed to protect the Roer River bridge sites, were used to establish an area defense behind the Rhine crossing sites. This gave adequate protection to the entire area and permitted staggered displacements forward to protect the advance of the ground forces without completely uncovering any vital objective in the rear. On March 24 the antiaircraft units on the Roer River were relieved by units of the IX Air Defense Command, and the Ninth Army units thus freed were then used in the Rhine crossing area defense. The 55th Antiaircraft Brigade, now commanded by Brigadier General Clarence H. Schabacker, provided initial antiaircraft protection for the Wesel bridge sites and progressively took over protection of other crossing sites southward as divisions and corps moved forward. Later, the brigade became responsible for both ground and antiaircraft protection for the Rhine bridges.

Antiaircraft units were given a high priority in the early crossings. One battery of self-propelled antiaircraft weapons was ferried across the river prior to the construction of any bridges. One battalion crossed before bridges were open to general traffic. As the divisions moved over, they picked up their antiaircraft battalions which had previously been disposed for defense on the west bank. Immediately on crossing, these were emplaced on the east bank to complete the defense. After the crossing of the initial divisions, heavy antiaircraft gun batteries were moved to the east shore to complete the defense against high-level air attack. Barrage balloons, to provide additional defense against strafing and low-level bombing raids, were emplaced and ready for action by the night of March 24. By March 25 the equivalent of two and one-half automatic weapons battalions and one antiaircraft gun battery had been crossed to form a complete defense of the bridges so far erected and the troops which had already crossed. As the divisions moved forward in the attack and took their antiaircraft units with them, other antiaircraft units were crossed to the east bank to maintain adequate coverage. Within three days the complete antiaircraft defenses included three gun battalions, ten automatic weapons battalions, one and one-half searchlight batteries, and fifty barrage balloons.

The secondary mission of antiaircraft guns was to fire upon targets of opportunity floating down the river. A searchlight battery was so disposed that it could provide night illumination of the crossing sites in addition to the performance of its normal mission. Fifteen tank-mounted searchlights furnished illumination for the booms. The effectiveness of the antiaircraft protection of the Rhine River bridges is evidenced by the fact that no bridges were damaged by aerial attack or enemy-directed floating obstacles, while antiaircraft units shot down 22 of the estimated 82 aircraft which attacked the crossings during the first four days.

Chemical smoke generator units maintained smoke cover for troop movements and bridging operations from 5:00 A.M. until dark on D-day, except for the period from 8:30 in the morning until noon, when the smoke was temporarily discontinued to avoid interfering with the airborne operations. For the next two days a continuous and effective screen was provided during all daylight hours. On the subsequent two days the weather made smoke necessary only in the early morning and late afternoon.

Throughout the first day of the assault, the fighter-bombers of the XXIX Tactical Air Command maintained constant air patrol, but no German aircraft entered the bridgehead to engage them. Only five German planes were observed by XXIX Tactical Air Command pilots during the entire day, a day that saw our fighter-bombers in the air at 6:00 o'clock in the morning to fly a total of 800 sorties, the Tactical Air Command's greatest effort in the war to date. Ranging well beyond the Rhine, the fighter-bombers claimed destruction or damage of large numbers of motor vehicles, locomotives, railroad cars, and tanks, as well as the silencing of 62 gun positions and the destruction of 54 enemy aircraft which they caught on the ground at an airfield at Dorsten.

On the night of the 24th, 43 raids were staged by the German air force against the bridge sites, with 41 of them made by individual aircraft. All attacking planes flew twisting irregular courses and took violent evasive action in the face of antiaircraft fire. Although but one plane was claimed destroyed by antiair-fire that night, there was no damage to any bridge.

The home front and posterity were not neglected by Ninth Army on the historic day of crossing. Signal Corps photographers accompanying the assault troops recorded 521 still pictures and over 15,000 feet of motion-picture film. On the following day a Ninth Army photographer, Sergeant D. W. Miller, scooped all of his colleagues when he obtained the only picture of Great Britian's Prime Minister, Winston Churchill, crossing the Rhine River in a landing craft. The film of this famous shot was carried back forty miles, developed, printed, censored, and transmitted direct from Army Headquarters by radio facsimile to New York in less than five hours. The picture was thus available to the evening editions of the newspapers in the United States on the same day it was taken.

On the second day of the attack, March 25, both assault divisions again made good progress. (*Map No. 12.*) The 79th Division, with the 134th Infantry Regiment of the 35th Division attached, now turned its attack southeastward into the fringe of the densely populated Ruhr industrial area in order to deepen the most shallow portion of the bridgehead and remove the artillery fire which was interfering with bridging operations at the southern bridge site. Generally, the attack of this division met light to moderate opposition from small-arms and automatic-weapons fire, although one regiment ran into stiff resistance in the vicinity of Wehofen, about four miles east of Orsoy, where fire from dug-in tanks held up the advance. Farther north, gains of up to three miles were made, and the towns of Letkampshof and Hiesfeld were taken. Six field artillery battalions moved across the river on this day to lend close support to the 79th Division. The 30th Division, while building up its strength with five more field artillery battalions and one tank destroyer battalion, pushed well to the east, reaching a point on the Lippe Canal just south of Gartrop, an advance of as much as five and one-half miles on some portions of its front. The resistance against the 30th continued light. The Army bridgehead was expanding quite satisfactorily and now measured as much as ten miles deep over a nine-mile front. Whereas on the first day of battle the 180th Infantry Division had been the only large enemy unit contacted, on this second day of the attack elements of the 116th Panzer Division put in their appearance. Both of these units were known from intelligence sources to be in this area.

Resistance continued to be stronger in the zone of the British Second Army, but the XVIII Airborne Corps was able to expand its area some two miles to the east while mopping up and consolidating its original positions. Of great importance was the completion of the job of clearing Wesel, for this was the most important bridging site of the entire 21 Army Group effort. The final mopping up here was assisted materially by the action of the colored troops of the 1698th U.S. Engineer Combat Battalion which had crossed the river with their heavy equipment to open routes through the rubble-clogged city. Before carrying out their primary mission, they lent a hand to the British Commandos in reducing the last strongpoints within the city. Beginning at 9:15 A.M. on the 25th, American engineer units under the direct control of Ninth Army began construction of the three floating bridges scheduled for installation at Wesel. One was a floating Bailey bridge, one a 25-ton reinforced ponton bridge, and one a treadway bridge. In addition, they initiated work on the establishment of a Class 70 prefabricated sectional barge ferry.

Again, on the 25th, the XXIX Tactical Air Command was out in full strength, flying 829 successful sorties and claiming hundreds of locomotives and railroad cars destroyed. In direct support of the ground troops a number of gun positions and strongpoints were effectively attacked. In one instance, the dive bombers were directed to a concentration of enemy armor with the astounding results of 29 tanks claimed destroyed and an additional 29 claimed damaged.

The German air force returned to the Rhine on the night of March 25, and though its efforts were no more successful than on the previous night, its losses were much higher. The antiaircraft gunners protecting the vital Rhine bridges in the Army zone claimed 24 aircraft destroyed or probably destroyed during a total of 68 attacks, even though enemy action was characterized by a refusal to press the bombing attacks home and by a contentment in most cases to limit the attack to strafing.

On the afternoon of March 25 work was started on the approach roads for another bridge in the vicinity of Mehrum, a Class 40 floating Bailey bridge with such additional booms as were required for its protection. Construction of the bridge began the following morning at 8:00 o'clock and was completed by daylight on March 28. Construction proceeded twenty-four hours a day with full use of lights during the hours of darkness and with interruption only during periods of enemy aerial activity. Some enemy strafing and shelling were directed against the bridging, but no casualties were suffered. At the same time, work was started on a similar bridge at Wallach. This was completed at 8:00 o'clock on the morning of March 29. These bridges were extremely long (the one at Mehrum, 1428 feet, and the other, at Wallach, 1739 feet) to accommodate possible river flooding and still remain operational.

March 26 saw continued advance once again all along the front. The 79th Division on the south was now inching its way forward in difficult terrain against stiffening resistance, particularly the fire of self-propelled guns and of antiaircraft weapons employed in a ground role. The woods in the center of the division zone were cleaned up on this day, the principal resistance in the vicinity of Wehofen was broken, and 79th Division troops were fighting in the town by the end of the day. The 30th Division progressed less rapidly, too, as the number of enemy mines and booby traps, and the fire of artillery and automatic weapons increased. The communications center of Hunxe was captured and the bridge there over the Lippe River was found to have been demolished. By the end of the day forward elements of the division were fighting in Gahlen, six miles farther to the east. Elements of the German 2d Parachute Division appeared this day, as well as some units of the 190th Infantry Division. The 2d Parachute Division, which had been reconstituted after its destruction at Brest by the VIII Corps, had an extremely fine reputation, and its appearance in this area meant that the German high command intended to battle it out to the bitter end. XVI Corps forces in the bridgehead were enlarged on March 26 as the 290th Infantry Regiment of the 75th Infantry Division entered the battle attached to the 30th Division, and the 35th Infantry Division completed the assembly of all its infantry battalions, a tank destroyer battalion, a tank battalion, and five field artillery battalions east of the Rhine, prepared to initiate its attack on the following day on the left of the 79th Division. On this day, too, the 8th Armored Division began its movement into the bridgehead.

For the third successive night the enemy again tried to destroy or damage the Rhine bridges from the air. Again, however, he failed to make a coordinated effort, although some ninety single attacks came from all directions and altitudes. Antiaircraft searchlights proved their effectiveness on this occasion when five planes were shot down while caught in their beams. Few bombs were dropped and no serious damage was inflicted on any bridge. Destroyed or probably destroyed were thirty German aircraft, one-third of the attacking force. This was the last air attack of any magnitude launched against the Rhine bridges. The Luftwaffe effort to defeat the crossing operation at its most vital point had failed dismally.

Prior to the crossing of the Rhine, Army supply points had been established as close to the west bank of the river as possible, and unit trains were heavily stocked in an effort to hold supply traffic adjacent to and across the river to the minimum. For the first forty-eight hours after the attack began, the only movements across the river were those of tactical units; then, as tactical moves permitted, service units and supply trucks were fitted into the traffic crossing the river. On March 26 one hospital unit of a field hospital was set up east of the river at Friedrichsfeld in support of the 30th Division. By March 29 a total of two evacuation hospitals, three hospital units of field hospitals, and a chemical supply point were east of the Rhine. On March 30 an additional evacuation hospital, a food and gasoline supply point, and an ordnance ammunition supply point were established in the bridge-head.

A major factor in relieving the amount of supply traffic that had to be routed over the Rhine bridges was the rapidity with which Advance Section, Communications Zone, extended the gasoline pipeline from its former terminus at Alpen, southwest of Wesel. The pipeline was crossed over the Rhine on one of the floating bridges almost as soon as the bridge was completed, and a new tank farm was constructed at Wesel. From that point, gasoline was transported in tank trucks to a decanting station, which was established at Erle, northeast of Wesel, on April 3.

At the end of the third day of the attack, March 26, on the left of the Army, XVIII Airborne Corps' 17th Airborne Division had made good progress along a six-mile front and now firmly held a position running north from Hunxe, on the Lippe River, to Brunen. South of the Lippe, the Ninth Army bridgehead, now eleven miles wide and thirteen miles deep, was not expanding with outstanding rapidity, but the troop build-up was good and four bridges were in operation in the Army area, in addition to two completed by Ninth Army engineers at Wesel. XVI Corps had three complete infantry divisions in the bridgehead, part of a fourth one, and substantial numbers of supporting troops, and had now initiated the movement of its armored division.

Since the bridges at Wesel were reserved for use by the British, except for five hours daily for Ninth Army, the routes across the Rhine that were available to the Army were little more than adequate for logistical support of the forces already across the river. Also, the battlefield area was rapidly becoming congested. However, measures were now being taken to concentrate the XIX Corps and prepare it for commitment on the left flank of the XVI Corps just as quickly as clear routes could be obtained to bring it in. It was estimated that the fairly strong resistance which was holding the advance to a few miles a day was, in reality, a shell, and once this shell was broken, armor and motorized infantry would have an opportunity for exploiting deep into the northern plains of Germany. So on March 26 the disengagement of XIX Corps along the west bank of the Rhine and the assumption of responsibility for that area by XIII Corps was ordered. (*Map No. 11.*) A simple "paper relief" was effected, with XIII Corps taking over command from XIX Corps of the 95th Infantry Division

and the 113th Cavalry Group, the forces which had been holding
this sector since it was taken over from First Army shortly after
reaching the Rhine. XIII Corps then held the river line south to
the inter-Army Group boundary at Worringen some ten miles
south of Düsseldorf.

German resistance continued to increase on March 27, the
fourth day of the operation. Recovering from the initial stunning
effect of the heavy artillery and air bombardment and appreciating now the scope and location of the assault across its river
barriers, the enemy began to fight back strongly, making small
but determined counterattacks and bringing some of his depleted
reserves into the battle area. The Army advance took on more
of the pattern of the slow slugging attack west of the Roer than
of the rapid open maneuver of the advance between the Roer and
the Rhine. It had always been appreciated that this area between
the northern face of the Ruhr industrial area and the Lippe River
was a dead-end street, offering little opportunity for maneuver
and exploitation, but forcing the attacker, rather, to push his way
slowly forward against numerous man-made obstacles and the
naturally unfavorable, swampy terrain. On the right (south),
the 79th Division continued its initial progress, gaining from one-
half to two miles against varying resistance, particularly from
strong enemy infantry action. (*Map No. 12.*) Elements of the
division succeeded in crossing the Emscher Canal on the extreme
right and cleared three small towns farther east, including Wehofen. The 35th Infantry Division, committed as a unit for the
first time in the operation, moved into the center of the line and
advanced through strongly defended woods to gain from one to
three miles to the east. On the north, the 30th Infantry Division
continued the battle along the Lippe River and Canal about half
way between the important road centers of Hunxe and Dorsten,
but throughout the day ran into heavy resistance including tank
and artillery fire as well as the usual small arms and machine gun
action. Five miles behind the 30th, and crowding its rear area,
the 8th Armored Division completed its assembly in the area
south of Hunxe. Troops were a-plenty, but they were massed in
a restricted area which made mere numbers more of a liability
than an asset.

Bad weather had set in, too, which limited the assistance that
XXIX Tactical Air Command could give. On March 27 there

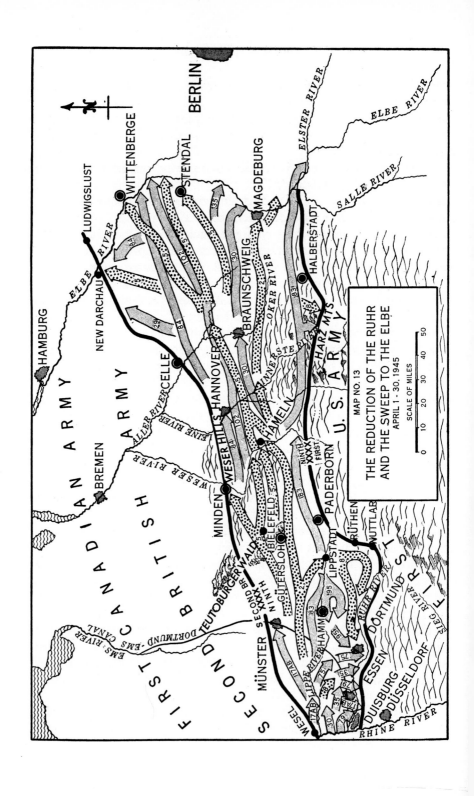

MAP NO. 13

THE REDUCTION OF THE RUHR
AND THE SWEEP TO THE ELBE
APRIL 1 - 30, 1945

SCALE OF MILES

0 10 20 30 40 50

were no air operations whatsoever, and indeed the fighter-bombers were able to do little throughout the rest of the month. They did get into the area south of Dorsten on the 28th to bomb enemy troop concentrations and suspected armor assembly areas. However, weather made their damage difficult to assess. With the exception of a good strike by 405th Group on the German air base at Gütersloh (*Map No. 13*), where 56 enemy aircraft were claimed destroyed or damaged, there were few successful missions flown in the closing days of the month.

At noon on March 27 when the Army took over direct responsibility for all Rhine bridging, traffic control, and security of the installations within the Army zone, the bridging program had developed very satisfactorily. (*Map No. 12.*) In the 79th Division zone the treadway bridge at Milchplatz had been completed and was carrying traffic. In the 30th Division zone the treadway bridges at Mehrum and at Wallach were finished and in operation. The 25-ton ponton bridge at Wallach was also carrying traffic. Construction of the floating Bailey bridge at Mehrum was approximately sixty per cent complete, and construction of the similar bridge at Wallach was well under way. At Wesel, where British Second Army still controlled the routes, the treadway bridge and the 25-ton bridge were completed and carrying traffic, and the floating Bailey bridge was nearing completion.

Ninth Army's greatest engineering task on the Rhine commenced with the initiation of work on the fixed timber pile highway bridge to be constructed at Wesel. The mission of building this structure was assigned to the 1146th Engineer Combat Group whose three combat battalions, light equipment company, and dump truck company were augmented by a naval construction battalion maintenance unit, detachments from two engineer port construction and repair groups, and a detachment of the Army engineer topographic battalion. Extra equipment was provided, too, including heavy steam pile-driving rigs, extra cranes, air compressors, welding and cutting sets, and generators. The site finally selected required the spanning of both the Rhine and the Lippe Rivers and the construction of two bridges—the Rhine Bridge, 1814 feet long, and the Lippe bridge, 411 feet long. On March 28 old Fort Blücher on the west bank of the Rhine was demolished to provide rubble for approach roads. On the 29th test piles were driven, and on April 1 work was begun on the bridges proper.

The great bottleneck in the flow of troops and supplies across the Rhine was the situation on the routes through Wesel. Communications Zone engineers were to begin construction of the railroad bridge at Wesel on March 29, and although much of the supplies and equipment needed for that structure was brought in by rail, some use of the Venlo–Geldern–Wesel road was necessary. British Second Army was already using the routes through Wesel to the extent that serious delays in the completion of both fixed bridges were experienced by American engineers who, many times, were unable to move their trucks past British vehicles double-parked along miles of the road.

Of even greater importance was the restrictive effect of the Wesel bottleneck on the impending commitment of XIX and XIII Corps. Seeking a solution to the virtual impasse which was developing, General Simpson assembled his corps commanders on the afternoon of March 27 at the command post of XVI Corps at Lintfort. Major General Matthew B. Ridgway, commanding XVIII Airborne Corps, was also present to give a firsthand account of progress just north of Ninth Army's zone on the other side of the Lippe River. Both the U.S. 17th Airborne Division and the British 6th Airborne Division were beginning to break loose against crumbling enemy resistance in their zones, but the extremely crowded conditions of the routes north of the Lippe gave little promise of permitting Ninth Army to pass troops through the right of the British Second Army zone in order to outflank the resistance on its own front.

More than a week before, on March 19, after considerable discussion with reference to the use and regulation of the road net of which Wesel was the hub, Field Marshal Montgomery had ruled the following procedure:

> During the period from the present time (March 19) until the completion of the floating bridges at Wesel, Ninth Army will have control of the route with running rights to Second Army.
> From the completion of the bridges until the completion of Phase One (the seizure of the Dorsten–Borken line) and until the build-up of 8th British Corps is complete, Second Army will have control of the route with certain running rights to Ninth Army.
> Subsequently, Ninth Army will have control of the route with certain running rights to Second Army. Both Armies will have traffic control parties throughout. Both Armies will share the use of the route during all three phases.

Because of the slowness of their bridging operations at Xanten and Rees and because German paratroopers put up bitter, time-consuming resistance at Emmerich, the British transferred the bulk of their cross-river traffic to the Wesel area. Ninth Army was also crowding the maximum possible number of tactical and service units and supply vehicles over the Wesel bridges during the five hours daily the Americans were allowed to use that route. At the same time, the expansion of the bridgehead north of the Lippe was progressing much more favorably in its southern portion than in the northern, so that the Dorsten–Borken line would soon be reached with the northern flank still relatively unexpanded. British Second Army, at this stage of operations, on March 27, was quite unwilling to provide sufficient running rights over the Wesel routes to permit General Simpson to commit additional troops over that route. Consequently, he sought another solution. He decided to risk further crowding of his own limited bridgehead and overtaxing of the capacity of the bridges in his own zone and ordered that XIX Corps commence movement into the bridgehead by crossing the Rhine at Wallach and concentrating south of the Lippe River and Canal, prepared to move north as soon as bridges over these obstacles could be constructed. General Ridgway was strong in his belief that the area north of the Lippe River could not stand further build-up of troops. Its road net and troop concentration area were simply taxed to the limit already. However, should the action of XVIII Airborne Corps continue favorably for another couple of days this situation might well be eliminated, and the Army Commander was most desirous of getting an exploiting force close up and ready to drive east should the breakthrough occur. In the meantime, General Simpson presented a strong plea to General Dempsey, Commander of British Second Army, and to Field Marshal Montgomery that he be permitted the exclusive use, at the earliest possible date, of the Geldern–Wesel road, including the bridges at Wesel, and of the main highway leading out of Wesel to the east toward Haltern. Once these key facilities were granted to Ninth Army, XIII Corps too could be committed east of the Rhine.

To provide mobility in the anticipated pursuit, six quartermaster truck companies were attached to XIX Corps and a similar number to XIII Corps to permit the motorization of infantry elements. Another company was provided to supplement the organic transportation of XIX Corps' 2d Armored Division, spearheading the operation. Finally, two more truck companies were utilized to motorize hospital units and other small supporting units in order that they might keep up with the expected rapid advance once it got under way.

On March 28, in the bridgehead, the 79th Division found enemy resistance spotty and considerably lighter than it had been, and was able to push forward from one to five miles in its zone of action. (*Map No. 12.*) Particularly noteworthy was its advance on its right flank along the Rhine River to the Rhein–Herne Canal, thus reaching for the first time the limit of Ninth Army's bridgehead as defined in the attack orders. The 35th Division, too, gained from one to four miles in its zone in spite of the strong small-arms, mortar, and artillery fire it encountered. It captured Rentfort and by nightfall was fighting in the western outskirts of Gladbeck.

In the northern portion of the Army bridgehead, XVI Corps prematurely attempted to gain a breakthrough by passing the 8th Armored Division through the 30th Infantry Division. It was hoped that an armored division, fresh and at full strength, might provide the drive to punch a hole through the enemy's shell. However, the restricted maneuver room, the swampy terrain, the numerous antitank obstacles which dotted this area, and the bitter fighting of the German defenders stalled the two combat commands which were leading the attack. Their advance was limited to three miles, and at the end of the day German forces were offering a strong fight for the important communications center of Dorsten.

North of the Lippe in the zone of British Second Army, XVIII Airborne Corps, now reinforced by the British 6th Guards Tank Brigade, was developing the breakthrough General Simpson had foreseen. Paratroopers of the 17th Airborne Division mounted the Churchill tanks of the tank brigade and raced seventeen miles to the vicinity of Haltern. Other elements pushed out seven miles to Wenge. The British 6th Airborne Division also broke loose and advanced east as far as Lembeck.

On March 28, too, Field Marshal Montgomery issued a directive to govern the continuation of the battle. He painted a picture of an extremely disorganized enemy and a great opportunity for exploitation if the Allied attack were now pressed home. He laid

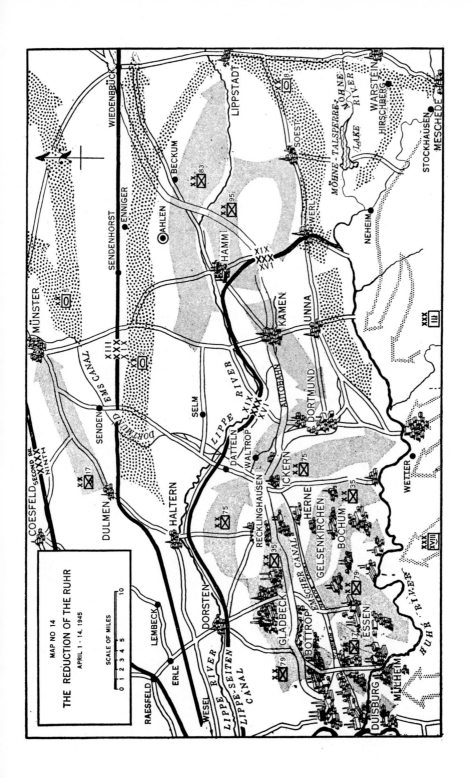

MAP NO 14

THE REDUCTION OF THE RUHR

APRIL 1 - 14, 1945

SCALE OF MILES

0 1 2 3 4 5   10

down his intention "to exploit the present situation rapidly and to drive hard for the line of the River Elbe so as to gain quick possession of the plains of northern Germany." (*Map No. 13.*) His plan was to continue the advance to the Elbe with Ninth Army and Second Army abreast, lining up along the Elbe between Magdeburg on the south and Hamburg on the north and halting at that point. The boundary between the two armies was established from Wesel, northeast through Münster and Minden, both of which were included to Ninth Army, through Celle, a road hub to be shared by both armies, and on to the Elbe at, initially, Wittenberge. He prescribed that one corps of Ninth Army remain in position along the northern face of the Ruhr to insure that no threat could be developed by the enemy to jeopardize the security of the Rhine River bridges, which were vital to supply the extensive operation in view. As soon as contact was effected with First Army beyond the Ruhr area, Ninth Army was to cooperate with First Army in the reduction and occupation of the Ruhr itself. The Rhine operation, as such, was rapidly nearing completion and these were, in effect, the orders for Ninth Army's next two operations—those of reducing the Ruhr and advancing to the Elbe.

Most important of all to General Simpson's plan for early exploitation was a definite decision regarding the assignment of the supply route and road net. Field Marshal Montgomery directed that "The road Erle-Lembeck-Coesfeld (*Map No. 14*) will be available to Second Army until 0700 hours on Friday, 30 March," thus giving the vital roads north of the Lippe River and east of Wesel to Ninth Army after that time. And finally, to clear the muddled situation of the route through Wesel, he ordered that the "Wesel bridges will pass from Second Army to Ninth Army at 0700 hours on Saturday, 31 March. Until that time Ninth Army will have the use of the bridge for a total of five hours per day of twenty-four hours."

With these definite decisions available to him, General Simpson was able to round out the plan he had been making, to confirm instructions already given to his corps commanders, and to issue complete orders for the ensuing operations. On March 29 he issued the Letter of Instructions for the operations. XIX Corps, which was to be composed of the 30th, 83d, and 95th Infantry Divisions and the 2d and 8th Armored Divisions, when regrouping was completed, was given the following mission (*Map 14*):

(1) Employing initially one armored division, one infantry division and necessary supporting troops, cross the Rhine and Lippe Rivers without delay, attack to seize Hamm and continue the advance to the east in its zone.

(2) Protect the Army right flank east of Datteln and establish contact with elements of the 12th Army Group in the vicinity of Paderborn. (*Map No. 13.*) Thereafter maintain contact with elements of 12th Army Group.

(3) Be prepared, on Army order, to release to XVI Corps elements protecting the right flank west of Paderborn.

(4) Maintain contact with elements of British Second Army prior to the commitment of XIII Corps east of the Rhine.

(5) Assume operational control of the 8th Armored Division upon the establishment by the 8th Armored Division of bridgeheads over the Dortmund–Ems Canal, the Lippe–Seiten Canal, and the Lippe River in the vicinity of Datteln. (*Map No. 14.*)

(6) Assume command of the 30th Infantry Division effective 6:00 A.M., March 30.

After regrouping XIII Corps was to be composed of the 17th Airborne Division, the 84th Infantry Division, the 102d Infantry Division and the 5th Armored Division. The following mission was given to XIII Corps:

(1) Employ initially one armored division, one infantry division and necessary supporting troops, cross the Rhine River over the Wesel bridges, and attack to seize Münster and the airdromes in the vicinity of Münster and continue the advance to the east in its zone. Be prepared to initiate movement across the Rhine River at 7:00 on March 31.

(2) Upon commitment east of the Rhine, establish and maintain contact with elements of British Second Army.

(3) Be prepared to assume command of the 17th Airborne Division on Army order.

The 29th, 35th, 75th, and 79th Infantry Divisions were to be under the command of XVI Corps after regrouping was completed. The mission given to XVI Corps was:

(1) Construct two two-way Class 40 routes over the Lippe River and the Lippe–Seiten Canal, one in the vicinity of Hunxe (*Map No. 12*), and the other in the vicinity of Dorsten.

(2) Clear its zone to the line of the Rhein–Herne, Emscher, Dortmund–Ems Canals. (*Map No. 14.*) Thereafter defend aggressively along this line with minimum forces, retaining a reserve of at least one infantry divison, which will be committed only on Army order.

(3) Be prepared to resume responsibility for the protection of the Army right flank to Paderborn, on Army order, and to assume command of the elements of XIX Corps released to XVI Corps in place along this flank.

(4) Be prepared to assume responsibility for the security of the Army rear area east of the Rhine River as the rear boundaries of XIX and XIII Corps are advanced to the east.

(5) Release operational control of the 8th Armored Division to XIX Corps upon the establishment by the 8th Armored Division of bridgeheads over the Dortmund–Ems Canal, the Lippe–Seiten Canal, and the Lippe River in the vicinity of Datteln.

(6) Release the 30th Infantry Division to XIX Corps effective at 6:00 A.M. March 30.

All troops were instructed that enemy airdromes were high priority objectives. Corps were ordered to report promptly to Army Headquarters the location, condition, number, and length of runways of all captured airdromes.

To insure the security of the Rhine River bridges against ground attacks, attacks by paratroopers, and against the destructive possibilities of floating mines, swimming saboteurs, and river craft of all types, the entire mission was given to one unit, the 55th Antiaircraft Artillery Brigade, directly under Army command.

XIX Corps was losing no time effecting its build-up east of the Rhine. Acting on the oral orders of the Army Commander on the afternoon of March 27, it was able to move Combat Command A of the 2d Armored Division, with the 377th Regimental Combat Team of the 95th Infantry Division attached, to an assembly area southeast of Hunxe early on March 28 and to concentrate the remainder of the 2d Armored Division in the vicinity of Lintfort preparatory to crossing the Rhine. (*Map No. 12.*)

Then, on the 28th, moving over the Lippe River bridges constructed by the XVI Corps near Hunxe, Combat Command A moved north of the Lippe. The rest of the 2nd Armored Division crossed the Rhine and prepared to follow the leading combat command. Farther back, the 83d Infantry Division, now designated as the follow-up unit behind the 2d Armored Division, got under way, moving north from München-Gladbach to the Rhine River bridges. The roads were filled with eager troops moving east across the Rhine and onward to the plains of northern Germany. Now all roads led to Berlin.

The attack to expand the bridgehead to the east and southeast continued hand in hand with the feverish activity to build up the forces for the exploitation phase. On March 29 a second regiment of the 79th Division closed along the Rhein–Herne Canal and established positions overlooking the Ruhr Valley. Sterkrade was cleared, and in an effort to probe the defenses of Duisburg, patrols were sent across the canal toward the city. They met heavy fire from the houses along the south bank of the canal, however, and were forced to retire. The 35th Division made advances of one-half to two miles and cleared Gladbeck. Again the 8th Armored Division continued to meet very heavy opposition, but pushed forward some two to four miles and cleared the towns of Dorsten and Feldhausen. Dorsten was particularly important because of its choice as a site for bridging the Lippe.

At 9:00 o'clock in the evening the first trickle of the stream of armor and motorized infantry that was to sweep to the Elbe began moving to the east from vicinity of Haltern—the reconnaissance elements of the 2d Armored Division were striking out of the Rhine bridgehead.

The 79th Division completed its labors in the bridgehead on March 30 by closing to the Rhein–Herne Canal throughout its zone. The 35th made good progress, too, pushing on beyond the prescribed bridgehead limits on March 30 and 31 to reach within two miles of Recklinghausen. In the difficult terrain just south of the Lippe, XVI Corps began the substitution of infantry for armor in the advance. On March 30 one regiment of the 75th Infantry Division operated with the 8th Armored Division, and on the last day of the month the 75th Division passed through the 8th Armored and drove from four to five miles to the east to complete entirely the original bridgehead prescribed in the Rhine

River attack order. In eight days this corps had crossed the greatest water barrier encountered since the invasion of the Continent, and had driven through unfavorable terrain, well adapted to the enemy's defenses, to establish a bridgehead more than twenty miles deep and ten miles wide and set the stage for the exploitation operations which were soon to result in the unconditional surrender of Germany.

XIX Corps struck to the east on March 30 with its 2d Armored Division from the vicinity of Haltern and Dülmen. (*Map No. 14.*) Delayed only a few hours by blown bridges over the Dortmund–Ems Canals, as the month ended the division was rolling east, almost without opposition, toward the link-up with First Army and the encirclement of the Ruhr. XIII Corps, poised with its 5th Armored Division and 84th Infantry Division, began movement across the Wesel bridges as soon as they passed to Ninth Army control on the morning of the 31st, preparatory to taking its place on the left flank for the next operation. West of the Rhine, U.S. Fifteenth Army had initiated its progressive relief of Ninth Army in territory on that side of the river, utilizing for the time being the 102d and most of the 95th Infantry Division for the task.

Ninth Army now entered into a new phase of operations. The crossing of the Rhine had been effected successfully and economically, with less than 3,000 casualties, the bridgehead won, the enemy thrown into disorder. Over 9,000 prisoners had been taken in the period from March 24 through the 31st. Two major campaigns were yet to be fought, the reduction of the Ruhr industrial area and the great race to the Elbe River. The industrial heart of Germany was in imminent danger of encirclement and complete strangulation. The most direct route to Berlin lay straight ahead, barred only by the densely wooded low mountain range, the Teutoburger Wald, and by two major rivers, the Weser and the Elbe. The vaunted Luftwaffe was in the throes of death, and the Germany Army was broken and divided, physically and in spirit.

CHAPTER 7
THE RUHR AND THE ELBE

EASTER Sunday, April 1, 1945 was a major milestone in the war against Germany. On that date the Ruhr pocket was formed by the link-up of U.S. Ninth and First Armies, which has been called the greatest encirclement in military history. The eventful contact was established at 4:00 o'clock in the afternoon at Lippstadt, Germany, seventy miles east of the Rhine. (*Map No. 13.*) Here it was that Combat Command B of XIX Corps' 2d Armored Division, circling to the north of the Ruhr Valley, met elements of the 3d Armored Division of First Army's VII Corps which had struck north and east after breaking out of the Remagen bridgehead.

The meeting of the two armies had a significance whose import could not be overestimated. Battered though it was by heavy bombing throughout the war, the Ruhr still contained the heart and sinew of the Reich's industry. Moreover, within the armed cordon now encircling the Ruhr Valley were nearly one-third of a million German soldiers—Field Marshal Model's Army Group B with the greater part of the Fifth Panzer and Fifteenth Armies as well as elements of the First Parachute Army. These forces included a total of seven corps and the major elements of nineteen divisions, augmented by some one hundred thousand antiaircraft personnel. The destruction or capture of this great military force would deal Germany a major blow. The huge pocket embraced an area of some 4,000 square miles lying generally between the Sieg River on the south and the Lippe River on the north and measured 55 miles from north to south and 70 miles from east to west. The pocket was bounded on the west by the Rhine River. It was now inclosed by United States forces on all sides.

The Ruhr had always been a major consideration in Allied plans. Operation Overlord, the master plan for the invasion of the Continent, called for the envelopment of the Ruhr in the final phase. Now it had become a reality. But important as the Ruhr pocket was, it nevertheless was only a part of the great battle in which Ninth Army now engaged. Field Marshal Montgomery, in his battle order of March 28, had directed the Army to "operate strongly to secure the line of the Elbe River between Magdeburg and Wittenberge"; . . . to "hold a secure right flank facing the Ruhr as far east as Paderborn" (to obviate an enemy threat from the south flank against the eastward move to the Elbe until junction with 12th Army Group was effected in the vicinity of Paderborn); and to "assist 12th Army Group in mopping up the Ruhr." Now with the Ruhr sealed off, Ninth Army engaged in two simultaneous operations of great magnitude—the drive to the Elbe by XIII Corps and the major part of XIX Corps, and the reduction of the Ruhr by XVI Corps and elements of XIX Corps. From April 1 to April 14, when the last Ninth Army objective in the Ruhr was taken, the Army's operations were in continually diverging lines and of sharply contrasting types—slashing east in armored and motorized infantry operations of extreme rapidity and wide scope, and simultaneously driving to the south and southwest through the thickly populated, highly industrialized Ruhr, fighting from town to town, street to street, and building to building.

Let us consider, first, the grinding, slugging fight to reduce the Ruhr in conjunction with First Army. On April 2 representatives of the two armies met at First Army Headquarters to plan and coordinate the joint attack on the huge pocket. The boundary between armies was set as the Ruhr River as far east as Nuttlar and then north to Ruthen and east to Paderborn. (*Map No. 13.*) This gave to Ninth Army the densely-populated, heavily built-up industrial section north of the river, and to First Army the rugged terrain to the south.

Ninth's Army's plan of attack was simple. (*Map No. 14.*) The operation called for a converging attack by two corps aimed at the heart of the Ruhr. XVI Corps was to attack south to the Ruhr River from its current positions north of the Rhein–Herne Canal. XIX Corps forces, striking from the Hamm and Lippstadt areas, were to drive southwest to the Army south boundary. At the same time, First Army forces would be driving north and northwest to effect a junction with Ninth Army all along the Ruhr River.

General Simpson's decision to have XIX Corps participate in the reduction of the Ruhr at the same time that it launched a strong attack eastward to the Elbe was made with full recognition of the difficulties thereby imposed on the corps. It was necessary to strike southwest into the Ruhr from the Hamm–Lippstadt area so as to thicken the eastern wall of the pocket and thwart any enemy attempt to break out to the east and northeast. XIX Corps elements already held the positions from which this could be done. Furthermore, it was apparent that lateral communication, command, and control of the entire Ruhr River drive by XVI Corps would be most difficult in view of the distances involved. XIX Corps was in a position to control both its attack into the Ruhr and its advance to the east. Since the Ruhr attack would be on converging lines, XVI Corps could take over full responsibility when the forces had advanced sufficiently to make command and control feasible for a single corps. To give XIX Corps additional forces, the 8th Armored Division was passed from XVI Corps to XIX Corps on March 31 and began assembling in the vicinity of Selm. The 95th Infantry Division, less one regiment which had already accompanied the 2d Armored Division on its drive to the east, returned on April 1 from the operational control of Fifteenth Army west of the Rhine. The division was now attached to XIX Corps, and moved to an assembly area north of Hamm on April 2. Thus XIX Corps was given the means to execute its mission in the Ruhr, but before the corps was relieved of that responsibility, it had troops fighting on fronts which were 125 miles apart.

Immediately after the link-up at Lippstadt, regrouping of forces began so as to allow both Ninth and First Armies not only to capture the prized Ruhr industrial area but also to continue the rapid advance deep into the heart of Germany. In Ninth Army's XIX Corps zone, along the northeast wall of the pocket, Combat Command B of the 2d Armored Division was relieved by elements of the 83d Division, enabling the combat command to rejoin its division and to resume the race eastward to the Weser and the Elbe Rivers. The south flank of XIX Corps was protected along the twenty-mile front from Lippstadt to the vicinity of Hamm by the 83d Division. The 8th Armored Division and the 95th Infantry Division were to pass through the 83d Division and attack into the pocket. When thus relieved, the 83d Division would be motorized for the XIX Corps drive to the east. The 15th Cavalry Group was screening the corps flank from Hamm 18 miles west to the Dortmund–Ems Canal and the east flank of XVI Corps.

At the time the Ruhr pocket was formed, the XVI Corps was already fighting south and east out of its Rhine bridgehead into the densely populated area of the Ruhr. The corps front from west to east was held by the 79th, 35th, and 75th Infantry Divisions. The 79th had closed up to the Rhein–Herne Canal, and was holding positions along the canal from the Rhine 14 miles eastward. Patrols had already crossed the canal in the face of heavy opposition. The 35th Division, attacking southeast, was rapidly moving up to the canal. The 75th was eleven miles from the Dortmund–Ems Canal. Strong artillery support was available to back up the XVI Corps attack. The Army's 34th Field Artillery Brigade was still attached for operations. In all, the corps had a total of 21 non-divisional field artillery battalions, in addition to organic division artillery, for use in reducing the pocket.

On the south of the pocket, First Army began disengaging VII Corps from the Ruhr area immediately, so as to free the corps and its divisions to spearhead First Army's attack eastward. III Corps, with the 9th and 99th Infantry Divisions and the 7th Armored Division, took up positions along the eastern wall of the pocket. Along the southern edge, XVIII Airborne Corps Headquarters, fresh from its successful operations east of Wesel and relieved from British control, was in process of forming for an attack north with the 97th, 78th, and 8th Infantry Divisions under its command.

Thus the reduction of the Ruhr was begun by four corps— XVI and XIX of Ninth Army and III and XVIII Airborne of First Army. It cannot be said that the operation began on any certain day, for even before the link-up, both armies were hammering the German defenses of the area. Now, however, with a coordinated effort, the hammering could be renewed with increased intensity and continued until the Ruhr pocket was wiped out.

Pressing against the north face of the Ruhr, the three infantry divisions of XVI Corps were well suited for the task that lay ahead, which was largely one for foot soldiers. The battlefield was composed of industrial, urban, suburban, and rural areas studded with strong points which had to be thoroughly reduced and then finely combed for last-ditch defenders and possible saboteurs. Ahead were key cities with large pre-war populations, such as Essen, 668,000; Dortmund, 550,000; Duisburg, 457,000;

Gelsenkirchen, 322,000; Herne, 96,000; and Bottrop, 86,000.

In XVI Corps on April 1, the 79th Division found the enemy along the northern perimeter of the pocket extremely sensitive to all efforts to cross the Rhein–Herne Canal and made no advance. The 35th Division fought its way four miles east and captured Recklinghausen. Along the Corps' east flank the 75th Division pushed forward nine miles against varying resistance and by night was within two miles of the Dortmund–Ems Canal. On April 2 there was little major action in the XVI Corps zone as the divisions consolidated their gains and cleaned up overrun areas. In the XIX Corps portion of the pocket the 8th Armored Division, which had been moved east from the Selm area, now passed through one regiment of the 83rd Infantry Division and attacked towards Soest from the Lippstadt-Paderborn area. It gained four miles against bitter and determined resistance. The 116th Panzer Division, an élite German unit which had opposed the initial XVI Corps attack across the Rhine, had disengaged from contact near Recklinghausen and moved east to spearhead an attempt to break out of the pocket. It was on April 2 that the 8th Armored first met the 116th Panzer; from this time on, the two units were in contact until the 8th finally drove its opponents out of the Army zone and south of the Ruhr River. During that night the enemy attempted an abortive counterattack south of Hamm. Additional efforts of this nature were expected hourly as enemy forces were known to be concentrating in the Lippstadt area, as well as in the eastern portion of the First Army zone. If successful, such attacks would have a two-fold result. They would smash open an escape route from the trap and in doing so might hope to relieve the pressure on the German forces attempting to hold the northern and southern flanks of the pocket.

On April 3 the 8th Armored continued to attack toward the key German communications center of Soest, and while reconnaissance elements maintained contact with First Army units, the division drove four miles deeper into the pocket. The enemy continued his escape efforts, probing into the eastern wall in an attempt to locate a weak point. Favorable terrain, well suited for a stubborn defense, aided the miscellaneous German forces in limiting the XIX Corps advance. The 95th Infantry Division relieved the two remaining regiments of the 83d Infantry Division along the Lippe River, thus releasing the entire 83d Division for movement to the east and placing the 95th Division west of the 8th Armored Division to attack into the pocket in conjunction with it. The same day, in the XVI Corps zone, the 75th Division, attacking across the Rhein-Herne and Dortmund–Ems Canals with three regiments, scored gains of two to five miles. Considerable small-arms and automatic-weapons fire resisted the advances in the XVI Corps zone, but German artillery fire was light, as it generally was all during the Ruhr operation. The small amount of fire was usually harassing and interdictory in nature and was generally delivered against front-line elements and forward road intersections.

The Ruhr district, however, was plentifully supplied with heavy antiaircraft guns for the air defense of the great industrial plants. The employment of these guns in a ground role, both for direct and indirect fire, often presented an extremely stubborn and bitter defense, which was crushed only after sharp and skillful fighting by our troops. Similar conditions were to be met by XIII and XIX Corps in their drive east, where the antiaircraft defenses of principal cities, key communications points, and industrial sites often presented major resistance.

Ninth Army reverted to the control of 12th Army Group on April 4, thus bringing under 12th Army Group all troops engaged in the reduction of the Ruhr. On the same day the new Ninth Army–First Army boundary, following the Ruhr River, went into effect. In the XIX Corps zone during the day, while the 8th Armored Division continued to fight against stiff opposition, the 95th Division launched an attack south over the Lippe River and drove forward four miles against varying opposition. The 378th Infantry Regiment of this division ran into a hornet's nest at Hamm. Here strong resistance was met as the Germans battled bitterly to hold on to the key rail center. Even though it was useless to the Germans, they could see the value it held for Ninth Army, which was vitally interested in the rehabilitation of railroad lines eastward. Fighter-bombers of the XXIX Tactical Air Command, supporting the armored and infantry advance, dive-bombed an enemy troop concentration near Soest, killing an estimated 300 German soldiers. In contrast to the resistance in Hamm, many small towns in the area surrendered during the day as *Bürgermeisters* waving white flags came out to meet the advancing troops. With the XIX Corps striking heavily and more deeply southwest into the pocket, any possible enemy plans for an organized breakout in the area southwest of Lippstadt were dissipated. As the chance vanished for carving out a large-scale escape route to the east, repeated efforts were made by individuals and small groups to infiltrate through the lines and reassemble outside the pocket. Captured enemy personnel stated that they had been ordered to rejoin the beleaguered forces vainly striving to stem the onrushing Allied attack now smashing into central Germany.

Only limited gains were made in the XVI Corps zone on April 4. Heavy fire of all types held up the attacking forces of the 75th Division in the built-up area south of Waltrop and in the northern outskirts of Ickern. Along the Rhein–Herne Canal in front of the 79th and 35th Divisions, the enemy indicated his determination to defend against our southward advance into the Ruhr by blowing all bridges over the canal.

April 5 and 6 found substantial advances in the XIX Corps zone by the 95th Division and the 8th Armored converging on Soest from the northwest and northeast respectively. The city fell to the 95th Division on the 6th. Elements of the armored division advanced five miles to a point just east of Soest on the same day while Combat Command B, driving south of the city, by-passed the resistance and advanced eleven miles west. Farther to the north the 378th Infantry Regiment of the 95th Division cleared two-thirds of Hamm. On the east flank of the pocket the 194th Glider Infantry Regiment, now attached to the 8th Armored Division from the 17th Airborne Division, drove south over the Möhne River into the heavily forested area that lay between the Möhne and the Ruhr. The object of this attack was not only to clear this area of all resistance, but also further to thicken the eastern wall of the pocket. Gains up to four miles were made by the sky troopers, and two counterattacks were beaten off. Statements from prisoners indicated that large numbers of enemy troops were withdrawing into the hills south of the Möhne-Talsperre Lake.

Ninth Army Letter of Instructions No. 19, dated April 7, confirmed verbal orders that General Simpson had given to his corps commanders. XVI Corps was ordered to continue the attack to reduce the Ruhr in conjunction with the XIX Corps and First Army; to be prepared to assume command, on Army order, of all XIX Corps troops operating in the Ruhr area; to secure industrial targets and displaced persons' camps in the area; and, upon elimination of enemy opposition, to employ two infantry divisions to occupy, organize, and govern the Ruhr industrial area within the Army zone of action. The same Letter of Instructions directed XIX Corps to clear the Ruhr pocket in its zone and to be prepared to release to XVI Corps, on Army order, those units currently fighting in the Ruhr. Further instructions to XIII and XIX Corps were concerned with the drive to the east.

In order to concentrate more strength along the XVI Corps front, the 17th Airborne Division (less the 194th Glider Infantry), which had been fighting in Münster under XIII Corps, was now transferred to XVI Corps, and on April 5 and 6 the division went into line on the XVI Corps west flank as the 79th side-slipped to the east. By the night of April 6 the stage was set for a second attack south across the Rhein–Herne Canal. At 3:00 A.M. on April 7 the 79th Division crossed the canal and drove forward two and one-half miles along a four-mile front through the built-up area between Essen and Gelsenkirchen. The 35th Division maintained its positions on the north bank of the Rhein–Herne Canal, preparatory to launching a strong attack over the barrier on the following day. On the eastern flank of the corps front the 75th Division continued its advance southeast and pushed into the suburbs of Dortmund. One small counterattack was repulsed.

XIX Corps, in order to unify command among its forces driving into the shrinking pocket, formed Task Force Twaddle on April 7. This task force, commanded by Major General Harry L. Twaddle of the 95th Division, was composed of the 95th and the 8th Armored Divisions, the 194th Glider Regiment, the 15th Cavalry Group, and supporting troops. On April 7 the 95th Division completed the clearing of Hamm, captured large stores of abandoned enemy equipment in the city, and advanced two to four miles southwest of the city. The 8th Armored Division advanced three to five miles, cleared Warstein, and reached the north bank of the Möhne-Talsperre Lake.

April 8 found Task Force Twaddle pushing steadily west. All along the 22-mile front gains up to eight miles were registered. On the east flank, Hirschberg and Meschede were reached, and at Meschede contact was established by the 194th Glider Regiment with the 9th Infantry Division of First Army's III Corps, thus substantially reducing the size of the pocket.

The 17th Airborne Division joined the XVI Corps attack on April 8, when elements of one of the parachute regiments passed through the Rhein–Herne Canal bridgehead of the 79th Division and attacked southwest. The 79th fought its way into the outskirts of Essen against increasing resistance. Experiencing stiff but brief opposition, the 35th hurdled the Rhein–Herne Canal and by the end of the day forces of the division had entered Gelsenkirchen. All divisions of XVI Corps were now south of the canal. Several counterattacks along the corps front were repulsed with considerable loss to the enemy. In the dogged fighting in these urban and suburban areas, our infantry was supported by heavy artillery fires, but despite this support, the advances were generally slow. Although heavy artillery concentrations on the cities were effective in neutralizing some of the enemy's strength, once the troops entered the built-up area each separate house had to be cleared by infantry.

Paralleling the Ninth Army's advance was the drive of First Army with III Corps pushing generally west and XVIII Airborne Corps north. Resistance against First Army's forces varied greatly. On April 4 a total of ten counterattacks, all of them unsuccessful, were launched by the enemy at various points along the eastern perimeter. On April 6 substantial gains were made by the attacking forces in the east, but opposition in the south continued stubborn. Resistance slackened in the south on the 7th and good progress was made while several ineffective counterattacks were repulsed. This deterioration of resistance suggested a planned shortening of the enemy's lines, but several towns were cleaned out only after bitter fighting during which German civilians fought side by side with their army. On April 8 gains of three miles were made after particularly stiff fighting.

At noon on April 9 all Ninth Army forces fighting in the Ruhr Valley came under the command of XVI Corps when Task Force Twaddle was transferred from XIX to XVI Corps. The Army's converging attack on the Ruhr pocket had now advanced sufficiently to permit the entire front to be controlled by one corps. This move not only brought unification of command and closer coordination to the forces fighting in the pocket, but also enabled

XIX Corps to devote all its time and effort to its "eastern front" and the race to the Elbe River. Moreover, the success of both XIX Corps and First Army's III Corps pushing southwest and northwest into the Ruhr was such that the Germans were no longer deemed capable of smashing out of the great trap.

April 9 found a general enemy movement to the south, even though the defense of the large metropolitan areas remained strong. The XVI Corps attack met varied resistance. One regiment of the 79th Division pushed a deep salient into the enemy lines within two miles of the Ruhr River. Prisoners taken when the 35th Division captured Gelsenkirchen stated that high-ranking SS officers were falsifying pay books and changing into German army uniforms in the hope of being captured and evacuated without detection as SS personnel. Task Force Twaddle made rapid progress. The 95th Division advanced six miles along an eight-mile front. Elements of the 8th Armored Division reached the junction of the Ruhr and Möhne Rivers just north of Neheim while other elements cleared Werl, held up only by scattered strongpoints and defended roadblocks. Southeast of the Möhne-Talsperre Lake, opposition to the advance of the glider troops was spotty and consisted mainly of roadblocks, mines, and booby traps.

Essen—proud city of the Ruhr, "the Pittsburgh of Germany," and site of the great Krupp works, heart of the German armament industry—was captured and cleared on April 10 by the 79th Infantry and the 17th Airborne Divisions without major contact with the enemy. The city had been evacuated by the German Army, but passage was difficult because of the many blown and blocked intersections and underpasses and the extensive damage wrought by long months of aerial bombardment. Also on April 10 the 79th Division entered Bochum, and the 35th Division captured Herne. The 75th was still meeting tough resistance west of Dortmund, but late in the afternoon there were indications that this city might also be evacuated. Although light to heavy opposition by fire of all types harassed the westward movement of Task Force Twaddle, the 8th Armored gained five miles and cleared Unna, an important communication center. Fighting in the town was severe, but with the feinting of an attack from the west, while the main effort of the 8th Armored came from the south, the enemy was caught off balance and by nightfall the town was cleared.

East of Unna a sharp enemy counterattack was launched against the 8th Armored Division late in the afternoon by a battalion of SS infantry supported by Tiger tanks. The counterattack was beaten off without loss of ground. The 95th Division gained three to eight miles and entered Kamen. The 194th Glider Regiment completed its mission of clearing the heavily wooded areas between the Möhne and Ruhr Rivers.

With the fall of Bochum, Essen, and Unna, and with the report that the Duisburg area was only lightly held, the only major objective left in the Ninth Army portion of the Ruhr pocket was Dortmund. On April 11 the 75th Division reached the western outskirts of the city and the 95th Division began attacking toward it from the east. Little progress was made during the day. According to statements by prisoners of war, evacuation had been halted and the city was to be bitterly defended. The 17th Airborne Division, pushing south and west from Essen against crumbling resistance, reached the Ruhr River, captured a bridge intact at Mülheim, and against comparatively heavy enemy artillery fire, established a small bridgehead on the south bank. Much of the Ruhr River line was now held by XVI Corps, which was rapidly clearing its zone. The 17th Airborne was closed up along the river from the Rhine six miles to the east, the 79th Division held a stretch of about twelve miles, and the 35th and 75th each held four miles. Task Force Twaddle had cleared an additional six miles of the north bank.

The enemy continued his tenacious defense of Dortmund on April 12 by bitter house-to-house fighting in an effort to keep open a bridgehead south of the city through which he could evacuate his troops under the cover of a determined rearguard action. Roadblocks, mines, and artillery and mortar fire augmented the heavy small-arms fire laid down by the defenders of the city. Farther west, combat patrols from the 17th Airborne Division entered Duisburg and found the city evacuated.

Air operations against the Ruhr pocket were discontinued on April 12 when XVI Corps no longer had a battlefield over which fighter-bombers could effectively operate. In fact, during the preceding week there was little that the planes could do in this area other than aiding ground forces in the reduction of isolated strongpoints, since the season had been closed on one of the main sources of game for the hunters of XXIX Tactical Air Command when a directive was received from Ninth Air Force early in April prohibiting attacks on stationary railroad cars and locomotives within a radius of fifty miles of our front lines. This ban, affecting the entire Ruhr pocket, was issued for the purpose of saving from destruction all rolling stock which might possibly be used later by Allied forces.

By April 13 Ninth Army's role in the reduction of the Ruhr had reached the mopping-up stage. Task Force Twaddle was dissolved on this date. The 75th and 95th Divisions cleared Dortmund. Duisburg was taken over by a battalion of paratroopers, and the Ruhr River line in the Army zone was completely cleared except for one small five-square-mile pocket in the zone of the 79th Division. At the close of the day, sporadic small-arms fire and scattered artillery fire constituted the enemy activity in the zone, with the exception of light resistance in the one remaining enemy bridgehead north of the river. Units were now strengthening their hold on the north river bank and waiting to contact the advancing forces of First Army.

The last resistance was easily cleared on April 14. The day was spent in mopping up all isolated resistance in the zone and in searching for hidden enemy troops, matériel, and supplies. Ninth Army had completed its assigned share of the reduction of the Ruhr pocket. Just fourteen days earlier, its troops had been fighting along the entire 75-mile northern edge of the Ruhr pocket. XVI Corps began extensive regrouping for the corps security and military government mission, and to release forces for the Elbe River front, some 175 miles to the east. The 35th Division had begun moving to XIII Corps on April 13, and on April 14 the 8th Armored Division likewise moved east, to the vicinity of Braunschweig (Brunswick), where it was placed in Army reserve.

Meanwhile, the advance had continued in the First Army zone. The perimeter of the pocket was shrinking but only grudgingly in places. This was particularly true along the still sensitive eastern wall. On April 9 resistance slackened appreciably and gains were made in the south, while on the eastern flank, even though the opposition had diminished, difficult terrain held up the advance. On the 10th, strong local enemy counterattacks were launched, but efforts were repulsed. By April 10, too, the 86th Infantry Division and 13th Armored Division, newly arrived, had been committed by XVIII Airborne Corps, and the 5th Infantry Division had joined the battle ranks of III Corps. Enemy defenses deteriorated badly on April 12 as First Army forces made gains up to twelve miles.

The Ruhr pocket became two rapidly vanishing small pockets late in the afternoon of April 14, when contact was established between the 79th Division of XVI Corps and the 8th Infantry Division of XVIII Airborne Corps just south of Wetter. On the same day the five divisions of the Airborne Corps pushed north and made gains of five to ten miles. Very little of the original Ruhr pocket remained, although enemy resistance on the front of III Corps in the "eastern" pocket showed a decided increase on April 15, particularly in towns and on key terrain features.

As the Ruhr pocket shrunk, special precautions were taken by XVI Corps and First Army units regarding artillery "no fire" lines. With two friendly forces compressing the pocket and pushing closer together, it was necessary for each to exercise extreme care in shooting toward the other's lines. The exchange of liaison officers and the strict supervision of artillery fires insured successful accomplishment of artillery support without endangering approaching friendly troops.

In the reduction of the Ruhr and the operations east of the Rhine, artillery ammunition, other than white phosphorus and colored-smoke shell, was unrationed for the first time since Ninth Army started operations. Difficulties were encountered, however, in placing ammunition and supplies within easy reach of the artillery units because of transportation problems. Fortunately, XVI Corps, with the greater need, was better located than either of the other two corps, since it was considerably closer to the source of supply. During the fourteen days required to reduce the Ruhr, XVI Corps field artillery units fired 259,061 rounds of ammunition. In contrast, during the same period, XIX Corps, fighting both in the Ruhr and on the Army's eastern front, fired 112,612 rounds of ammunition, while XIII Corps, racing eastward, fired only 33,440 rounds.

Resistance ceased in the "eastern" pocket on April 16. Ninth Army prisoner-of-war totals were swelled as First Army continued to press northward. An imposing list of officers led their commands into the enclosures. They included Generaloberst (General) Josef Harpe, former commander of Fifth Panzer Army; Generalleutnant (Major General) Beyerlein of LIII Corps, formerly commander of Panzer Lehr Division; General der Panzer-truppen (Lieutenant General) Lüttwitz of XLVII Panzer Corps; Generalmajor (Brigadier General) Klosterkemper of the 180th Infantry Division; Generalleutnant Hammer of the 190th Infantry Division; Generalmajor Denkert of the 3d Panzer Grenadier Division; Generalmajor Ewert of the 338th Infantry Division; a Colonel Zollenkopf with remnants of the once powerful 9th Panzer Division and Generalmajor Von Waldenburg of the 116th Panzer Division.

In the Ruhr pocket the proud 116th Panzer Division, which had spearheaded the southern prong of the German Ardennes counteroffensive in December, had finally encountered a trap from which it could not escape. In its withdrawal to the south from Soest, Werl, and Unna in the face of the 8th Armored Division, it had taken along as prisoners of war two officers and two enlisted men from the 8th Armored Division. It was particularly fitting that even after the 8th Armored had left the Ruhr area and moved eastward into Army reserve, its men who were held as prisoners of war by the 116th Panzer should lead that division's surrender parties into the American lines.

Still other notables continued to pour into the prisoner of war cages. Among those captured were General der Artillerie (Lieutenant General of Artillery) Loch, artillery commander of Army Group B; Generalleutnant Lange, former commander of the 183d Infantry Division (VG); and Oberstleutnant (Lieutenant Colonel) Guderian, son of the German Army Chief of Staff, and operations officer on the staff of the 116th Panzer Division. A prize political prisoner fell into Ninth Army hands when a small patrol from the 194th Glider Regiment found Franz von Papen in a secluded hunting lodge near Stockhausen. Von Papen, whose last known assignment was that of Ambassador to Turkey, was a notorious international intriguer of both World Wars.

As the Ruhr pocket was reduced, XVI Corps occupied, organized, and governed its portion of the great industrial area. Moreover, with the rapid advance of XIII and XIX Corps to the east, the Army rear area east of the Rhine became so large that it had been necessary on April 12 to assign to XVI Corps the responsibility for security and military government of this area. Responsibility for ground protection for all Rhine bridges in the Army zone was transferred to XVI Corps from the 55th Antiaircraft Brigade, which continued to provide antiaircraft protection for the bridges. Available to XVI Corps for its security and military government mission were the 17th Airborne, and the 75th, 79th, and 95th Infantry Divisions, but the corps was directed to be prepared to release to Fifteenth Army the 17th Airborne and the 79th Infantry Divisions and the territory which they occupied.

Previous to this time the 29th Infantry Division, under direct Army control, had been assigned the rear area security and military government mission in the zone between the Lippe River and the inter-Army Group boundary from the Rhine River east to Bielefeld. (*Map No. 13.*) In this large zone the division had speedily organized and operated displaced persons' camps, guarded vital intelligence and supply installations, and maintained the security of the lines of communication. The 29th Division now passed from direct Army control to XVI Corps, but the corps was ordered to be prepared to release the division for employment by XIII Corps.

By midnight of April 17 the Ruhr pocket was no more. The First Army had closed with Ninth Army all along the Ruhr River and organized resistance was at an end. The reduction of the Ruhr had cost Ninth Army 2,452 casualties, including 341 killed, 1,986 wounded, 121 missing, and 4 captured. In contrast to these losses, the Army had taken 36,960 prisoners in the Ruhr alone in the first fourteen days of April. The entire fabulous area had been captured in what began on April 1 as the greatest double envelopment in military history and ended a little over two weeks later with a loss to Germany of not only her most vital industrial establishments and an inestimable amout of matériel but also a great part of her fighting forces.

When the prize of the Ruhr fell to Ninth Army troops, although seemingly complete destruction was the first impression, the years of aerial bombing and the recent fighting had by no means knocked out the potential productive capacity of one of the richest industrial areas in the world. Many of the great plants were in fair shape and capable of continued operation. Although most installations showed considerable damage, machines and other facilities were often in surprisingly good condition; some were continuing to operate, and others could be put into operation after a few repairs. With typical German thoroughness, building supplies were usually available nearby to repair damages, and raw materials were generally on hand to continue production. In many cases, whole sections of plants either had been moved to protected places or had been so sheltered from bombing and artillery fire that production could continue up to the time they were overrun by our troops. The more vital materials and equipment had ofttimes been dispersed to give greater security from bombing. Thus some industries were extended over a wide radius, with special shops located in isolated spots not charted by the Allied Air Forces. A large barn, warehouse, or other unimpressive looking building might house a complete department of a major industry. Many vital plants on the fringe of the district were practically intact and proved very valuable in supplying needs for Ninth Army. A case in point was the Westphalia Separator Company, which soon was making many badly needed ordnance parts. In summary, on the Army's occupation of the heart of the Ruhr, industry was estimated to be operating at an average of better than fifty per cent capacity, and this probably could have been raised to eighty-five or ninety per cent within four to six weeks.

The seizure, safeguarding, and exploitation of the Ruhr industrial facilities and of the research establishments connected therewith were all a part of an elaborately worked out system for securing "intelligence targets." Long before the advance into Germany, voluminous and detailed plans had been made by the higher Allied headquarters for the intelligence target program. Broadly speaking, intelligence targets included everything which was of particular importance in assisting the Allies to continue the prosecution of the war against both Germany and Japan, and in indicating the enemy's future intentions and capabilities. Intelligence targets thus covered an almost unlimited scope of scientific and military interest, ranging from such "subjects" as an obscure professor working on a new chemical formula to the great Krupp works, near Essen, where completed instruments of war were produced. From Allied intelligence sources both the general categories of intelligence targets and the actual or suspected locations had been obtained. These were broken down into such classifications as specific military and political headquarters, manufacturing plants, research laboratories, proving grounds, stores of various types of war matériel and raw materials, underground factories, records, archives, secret documents, master files and plans, and particular key personnel and alleged war criminals.

Both of the Army Groups furnished dossiers of information on selected intelligence targets and, to a considerable extent, specified who would be authorized to exploit certain ones and the priority in which they would be exploited. Army headquarters broke all targets down into groups depending upon their locality. These were then sent to the troop units operating or expected to operate in the area. A unit was therefore able to study its targets in detail and was in a position to capture and guard them promptly. In the exploitation of intelligence targets the Army was assisted by the main portion of a special 12th Army Group force, known as T Force, which operated with Ninth Army during the month of April. In addition, special technical intelligence teams were attached to the Army and worked through and with the Army and subordinate unit technical services and intelligence agencies. It was anticipated that long-range intelligence would be uncovered, some of which might require years to exploit fully. All information obtained was to be made jointly available to the American and British branches concerned and, in appropriate cases, to American and British scientists, industrialists, and economists who could use the information in furtherance of the Allied war effort.

To systematize the task of assembling the vast body of information and disseminating it to all concerned, the Army published a detailed *Daily Intelligence Target Report,* which was distributed to higher headquarters and to lower headquarters to include brigades. Information was thus made available on the discovery of targets and their location, character, and condition. On succeeding days the progress of exploitation was recorded, until each target was closed. The system permitted consistent and effective follow-up by Army intelligence personnel so that, in spite of numerous and frequent changes of units guarding the targets, no target was "lost." Once a target was located, it could be protected and eventually exploited even under the most trying tactical and administrative conditions.

Turning now to the sweep to the Elbe, the planning for the great operation had long since been accomplished. Preceding the assault of the Rhine River line, the staffs, not only of Ninth Army but also of XIII and XIX Corps, had engaged in studying the operation. It had been decided long before that both XIII and XIX Corps would be employed in breaking out of the bridgehead once it was established by XVI Corps. XIX Corps, with one or two armored divisions and two or three infantry divisions, was to be the southern prong of the two-headed drive eastward. XIII Corps, to be composed of one armored division, two infantry divisions, and possibly one airborne division, would be the northern prong, attacking eastward between XIX Corps and British Second Army. The plan envisioned a fast armored drive assisted by motorized infantry divisions. Armored units were to sweep ahead as rapidly as possible to the east, aiming their tanks at Berlin, the coveted goal of all Allied forces. The infantry would follow, clear all rear areas, reduce strongpoints, and assist in river crossings. Enemy resistance was not expected in enough force to withstand this powerful two-pronged attack. The greatest difficulties to be overcome would be the natural barriers obstructing eastward movement and the necessity of stretching supply lines almost to the breaking point.

The final phase of the European campaign offered an opportunity to the Army to capitalize to the utmost on the mobility and fire power characteristics of armored forces. The terrain and the weather were ideal. The first assault across the Rhine and the subsequent drive eastward had rolled up the German defenses and had foreshadowed the disintegration which would open the way for the armor to break out and pour forward across the Reich. The static situation which had prevailed for the two-week period before the crossing of the Rhine had given ample time for armored units to put vehicles in first-class condition, to replenish supplies, and to rest veterans and train reinforcements. All units were brought up to full strength in vehicles, and a substantial Army reserve was ready for immediate replacement. The effect of the armored onslaught, flanked and assisted by hard-driving motorized infantry, equalled and exceeded the anticipations of the most enthusiastic proponents of armor as a weapon of exploitation.

Once the north face of the Ruhr had been sealed off by the junction of Ninth and First Armies, the entire north German plain was laid open to attack. (*Map No. 13.*) The southern fringe of the plain, across which Ninth Army would attack, was moderately hilly. It was broken by the formidable wooded and rugged region of the Teutoburger Wald and the Weser hill country. In addition to numerous canals, six main rivers, flowing generally northward, presented potential obstacles to the eastward advance. These were the Weser, the Leine, the Innerste, the Oker, the Aller, and the Elbe. The larger cities such as Münster, Hannover, Braunschweig, and Magdeburg could provide troublesome pockets of resistance. In the southern part of the Army zone the rugged Harz Mountains and Forest, lying astride the Ninth-First Army boundary, offered possibilities for a prolonged defense.

The period of the drive to the Elbe was characterized by broken withdrawals on the part of the enemy, intermingled with periods of moderate to bitter resistance when the beleaguered German Army found time and matériel sufficient to organize local stands. The attacking forces of Ninth Army generally met units made up of battle groups, service troops, flak personnel, replacement and training units and other spare parts, and a few hastily organized, under-manned, stop-gap "divisions." Nearly all of the first-line field divisions, against which the Army had been battering since the Rhine crossing, were bottled up in the Ruhr pocket. But the Germans, scattered and dispersed though they were, often fought bitterly with any forces they could scrape together. In an attempt to stem the rapid advances, they even threw into the line some special units made up of rehabilitated individuals. These were identified by such descriptive names as "Stomach Battalions," indicating that the unit was composed of personnel suffering from stomach ailments. Troops had thus been gathered into special units both to simplify their medical care and to label their probable fighting ability. Commitment of such units was clearly indicative of the strained and tightened manpower conditions with which the German Army was faced.

Similarly indicative was the increased appearance of Volkssturm units, the hastily organized German home guard of old men and boys. The Volkssturm had been first met in appreciable numbers by Ninth Army in its drive from the Roer to the Rhine. In the advance deeper into Germany they were encountered in considerable strength. Their fighting ability varied greatly. Always equipped with a wide variety of weapons and wearing everything from hastily converted civilian clothing to a mixture of German Army and Nazi Party uniforms, some put up fairly stiff resistance, while others lasted only as long as SS troops stood back of them, ready to shoot them down if they faltered. Under Ninth Army

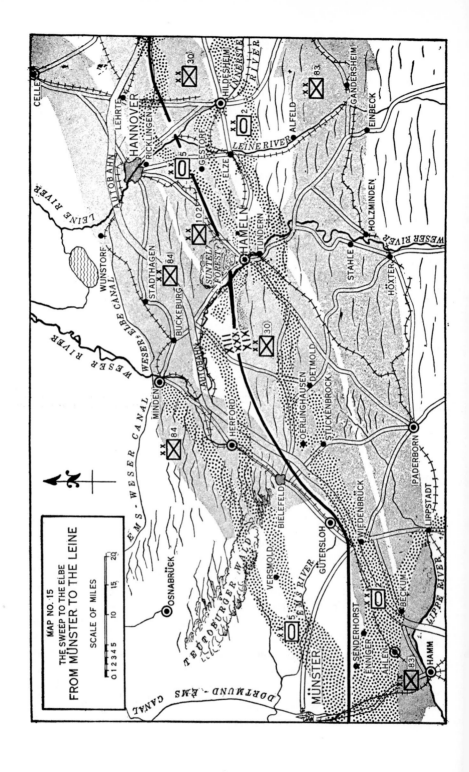

MAP NO. 15
THE SWEEP TO THE ELBE
FROM MÜNSTER TO THE LEINE

SCALE OF MILES

0 1 2 3 4 5   10   15   20

policy, established when the units were first encountered, Volkssturm prisoners were habitually disarmed and disbanded in place and were returned to their civilian occupations, to prevent clogging the prisoner-of-war channels.

By the beginning of April the German air force had given up trying to knock out the Rhine River bridges and had shifted to its old pattern of harassing attacks against forward elements. The rapid advance of the Army was destined to overrun many airfields, and those that did remain in German hands were continually under attack by XXIX Tactical Air Command. It was surprising that the enemy was able to offer even the degree of aerial resistance that he did during April.

Considering now in detail the operations of XIII and XIX Corps in the drive to the east out of the Rhine bridgehead (*Map No. 14*), on March 30 XIX Corps was attacking eastward from the Haltern–Dülmen area with the 2d Armored Division reinforced by two motorized infantry regiments, one from the 30th Division and one from the 95th Division. The corps was also engaged in positioning the remainder of its combat forces for the attack. The 30th Division passed from XVI Corps to XIX Corps command on this date and the major portion of the division was assembling along the Lippe River southwest of Dorsten. The 83d Division, with the attached 15th Cavalry Group, was assembled near Haltern, preparing to follow and mop up behind the 2d Armored. The 113th Cavalry Group had also moved over the Rhine and was assembled in the troop-jammed area along the Lippe River. XIX Corps was ready for a powerful thrust to the east.

The 2d Armored Division roared eastward almost unopposed on March 31. Blown bridges over the Dortmund–Ems Canal proved to be but a slight obstacle as division engineers quickly spanned the barrier. The end of the day found the division thirty to thirty-five miles to the east. Sendenhorst, Enniger, Ahlen, Beckum, and Wiedenbrück were cleared during the day.

Culminating a breath-taking advance of fifty miles in less than three days, Combat Command B of the 2d Armored veered off to the southeast and established contact with First Army troops at Lippstadt on April 1. Combat Command A, on the division's north flank, sped fifteen miles northeast along the *Autobahn*, advancing as far as Stukenbrock. (*Map No. 15.*) The 113th Cavalry Group was committed along the XIX Corps' north flank and maintained contact with XIII Corps. The 83d Division began moving forward to relieve the elements of the 2d Armored along the northeast face of the newly formed Ruhr pocket.

Meanwhile, XIII Corps had been building up its forces east of the Rhine. (*Map No. 14.*) On March 31, as the Rhine bridges at Wesel passed to Ninth Army's control, the 5th Armored Division began crossing the river and moving into a forward assembly area near Senden, eight miles southwest of Münster. Late in the evening of March 31, the 11th Cavalry Group crossed the Rhine, and on April 1 the bulk of the 84th Division was likewise assembled southwest of Münster. The 102d Infantry Division remained west of the Rhine under Fifteenth Army's control, but was destined for return to XIII Corps as soon as additional forces could be made available to Fifteenth Army. The 17th Airborne Division, which had passed to Ninth Army and XIX Corps from British Second Army and XVIII Airborne Corps on March 30 as it was advancing on Münster, again changed hands on March 31 when it passed in place in the Münster area from XIX Corps to XIII Corps.

At 6:00 A.M. on April 1, XIII Corps unleashed its attack north of and parallel to that of XIX Corps. The 5th Armored jumped off from a line of departure near Senden, and by midnight had raced eastward 25 miles. Initial resistance was slight, but late in the day German defenses stiffened appreciably. In Münster the Germans were clinging tenaciously to the town; the 17th Airborne Division advanced in the bomb-shattered city, block by block, against dogged resistance from machine guns, mortars, and antiaircraft weapons. Two field artillery groups comprising five battalions of XIII Corps artillery were placed in support of the airborne division. The 11th Cavalry Group screened the corps' north flank and maintained contact with the British forces northwest of Münster.

In XIX Corps on April 2 (*Map No. 15*), Combat Command B of the 2d Armored Division, now relieved on the Ruhr front by elements of the 83d Infantry Division, again turned eastward and scored an eleven-mile gain. Combat Command A was held up in the wooded and mountainous Teutoburger Wald, where opposition was met from small groups of infantry supported by some armor and antitank weapons. The 30th Infantry Division began moving into the Wald to clear passes for the armor. The race eastward in the XIII Corps zone continued without cessation as the 5th Armored Division roared on 15 to 25 miles, clearing Versmold and reaching the *Autobahn* northeast of Bielefeld. Herford was defended by several hundred foot soldiers supported by a number of 88mm self-propelled guns, but this opposition was quickly overcome. Meanwhile the 17th Airborne Division, fighting on in Münster, cleared two-thirds of the city by the end of the day.

The XIX Corps advance was again held up on April 3, as the infantry battled on in the Teutoburger Wald. Late in the day, however, three mountain passes were cleared, and one combat command from the 2d Armored passed through to clear Oerlinghausen. In the XIII Corps zone the 5th Armored Division struck forward again and reached the Weser, the next major river barrier which separated Ninth Army forces from Berlin. After an advance of eleven miles, the tankers drew up along the west bank of the river south of Minden and consolidated their positions while the 84th Infantry Division was brought up so that the joint forces could force a crossing of the river. Consistent with precedent, the fleeing Germans had blown the Weser bridges. Back at Münster, the last opposition in the city was crushed, and the 17th Airborne turned over the city to military government administrators and began moving south to join the ranks of XVI Corps in the battle to clear the Ruhr. However, north of Münster, the situation was anything but quiet, as the 11th Cavalry Group learned. As the group command post was displacing forward to a site some ten miles northeast of the city, the headquarters personnel were forced into a pitched battle to clear the area. By the end of this short but sharp conflict, two hundred Germans had been killed and another hundred captured in the immediate vicinity of the new command post. Such isolated and small but bitter engagements were to be characteristic of the fighting from now on.

In the XIX Corps zone April 4 saw the remainder of the 2d Armored Division, utilizing the hard-won passes through the Teutoburger Wald, smash ahead some 32 miles to the Weser near Hameln (Hamelin), the Pied Pipers town. The 30th Division turned its attention to a thorough mop-up of the Teutoburger Wald and made good progress in clearing the city of Detmold. The 83d Division, having been relieved in the Ruhr pocket by elements of the 8th Armored and 95th Infantry Divisions, was now moving into position southwest of the armored spearhead and beginning to attack east on a wide front. On the same day, in XIII Corps, the 5th Armored strengthened its grasp on the west bank of the Weser. The 84th Division continued to move forward, and elements of the division cleared Bielefeld. To the north of the corps British forces had also reached the Weser and had captured Minden, where contact was now established between the Americans and the British. The day also saw the return of the 102d Division to XIII Corps from the Fifteenth Army, and the division began assembling at Lembeck, just west of Haltern. (*Map No. 14.*)

Thunderbolts of XXIX Tactical Air Command gave invaluable assistance to both corps on April 4 as the fighter-bombers razed strongpoints near Detmold and Minden. (*Map No. 15.*) Weather conditions in the first three days of April had been far from favorable for fighter-bomber activity, but as the weather cleared, more and more German installations felt the fury of the bombing attacks.

On April 4, also, a small tactical headquarters of the forward echelon of the Army Headquarters moved from München-Gladbach and established the first Ninth Army command post east of the Rhine, in the dwellings and local school building of the small village of Haltern, so that closer contact could be maintained with the fast-moving operations. The bulk of the forward echelon remained at München-Gladbach, and Army Headquarters operated in three echelons—tactical at Haltern, forward at München-Gladbach and rear at Rheydt—until the two elements of the forward echelon were reunited at Gütersloh on April 12. These frequent moves of the various elements of the Army command post were accompanied by frenzied and intense activity on the part of the Army signal troops. Normally, three days were needed to install the necessary switchboard and carrier facilities for the numerous telephone installations at a new headquarters, and the checking, correcting, and expansion of these facilities required an equal amount of time after the new command post opened. Since the command post was destined to move three times in the next twenty days, this activity was to be continuous.

April 5 found XIX Corps moving over the Weser River (*Map No. 15*), as the 2d Armored drove on through Hameln, crossed the river at three places, and established a bridgehead three miles deep and four miles wide. Reconnaissance elements of the division pushed on an additional five miles and established roadblocks to protect the bridgehead from counterattack. A task force of the division cleared Tundern. The 2d Armored had moved through Hameln so swiftly that many strongpoints were bypassed. The 30th Division was moved quickly and cleared the town against bitter and suicidal opposition. The citizens of Hameln watched helplessly, just as their ancestors had done when the Pied Piper had cleared the town many years before. XIII Corps also forced a crossing of the Weser on April 5, when the 84th Division passed through elements of the 5th Armored holding the river line just south of Minden. Artillery fire from the 84th, the 5th Armored, and XIII Corps Artillery supported the attack, and night found the 84th Division holding a firm and solid bridgehead east of the Weser. The miscellaneous German forces defending the Weser River line in front of both corps fought stubbornly with small arms, mortars, antiaircraft and self-propelled guns, and tanks, but were unable to resist the skillfully handled attack or to prevent the rapid expansion and consolidation of positions east of the river.

The 2d Armored shook loose from its Weser bridgehead on April 6 to knife forward thirteen miles to reach the next river barrier, the Leine, at Elze, about eight miles west of Hildesheim. To the south of the armored division, the 83d Infantry Division, sweeping over a broad front, closed up to the Weser in the Stahle–Höxter area, and crossed elements of one regiment over bridges in the 2d Armored Division zone south of Hameln. To the north in the XIII Corps zone, the 84th Division was still pushing out in all directions from the site of the Weser bridgehead, and by the end of the day two regiments had secured a twenty-square mile area east of the river. In the face of sharp resistance from antiaircraft and artillery fire, two bridges across the Weser were completed and placed in operation.

Ninth Army Letter of Instructions No. 19, dated April 7, has already been mentioned insofar as it pertained to the reduction of the Ruhr. In this same letter General Simpson confirmed verbal instructions previously issued for the drive of XIII and XIX Corps to the east. XIX Corps was ordered to seize the line Einbeck (exclusive)–Alfeld–Gestorf (exclusive), maintaining contact with First Army on the right and XIII Corps on the left and protecting the right flank of Ninth Army. XIII Corps was ordered to seize the line Gestorf (inclusive)–Wunstorf, protecting the right (south) flank of 21 Army Group and assisting its rapid advance to the Leine River. Both corps were ordered to eliminate pockets of resistance in their zones west of the Weser River and to be prepared to continue the advance east to the Elbe River and for further advance, beyond that, to the east or northeast.

German demolition experts and engineers were caught napping by the 2d Armored on April 7 as tanks, advancing seven to ten miles eastward, crossed both the Leine and Innerste Rivers on bridges captured intact. From now on engineer troops, as well as ordnance bomb-disposal squads, were kept busy in removing demolition charges which the retreating Germans had placed on bridges and abutments but had failed, for various reasons, to detonate. On April 7 the 83d Infantry Division continued its crossing of the Weser and began moving east to the Leine River against light resistance. On the same day, XIII Corps forces engaged in further expansion of their Weser bridgehead east of Minden, and elements of the 84th Infantry Division advanced as much as eight miles to Bückeburg and Stadthagen. The 102d Infantry Division moved forward over a wide front in the corps rear areas, searching out and overcoming by-passed pockets of resistance.

April 7 proved to be one of XXIX Tactical Air Command's best days during the operation. Four hundred and thirty-two sorties were flown, and twenty-three armored vehicles and large quantities of railway rolling stock were claimed destroyed by the Thunderbolt pilots. An attack was carried out against a military objective in the town of Halberstadt, east of the Harz Mountains (*Map No. 13.*). Evidently the buildings attacked were storehouses containing vast quantities of high explosives, for the fighter-bombers touched off an explosion whose concussion was felt by planes at an altitude of 5000 feet. One entire section of the city was completely leveled.

Both infantry and armor made notable advances on April 8. (*Map No. 15.*) In the XIX Corps zone the 83d Division, gaining twelve miles and capturing numerous towns, had its advance elements seven miles east of the Leine River. Elsewhere in the corps zone, one combat command of the 2d Armored captured Hildesheim before noon. In XIII Corps it was a banner day for the 84th as the division struck east for the great city of Hannover. By the

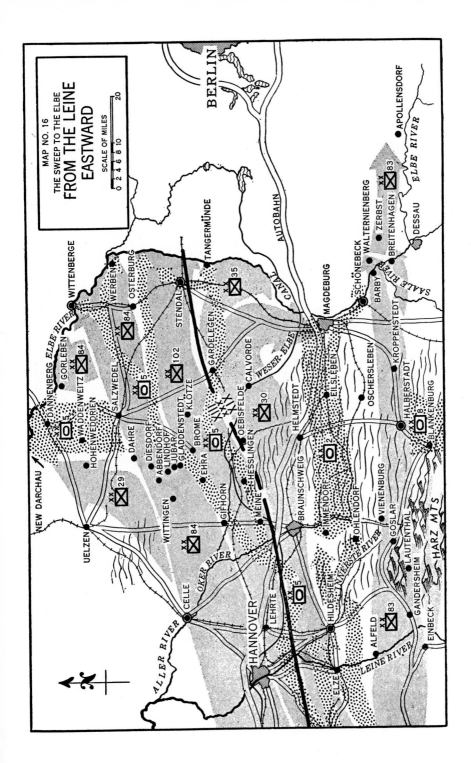

MAP NO. 16
THE SWEEP TO THE ELBE
FROM THE LEINE
EASTWARD

SCALE OF MILES

0 2 4 6 8 10   20

end of the day, twenty-five miles lay behind the forward elements and Hannover was only five miles ahead. One regiment of the division dashed fifteen miles east and crossed the Leine River at Ricklingen, just south of Hannover, using a bridge which had been taken intact by the 11th Cavalry Group. Division reconnaissance elements were seven miles northwest of the city. Over 3,000 prisoners were taken by the 84th Division during the day. XIII Corps again turned loose the 5th Armored, and the division sent elements south into the XIX Corps zone, where the Weser River was crossed using the Hameln bridges. Once over the river, the attack turned quickly northeast into the XIII Corps zone of advance and the tanks rumbled on fifteen miles to Gestorf.

After capturing Hildesheim, the 2d Armored Division was halted in place, for Ninth Army had been directed by 12th Army Group to hold up its eastward advance to permit the other armies on its flank to come abreast. Accordingly, on April 9 the armored division paused and consolidated its gains in the center of the XIX Corps zone. The 30th Infantry Division pulled into position on the north of the 2d Armored. To the south, the other flanking infantry division, the 83d, continued its advance east of the Leine, overrunning Gandersheim, which, together with Einbeck, had been captured earlier in the day by the 113th Cavalry Group. Thus the XIX Corps quickly consolidated positions, mopped up rear areas, and completed its planning to push on to the Elbe and Berlin should orders from higher headquarters so direct.

The progress of the 5th Armored in the XIII Corps zone was accelerated on April 9 and the close of the day saw the corps' major elements midway between the Rhine and Berlin. Combat Command R jumped off early in the morning from the Gestorf area, headed northeast. After advancing eleven miles, a stubborn pocket of resistance containing flak guns temporarily halted the advance. The combat command wheeled south into the XIX Corps zone, skirted the resistance, turned northeast again, and crunched ahead an additional 23 miles for a total advance of 34 miles for the day. Leading elements had severed the *Autobahn* and other principal roads between Hannover and Braunschweig (*Map No. 16*) and were just seventeen miles short of Braunschweig. The 84th Infantry Division assembled a few miles outside Hannover and took a well deserved pause, while *Parlemen-*

taires from the division approached the local Gauleiter with a demand for the surrender of the city. When the demand was refused, plans were completed for the reduction of Hannover the following day. The 102d Division, continuing its mop-up of the corps rear area, had worked up to and crossed the Weser River, although several spots of heavy resistance were found. Such pockets of opposition proved time and again to be very troublesome to supply and signal troops. Vehicles carrying rations and ammunition forward were constantly harassed. Temporary telephone and telegraph circuits offered excellent opportunities for sabotage, and accessible wire lines were often cut, temporarily disrupting communications between Army, corps, and divisions.

The waiting Ninth Army forces got the go-ahead signal from 12th Army Group and on April 10 XIX Corps was again unleashed to drive east. (*Map No. 16.*) The motorized infantry of the 83d Division made the main advance as they covered as much as 22 miles to reach Lautenthal, Goslar, and Vienenburg. The Germans offered little or no resistance. The 2d Armored led off from north and south of Hildesheim with two combat commands abreast. Combat Command A, after moving 12 miles, ran into brief but strong resistance west of the great Hermann Goering Steel Works at Immendorf, where the many antiaircraft guns sited for the defense of the industrial area were depressed for ground fire in an effort to halt the onrushing tankers and armored infantrymen. Sixty-seven antiaircraft guns, ranging from 50mm to 128mm in caliber, were destroyed or captured in this action. Combat Command B found the going easier and rolled almost unopposed for twenty miles, clearing Ohlendorf. The 30th Division, on the corps north flank, was also pushing ahead vigorously and made gains of 12 to 20 miles. Leading elements of one regiment were within four miles of Braunschweig.

The 84th Division threw all three infantry regiments into Hannover on April 10, and after a brief but bitter struggle, captured and secured the city. Back in the Ruhr pocket, XVI Corps captured Essen. Thus to Ninth Army, on the same day, fell two of the Reich's largest and most important cities. Elsewhere, in the XIII Corps zone, the attack continued unabated. The 5th Armored, racing ahead to the east, advanced another 15 miles, reaching the little town of Meine, seven miles north of Braunschweig and some 33 miles east of Hannover.

In the operational history of Ninth Army, no day is more memorable than April 11, 1945. Early in the day, division, corps, and Army all lost contact with the 2d Armored Division's Combat Command B, which was headed east in two parallel columns from the vicinity of Ohlendorf. Shortly after 8:00 o'clock that evening came a laconic report from the combat command that electrified everyone. "We're on the Elbe." The roaring Shermans had covered 57 miles since morning. The northern column of Combat Command B was at the outskirts of Magdeburg; the southern column was on the Elbe at Schönebeck. The 2d Armored Division had crashed across 200 miles of German soil since it had first attacked from the vicinity of Haltern fourteen days earlier. Ninth Army was the first Allied army to reach the Elbe. In nineteen days, it had fought its way 226 miles from the Rhine. It was truly "the blitzkrieg in reverse." The only things that moved faster than the Ninth Army in those nineteen days were a few fleeing remnants of the broken, battered, and beaten German Army.

On April 11, while the armor was reaching the Elbe, the 83d Division also cut loose. At the end of the day, when gains up to 32 miles had been registered, the division was referring to itself as the 83d "Armored" Division. Halberstadt and Kroppenstedt fell to the doughboys. To the north, the 30th Division, smashing into Braunschweig, was engaged in a bitter struggle. Resistance was extremely stiff along the canal just west of the city where the defense was studded with 88mm dual-purpose guns, railroad guns, and other artillery of a variety of calibers. These weapons poured in heavy fire on the attackers, but after a violent action, the line was forced and the enemy lost more than sixty 88mm guns. As the attack pressed in toward the heart of the city, resistance slackened and crumbled. One-fourth of the city had been secured by nightfall.

The advance in XIII Corps did not slow on the 11th. The 5th Armored reached Hesslingen and Ehra after gains of ten to twenty miles. Scattered enemy strongpoints and roadblocks offered the only opposition to the advance. The 84th Division mopped up Hannover while the 102d, employing all three regiments, continued its clearing of the corps rear area. One by-passed group of German fanatics in the heavily wooded Weser hills offered desperate resistance to the clean-up force of the 407th Infantry Regiment.

Even though the Elbe had been reached in the XIX Corps zone, the attack continued without let-up on April 12. The 83d Division raced on 25 miles and reached the Elbe at Barby. One regiment had been dropped off far to the west to probe into the Harz Mountains, attempting to push through to the south and effect contact with First Army, which was clearing north into the mountains. Heavy and bitter resistance was offered by the German forces holed up in this formidable terrain feature. In the 2d Armored Division zone the Elbe River bridge at Schönebeck was blown by the Germans on the morning of April 12, but late that evening the division ferried two battalions of armored infantry across the river and thereby crossed the last river barrier before Berlin. The crossing sites came under heavy enemy small-arms and artillery fire, and stiff opposition was met on the east bank of the river. Work was commenced immediately on bridging the Elbe, but the enemy artillery fire made construction extremely difficult. Early in the day the 30th Division secured all of Braunschweig. Leaving only one battalion behind in the city, the remainder of the division pushed on to Calvorde, 33 miles to the east and only 21 miles northwest of Magdeburg, where the 2d Armored was by this time negotiating for the surrender of the city.

XIII Corps moved up to the Elbe on April 12. Combat Command A of the 5th Armored took off from the Hesslingen area, and after a flying advance of 50 miles, the tanks drew up at Tangermunde, just 53 miles from Berlin. The bridge over the Elbe at this point was intact when the tankers reached it, but as they attempted to swarm across, the bridge was blown. The 5th Armored Division had spearheaded the XIII Corps advance of over 200 miles in thirteen days, to reach the Elbe closer to Berlin than any other American unit. In the last stages of the advance, elements of the division made effective and typically American use of their own soldiers who spoke German. As each town was taken, they phoned the next town ahead for the Germans there to get ready to receive the advancing columns—a field application of psychological warfare that often bore fruit in withdrawals or surrenders. Along the Elbe River the 5th Armored immediately fanned out north and south to clear the west bank and began laying plans to assault over the river.

Ninth Army now had strong elements of both XIII and XIX

Corps on the Elbe. The entire advance had been a striking demonstration of highly skilled, well equipped professional troops performing a task for which they were fully prepared and admirably trained. Everyone knew his job. There was no hesitation, no indecision. This was the culminating battle toward which all efforts had pointed. The response from all ranks was superb.

The daring thrusts of armor and motorized infantry might be described by tacticians as "exploiting the enemy's rear areas after breaching his frontal positions." The men of the divisions had a simpler name for it—"rat race." It was the kind of war many of them knew well, from the advances across France. The tanks, half-tracks, and motor columns kept running off the maps. Commanders relentlessly pushed their advance to keep the enemy off balance and to break through his resistance each time before he could build up strength. No one stopped to eat, no one stopped to rest, no one did anything but shoot and push on. People got tired and needed sleep. But they usually did not get it. "Would you trade sleep for blood? Get up and get going!" was the reply given by an armored combat command leader when an attached unit leader protested at having his troops routed out to move on at 2:00 o'clock in the morning.

On April 12, in the XIII Corps zone, while the 5th Armored was striking to the Elbe, the 84th Division also moved rapidly east from the Hannover area in multiple columns, utilizing all east-west roads in its zone. Gains of ten to fifteen miles were made, and one regiment reached Celle, where contact was made with British Second Army. The 102d Division now up front, likewise attacked east during the day, through the zone overrun by the 5th Armored, and pushed out 15 miles to Gifhorn and Meine. One regiment of the 102d, the 407th Infantry, passed to XIII Corps reserve to clear a stubborn pocket of resistance far to the rear in the Suntel Forest (*Map No. 15*).

The forward echelon of Army Headquarters moved on April 12 to Gütersloh. Here the small tactical headquarters from Haltern merged with the remainder of the forward echelon, which moved up from München-Gladbach. In Gütersloh the headquarters took over the Luftwaffe Signal Corps Barracks, a large, well built permanent installation consisting of numerous two-story brick buildings, many joined by covered walks. Located on its own enclosed military reservation on the outskirts of Gütersloh, it had been a training center for German air force signal personnel and provided excellent facilities for the Army command post.

At Gütersloh an augmentation was made in signal communications with 12th Army Group when a new high-speed radio net was placed in operation. Prior to this installation there were only two other nets in Europe employing similar equipment. The new set, using the Boehme system of high-speed automatic transmitting and recording, was capable of operating up to 400 words per minute. Equipped with a transmitter four times as powerful as any previously available, it was able to override the clutter of other signals in the air. Since 12th Army Group Headquarters was so far distant at this time, it had often been difficult to make teletypewriter contact, and a great portion of this type of signal traffic was now diverted to the new station, which proved a valuable aid to the signal operations of the Army.

Air operations of XXIX Tactical Air Command reached a critical stage in early April. Adequate airfields existed only west of the Rhine. Captured Luftwaffe bases at Münster, Gutersloh, Paderborn, and Braunschweig (Map No. 13) were destroyed to such an extent that only emergency strips could be made ready without extensive construction and repairs. Then too, there were stupendous supply problems, complicated by the thousands of tons of bombs and ammunition plus the millions of gallons of gasoline necessary to sustain the greedy fighter-bombers and tactical reconnaissance planes. General Nugent's aviation engineers and supply personnel completed all plans for a permanent move to new bases, and he presented his needs to the Army Commander. The controlling factor was the tonnage crossing the Rhine River. With full knowledge that he would be giving up the major portion of the support afforded by XXIX Tactical Air Command, General Simpson decided that he could not spare sufficient tonnage, from that needed for gasoline and food for his racing troops, to permit the Tactical Air Command to move its bases forward. He judged that the German disintegration was such that it was more vital to keep the ground troops moving with great speed than to maintain the complete continuity of air operations.

The Tactical Air Command's operations therefore became restricted. Carrying two wing tanks or a single belly tank, the planes could reach the front lines but could carry on only very limited operations once there. Although two emergency refueling strips set up at Münster and Gütersloh aided somewhat in easing the long hauls, the facilities of these two fields could refuel and rearm only a squadron or two at one time. With upward of fifteen squadrons operating simultaneously, many aircraft still were forced to make the long round trip from behind the Rhine to the Elbe without refueling. When eventually the logistical situation permitted the fighter groups of XXIX Tactical Air Command to be moved up to bases within operational distance of the front line, the international air boundary between the Russian air forces and the American air forces all but coincided with the front lines of Ninth Army, and the Army had virtually ceased all offensive operations to the east.

On April 13 a second bridgehead was established east of the Elbe in the XIX Corps zone when two battalions of the 83d Division fought their way across the river east of Barby and two miles inland to capture the small but important road center of Walternienburg. (*Map No. 16.*) Opposition was heavy and German artillery fire increased. From the time of the initial crossing, the Germans launched frequent counterattacks, using tanks to bolster their infantry. To the north, the 2d Armored bridgehead expanded to six square miles, and an infantry battalion from the 30th Division was moved across to reinforce the two armored infantry battalions already east of the river. All activity by XIX Corps east of the Elbe was bitterly assailed by the Germans, who bestirred themselves to defend the last natural barrier before Berlin. Three new enemy "divisions" appeared. All were recently formed scratch outfits at best, and were labelled Division Scharnhorst, Division Potsdam, and Division Von Hütten.

Enemy air attacks against the Elbe bridgehead were the most sustained of any encountered by Ninth Army. The Luftwaffe had been unable to stop the crossing of the Roer, the Rhine, and the Weser and had soon given up all attempts to do so, but he kept up his attacks at the Elbe for a full week after the crossing. Previously, every Ninth Army bridgehead had expanded so swiftly that air attacks could have no critical effect. The advances had been too rapid to permit air power to isolate and destroy the troops on the far shore. The German pattern of attack against each river crossing had been the same all the way through—a slow reaction, a build-up in intensity, and then an abrupt cessation of attack, usually in response to an urgent call from some other threatened zone. However, the Elbe River bridgeheads presented an entirely different picture. The threat to Berlin was too strong to be ignored. A total of 421 German planes attacked the bridgeheads during the first week, and Ninth Army antiaircraft units set up their best over-all record in destruction. Thirty per cent of all attacking planes was either destroyed or claimed destroyed. By April 21 enemy air activity began to dwindle as the advances of the Allied armies robbed the Luftwaffe of operational air fields.

XIII Corps rapidly expanded and strengthened its hold along the west bank of the Elbe. On April 13 elements of the 5th Armored reached Werben and Wittenberge. The latter town was 40 miles downstream, or north, of Tangermunde. Stendal was captured. Farther back on the flank, the 84th Division, operating along an eight-mile front, advanced some twenty miles and by evening held a line from Gladdenstedt to Wittingen. The 102d Division, sweeping forward over by-passed areas, advanced to the east and southeast to Klötze.

The Germans continued to throw all of their remaining resources at the two potentially dangerous bridgeheads across the Elbe in the XIX Corps zone. On the morning of April 14 a heavy counterattack was launched against the northern bridgehead of Combat Command B of the 2d Armored, which had not been able to get tanks across the river into its infantry-held bridgehead. The Germans contested all river-crossing operations with well placed artillery fires, supplemented by direct fire from large-caliber antiaircraft guns used in a ground role. Efforts to complete bridging against the strong resistance proved unsuccessful. During the day the enemy counterattacks against the bridgehead mounted in such fury and intensity that it was decided to withdraw the troops, and by mid-afternoon the combat command, protected by fighter-bombers of XXIX Tactical Air Command, had succeeded in pulling back to the west bank of the river. Despite the ferocity of the German counterattacks, which were supported by air, heavy artillery, and tanks, the losses suffered by the 2nd Armored were light and the withdrawal was orderly. Tactically speaking, the loss of the northern XIX Corps bridgehead was not important, for the southern bridgehead was firm, and on this same day the corps attached Combat Command R of the 2d Armored Division to the 83d Division, and the combat command moved east of the river over the Class 40 bridge now in operation at Barby.

The 30th Division was rapidly closing up to the Elbe north of Magdeburg, which still held out against our forces. The 35th Division, fresh from its fighting in the Ruhr, was now attached to XIX Corps for operational control only, and one regiment began occupying the north portion of the 30th Division zone along the XIX–XIII Corps boundary. The 35th was eventually to pass to XIII Corps control, and after it had been introduced into the line between the two corps, the boundary would be shifted south so as to bring the 35th into the zone of XIII Corps. On April 14, XIII Corps' 102d Division made a general advance of twelve miles from its positions east and southeast of Klötze, reaching a line between Osterburg and Stendal. The 84th Division, still moving under full steam, pulled up for the evening six miles short of the Elbe after an advance of 32 miles.

With the Army now rapidly closing up to the Elbe throughout its entire zone, the pressing question in the mind of the Army Commander was of course the continuation of the advance to Berlin. On April 15 General Simpson conferred with General Bradley at 12th Army Group Tactical Headquarters, now at Wiesbaden, Germany, and presented his plan for the continued expansion of Ninth Army's Elbe bridgehead and a strong drive on to Berlin. By direction of the Supreme Allied Commander, however, Ninth Army was ordered to hold its zone on the line of the Elbe and await the the advance of the Russian forces. The bridgehead east of the Elbe could be maintained, at General Simpson's discretion, as a threat to the Germans and as a base from which to contact the Russians. The end of the war was now clearly in sight. General Simpson returned to his headquarters and issued the necessary orders for the consolidation of the Army's positions. The great advance was completed. Now the Army must close up to the Elbe elsewhere in its zone, consolidate its gains, and wait.

In the meantime, on April 15, in the XIX Corps zone the 83d Division, reinforced by Combat Command R of the 2d Armored Division, had expanded the bridgehead to an area of 30 square miles. Other elements of the 83d crossed the Saale River along the Army south boundary to gain up to three miles along a six-mile front. The remainder of the 35th Division completed moving into line along the Elbe north of the 30th Division, and the 35th passed to XIII Corps control. During April 15 and 16 the 2d Armored and 30th Infantry Divisions continued clearing and patrolling the west bank of the Elbe in their zones, and contained and prepared to reduce the city of Magdeburg.

Action was virtually at a standstill in XIII Corps on April 15. The 102d completed clearing its area and assembled at Stendal and Osterburg, and the 84th cleared its zone and moved in behind the 5th Armored, which held virtually the entire corps front along the Elbe. On April 16 the 84th and 102d Divisions relieved the 5th Armored, which then engaged in clearing areas which had been by-passed in the rapid advance to the Elbe.

April 16 and 17 proved to be eventful days for XXIX Tactical Air Command. During these two days, certain of the airfields remaining in German hands, crowded with the remnants of the Luftwaffe, were attacked by the fighter-bombers. One hundred and forty-seven German airplanes destroyed and 85 damaged were the claims for the two days. In addition, buildings, hangars, barracks, and runways were levelled or destroyed by fire and explosions.

The Air Forces also participated in the reduction of Magdeburg, which was still a sore spot on the Ninth Army front. Since the city refused to surrender to the 2d Armored, General Simpson gave orders for its reduction. A huge air attack was planned by XXIX Tactical Air Command in cooperation with the ground effort. In addition to all XXIX Tactical Air Command fighter-bombers, IX Bombardment Division of Ninth Air Force was called on to lend medium-bomber effort. Because of the complete lack of medium bomber targets anywhere else along the Western Front, IX Bombardment Division placed its entire strength of eleven groups of mediums at the disposal of Ninth Army and XXIX Tactical Air Command. The air plan called for the fighter-bombers to attack the city immediately before and after the assault by the mediums. The attack preceding the medium effort was intended to keep the German defenders inactive and under cover and thus deny to them the knowledge that portions of the ground forces were pulling their forward elements back to a safe distance from the air strike by the medium bombers. The attack to follow the medium assault was planned to continue the pressure on the enemy and thus allow the ground forces to cross the safety area they had evacuated earlier.

Shortly after noon on April 17 the air assault began. The medium bombers shattered the city with 775 tons of high explosives. XIX Corps Artillery fired counter-flak missions prior to the air strike and then supported the ground advance. The effectiveness of the counter-flak program was indicated when not one out of over 360 planes taking part in the operation was lost due to flak. Immediately following the strike by the mediums, the 30th Division began moving against Magdeburg from the north and west and the 2d Armored attacked from the south and west. Initially, strong enemy resistance was met and fire of almost every description was encountered, but by the afternoon of April 18 the city, then a shambles, had been cleared.

The Elbe was bridged a second time in the 83d Division zone when a Class 40 bridge was completed at Breitenhagen on April 18. An especially heavy German counterattack against the bridgehead on the 18th was repulsed after a slight loss of ground.

Ninth Army's Letter of Instructions No. 23, April 20, confirming verbal orders of the Army Commander, directed XIII and XIX Corps rapidly to clear the pockets of resistance in their respective zones to the Elbe and to hold the river line with a minimum of infantry forces disposed in depth. The armored divisions were to be pulled back and assembled in the central or western part of the corps zones. XIX Corps was further ordered to hold its Elbe bridgehead as a threat to Berlin.

In the meantime both corps had been fighting their own little private wars in their rear areas far to the west of the Elbe. XIX Corps had a bitter fight on its hands back in the mountainous Harz Forest area. The 330th Infantry Regiment of the 83d Division was the initial force to penetrate into the gloomy woods. The regiment smashed forward two miles into the forest and established contact with First Army on April 14. For the next several days, the 330th, attacking east, made steady but limited progress. At XIX Corps' request, "Mount Olympus," a rugged mountain-top stronghold where the enemy resisted bitterly, was dive-bombed and strafed on April 18 by 41 fighter-bombers of XXIX Tactical Air Command. The observation tower, railroad station, and the tunnel leading to the installation were destroyed. But in spite of air and artillery support, the going was extremely difficult; the enemy resistance was strong, and the terrain favored the Germans. Dense woods and high hills characterized the

Harz area. It was soon evident that the task was far too great for one regiment of infantry, for the junction of the Ninth and First Armies had cut off and bottled up remnants of the German Eleventh Army in the Harz. Earlier in the month the 8th Armored Division had been brought up from XVI Corps and placed in Army reserve near Braunschweig. One combat command had been attached to XIX Corps and had performed corps rear-area security missions and protected the corps south flank. The remainder of the division was now passed to XIX Corps. On April 20 the 8th Armored attacked south into the mountains from the Halberstadt area, gaining two miles and clearing the central town of Blankenburg. April 21 found all organized resistance cleared as the armored division quickly moved south to the Army boundary. The Germans, cut off and disorganized, were in no position to take further advantage of the almost limitless possibilities the Harz offered for defense.

In the XIII Corps zone, despite the closing to the Elbe River, there were still Germans—and a large number of them—to be found in rear areas. These forces combined and attempted one last counteroffensive, a pathetic effort, but one which nevertheless caused some confusion in the corps rear areas. For six days following April 16 the corps was engaged in flushing German marauders out of the all-too-numerous wooded areas radiating generally west from Klötze, the corps command post. In will-o'-the-wisp fashion, small but determined enemy groups filtered down from the British Second Army area, possibly headed towards a sanctuary in the Harz Mountains. These groups began harassing supply columns along main routes, shooting at vehicles, interrupting communications, and generally disrupting activity behind the XIII Corps front lines. All telephone cables from Army to corps were cut and motor messenger service was suspended for two days. The only sure communication with the corps was by radio and airplane messenger. No sooner would one wooded area be cleared than the Germans would reveal their presence elsewhere. On April 16 an enemy force of 500 to 600 men, 18 armored vehicles, and two tanks entered the town of Jubar. Here they captured 13 trucks and jeeps and 47 American soldiers. On April 18, another enemy force of 20 to 25 tanks, six 75mm self-propelled guns, 25 to 40 armored half-tracks, and 1,000 infantry launched an attack near Lindhof. Other small enemy units, possibly elements of larger groups, were contacted from time to time.

To stamp out this resistance XIII Corps took the 335th and 407th Infantry Regiments from the 84th and 102d Divisions. In addition to this force, Combat Command B of the 5th Armored, which had been pulled back from the Elbe, and the 11th Cavalry Group were employed to clear the various pockets. The cavalry destroyed one small enemy force southeast of Klötze, and a tank force from Combat Command B wiped out a detachment of German armor in a spirited clash at Brome. Other pockets were reduced at Diesdorf and Abbendorf. By April 22 all remaining Germans were virtually trapped in the Klötze Forest, and after being subjected to a severe pounding by artillery, armor, and infantry, the German resistance was wiped out. In the last stages of the Klötze battle, artillery fire was adjusted and directed from General Gillem's bedroom window in the town of Klötze—much to his amusement. The 29th Infantry Division, which on April 17 had been transferred to XIII Corps from its military government duties with XVI Corps, furnished one regiment to assist in the final kill in the Klötze Forest.

On the front along the Elbe, major activity had ceased in the XIX Corps zone with the capture of Magdeburg on April 18. The corps maintained its bridgehead east of the Elbe, patrolling actively therefrom, and redisposed its forces. On April 21 the 2d Armored Division was relieved along the Elbe by the 30th Division and moved back to the Braunschweig area, where it took over a military government mission and prepared for its part in forming a task force to be sent later to Berlin. The 8th Armored Division, on completing its Harz Mountain fighting, took over a military government mission south of the 2d Armored. XIX Corps, then, with the 30th and 83d Infantry Divisions as its major elements on the Elbe, patrolled out of its bridgehead and awaited, on order, the westward advance of the Russians.

It fell to XIII Corps to carry out the last offensive operation of Ninth Army. On April 20 a new 12th Army Group–21 Army Group boundary, running northeast from Celle to Ludwigslust east of the Elbe (Map No. 13), gave Ninth Army and, in turn, XIII Corps, another thirty miles of Elbe River frontage. This new triangular area was still teeming with German forces. XIII Corps had made plans to capture the area and selected the 5th

Armored and the 29th and 84th Infantry Divisions for the task. The 34th Field Artillery Brigade, with two heavy battalions, was brought up from the XVI Corps area and attached to XIII Corps for the operation. XIII Corps planned to sweep the west bank of the Elbe as far north as Neu Darchau. The attack was launched on April 21 using the 84th Division on the east, the 5th Armored in the center, and the 29th Division on the west. (*Map No. 16*). Against varied resistance, the 84th Division advanced eleven miles to reach the Elbe at Gorleben. The 5th Armored, meeting stubborn resistance and many mines, drove ahead along a wide front, gaining up to 13 miles and reaching Waddenweitz. The 29th Division, after gains up to eight miles, held a line from Hohenweddrien to Dahre.

The following day, April 22, saw the advance virtually completed. The armor plunged ahead 17 miles to make contact with British forces on the Elbe at Neu Darchau and at Dannenberg. The advance of the 5th Armored, however, was not an easy one. The Germans resisted stubbornly with fire from mortars, *Nebelwerfers* (the German multi-barrelled rocket-projector), and *Panzerfausts* (the heavy one-shot antitank weapon, similar to the bazooka). Marshy ground hampered the advance and greatly restricted vehicular movement. The 29th Division moved in behind the 5th Armored and advanced rapidly, encountering heavy minefields but little ground resistance.

Final mopping up was completed on April 24, and the 29th Division relieved the 5th Armored Division, which withdrew to corps reserve north of Braunschweig. Farther south in the corps zone, the 35th Division was relieved by the 102d on April 26, and thus the XIII Corps front was held by the 29th, 84th, and 102d Divisions in order from north to south. The 35th Division moved to the vicinity of Hannover, where it received an area mission for security and military government.

Back in the Ruhr, in the vastly populated area assigned to XVI Corps, the military government and occupation program of that corps was in full swing. On April 22 the Ninth Army boundary with First Army was shifted south so as to coincide with German political boundaries in that area, and the 75th Division's occupation zone was expanded to include the new territory. In the entire Ninth Army area west of XIII and XIX Corps, occupational districts were being governed by the various elements of XVI Corps, including the 17th Airborne, 75th Infantry, 79th Infantry, and 95th Infantry Divisions, the 55th Antiaircraft Brigade, and XVI Corps Artillery. On April 25 the 17th Airborne Division, together with the division's occupation area in the Essen vicinity, passed to the control of Fifteenth Army.

The forward echelon of Ninth Army Headquarters again had moved its command post, leaving Gütersloh and opening at Braunschweig on April 23 in a former German Luftwaffe headquarters building. This headquarters, named for Hermann Goering, was an enormous, sprawling four-story stucco office building, roughly Z-shaped. Located on the edge of Braunschweig and camouflaged a dull gray-green, it had escaped damage from numerous Allied bombings of the city proper. Its interior, lavish with marble, plate glass, and bright metal work, illustrated the completeness with which the Nazi regime equipped itself and the luxury with which its leaders were surrounded. The building provided ample and convenient space for the forward echelon of the Army Headquarters.

Conquer Rear, which had remained at Rheydt while the forward echelon moved to Haltern and Gütersloh, had moved on April 18 to the Hermann Goering Rest Center, an elaborate establishment comprising many stucco and concrete buildings on the outskirts of the city of Münster. Originally a rest center for German military personnel, during the war it had become a training center for antiaircraft troops and also accommodated an aircraft assembly plant, which was the only part of the installation damaged by Allied bombing. The remainder of the buildings provided excellent facilities for the Army rear echelon, which was to remain at Münster until May 15, when it moved to the Gütersloh location vacated by the forward echelon.

Extraordinary logistical and administrative situations confronted the Army in executing simultaneously the reduction of the Ruhr and the drive to the Elbe. Transportation facilities bore a tremendous burden. Two corps breaking through to the east had to be supported, and a third corps had to be supplied while fighting in the rearward part of the rapidly expanding Army area. There were no shortages of supplies or equipment; the build-up preceding the crossing over the Rhine had been farsighted and successful. The supplies were in the depots and railheads, but the spearheading armored divisions accompanied by motorized infantry divisions went east so fast that it was impossible to leapfrog the storage installations often enough. The problem lay in getting the materials where they were needed. Every possible transportation expedient had to be employed.

With troops fighting on the tip ends of overextended supply lines, the Army began to resort to supply by air. Gasoline and ammunition were thus delivered to the troops at forward fields. The expedient did not prove wholly satisfactory or reliable, since it hinged entirely on prevailing weather conditions and it was never possible to ascertain in advance whether or not delivery would be forthcoming. CATOR, the Combined Air Transport Operations Room in Paris, controlled all cargo planes in the theater. Each day the requirements for the following day were telephoned to CATOR by the Army. During the night the requests were transmitted by Paris to the various air bases in the United Kingdom and on the Continent. Priorities for the supply of the various armies were fixed by 12th Army Group. After missions were assigned by CATOR, the weather might close in over certain fields, and planes based there would not be able to fly their missions. Consequently, complete reliance could not be placed on air supply, and Ninth Army used it only to augment truck and rail.

Air evacuation of the wounded worked more successfully, however, and proved of tremendous assistance in the widespread operations. Already extensively used in previous campaigns of the Army, air evacuation reached its peak at this time. The Douglas C-47 cargo planes flew shuttle service from advance landing fields selected and rehabilitated through the cooperative efforts of Ninth Army and the Air Forces, carrying patients back to Communications Zone hospitals. Fields were selected as far forward as possible, to reduce the ambulance haul, which otherwise would have required round trips of several hundred miles and would not have permitted adequate clearing of the Army evacuation hospitals.

At the beginning of April the Army had established one air strip for evacuation of casualties at Rheydt, west of the Rhine. At this strip, as on those later established, an Advance Section hospital functioned as a holding unit for patients until the planes arrived. As the advance progressed, additional sites were selected at intervals by the Army Surgeon. Air Force engineers prepared the strip and a hospital was rapidly moved to it. Strips were established successively at Kirchhellen (*Map No. 12*) to support the reduction of the Ruhr, and at Hildesheim and Helmstedt (*Map No. 16*) for those troops operating eastward to the Elbe. With the exception of a few special cases, all patients evacuated from Army hospitals to Communications Zone hospitals during the drive from the Rhine to the Elbe left the Army area by plane. These totalled 11,085 for the month of April. For the entire period of greatest air evacuation activity, from mid-March to the end of the Army's operations in Europe, 19,490 patients were evacuated by air.

During the advance into Germany and until the Army ceased operations in that country, three additional cemeteries were established for the burial of enemy military personnel. At no time, however, did the Army bury American soldiers on German soil. It was therefore necessary to transport the bodies across the Rhine and the German frontier to the Army cemetery at Margraten in the Netherlands. Although this became more difficult each day with the swift advance of our troops, the policy completely justified itself by obviating later disinterment and reburial.

Truck transportation bore a tremendous burden during the Ruhr–Elbe operations. The Army had 43 quartermaster truck companies assigned. Of these, eight were attached to the various corps and four were attached to the Army's armored division. Thirteen companies were used throughout the period to motorize infantry divisions. Eighteen truck companies thus were retained under direct Army control, and these were supplemented by 16 ten-ton truck companies on dispatch from the Advance Section of Communications Zone. Even with this relatively large amount of transportation, every truck was running night and day, often without pause for maintenance and with only the minimum number of stops necessary to give essential rest to drivers. Although central control and dispatch of trucks had to be relaxed to gain flexibility in some few instances, in general the closest supervision was maintained by Army headquarters. Only through strict control could it be insured that supply items of greatest need were receiving first priority for transportation to the onrushing forward troops. In view of the long hauls as the supply lines were stretched farther and farther, the use of even a few trucks for a particular item of supply had to be weighed against other demands, and the decisions made at Army Headquarters.

The evacuation of prisoners of war from the front-line area was a major operation in itself. For example, from April 1 through April 14th, 70,464 prisoners of war were sent to the rear, principally by truck transportation. This large number called for the use of every expedient. Prisoners were normally evacuated by supply trucks returning to the rear areas, but groups of prisoners were now to be found under almost every tree. With collecting points springing up in profusion, it was next to impossible to keep truck drivers informed of the locations. Officers of the transportation section of the Army Headquarters went into the forward areas in a roving capacity, stopping empty trucks and diverting them to the nearest collecting point to pick up a load.

The great influx of prisoners, together with their general attitude of docility once they were captured, brought a decided change in their handling. Where formerly combat units had sought to secure prisoners for intelligence and security reasons, now they often could not be distracted from their rapid advance to receive individual surrenders, preferring to keep going and let the next outfit take over the disarmed Germans. In more than one instance individual German soldiers tried to turn themselves in for many hours, or for a day or two, before they were successful in obtaining PW status to get food. German civilians would not ordinarily feed or hide them for fear of American action if apprehended. Formerly, prisoners had been kept under careful and close guard. Now large convoys containing hundreds of German ex-soldiers often made their way to the rear shepherded by a lone MP in a jeep. Frequently the truck drivers themselves were the only guards, sometimes to their quite apparent unhappiness.

One unknown hero of the PW evacuation was the first truck driver who discovered a simple expedient for loading his truck to overflow capacity. Load up, move forward a few yards, and stop quickly. Inertia carried the loaded prisoners forward in the truck, and by quick action an additional dozen or so could be loaded in the space left vacant. A rough but effective method, necessary to make maximum use of every square foot of truck space; every prisoner carried to the rear meant that much less food for the straining transportation system to bring forward. Prisoners were jammed into the trucks so tightly that individual movement was impossible, but they were generally only too happy to get out of the combat zone quickly. The big ten-ton trucks from the Communications Zone provided a colorful spectacle as they rolled down the roads with as many as 130 prisoners packed standing in each one.

In the rapid expansion of the operations east of the Rhine, traffic across the Rhine tactical bridges was heavy from the time they were opened until April 9. Traffic began to decline from this day on, since the railroad bridge was then completed and the major portions of the Army's combat elements were across the Rhine. The heaviest traffic loads were carried by the Wesel bridges, because they were served by the most favorable road net east of the river. Maximum hourly traffic counts at Wesel tallied 573 vehicles for the Bailey bridge, 523 vehicles for the 25-ton ponton bridge, and 427 for the treadway bridge.

By April 8 the Advance Section of Communications Zone had rehabilitated rail lines up to the west bank of the Rhine and as far as Münster east of the Rhine. Advance Section's construction of the semipermanent pile trestle railway bridge at Wesel had proceeded on a 24-hour-a-day basis since March 30, and this, the first rail bridge over the Rhine, was completed the night of April 8. The first railroad train of supplies to be moved over the Rhine by Allied forces in World War II crossed at 12:30 A.M. on April 9. In the rail construction program east of the Rhine, 220 miles of main line and 75 miles of spur and branch line trackage were open for operation by April 13, and five major rail bridges, exclusive of the Rhine bridge, had been built and were in operation in the Army zone.

Early in April rail lines were opened as far east as the Weser River, and work on a Weser rail bridge was expedited. When some of the rails east of the river were found to be in an operative condition, it was decided not to wait for completion of the Weser bridge. By resorting to a rail-to-truck-to-rail procedure to cross supplies over the river, rail lines were employed on both sides, resulting in a material saving in truck miles. Once again, the Army policy of intensive reconnaissance of rail lines and of securing Advance Section's cooperation in pushing railroads rapidly behind the advancing troops was paying dividends. Undoubtedly this program made it far easier to supply the forward elements. Instructions were issued to German rail representatives for the opening and operation of the line Lehrte–Braunschweig–Eilsleben–Magdeburg (*Map No. 16*), and work was pushed rapidly. All labor was performed by German civilians under the supervision of the Military Railway Service and Ninth Army. The Weser rail bridge was opened for traffic late in the afternoon of April 25, giving the Army continuous rail lines as far east as Obisfelde, northeast of Braunschweig. Additional lines were opened shortly thereafter into Magdeburg and to Uelzen on the north flank. By the end of April, sixteen railheads were in operation in the Army area.

In the rehabilitation of railroads, invaluable assistance was received from an unexpected source. Army rail transportation officers located in Braunschweig a Dr. Frohne, who was the senior non-Nazi official in the division of the German railway system which lay in the Army area. Dr. Frohne's superior, a Nazi official, had fled, but the Doctor, who was able to furnish conclusive proof that he was not a member of the Nazi Party, remained at his position and cooperated willingly with the Army. Not only did he himself agree to serve, which was a stroke of fortune, for he was an excellent construction engineer as well as an operating expert, but also he located other key personnel whom he was able to vouch for as not being affiliated with the Nazi Party and who also agreed to serve. Through his efforts a complete organization of trained German rail transportation operating and construction personnel was created, the integrity and clear record of each man being guaranteed by his immediate superior. Dr. Frohne and his executives were furnished with captured motor vehicles for their use, and all railroad employees were exempted from curfew and travel restrictions in the Army area. Their contribution was of inestimable value and was rendered throughout the remaining period of the Army's operations without a single violation of good faith.

Additional benefits of theater-wide importance were provided in Dr. Frohne's organization in the uncovering of thousands of freight cars in Germany. Cars were critically short all over the Continent, and those located in Germany offered a much-needed cushion in rail transportation. Wherever found, cars were immediately taken over, unloaded on the spot, marshalled, reloaded with prisoners or displaced persons for dispatch to the Communications Zone or with supplies and equipment for dispatch to other localities within the Army area.

The most critical point in rail operations remained, naturally, the Rhine bridge at Wesel, a single-track structure over which all rail movements across the Rhine in the Army area had to pass. Not only Ninth Army supplies but also some destined for First Army came in over the bridge. With a bridge capacity of only fifty trains per day, it was obvious that to get supplies across in the order needed, and to insure that each Army received its fair share, priorities were required for the movement of various classes of supplies. The priority system, however, pyramided the problem. Supplies were put into the "pipeline" by the Communications Zone depots, necessarily without regard to the priorities set up by Ninth Army, and consequently did not arrive at Wesel in the order in which they were to cross. Rail facilities in the vicinity of the bridge were not adequate to permit the marshalling of trains and the segregation of supplies. It was found necessary, therefore, to begin control in the rail yards of München-Gladbach, where a central board was set up to supervise the marshalling and dispatch of trains.

Advance Section's rapid installation of a gasoline pipeline across the Rhine at Wesel was a valuable asset to the Army supply system. Opened on April 3, by April 6 the pipeline had made large deliveries, and 800,000 gallons of gasoline were on the ground at the decanting station at Erle (*Map No. 14*). It was estimated that the gasoline delivered by the pipeline saved the Army the equivalent capacity of one highway bridge across the Rhine. As soon as rail lines forward were sufficiently rehabilitated, railroad tank cars were used to transport gasoline from the pipeline terminus at Wesel to a new decanting point at Gütersloh. For a brief period a shortage of railroad tank cars threatened to hinder operations, but this situation was effectively relieved by rounding up all available German tank cars. Insufficient storage space at Gütersloh made it necessary to transfer the gasoline, after decanting, to a near-by Army gasoline depot. Later, as the Army advanced farther east, decanting operations were transferred to Hannover, which had ideal facilities for Advance Section's decanting and for storage.

The magnitude of all supply and transportation operations is best illustrated by figures. From the initial assault crossing of the Rhine to April 13, a total of 141,961 tons of supplies was moved across the Rhine to supply Ninth Army forces. This tonnage breaks down as follows: food—14,600 tons, a total of 6,163,936 rations; gasoline and allied products—53,400 tons, including 14,000,000 gallons of gasoline; ammunition—42,100 tons; other equipment and supplies—31,861 tons. This total tonnage moved east of the Rhine was transported by Army means an average distance of 77 miles, making a total of 10,930,997 ton-miles. The tonnage transported represents the combined lift of 46,108 2½-ton trucks. Issues to troops of the Army during the period from March 31 to May 9 totaled 24,447,365 rations (72,280 tons), 23,495,830 gallons of gasoline (84,159 tons), and 702,741 gallons of Diesel oil (2,740 tons). Lack of rail facilities during the early part of the period, the long supply lines, and the extensive employment of armor are reflected in the high consumption of gasoline and Diesel oil.

The swift eastward movement of the Army and the congestion present in the Ruhr region required extensive engineer effort. The long months of aerial bombardment to which the Ruhr had been subjected necessitated unceasing measures to clear rubble and debris from the city streets to permit the passage of military traffic. Extensive rehabilitation of roads and bridges was necessary. Prior to the reduction of the Ruhr, work was commenced immediately to develop crossings of the Lippe River and the Lippe-Seiten Canal to provide routes south into the XVI Corps area from the Wesel–Haltern–Münster main arterial highway. (*Map No. 12.*) As finally developed, these routes consisted of two traffic lanes south from Wesel, two lanes south of Dorsten, and two at Haltern.

Reconnaissance of the *Autobahn*, the four-lane superhighway, in the Ruhr area showed that demolition was so complete that the construction of twenty-two bridges would be required in the first twenty-five miles. It was therefore decided that the section of the *Autobahn* west of Hamm would not be used as a main supply route, although the route would follow the *Autobahn* east of that city. Easterly from Hamm to the Weser River, the *Autobahn* was repaired as rapidly as possible and was put into service as a main supply road by the end of April. This was an invaluable addition to the road net. While a semipermanent highway bridge was being constructed across the Weser, repair work proceeded on the *Autobahn* to the east, and in May the route was opened all the way to Magdeburg.

During the advance of XIII and XIX Corps, combat bridging activities became a constant succession of placing tactical bridges, taking them up as soon as the foremost divisions had passed, replacing them with semipermanent timber bridges, and getting the tactical bridges still farther forward to have them available for the next river crossing. As the advance increased the Army's area, it was necessary constantly to stretch the areas of general responsibility for engineer work of all of the Army engineer groups to free the corps engineer troops for their all-important task of providing stream crossings. Army engineer groups were kept close behind the advancing corps and took the responsibility for engineer work well forward of the corps rear boundaries. Prior to the Rhine crossing, the average area assigned to one group had been 12 by 18 miles. During the race to the Elbe, areas were as large as 40 by 70 miles. Furthermore, the limit of area advance for the Communications Zone had been set at the border between the Netherlands and Germany, and the engineers of the Advance Section could no longer extend their areas forward in relief of the Army engineers.

With a large-scale crossing of the Elbe and an entry into Berlin always in mind, engineer stream-crossing units and equipage were initially kept well forward preparatory to forcing a crossing. When orders were received that no further advance was to be made, engineers could turn more attention to the task of improving the existing routes in the Army area. Naturally, more and more highways became available as the advance continued; 1,343 miles of road and highway were eventually used in the supply of troops, and 632 miles of these roads were designated as main supply routes between the Rhine and Elbe.

In the entire program of preparation of routes it was necessary to construct 59 tactical bridges and nine fixed bridges over the principal waterways, in addition to the nine tactical bridges and one fixed bridge over the Rhine. Among the outstanding semipermanent bridges completed were the 1813-foot timber pile trestle bridge over the Rhine at Wesel, opened to two-way traffic on April 18 and dedicated as the "Franklin D. Roosevelt Memorial Bridge," and the 411-foot timber pile trestle bridge connecting the *Autobahn* over the Weser south of Minden, opened to one-way traffic on May 1 and to two-way traffic on May 3. Later, on May 31, a 440-foot steel trestle bridge across the Elbe at Magdeburg was opened, and was dedicated as the "Friendship Bridge" in a joint ceremony of representatives of American, British, and Russian armies.

The system of map distribution from Army engineer map depots to corps depots proved itself during the simultaneous Ruhr–Elbe operations. Each corps map depot was stocked with the necessary maps for its particular operation. Practically all the maps for the Ruhr area were turned over to the XVI Corps map depot, leaving the Army with the necessity of stocking only those needed by XIII and XIX Corps. Nearly 800,000 copies of maps of all scales of the Ruhr Valley were distributed from the Army depot to XVI Corps. Approximately 600,000 copies of various scale maps and 50,000 special maps and town plans were reproduced during the first two weeks in April. Town plans of the larger cities in the Ruhr Valley were reproduced both by topographic units within the Army and by topographic units of higher echelons. Many town plans consisted of aerial photographs with street names and important buildings drafted onto the photographs. These proved to be of enormous value to the attacking troops. Two million, seven hundred thousand copies of 1:25,000 and 1:50,000 scale maps of the area between the Rhine and Elbe Rivers were reproduced, and all but 300,000 of these were distributed to Army troops and corps map depots.

Signal Corps troops encountered great difficulties, and wire-laying was sometimes almost impossible. The heavy vehicle traffic caused numerous troubles in vital ground communication lines, particularly at traffic choke points. The use of civil communications was impeded in the vicinity of the Ruhr industrial area, where frequent bombing and heavy fighting had almost completely disrupted the German system. Demands for communication facilities, moreover, were heavier because the traffic control points and numerous military government agencies all required communications aid in accomplishing their tasks. Signal Corps cable splicers worked long hours to locate and repair the damaged German lines and equipment. In the eastward advance, the VHF radio link again proved invaluable, often providing the only telephone communications to the fast-moving corps many miles away and to other headquarters far to the rear. Radio relay teams, as well as messengers and construction crews, were constantly working alone in areas teeming with German troops by-passed in the drive to the Elbe, and some lost their lives in getting the messages through.

Later, as the rout of the enemy became more complete, the condition of his abandoned fixed communication equipment became better and better. The enemy was no longer attempting to destroy his telephone and telegraph equipment. Sometimes he tried to render the equipment inoperative in a way that was difficult to find but easy to repair. More often, however, the equipment was found intact in the hands of skilled civilian technicians. At Braunschweig, for example, when signal troops arrived to prepare for the movement of Army Headquarters there, the big switchboards in the Luftwaffe headquarters building were in full service with the regular German operators on duty. It appeared that the Germans knew that the end was near and felt that they might benefit from the safekeeping of facilities which, once destroyed, would be difficult if not impossible to replace. As the Army area became larger and larger, it was impossible either to supply American signal equipment or to man it with American personnel. Much German equipment was pressed into service at switching centers and repeater stations, and German technicians, under close military supervision, serviced and operated the equipment.

Extended supply lines placed a heavy overload on Army ordnance resources and supplies, and the maintenance of all forms of transportation became critical. In the continuous truck operations, runs of several hundred miles were common. The long distance traversed at maximum or excessive speeds, without time out for preventive maintenance, increased the need for shop maintenance enormously. Sufficient ordnance maintenance companies were not available to furnish the usual support over the extended distance of the Army area and at the same time provide adequate maintenance along the routes of advance. Consequently, the maintenance companies of one ordnance group were assigned to support front-line tactical troops, while the other groups echeloned companies in depth to provide support over the principal arteries of the road net. These companies in turn were split into platoons and set up roadside service stations providing emergency repairs and continuous road patrols between adjacent stations. The resulting distribution made possible the establishment of service stations at regular intervals along the *Autobahn* and other main roads. Roadside billboards and refreshment stands were the only things lacking to remind one of the highways back home.

In spite of all special maintenance measures, the heavy demands made upon the trucks caused their mortality to increase tremendously. In order to keep transportation rolling, complete vehicle overhaul and rebuild plants were set up in the industrial city of Hamm. To provide a source for certain spare parts which were not obtainable in the theater, Army ordnance took over and operated a complete German factory. This proved to be a paying venture and took many vehicles and weapons off the deadline. The increased maintenance service required other parts which were in the process of being moved across the Rhine by rail or awaiting shipment from Communications Zone depots. These supplies had to wait their turn on priority, which was low compared to food and fuel supplies. Fortunately, units were able to exist on a well built-up stock of parts which had been accumulated prior to the operation. This was particularly true of armored units, which had moved long distances at maximum speeds. Many sets of tank tracks became unserviceable after a few miles of operation, because of failure in the synthetic rubber composition. Moreover, rebuilt engines, which had been counted on as serviceable stock, were found to be unserviceable due to faulty rebuild in European shops. Critical items had to be located, and any available transportation sent to haul them to the points where required. Evacuation of major units such as engines, transmissions, and axles became a prime factor, and at one time there were two hundred carloads of these units awaiting shipment to Communications Zone depots for rebuild. Shipment of prisoners of war had to be given priority over evacuation of these units, yet resupply was dependent on getting the units back to the rebuild plants for repair.

With the Army deep in Germany, the continuous search for chemical producing plants and large toxic gas depots was well rewarded. Earlier estimates regarding Germany's large-scale war-gas production were confirmed when several factories were found actually producing toxics. Two depots, each containing approximately 75,000 shells and bombs filled with gas, were found. Other depots containing gas-filled shells and bulk toxics were discovered at numerous sites throughout the overrun area.

Military government shouldered a huge burden, particularly in thickly populated industrial areas with their hordes of displaced persons used as slave labor. As the tide of combat moved forward, Military Government detachments immediately set to work organizing and governing each community. In the Ruhr, because it was the eventual occupation zone of the British, principal cities were governed by British Military Government detachments which had been supplied to the Ninth Army and which entered the Ruhr under the control and direction of XVI Corps. Ninth Army sent its own Military Government provisional detachments into the area with XVI Corps to govern those towns not covered by the British. In the great industrial district the detachments found the destruction and the misery that were now being faced everywhere throughout Germany. In the Ruhr alone, 300,000 displaced persons were liberated from their enforced slavery. It was a hectic period. Streams of liberated displaced persons lined every road, utilizing every means of transportation to get themselves and their pitifully few possessions into free territory and a few miles closer to home. They were on the roads twenty-four hours a day, columns of people loaded in battered charcoal-burning vehicles, riding bicycles, pushing wheelbarrows, pulling carts and wagons and every possible kind of homemade contraption that could be made to travel on wheels—anything to relieve the burden that most of them had to carry on their backs. It was a staggering task for the Army to restore order, gather the people into camps, and take steps for their repatriation.

During the operations to the Elbe it was impossible for Military Government to keep pace and effect an immediate and complete reorganization of each area or community captured. Spearhead Military Government detachments went forward with the divisions and thus insured that the minimum security demands of the tactical commanders, such as curfews and restrictions on the circulation of the local population, were immediately made effective. Once the system was set up and in operation, the detachments sped on to new forward locations, and the more detailed measures of military government and long-term occupation were instituted as tactical conditions permitted.

The Army Military Government agencies, almost automatically

now, but on a far vaster scale than ever before, took measures to insure that the civilian populace had a minimum standard of food. In an area whose population was numbered in millions, swift measures for control of food stocks and the system of distribution were vital. Experience gained west of the Rhine in meeting similar but smaller situations stood Military Government agencies in good stead. Particular attention, too, was given to the future feeding of the German people, principally through their own efforts. Army food experts immediately instituted surveys of seed stocks and crops in the area. The crop situation was generally found to be surprisingly good. The German farmer had managed to plant before we crossed the Rhine and seemed to have utilized every square inch of tillable land. He placed milk cows before his plow if he had nothing else. All available hands, including women and children, were working in the fields. There was no doubt that the farmer knew that he had to work for all he was worth or starve.

Thousands of Allied prisoners of war of all nationalities were liberated from prison camps spread throughout the Army zone. The more prominent of these were near Dorsten, Münster, Paderborn, Soest, Lippstadt, Hameln, Hildesheim, Immendorf, Stendal, and Wolfenbüttel. Generally, each camp contained predominantly prisoners of one nationality, but some camps held a mixture of American, British, Russian, Belgian, Italian, French, Polish, Jugoslav, Roumanian, New Zealander, Australian, South African, Serb, Czech, Greek, Indian, Dutch, and Canadian personnel. The majority of the prisoners had been housed in insanitary and poorly ventilated buildings; they slept in triple-decked wooden bunks. The accumulation of filth and disease in the camps was far worse than had been anticipated. Upon uncovering each installation, swift measures were essential to convert it into a livable place until the prisoners could be moved elsewhere and repatriated. Medical supplies, pure water, and food were brought in, and within a short time the ex-prisoners were being fed and cared for. Evidence of marked improvement was quickly apparent.

The Army was confronted with many situations in processing, caring for, and evacuating the thousands of liberated Allied prisoners. Two early instances are typical. A small group of 65 liberated British prisoners, who had been captured at Dunkirk and in North Africa, testified that they had been marching westward from Poland almost continually for three months under guard of SS troops. Their daily ration had consisted usually of one potato per man per day. From lack of food and proper rest, many had become too weak to continue the march and were shot by the SS guards or left to die along the roadside. One needed only to look at the surviving 65 to realize the suffering they had experienced. Immediately after liberation, the ex-prisoners were evacuated to Stalag VI-J, a former German prisoner-of-war camp near Dorsten, which had been rehabilitated for this purpose. Here the men were bathed, fed, dusted with DDT powder, documented, and made ready for air evacuation to the United Kingdom. Several were unable to eat the ordinary Army food because of the extremely limited diet to which they had been subjected, and for these special food was prepared. Air lift was requested from SHAEF and within twenty-four hours after the prisoners had been liberated three British Dakotas roared down on the field and taxied up to the waiting men. The men shouted and cried at intervals—it seemed like a dream to them. Tears rolled down their gaunt, lined, faces as they talked to the pilots about home. Their desire to live showed in their wrinkled faces—their war was over.

In a second instance, reports received from recovered Allied prisoners indicated that additional thousands of American and British prisoners were in close proximity to our approaching front-line divisions. In order to provide facilities, a transient camp located near an airfield was necessary. The answer was found at Hildesheim, where there was a former Luftwaffe airfield with buildings capable of housing 10,000 men. However, heating, lighting, sewer, and water facilities were not operating. Immediate steps were taken by XIX Corps to convert the camp into a semipermanent air and rail evacuation center. A quartermaster bath unit was ordered in. Four Red Cross Clubmobiles moved to the camp site. A medical detachment was ordered in, and the Army opened an evacuation hospital. Engineer units worked twenty-four hours a day to restore the facilities. SHAEF was asked to fly in medical supplies, blood plasma, DDT powder, and 20,000 blankets. These supplies arrived within eighteen hours after they had been requested. A field artillery battalion took charge of the camp and procured 1,700 near-by German civilians to provide labor for cleaning and delousing the buildings.

Within three days nearly 600 American and 9,400 British prisoners had funneled into the Hildesheim camp. As each truckload arrived, each man was given a hot shower, dusted with DDT powder, and examined by a medical officer. Red Cross ditty bags given to each man contained soap, towel, comb, toothbrush, razor and blades, shaving soap, cigarettes, candy, and gum. The men were grouped in airplane load units of 22 and were quartered in barracks where cots and clean blankets were provided. Hot food was served at various messes throughout the camp. For personnel being processed during meal times, K and C rations, hot soup, and coffee, were served. Nothing was left undone to provide ease and comfort to the men who had suffered so much. Chaplains of each faith were in constant attendance. Writing materials, books, the daily *Stars and Stripes, Yank* and other magazines, ping-pong tables, and small games were provided. An Army Ground Forces Band gave a concert each morning and afternoon. In the evenings, a Special Service company band played dance music and the ex-prisoners danced with Red Cross girls. Two motion-picture theaters and a "live talent" Special Service show were open daily. British and American planes began arriving en masse. Sometimes seventy C-47s were on the field at one time. The planes would fly in with gasoline, food, or medical supplies and leave with happy American and British soldiers. Often men who arrived at the camp at 9:00 A.M. were boarding a plane by 2:00 P.M. The Hildesheim camp was but one of the many examples of what was done for liberated Allied prisoners of war.

The sudden liberation of the thousands of Allied prisoners and displaced persons, together with the mass surrenders of German troops, dumped into the lap of the Army the immediate necessity of feeding nearly four times as many mouths as it had been feeding. This situation strained to the utmost the facilities and service troops, which were of course provided only on the basis of the number to be fed in the Army itself. In the latter part of April the Army, with a troop strength of 485,000 had to feed over 1,700,000 people per day. The various categories which made up this total were:

U. S. Troops	485,000
Allied PWs	204,379
German PWs	124,618
Displaced Persons	924,500
Total	1,738,497

Supreme Allied Headquarters had laid down the policy that the German Government was responsible for the feeding and care of displaced persons, which was as it should be. But the hard cold fact remained that when a displaced persons' camp was overrun, say at 8:00 P.M., liberating some six to eight thousand hungry clamoring Poles, Czechs, Belgians, or any of a dozen different nationalities, their appetites could not be satisfied with policy. They had to be fed. Whenever possible, of course, they were fed from captured German food stores, but when these were not available, other provision had to be made. By international agreement, a seperate menu had been established for each nationality; these menus were made up from German stores as far as possible, and were augmented by Army stores only when absolutely necessary. When German food was not available, captured German soldiers were fed one-half of a K or C ration per day and displaced persons received two-thirds of a K or C ration per day. All these conditions arose at a time when rations for American troops were more critical than at any other time in the Army's history. The daily ration trains were coming from the distant Belgian cities of Liège and Charleroi; with the hectic conditions then prevailing, trains were easily sidetracked and "lost" for short periods. For the first time an issue of operational (canned) rations for all troops was forced on April 18 and again on May 8 and 10. But only on these days was it necessary to require all troops to use less appetizing canned rations instead of the more palatable standard meals.

Staggering medical conditions were met in caring for displaced persons, liberated Allied prisoners, and political prisoners of the Germans. Typical of the situations requiring immediate and rapid action was the political prisoners' camp discovered near Halberstadt on April 15. Advancing infantry uncovered some 1,400 French and Western Europeans existing in an inclosure in a deep forest. Although all were suffering from acute malnutrition, about 400 of the prisoners, fearing the return of the Germans, managed to leave the camp. Many died in the attempt. The Army medical service was presented with some 1,000 patients, all starved, 120 with severe diarrhea, 140 requiring surgery, 40 with pneumonia, and 33 with tuberculosis. They lay in small wooden shacks, two to a double-decked bunk, partly clothed in filthy shirts, too weak to raise their heads, much less to take care of their bodily needs. The floors were covered with a quarter inch of slime. In this place 2,000 persons had died in the past five months. Under the Germans, the medical care of the camp had been entrusted to a single Polish physician, himself a political prisoner. An Army field hospital, normally providing 300 beds, was immediately transported to a large barracks in Halberstadt, and was expanded to receive the patients. All individuals required bathing, disinfestation, and reclothing, but within forty-eight hours all had been transferred to the field hospital. The patients were in such debilitated states that special diets and careful nursing care were absolutely necessary. It was impossible to transfer them to civilian medical installations until they had recuperated to the point where they could stand an ambulance trip. This one camp required for two months the services of one of the five field hospitals available to the Army at the time.

On April 29 and 30, XXIX Tactical Air Command, Ninth Army, XIX Corps, and Army and corps antiaircraft units all cooperated in a unique project. For weeks previously, pilots of the German air force, accompanied by mechanics, "fiancées," and other odds and ends of the German population, had been bringing their planes behind the front lines for the purpose of landing them and becoming American prisoners. By this action, the pilots reasoned, they would escape falling into Russian hands. To induce more German air force personnel to surrender, XXIX Tactical Air Command prepared and dropped leaflets notifying the German pilots that an operational airstrip at Oschersleben, southwest of Magdeburg, had been set aside for them to land on and surrender. Antiaircraft fires along a specified corridor leading to the field were suspended. Although no pilots ventured into this haven of escape, a number landed at other points in the Army area and indicated that the leaflets had been widely read by air force personnel. It was generally believed that the remaining German flyers were too inexperienced to fly to the designated airstrip.

On April 30, XVIII Airborne Corps, with the 82d Airborne Division, 8th Infantry Division, and 7th Armored Division, was attached to Ninth Army for administration and supply only. The corps operated under command of British Second Army and was used to assist in establishing a bridgehead over the Elbe River north of the Ninth Army sector, advancing forty miles, and making contact with the Russian forces in northwest Germany.

Ninth Army provided two field artillery group headquarters, five field artillery battalions, one tank destroyer battalion, one engineer combat group headquarters, five engineer combat battalions, and some smaller engineer units, for the use of XVIII Airborne Corps. In addition, all logistical support for the corps was furnished by Ninth Army in accordance with the established procedure that U. S. troops, though under British command, should nevertheless be supplied by U. S. agencies. The distances involved in supplying the corps were great and necessitated opening a food supply point, a gas, oil, and lubricants supply point, an ordnance depot, and a chemical warfare ammunition point for the exclusive use of the corps. Quartermaster, signal, and engineer supplies were drawn from existing Ninth Army depots. Medical support was provided to include one medical battalion, a hospital unit of a field hospital, one evacuation hospital, and a medical depot. Quartermaster fumigation and bath and laundry units were also furnished the corps by the Army.

As Ninth Army troops held on the line of the Elbe, the great question was when and where the Army would meet the Russians who were driving west from Berlin. Everyday brought new rumors that the junction had been effected. On April 30 initial contact was made when the 125th Cavalry Squadron of the 113th Cavalry Group, probing out from the 83d Division bridgehead of XIX Corps, sighted Russian forces east of Zerbst. At the little town of Apollensdorf (*Map No. 16*) at 1:30 P.M. on April 30, troops of the United States Ninth Army and troops of the Russian 121st Infantry Division met and shook hands. Additional contact was established farther north in XIII Corps on May 2 when both the 29th and 84th Infantry Divisions met the Russians.

German troops continued to make their way across the Elbe River in attempts to reach American lines, and prisoner-of-war figures reached very high totals. For example, in the three-day period, May 2, 3, and 4, prisoners totaled more than 100,000 and surrenders continued to increase. Prisoners of note were taken into custody in wholesale quantities. Major General Kurt Dittmar, the German radio military commentator, crossed the Elbe and asked to speak with General Hobbs, the Commanding General of the 30th Division. Dittmar desired to surrender wounded military personnel and civilians to American troops. Upon receiving a negative reply, he started back toward the Elbe but changed his mind at the last moment and requested prisoner-of-war status for himself. Subsequently, a colonel crossed over, looking for General Dittmar, a major crossed looking for the colonel, and a captain came seeking the major. All remained with the 30th Division, at their own request.

The German Army's distintegration and the chaotic conditions in the area between Ninth Army's Elbe River front and the approaching Russian Armies were typified in the actions of the German forces whose chief of staff was General der Panzertruppen (Lieutenant General) Von Edelsheim. These comprised the German Twelfth Army, and remnants of the German Ninth Army which had been fighting on the Eastern Front—four corps with some 65,000 troops, 6,000 wounded, and some 100,000 civilians who had attached themselves to the military as the Russians advanced westward. General Von Edelsheim attempted to surrender the entire force to Ninth Army through the 102d Infantry Division. The Army did not accept the surrender, and General Von Edelsheim was informed that the Russians and Americans were allies—and that Ninth Army had all the German prisoners it wanted and more too. However, according to the Geneva Convention and the customs of war, individual elements that could cross the river at their own risk were received as prisoners of war by Ninth Army units on the west bank of the Elbe. No civilians were permitted; crossing parties were required to bring their own food; ambulatory wounded could be brought, but other wounded only if they were provided with German field hospitals deemed adequate for their numbers by Ninth Army medical personnel; individuals were required to be maintained in units under their own officers. The Germans came across the river in droves—some over a German-destroyed railroad bridge that they now repaired to make usable for foot troops, some on rafts, some by boat, and some swimming nude.

While the Ninth Army, its offensive mission completed, waited on the banks of the Elbe, the pressure from the Russians gradually narrowed the corridor in front of the Army until this sector in the heart of Germany was firmly sealed with Russian and American forces. By May 6 the Ninth Army bridgehead east of the Elbe had been turned over to Russian forces. Other Allied Armies pursued the disintegrating German Army. The forces in Italy were the first to capitulate, and units from the U. S. Fifth Army fighting north from Italy, and U. S. Seventh Army pushing south from Germany, made firm link-ups near Innsbruck in the Alpine provinces of North Tyrol. This juncture exploded the myth of the Austrian "redoubt" area which ostensibly would house a last-ditch defense by the Germans. Cut off from central command, supplies, and replacements, the German Army was no longer a unified military power; its position was hopeless.

In the early morning hours of May 7, 1945, at Supreme Head-quarters Allied Expeditionary Forces, in Rheims, France, envoys of the German High Command signed the complete and unconditional surrender of all German forces. The surrender became effective at 12:01 A.M., May 9, and the "cease fire" order went out to all Ninth Army troops. While the "cease fire" order marked the end of the war in Europe and May 8 was proclaimed as the long-awaited VE-day, it was largely a matter of form for Ninth Army. The Army had long since completed its fighting mission. Resistance in the Army's portion of the Ruhr had ceased on April 14. The Elbe had been reached and crossed by April 12. By April 24, the entire line of the river in the Army zone had been firmly secured. There the Army held, on order. In the great simultaneous operations of reducing the Ruhr and striking to the Elbe, Ninth Army had encircled, in conjunction with U. S. First Army, the enemy's greatest industrial area, and had conquered and occupied it, while at the same time Ninth Army forces striking from the Rhine to the Elbe had advanced more than 230 miles and had occupied more than 13,000 square miles of heavily populated German soil. Total Army battle casualties in the dual operations, from April 1 through May 9, were 1,358 killed, 5,572 wounded, and 878 missing. German prisoners of war taken by the Army totaled 584,450 for the same period. The Ninth Army had lived up to its code name—CONQUER.

By VE-day the active operations of these combat days were pushed into the background, at the moment, for Ninth Army was knee-deep in the multitudinous problems of occupying and governing its portion of conquered Germany.

CHAPTER 8
OCCUPATION AND MILITARY GOVERNMENT

ALTHOUGH the fighting was over and the war was won major tasks still faced the Allied Armies in Europe. The defeated nation was in chaos and to bring order out of this chaos, the Allies would have to administer and govern Germany. In addition, to prevent the German nation from ever again becoming powerful enough to wage war, the Allies proposed to occupy Germany for an indefinite period of time. Much thought and planning had been given to these paramount necessities long before the victory was won. The preliminary general plans had reached Ninth Army Headquarters in January 1945, as Operation Eclipse, the plan for the occupation of Germany. Eclipse was to begin on A-day, the day when major military operations against Germany came to an end. This could have come about through a formal surrender by the German Government, through a formal surrender by the German High Command, or through the total defeat and piecemeal surrender of the German armed forces. The general plan for Operation Eclipse contemplated two phases. The first envisioned the completion of military operations by the seizure of primary strategic objectives, such as key communication and industrial centers, and the occupation of the entire nation by the Allied armies; the second phase contemplated the withdrawal of the various armies, where necessary, from areas initially seized into their final respective national zones, and the long-term occupation of Germany. The whole of Germany was divided into four zones to be held by American, Russian, British, and French forces. Concurrently with the two general phases, military, governmental, economic, and social measures would be instituted to insure both the short-term and long-range objectives of the Allied powers.

Ninth Army began work on the detailed plans for Eclipse in January. After intensive study and conferences with other headquarters, both American and British, the first Army instructions pertaining to Eclipse were issued to the three corps on April 9, as Letter of Instructions No. 21, First Draft. This letter of instruction was twice revised, in accordance with changes received from

12th Army Group, and was issued in final form on May 15. In addition to the basic document, six annexes were attached, dealing with areas to be held and with intelligence, engineer, personnel, military government, and signal activities.

The occupation of Germany under the Eclipse plan could be compressed into a phrase—"occupy, organize, and govern." Carrying out the task, however, involved gigantic problems. Military measures had to be taken to insure the enforcement of the surrender terms, the security of the occupying forces, and the discipline and good order of the civilian populace. Military government must be securely established and the local civil government reconstituted. Intelligence measures were required to insure the apprehension of war criminals, subversive political personages, and common saboteurs, as well as the seizure and safeguarding of records, documents, or installations of intelligence value, particularly for the war against Japan. The disarmament of Germany and the disbandment of her military and semi-military forces must be achieved. The liberated Allied prisoners of war and the displaced persons must be cared for and repatriated. And all of these tasks had to be accomplished in a country completely disorganized and broken down—politically, economically, and socially.

It was a greatly enlarged Ninth Army that undertook the governing of its portion of Germany under terms of the Eclipse plan while at the same time preparing units for redeployment to the Pacific for the war against Japan. On May 6, to release Headquarters First Army for redeployment, 12th Army Group transferred to Ninth Army VII Corps comprising the 9th, 69th, 104th Infantry, and 3d Armored Divisions, and VIII Corps, comprising the 76th, 87th, 89th Infantry, and 6th Armored Divisions, together with a large number of corps and army troops. Ninth Army simultaneously assumed responsibility for all of the First Army area occupied by these units, which comprised the bulk of that Army, and for a small portion of Third Army's area. Within the next four days, the 70th and 78th Infantry Divisions were transferred to Ninth Army from Third and First Armies, respectively. Ninth Army now included five corps and twenty-two divisions and by mid-May reached a peak strength of over 650,000.

At the cessation of hostilities, the Army was already regrouping its forces for occupational duties and for the specific tasks set

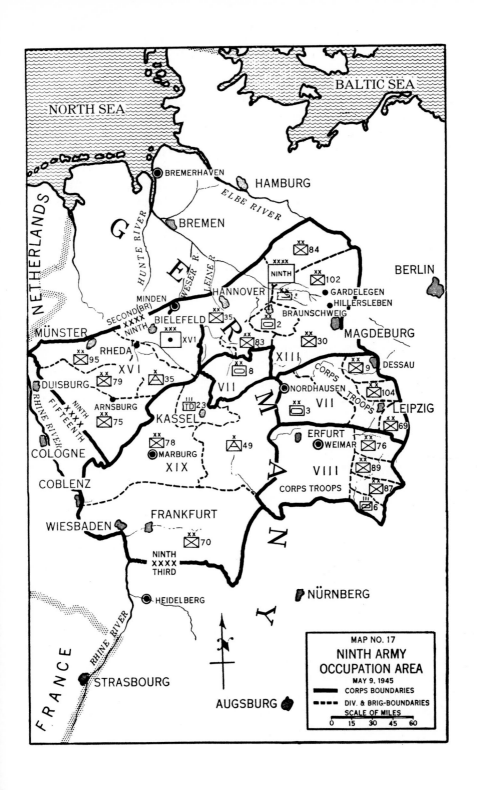

MAP NO. 17

NINTH ARMY
OCCUPATION AREA
MAY 9, 1945

CORPS BOUNDARIES
DIV. & BRIG-BOUNDARIES

SCALE OF MILES
0   15   30   45   60

forth in Operation Eclipse. On May 8, XIX Corps Headquarters took over the former First Army rear area, and the XIII Corps area was enlarged to include the former XIX Corps sector along the Elbe. On the same day, the 2d Armored Division, which was assembled south of Braunschweig, passed from XIX Corps to direct Ninth Army control, in preparation for the division's use as a task force, as provided for in Eclipse, to occupy the American sector of Berlin. Throughout the Army area, unit boundaries were adjusted, so far as practicable, to coincide with German political boundaries in order to simplify the conduct of occupation and military government. The dispositions of major units of the Army on May 9 were as shown on Map No. 17, and the Army organization, by corps and divisions, on the same date was as follows:

> *VII Corps*
> > 9th Infantry Division
> > 69th Infantry Division
> > 104th Infantry Division
> > 3d Armored Division
> > 8th Armored Division
>
> *VIII Corps*
> > 76th Infantry Division
> > 87th Infantry Division
> > 89th Infantry Division
> > 6th Armored Division
>
> *XIII Corps*
> > 30th Infantry Division
> > 35th Infantry Division
> > 83d Infantry Division
> > 84th Infantry Division
> > 102d Infantry Division
> > 5th Armored Division (assembled north of Braunschweig)
>
> *XVI Corps*
> > 29th Infantry Division (assembled east of Münster)
> > 75th Infantry Division
> > 79th Infantry Division
> > 95th Infantry Division
>
> *XIX Corps*
> > 70th Infantry Division
> > 78th Infantry Division
> > *2d Armored Division*

In addition to the above, the Army retained responsibility for the supply, evacuation, and administration of XVIII Airborne Corps, consisting of the 82d Airborne, 8th Infantry, and 7th

Armored Divisions, and supporting troops. This corps remained on loan to British Second Army and operated to the north of Ninth Army's area until May 22, when the corps headquarters was relieved from British Second Army and moved back to France. The 82d Airborne and the 8th Infantry Divisions continued occupation and military government activities under British control. The 7th Armored Division passed to Ninth Army on May 21 and was attached to VII Corps.

The prompt supplying of communications in the tremendously enlarged Army area was made possible by the efficient repair and use of the existing German telephone network and the prompt installation of signal corps VHF radio link circuits. By the time Ninth Army became responsible for the area of First Army, reliable telephone communication had been established to VII and VIII Corps as well as to First Army switch centrals at Cassel, Marburg, Erfurt, and Weimar, all over 120 miles distant. Radio link was used to parallel all important lines, and the radio system became more extensive than at any other time in Ninth Army's operations.

Under Operation Eclipse, the Army was responsible for two specific missions over and above the general provisions for the occupation of its assigned portion of Germany. These were the setting up of task forces for the Bremen area and for the U. S. zone in Berlin. The German ports of Bremen and Bremerhaven and the areas immediately adjacent to those cities had been designated as the U. S. Bremen–Bremerhaven Enclave for use, as soon as practicable after cessation of hostilities, as the supply ports for all U. S. occupational forces. Since the area was in the British zone of military operations, as well as in their eventual occupational area, SHAEF directed 21 Army Group to secure the area initially and later turn it over to United States forces.

For occupational purposes the U. S. Bremen–Bremerhaven Enclave was organized into and known as the Enclave Military District. The American force to take over the district was designated Task Force Bremen and the task force commander was also to be the Enclave Military District commander. Ninth Army was to prepare the detailed occupational plans, coordinating in this with 21 Army Group, British Second Army, Communications Zone, the U. S. Navy, and the U. S. Army Air Forces. Liaison was to be established with 21 Army Group to coordinate the movement of all U. S. forces into the Enclave, and Ninth Army was responsible for that movement as well as the maintenance of the forces. The task force, of one division with supporting troops, was to be prepared, five days after Eclipse conditions were declared to be in effect, to move into Bremen and take over control of the Enclave from British forces. An Air Task Force Bremen, composed of a fighter-bomber group, was also set up to move into the Enclave to relieve the Royal Air Force and provide air cooperation for Task Force Bremen. Similar forces for port area headquarters and for control of the harbors were designated by the Communications Zone and by the Navy.

Ninth Army Letter of Instructions No. 24, dated April 22, 1945, delegated the responsibility for the execution of the Bremen mission to XVI Corps and named Major General Harry L. Twaddle, Commanding General of the 95th Infantry Division, as Task Force Commander. The task force was composed of the 95th Division, together with a number of supporting troops, such as tank and tank destroyer battalions; ordnance bomb-disposal squads, depot companies, and maintenance companies; medical collecting, ambulance, and clearing companies, an evacuation hospital, and a medical depot; quartermaster truck, railhead, and service companies; military government and United Nations Relief and Rehabilitation Administration detachments; and various other miscellaneous units. The 95th Infantry Division continued its occupation duties under XVI Corps, meanwhile preparing for its mission as the principal component of Task Force Bremen. On May 1 one regiment of the 95th moved into Bremen as an advance detachment, although the area had not yet been cleared by the British and fighting was still in progress. On May 7 orders from 12th Army Group substituted the 29th Infantry Division, commanded by Major General Charles H. Gerhardt, for the 95th Division, which was now designated for early redeployment to the Pacific, and the 29th immediately began relief of the 95th elements in Bremen. The 29th Division command post opened in Bremen on May 10. The Enclave Military District was turned over by the British Second Army to Task Force Bremen at mid night, May 24, and at the same time the Task Force passed from XVI Corps control to direct Army control. Army engineer troops, not attached to the task force, were assigned areas in the Enclave where they performed all general engineer work. In addition to routine rehabilitation and maintenance of roads, they constructed semipermanent bridges across the Weser, Hunte, and Hamm Rivers.

A further provision of Eclipse called on Ninth Army to organize and hold in reserve a task force composed of the 2d Armored Division, with the necessary supporting troops, to be dispatched to Berlin on orders from Supreme Allied Headquarters to occupy the U. S. zone in that city. Upon arrival in Berlin, command of the task force was to pass to the U. S. Berlin District commander. Ninth Army Letter of Instructions No. 25, dated May 7, 1945 (revised May 15, 1945) designated the Commanding General, 2d Armored Division (Major General Isaac D. White), as the commander of Task Force Berlin and set up detachments of supporting troops—antiaircraft, tank destroyer, ordnance, medical, quartermaster, and intelligence. As has been noted, the 2d Armored Division passed from XIX Corps to direct Army control on May 8 in the vicinity of Braunschweig. There the division and supporting troops were assembled and the task force was made ready to occupy the Reich capital. It was not until July, however, after the unit passed from Ninth Army command, that the American occupation of Berlin was effected.

The general provisions of Operation Eclipse—to occupy, organize, and govern the conquered territory—had already gone into effect as the Ninth Army portion of Germany had been conquered. The detailed plan had been in the hands of corps commanders since early April. As military operations penetrated deeper and deeper into Germany, parts of the plan were put into effect in conquered areas, and substantial portions of Germany were being occupied and governed under Eclipse before the war in Europe ended. Libraries, archives, documents, persons of counterintelligence value, governmental ministries, industrial plants, and army, navy, and air force establishments had been seized. Fixed defenses and fortifications were destroyed. Rehabilitation of hospitals, fuel systems, port and landing facilities, and shelters for troops and displaced persons had begun. Many Allied prisoners of war had been retaken from the Germans and cared for. Control measures for the civilian populace had been put into effect as the territory was overrun. Military government had been initiated. Now it remained to expand and strengthen military government; to reconstitute local civil government as rapidly as possible;

to insure order and a return to a minimum standard of living for the civil populace; to reconstruct the civilian economy to meet the minimum needs of the community and of the occupying forces; and to disarm and demilitarize the conquered nation.

Shortly after the Army entered Germany it had become apparent that the number of Military Government detachments which had been made available from the European Civil Affairs Division would be inadequate to bring effective military government to Germany. Throughout the winter, the Army had carried on a detailed and intensive program of training for Military Government detachments at an Army Military Government Training Center at Tirlemont, Belgium. However, the large number of detachments thus trained by Ninth Army were deployed with American Armies on the basis of the permanent U. S. occupation zone, and Ninth Army occupied extensive territory which was in the eventual occupation zones of the Russians and the British. To alleviate the shortage of Military Government detachments, the Army activated a provisional Military Government regiment consisting of three companies of forty-nine detachments. Personnel for the unit were drawn from combat divisions and from corps troops, under a quota system set up by the Army. The officers and men thus selected had long known the Germans, since they had fought them on the Normandy beaches, across France, through the Siegfried Line, and into Germany. They knew that a fair but stern military government was necessary. At an Army Military Government Training Center in Bielefeld, the personnel were given an extensive and concentrated training course, which was a brief of the more detailed instruction formerly given at Tirlemont and was conducted by the same military government specialists wholly familiar with and long-experienced in the work. In all, some 450 officers and 800 enlisted men received training at Bielefeld. In a few short weeks more and more detachments were available to move forward and take over military government. Often they moved in and took over existing governments which had been set up as a stop-gap measure by infantry, artillery, antiaircraft, or other tactical units not engaged in actual combat.

Military Government detachments were stretched almost to the breaking point during the Army's advance east of the Rhine. The detachments were ordered to assume responsibility for many thousands of Germans as well as to operate displaced persons' camps, which were set up to accommodate the vast numbers of enslaved people freed by the advancing Ninth Army. Many of the detachments controlled areas and assumed responsibilities which under anticipated conditions would have been handled by two or three such units.

The detachments set up civil administration everywhere, chiefly on town levels. The new administration often required the complete reactivation of all departmental and municipal agencies. Police control and the feeding of displaced persons were prime necessities; occupation and post-combat conditions required such measures as the provision of billets for the occupying troops, the maintenance of public health and sanitation, the procurement of labor, and the supervision of restrictions on the movement of civilians. In reconstituting local government the detachments often found that the Nazi-controlled officials had fled; the immediate job was the appointment of new governmental officials. In other localities the Nazis remained and were immediately dismissed and arrested. These dismissals and arrests were typical of the de-Nazification program carried out in the Army zone. Finding replacements for dismissed officials was naturally much more difficult than discovering and ousting those with Nazi tendencies. The successors had to be acceptable, not only in willingness to cooperate with the military forces but also in ideological convictions in keeping with the principles of Democracy. Few such men were available, for the taint of National Socialism was found everywhere. Occasionally there was a feeble resurgence of Communistic and Social Democratic sentiment, but this was rare. At best, the officials selected by military government were capable technicians without political bias; at worst, they were administrative automatons without convictions of any kind, political or otherwise.

On VE-day there were 180 American Military Government detachments operating in the Army area, and five in the Bremen Enclave area. In addition, there were 29 United Nations Relief and Rehabilitation Administration detachments assisting Military Government. By June 14 provincial governments had been activated in Westfalen, Hannover, Kurhessen, Braunschweig, Lippe, and Schaumberg-Lippe; administrations on a *Regierungsbezirk* (several counties) level, were established at Münster, Minden,

Arnsberg and Hannover; and of the 163 *Landkreise* (counties) in the Army area, some 80 had completely new governments under an Army-approved head. The full-scale opening of American Military Government in Germany proved that the detachments had been adequately trained and were prepared to perform their mission. Although mistakes were made, this type of government demonstrated to the Germans that the American Army had come to Germany as a conquering power and proposed to rule the lives of the people until they were prepared to guide their own destiny in such a way that it would not be necessary for the United States or any other Allied power ever again to return to Germany by force of arms.

The attitude of the German people toward American occupation and military government can best be described by a single word—"docile." For the most part, after they had got over their initial fright, they were easily controlled and obedient. There were scattered and rare instances of trouble from youthful fanatics, but the widely advertised "Werewolf" underground terrorism failed to make its appearance. For years the Germans had had a strong central government from which the people received directives concerning their military, political, economic, and social lives. Detailed as these directives had been under the monarchy and the Weimar Republic, they became even more detailed under the Nazis. The completeness with which the Nazi government organized, supervised, and controlled all aspects of the daily life of the individual is well known. The resulting attitude of the people readily lent itself to the institution of the many specific measures necessary for military government and occupation by the Allies. In addition, the vast destruction of factories and homes, together with the physical and mental beating taken by the German people as a whole during the war, had produced a stunned effect on the populace. Added to this was the shock the German civilian received when he realized that the supposedly invincible German Army had been completely beaten in battle and captured almost in its entirety.

Notable differences in these general attitudes were found in the provinces of Lippe and Schaumburg-Lippe and in the city of Cassel. The two provinces were more thoroughly Nazified than any other which the Army occupied. So completely had they been Nazified that it was almost impossible to find suitable personnel for the various governmental functions at the city, county, and provincial level. Extremely careful screening of personnel was necessary. The city of Cassel, with a normal peacetime population of some 225,000, had suffered heavily from bombing. During one air strike the air-raid alarm failed to function. As a result, according to statements of the acting *Bürgermeister* immediately after the city was occupied, practically every family in the city had suffered casualties. All reports from MG agencies and from the occupying troops in Cassel indicated an understandable sullenness and hatred on the part of the inhabitants.

The Supreme Allied Commander had issued for Germany his general proclamation, together with various ordinances and laws which were binding legislation upon the German population and were enforced by Military Government courts. Ordinances and laws included those with regard to crimes, control of property and foreign exchange, abolishing the Nazi Party and affiliated organizations, abolishing or suspending certain German legislation, closing German courts and providing for how and when they should be reopened, and numerous other civil, administrative, and legal matters. Authority was delegated to the Army Commander to establish Military Government courts for the enforcement of Military Government regulations. He, in turn, delegated authority to establish all types of courts to each corps and division commander. Three types of courts were established: summary Military Government courts with authority to impose punishment not exceeding one year in prison and $1,000 fine; intermediate Military Government courts with authority to impose sentences not in excess of ten years and $10,000 fine; and general Military Government courts with authority to impose sentences up to and including death. The appointing authorities were the reviewing authorities. The Army Commander finally reviewed, however, all sentences in excess of one year or $1,000 fine, and all sentences in cases in which petitions for review were filed. Death sentences could not be executed without confirmation by the Army Group Commander.

The majority of cases in the Army area arose out of violations of curfew and circulation regulations and were tried by summary Military Government courts. There were a number of cases of German civilians harboring German soldiers during the earlier phases of the Army's fighting in Germany in which severe penalties were imposed. There were, however, only seven death penalties imposed in the Army area. Six of these were for espionage, and one was for resistance by a German soldier after VE-day. Two of the sentences for espionage were approved and executed. Action on the other five cases had not been completed at the time the Army became nonoperational.

The ordinance closing the German courts permitted their reopening after screening of personnel. By the time the Army became nonoperational, a substantial number of lower courts had been reopened and good progress had been made toward the reopening of others. The greatest difficulty, naturally, was the locating of judges and court personnel free from the Nazi taint.

One of the largest tasks which confronted Military Government was the care and repatriation of liberated displaced persons. Once freed, these French, Dutch, Belgian, Russian, Polish, Greek, and Slavic workers, forcibly brought into Germany to till the fields and work in the factories, often left the camps in which the Germans had segregated them and took to the roads. They dropped their tools and plows and began streaming eastward, westward, any direction that would carry them away from their place of long imprisonment. Moreover, many German farmers, who had been working on war production in the industrial centers, and city dwellers, who had sought refuge in the country from the incessant Allied bombings, wanted to return to their homes once the tide of battle had swept past them. Considering the serious consequences that might result from the standpoint of impeded military traffic, the counterintelligence difficulties, and the possibilities for looting and even organized guerrilla resistance if these masses of liberated slave laborers, mixed with thousands of German nationals, were allowed to move at will throughout the area, the Army early decided upon a general stay-put policy, which though difficult to enforce, offered the surest guarantee of effective control. To a great extent the problem was solved by the establishment of roadblocks and collecting points by the tactical units. Military Government rapidly organized camps throughout the area for the displaced persons and required all such individuals to remain in place until their repatriation became possible. In these camps, emphasis was placed on disinfestation and an orderly efficient administration. Whenever possible, personnel of the camps themselves were used in administrative positions.

The number of displaced persons uncovered by the Army was staggering. In all, over 1,250,000 displaced persons were repatriated. Over 37,000 people were shipped from the Army area in a single day, May 30. Citizens were returned to their home lands as rapidly as transportation permitted, not only for humanitarian reasons but also because their removal from the Army area released camp space, Military Government personnel, and large quantities of food for other purposes. UNRRA personnel, together with liaison detachments assigned to the Army from most of the countries involved, provided valuable help in repatriation. They assisted in making arrangements for medical care and supplies and for food and clothing, and aided in the control of the liberated people and in the provisions for their transportation to their home countries and reception there. Several countries provided part of the transportation for their nationals. France, for example, sent numbers of trucks into the Army area to take French men and women home.

The procurement and distribution of supplies for displaced persons was a tremendous undertaking. By VE-day, approximately 250,000 rations were being issued daily to displaced persons. About one-half of these rations were imported from the United States, while the remainder came from captured German food stocks. By the end of May, 400,000 rations were being issued daily from warehouses at Münster, Cassel, and Marburg, and from fifty to seventy per cent of this food came from the United States. The diet comprised approximately 2,000 calories per day and included such items as meat, bread, noodles, soup, milk, and chocolate. To supply fresh bread, German Army baking facilities in Cassel were taken over, and 10,000 three-pound loaves of bread were baked each day. In addition to food, there were supplied blankets, soap, clothing, cigarettes, toothpaste, and various other items, many of them captured from the Germans. To distribute the food and clothing and other supplies to the various camps, ten French truck companies were operated by the Army. All that was humanly possible was done for these wards of the United Nations, the freed slaves of the Third Reich.

For all of the displaced persons, liberation was accompanied by a spirit of festivity, often with unhappy results. Long celebrations were in order in the camps where the Germans had held them prisoners for so long, and the area was scoured for alcoholic beverages. The inability of the Eastern Europeans to read German labels and their faith in an apparently uneducated olfactory sense resulted in the consumption of large quantities of varnish remover, wood alcohol, "buzz bomb" fuel, and embalming fluid. These liquors were in most cases purloined in bulk lots from warehouses and tank cars. As a result, displaced persons' barracks on the "morning after" were many times changed to hospital wards filled with acutely ill and dead. Hundreds died and many more suffered the agonies of wood-alcohol poisoning. In some instances their benefactors, the American soldiers, suffered too. Members of the military detachments at the camps were invited to share the prize of a clandestine raid, which had often been poured from a five-gallon drum into bottles bearing the labels of fine cognac and champagne.

To aid in the production and distribution of food for the German population, the Army impressed thousands of captured German vehicles into service to form a transport system to carry produce from farm to market and from area to area. An Army Central Food Control Board was established to coordinate the supply and distribution of all food for all categories of people, exclusive of U. S. troops. The board organized the inventorying and reporting of all German food stocks, civilian and military, including large depot stocks of grain, sugar, and canned and dehydrated foods captured intact as our troops had overrun the area. Food stocks were inventoried and broken down into the various components of the prescribed menus and the Food Control Board directed the movement of stocks throughout the Army area. When certain food components were surplus in one area and lacking in another, surpluses were shipped into the areas which were short. Food offices were opened everywhere and ration schedules for the civilian population were announced. Food-processing plants were reopened. In Braunschweig, for example, a flour mill, two flour-products factories, and a meat-preserving factory resumed production.

While food control and production had first priority, other commercial activities were instituted on a limited scale for civilian use and to meet Army requirements. Shops specializing in agricultural machines and automotive repairs were given permission to resume business. A clothing factory at Warstein began making clothes for the German population. Other industries, such as automobile and steel plants and oil refineries, were directed to reopen and begin production to meet the special needs of the occupying forces.

The German financial and banking system had of course been thrown into chaos. It was necessary to get it into operation to permit day-to-day transactions in the routine business of living and to permit payments to industries needed by the occupation forces. To normalize banking and to make it possible for banks to meet current withdrawal demands, part of the *Reichsbank's* 700,000,000 *Reichsmark* currency reserve at Magdeburg was redistributed over the Army area as needed.

More than 450 German banks were reopened. Constant supervision was maintained over the currency situation in the entire Army zone. In industries and facilities which were essential to efficient occupation, such as the railroads and the Bremen shipyards, Army supervision and coordination was necessary to provide financing for the payment of the workers. Military Government financial agencies worked through municipal authorities, industrial management, and the *Reichsbank* to insure that funds were available to pay railroad employees and shipyard workers. The system of bank clearings was re-established, beginning in Hannover, and was gradually extended throughout other political subdivisions of the Army occupation zone.

More than a million dollars' worth of foreign exchange and bonds, together with 100 tons of silver bullion belonging to the Hungarian and Austrian governments, were removed from Magdeburg to Supreme Allied Headquarters now located in Frankfurt. Also to Frankfurt was sent a great collection of art treasures, religious vessels, and crucifixes, many of them comprising precious metals and jewels, looted by Germans from the cathedral of Poznan, Poland, and uncovered by our troops at Grasleben, Germany.

All during the occupation, the process of caring for, rehabilitating, and repatriating the long-suffering and newly liberated Allied prisoners of war continued at full speed. In all, the Army uncovered 592,000 Allied prisoners. Thirty thousand American and 41,000 British soldiers were liberated during the 64-day period after the Army crossed the Rhine, and in the same period 410,000 Allied prisoners of war of all nationalities were cared for, processed, and evacuated from the Army area.

Both displaced persons and Allied prisoners of war, as well as German political prisoners, were victims of German atrocities, and many had been inmates of the infamous concentration camps. The inhuman and unbelievable indignities that man was forced to suffer under the arrogant and bestial Germans are well known. Space will not be given here to a detailed account of the horrors and misery that had existed in the Army area. Suffice it to say that there were notorious concentration camps, such as Buchenwald, near Weimar, and Nordhausen, both initially captured by First Army, where conditions were terrible beyond description. Near Hannover a concentration camp was found where thousands of Russians, Poles, and Frenchmen had been systematically starved and then burned in large incinerating ovens. At Gardelegen one of the most shocking of the atrocities occurred. Some 1,100 political prisoners, wearing their pitifully clown-like striped uniforms, were rounded up by SS troops in anticipation of the American occupation of the town and herded into a large barn, the floor of which had been covered with gasoline-soaked straw. After the prisoners had been jammed into the barn and the doors closed, the building was set on fire. Prisoners who tried to rush the doors were killed by machine guns placed to cover each exit. American troops arrived at the scene before the SS had time to bury the still-smoking bodies, which were being piled into huge pits and trenches.

The Supreme Allied Commander personally directed that steps be taken to cause decent burial of persons of all nationalities who were atrocity victims and still unburied. Personnel who had been buried in mass graves and in pits were to be disinterred, if possible, and given individual reburials. Cemeteries would be placed in prominent spots, and the same grave markers would be used as were employed for the burial of Allied soldiers. The Supreme Commander further directed that German males of all classes, including a cross-section of prominent persons such as bankers, and lawyers, be required to perform the actual work of burial, or disinterment and reburial, and the maintenance of individual graves. This was to be an object lesson to all Germans.

When examples of Nazi brutality were brought to the attention of the German people they invariably murmured "*Nein, Nein.*" They had not known such things were going on, they said. In many cases they refused to believe the facts, labeling them propaganda. To show them that the atrocities actually had been committed, Ninth Army troops and Military Government units forced the citizens of towns near notorious concentration camps to dig up the bodies from mass graves and to give them decent burial in the neighboring villages. Citizens were also made to go through the torture chambers and view the instruments of torture. By direction of the Supreme Allied Commander, at Gardelegen a cross-section of the town's population was taken out to the barn where the bodies had been found, shown all of the shocking evidence, and made to give the victims decent burial in a cemetery to be maintained as a memorial in the city park. Each body was individually buried by a specified German citizen of stature in the community. Each German who buried a body is registered in the city hall and is required to maintain perpetual care of that grave. If the German dies or moves away the *Bürgermeister* is responsible for appointing a new caretaker for the grave. Four hundred and forty-two bodies were removed from the barn and 574 were disinterred from the trenches and pits.

In all of these atrocity cases, immediate investigation was instituted by the War Crimes Branch of the Ninth Army Judge Advocate's Section, under Colonel Stanley W. Jones, to determine responsible and guilty individuals and bring them to trial for their crimes. There was nothing more that the Army could do for the dead. As for the living, medicines, food, and clothing were rushed to the concentration camps to save those who could still be saved.

The magnitude of the medical problem confronting the Army can best be illustrated by a few figures. Displaced persons alone presented a medical situation of great seriousness. On May 7, 1945, there were some 2,500 camps for displaced persons in the Army area, with a total of 1,294,316 inhabitants. The crowded and insanitary conditions in these camps produced an increased incidence of disease, and in only a few was there adequate civilian medical personnel. The Army had to assume the medical care for all these camps. All hospitalization in the entire Army zone was, of course, an Army responsibility. On May 15 the Army controlled 468 German military hospitals, 30 hospitals for liberated Allied military personnel, and 16 hospitals for displaced persons. In these hospitals were 88,047 German military, 11,055 liberated Allied military personnel, 1,357 displaced persons, and 2,697 German civilian patients. The administration of these installations was supervised by personnel of Army medical units, who were responsible for the provision of rations and medical supplies.

The ever-present danger of typhus required the most careful attention. Because of its typically rapid spread, particularly in areas of lowered living standards and economic deterioration, this disease was expected to create a problem in occupied Germany. Using DDT powder, a vigorous campaign was initiated against lice, the carriers of typhus. Large groups of displaced persons and prisoners of war were deloused and carefully observed for signs of the disease. Typhus-control teams, operating from Army Head-quarters investigated all reports of the disease within the Army area and instituted methods of control. Areas found to be har-boring the disease were designated as typhus zones, and civilian traffic in and out was carefully regulated. Entry and departure of persons was kept to a minimum. Those traveling to another town were carefully examined and were dusted with DDT; noti-fication of their exposure to the disease was forwarded to authori-ties at their destination. To prevent the spread of typhus from central Germany to western Europe, the natural barrier of the Rhine was established as a *cordon sanitaire*. The limited crossing sites over the river permitted the Army accurately to control westward displacement of civilians. At all crossing sites were located DDT dusting teams whose function was to make certain that all persons crossing the *cordon* were free of lice. All U. S. personnel departing central Germany for leave areas or duties west of the Rhine were carefully examined for the presence of lice prior to departure. Thus the disease was kept more or less local-ized. The incidence in the civil population at no time reached alarming proportions and in the Army itself was nil.

To provide for the internment of alleged war criminals and other security suspects, four camps were set up in the Army area. The camp at Recklinghausen, on the northern edge of the Ruhr district, constructed soon after the Army crossed the Rhine, was typical. It was designed to permit segregation of internees of counterintelligence interest from other internees and war crimi-nals, and a further segregation of males and females. Accommo-dations were provided for 7,500 individuals. Army engineer troops constructed semipermanent type barracks, messhalls, and admin-istration buildings. While the camp was still in the process of being built, arrests began and internees started pouring into the camp. Each person arrested and brought to the camp was screened to determine if he properly should be interned. Those arrested were registered by name, identification number, date of arrival, and reason for arrest. Prominent internees included selected members of the SS; members of the Gestapo; persons on the SHAEF blacklist; certain high-ranking police and other public officials; Nazi Party officials; and high-ranking military personnel of the German General Staff Corps and equivalent air force and naval officers. In all, the Army interned about 18,000 such individuals during its operations in Germany.

Upon cessation of hostilities on VE-day, the Army prisoner-of-war cages were bulging with 400,000 German prisoners of war who had not yet been evacuated from the Army area. 12th Army Group now directed that no more prisoners of war be evacuated to the Communications Zone and that all prisoners in the Army areas be documented, processed, screened, and made ready for an orderly demobilization and return to civilian life. The Ninth Army plan for the demobilization and disbandment of the German disarmed military forces and certain semi-military organizations was announced on May 13, 1945. Corps commanders were ordered to establish concentration areas large enough to accommodate ten to fifteen thousand disarmed German soldiers. Each corps was made responsible for providing adequate guard and administrative personnel for all camps in its area and was encouraged to use German personnel to the utmost in carrying out administrative and maintenance functions under American supervision. The German prisoners were required to do the actual work of constructing their own concentration areas. American engineers furnished the materials and supervised the prisoners, who erected barbed-wire fences, dug latrines, and constructd machine-gun emplacements to be used by the American soldier guards. Once these measures were completed, each German constructed his own temporary improvised shelter.

Three days after the publication of the Army directive, the several corps were busy moving German forces into concentration areas, where nominal rolls and other statistical analyses were prepared. Within a short time all personnel had been documented and earmarked according to service, rank, sex, industrial and professional groups, nationality, residence, and availability for discharge.

Initially, only individuals who resided in the Army area and who were to be employed in agriculture, coal mining, or transport service were discharged. Later, such personnel who resided out of the Army area were discharged. Each person discharged was sent to the capital city of the *Landkreis* in which he lived. Here Military Government, with the aid of the *Bürgermeister* of the *Landkreis* capital, assumed the responsibility of releasing the individual to his actual residence.

German disarmed forces, other than the army, who were similarly documented and prepared for discharge included members of the SS, or *Schutzstaffel,* the protective guard of the Nazi Party; members of all units of the German Labor Service; members of *Organisation Todt,* the great German labor force; regular German air force personnel in the Auxiliary Home Air Defense Corps; members of all units of the Nazi Party Air Corps and the Nazi Party Motor Transport Corps working for the armed forces, together with personnel of their schools and training establishments; and other such semi-military personnel as it was necessary to handle through the armed forces machinery. Except for the SS, large numbers of members of all these units were discharged by Ninth Army. By direction of 12th Army Group, SS personnel, although prepared for discharge, were not actually discharged during the Army's operations in Europe. Highest priority was given to the disarmament and control of the fanatical *Waffen*-SS, the full-time military organization of the SS which had become a part of the German armed forces. Extraordinary precautions were taken. After preliminary disarmament, all SS officers and noncommissioned officers of the rank of sergeant and above were arrested and interned. The SS units were then disbanded, as such, and the personnel not arrested and interned were attached to regular German Army units. In effecting this transfer, care was taken to insure that a number of individuals who had previously served together in the same SS unit were not attached to the same Army unit.

The German penal units were also given high priority and special handling. Personnel of these units normally consisted of SS staff, army staff, and men undergoing sentence. The SS and army staff were carefully screened by counterintelligence personnel as possible war criminals and if cleared were disposed of through the established channels, as already indicated. The men undergoing sentence were divided into two classes according to the gravity of their offenses, in accordance with such information as was available at the time. Those who were under sentence for purely military or minor civil crimes were processed for demobilization as ordinary members of the German disarmed forces. Completion of the unexpired portion of their sentence was not required. Those who were under sentence for major civil crimes were transferred to such prisons as were convenient, pending investigation of their charges and sentences. If later released, these were discharged through the appropriate machinery.

Concurrently with the disbandment of the German armed forces, the collection, safeguarding, and intelligence appraisal of German war equipment were carried out. Great stores of material and equipment had of course been overrun and captured during combat operations. The responsibility for collecting, guarding, and reporting captured items had been delegated to corps. The various Army technical and supply services—ordnance, engineer, chemical warfare, quartermaster, medical, and signal—supervised the inventory and the technical and intelligence appraisal of German equipment, maintained files cross-indexed as to items and locations, and noted items of special interest to higher headquarters or to the Army. For example, large quantities of German Army signal equipment were captured, some of which was shipped to higher headquarters because of its intelligence value while some was retained by units for use in their occupational role. Items of intelligence value were thus saved, and by using other captured German equipment, units were able to clean, repair, and pack their organic signal equipment for redeployment.

In the exploitation of intelligence targets, large numbers of military and civilian technical specialists, together with scientists, economists, and industrialists brought from the United States, were now visiting the Army area to gain information and to assist in determining the results of the German scientific and industrial effort. The mass of visiting specialists required the establishment of a series of intelligence target visitors' camps, complete with messes and transportation facilities, capable of caring for 600 individuals. In the meantime, the Army's own documentation, recording, and appraisal of intelligence targets continued, on an ever vaster scale after taking over the First Army area.

Two German war research installations overrun by Ninth Army are worthy of special note. The German Air Forces Institute for Weapons Research, near Braunschweig, was one of the best technical finds of the war. Of particular importance was the aerodynamic range, together with its related facilities, comprising a cylindrical range 1330 feet long and 20 feet in diameter, from which the air could be evacuated to 2/100 of normal atmospheric pressure. Here the effects of high altitude and decreased pressure upon the firing of projectiles from aircraft in flight could be exhaustively studied. Equally important was the Hillersleben Proving Ground, the principal research and development establishment of the Wehrmacht, where items produced by such firms as Krupp were tested and further developed. At Hillersleben it was seen that, although the German government furnished ample facilities to the army, navy, and air force for research and development, these agencies often followed independent and uncoordinated lines. Moreover, Hitler always hoped for the miracle weapon; consequently many of the projects, such as devices for creating air disturbances of sufficient violence to destroy aircraft in flight, followed ill-conceived suggestions and inventions. In addition, the scientists received little military supervision and were prone to diverge on research only remotely connected with the war effort. The scientists at Hillersleben were found to be eager to divulge their findings to Allied investigators as their contribution to science, even though the research had been sponsored by a hostile government during the course of the war. With their aid, many items of value were found at Hillersleben, although much destruction had been wrought by an SS engineer battalion detailed for demolitions at the site, and by displaced persons, who had been quartered there.

Several infra-red ray instruments of special interest were discovered. A viewer, about 4 inches in diameter and 10 inches long, containing phosphorescent crystals, had been developed for use by patrols to indicate the use of infra-red rays by Allied troops and the approximate source-location of these rays. Long range photo-theodolites had also been developed. These had been used to photograph Dover, England, from across the English Channel, approximately 25 miles, with such clearness that the wires of the radio towers could be distinguished in the pictures. Similar instruments had also been located in the Harz Mountains to photograph the effects of artillery fire at Hillersleben, nearly 65 miles away.

Among the interesting installations at Hillersleben was the loading plant, which had many specimens of finned projectiles. Of special interest was the 15cm smooth-bore long-barrelled projector. Projectiles from this type of weapon had fallen in the vicinity of the rear echelon of Ninth Army Headquarters at Maastricht on December 16, 1944. One of these weapons was located on the Hillersleben Proving Ground range, and investigation showed why it could attain a range of about eighty miles. The 258-foot tube consisted of sections with five sets of two-booster powder-charge tubes installed at intervals along the main tube.

A trip over the Hillersleben firing ranges indicated the vast amount of testing that had been done and the nature of the tests. The large number of concrete test targets showed that much effort had been devoted to the development of concrete-piercing weapons and projectiles for attacking fortifications. A 1,000-foot tunnel leading to two heavily armored pillboxes showed experimental installations for the Siegfried Line. The presence of sample quantities of Allied armament showed that these items had been used for various tests. Data on firing effects of German weapons had been obtained by firing into shielded tunnels at close range, using reduced charges. Ingenious methods had been used to obtain data on the effects of recoil. While the Germans had carefully studied and tested interior ballistics, the exterior ballistics methods were based on a limited number of direct observations rather than on accurate scientific calculations. Range tables, for example, were obtained by photographing the trajectories of tracer projectiles at night. The results were inaccurate according to U. S. standards.

Advantage was taken of the Hillersleben Proving Ground to test and repair Ninth Army artillery weapons. All artillery pieces of major caliber were calibrated and inspected. Tubes and recoil mechanisms were replaced if necessary, and other repairs were made in order to render the pieces serviceable for shipment to the Pacific theaters.

Caves, mines, and other underground plant and storage facilities had been used to an amazing extent by the Germans. Over a large part of the area east of the Rhine, abandoned tunnels, mine shafts, and specially prepared underground areas housed complete plants for the manufacture and assembly of ammunition, bombs, and engines and for the storage of large quantities of valuable raw materials and finished products. For example, 3,500,000 yards of parachute silk were found stored in one salt mine. Large quantities of special documents had also been hidden away in these underground warehouses. In one mine intelligence teams found hidden sets of plans for special weapons to be used against Allied forces. In other mines several trainloads of records of various German cities were found. The underground establishments were often difficult of detection and even after their capture were sometimes difficult to enter and explore. Tunnels ran for miles, hundreds of feet under the surface. Without maps and with electric power cut off, their full exploration was often difficult. Moreover, the initial search of areas and of underground storage places often would result in only superficial findings, but as the search progressed and as additional information was obtained from displaced persons and German civilians, cleverly hidden passages revealed mass storage warehouses or large production facilities. Germany had literally gone underground.

One of the most important and interesting underground plants was that at Nordhausen, which had been overrun by First Army and later came under Ninth Army control. One of the main sites for the manufacture of V-bombs, the plant, complete in every detail, comprised an elaborate underground network of three miles of tunnels. The plant was laid out with great efficiency for the mass production both of V-bombs and of some types of aircraft engines. Cross tunnels opening into various main shafts provided arrangements similar to those of the most modern automotive plant, where the major product is assembled as it moves down a line and each sub-assembly is fed in at the right time and place. The tools, materials, and special equipment were capable of the most efficient modern production. Some of the special welding machines presented fine examples of the machine designer's art, built for special purposes and mass production. Originally devoted to the manufacture of V-1 bombs, the plant was almost completely converted to V-2 production at the time the American forces reached the area. Another month's delay in overrunning the territory might have seen the production of the formidable V-2 weapon in such numbers that tremendous damage to Allied facilities would have been possible.

Throughout the period, the Army continued the examination

and inventorying of the large stocks of finished and raw materials found in the factories and military installations in the Army area. Urgent calls were received daily from the Advance Section, Communications Zone, for lumber and housekeeping equipment for prisoner-of-war inclosures and for lumber, asphalt, plumbing fixtures, and other building supplies for the construction of assembly and staging areas in the redeployment of troops. Accordingly, everything that could be spared was made available. Twenty-one million linear feet of lumber and approximately 24,000 tons of tools, appliances, and plumbing supplies were collected and shipped to Communications Zone.

In inventorying the resources of the Army zone, quantities of materials for iron and steel production, tire and paper manufacture, and various valuable metals were uncovered and reported to SHAEF and the Communications Zone. From the reports submitted by the Army, the Communications Zone requested the materials it needed to support its continental manufacturing program and the Army assisted in procuring the selected items.

The Army had overrun one of the richest industrial regions in the world. While this area had been heavily bombed, many plants could be operated with the remaining facilities, and large stocks of materials were available. German industry had been so decentralized that sufficient subsidiary plants were often available to start production even if the main plant had been partially destroyed. Maximum use of these plants was made to manufacture needed items. For example, 125 *Volkswagens* (German jeeps) were produced under Army ordnance supervision for use by Military Government agencies. Other items produced under Army supervision included tires, tubes, and patches; industrial gases; bushings, gears, spindles, and special bolts, nuts and studs; and a variety of special gun parts and machine parts.

Activities of the Army engineers during the occupation period were many and varied. Demolition of many highway and railroad bridges had been prepared by the enemy but not executed. In locating and neutralizing emplaced explosive charges, information obtained from a captured civilian German demolition expert was found to be of much assistance. Minefields were cleared when necessary, but whenever possible were marked and left for future clearing by the Germans. Engineer photo-interpretation personnel were used to investigate captured aerial photographs to determine their suitability for future mapping operations. Reproduction of maps pertinent to the Army missions in Berlin and Bremen–Bremerhaven was continued as required. Army engineers assumed the responsibility for road maintenance and other routine engineer work in large portions of the areas of the various corps, inasmuch as the entire Army area had been divided among the corps.

Even though hostilities had ceased, rations and gasoline were in greater demand than ever because of the increased strength of the Army and the necessity for feeding and transporting displaced persons and released Allied prisoners of war. During the period May 10 to June 14, inclusive, 34,756,871 rations (102,000 tons) ; 22,717,566 gallons of gasoline (83,850 tons), and 523,575 gallons of Diesel oil (2,040 tons) were issued.

On May 30 impressive memorial services were conducted at the Ninth Army Military Cemetery located at Margraten. An estimated 50,000 citizens of the Netherlands Province of Limburg were present. Army personnel and civilian dignitaries included sixteen general officers representing divisions whose dead were interred at the cemetery, the Governor of the Province of Limburg, as well as the mayors of all cities in the province. A voluntary committee of the citizens of Maastricht had previously formulated plans for the decoration of each grave. This program was carried out during the previous night and early morning hours by school children of the province. Prayers were offered by chaplains of each faith. General Simpson gave a short address and placed a wreath on the grave of an unknown soldier. Other general officers present placed wreaths upon the graves of soldiers of their units. A battery of field artillery and a composite rifle platoon made up of members of each division whose dead were interred at Margraten fired commemorative salutes.

The Margraten Military Cemetery was turned over to the Channel Base Section of Communications Zone on June 1. During the seven-month period that this cemetery was operated by Ninth Army, 10,095 Americans, 700 Allied, and 3,000 Germans were buried there. Of the Americans interred, 755 were unknown at the time of burial. Identification of these was a continuing process. Every effort was made and all sources were exhausted in attempts to identify the bodies. At the time the operation of the cemetery was turned over to the Communications Zone, only eight-tenths of one per cent of the total buried were still unidentified. When control of the cemetery was relinquished, all available information concerning the remaining unidentified bodies was forwarded to higher headquarters for further study and attempt at identification.

At the same time that the Army engaged in all the varied and diverse tasks of occupation, redeployment of units for the war against Japan proceeded at full speed. Involved in redeployment, too, was the necessity for removing individuals with long service from the various units. With the announcement, in late May, of critical point scores for the release of individuals from the service, all units were screened for personnel with the required number of points. These persons were then transferred to units scheduled for early return to the United States for inactivation or were shipped to Communications Zone installations for return to the United States as individuals. Units alerted for redeployment to the Pacific were brought up to strength with personnel having low-point scores. Alerted units were relieved of occupation duties, brought to full strength, re-equipped, and prepared to perform their primary mission in the Pacific Theater of Operations. Redeployment made the regrouping of forces for occupational roles a never-ending task. No sooner would the divisions and corps be settled down than a major unit would be alerted for redeployment and the regrouping would begin again. The remaining units would have their occupation areas redefined. Always present was this constant shuffling and thinning out of troops.

With the cessation of hostilities and the announcement of the critical score for release from the service, major changes occurred in the daily routine of the lives and in the thoughts of individual soldiers. Personnel of frontline units, who prior to VE-day had been chiefly concerned with living from day to day, now found life more comfortable and had time to devote serious thought to the future. For many, with long service and much time in combat, there was the exciting prospect of an immediate return home. Others, who had accumulated fewer points, could look for quick redeployment to the Pacific war against Japan or to a period of service in the military occupation of Germany. For all, there were liberal leaves and furloughs and opportunities to travel to points of interest on the Continent. General Simpson gave his personal attention to the development of an educational, recreational and leisure-time program to help the men through their period of waiting. The maximum number of leaves and furloughs were granted to England, to Brussels and Paris, and to the Riviera in southern France, as well as to the Army rest centers in the Netherlands. Sightseeing tours were scheduled throughout western Germany. Library facilities were increased, day rooms established, and athletic programs and academic courses of instruction were made available to those men not required full-time for occupational or redeployment duties.

After VE-day the Army became dress-conscious. Clean, neat, pressed uniforms were the order of the day. Now that the Americon soldier had given up his lease on his foxhole and was quartered in German houses, in barracks, or in tents, the German people must be shown that the tough, dirty, and sometimes unshaven combat soldier was, in fact, an educated and civilized American. Plans were formulated to issue wool field jackets—better known as the Eisenhower jacket—ties, and garrison caps in lieu of steel helmets. During the rapid movements from the Rhine to the Elbe it had been impossible, with the limited laundry and salvage repair companies assigned to the Army, properly to launder, classify, repair, and reissue clothing and equipment received at salvage collecting points. The salvage had been shipped to Communications Zone for processing. Now, however, a static salvage processing center was established at Rheda, Germany, consisting of a laundry and dry cleaning plant and repair facilities. There approximately 200 German civilians were employed to recondition clothing under the supervision of Army laundry and salvage repair personnel.

Concurrently with the shifts of troop units for redeployment, the areas occupied by the Army in the final occupation zone of the British and the Russians were turned over to those forces. In Ninth Army Letter of Instructions No. 21, Third Draft, dated May 15, 1945, which has already been mentioned as the final Eclipse instructions, corps commanders, in addition to occupying, organizing and governing their assigned areas under the provisions of Eclipse and to preparing their forces for redeployment as directed, were further ordered to turn over the areas they held in the final Russian zone of occupation to the forces of the Union of Soviet Socialist Republics and the areas they held in the final British zone of occupation to the forces of the United

Kingdom. British units immediately began relieving XIII and XVI Corps units from north to south progressively. As American units were relieved they were either redeployed, sent to another Ninth Army Corps, or dispatched to Third or Seventh Armies. By June 11 British forces had taken over the whole of the former XIII and XVI Corps areas and a small portion of the VII Corps area.

Upon relief by the British, XVI Corps Headquarters left Ninth Army's command and moved to Chantilly, France, where it passed to the control of the Assembly Area Command of the European Theater of Operations, with the mission of processing redeploying units. XIII Corps Headquarters, after relief, moved to Le Havre, France, for embarkation to the United States for redeployment through the United States to the Pacific. Word was received on June 6 that VII Corps was also to be redeployed and on June 11, XXI Corps Headquarters, commanded by Major General Frank W. Milburn, was assigned to Ninth Army from Fifteenth Army, and took over the VII Corps area and troops. VII Corps Headquarters departed for Le Havre, France, on June 13. June 13 also saw the first Russian relief of Ninth Army forces when elements of VIII Corps' 76th Division were relieved east of the Mulde River by Red Army Forces.

Throughout the period of occupation—in fact, from the time contact had first been made with the Russians east of the Elbe on April 30—the forces of Ninth Army and those of the Russian Army exchanged visits of courtesy. Commanders of all corresponding ranks, together with individual soldiers, were invited to each other's headquarters. Many colorful ceremonies took place, as the forces of the victorious nations joined to celebrate their triumphs. At his headquarters in Braunschweig, General Simpson was host to prominent Russian commanders and their staffs, and the Army Commander and his staff were cordially received and extensively feted by Russian commanders in their territory across the Elbe. The large maneuver field adjacent to the Hermann Goering Luftwaffe headquarters building in Braunschweig —formerly the site of Nazi ceremonies—became the scene of reviews and parades by troops of Ninth Army while overhead planes of XXIX Tactical Air Command swooped low to display the might of American air power or flew high to spell out the initials USSR.

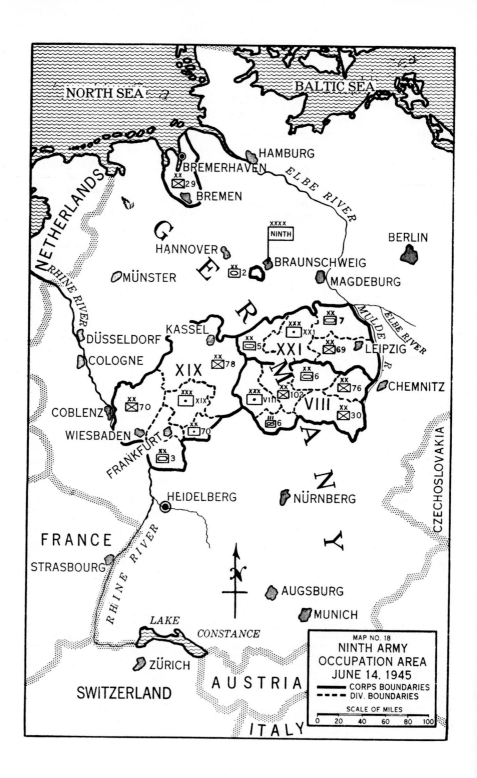

NORTH SEA

BALTIC SEA

NETHERLANDS

HAMBURG

BREMERHAVEN

XX 29

BREMEN

ELBE RIVER

BERLIN

G
E
R
M
A
N
Y

XXXX
NINTH

HANNOVER

MÜNSTER

RHINE RIVER

BRAUNSCHWEIG

XX 2

MAGDEBURG

MULDE RIVER

ELBE RIVER

DÜSSELDORF

KASSEL

XXX 7

XXX XX1

XXI

XX 5

XX 69

LEIPZIG

COLOGNE

XX 78

CHEMNITZ

XIX

XXX XIX

XX 6

M

VIII

XX 76

COBLENZ

XX 70

XXX VIII

XXX 102

XX 30

WIESBADEN

XX 70

FRANKFURT

XX 6

XX 3

HEIDELBERG

NÜRNBERG

FRANCE

RHINE RIVER

STRASBOURG

AUGSBURG

MUNICH

LAKE

CONSTANCE

CZECHOSLOVAKIA

ZÜRICH

AUSTRIA

SWITZERLAND

ITALY

MAP NO. 18
NINTH ARMY
OCCUPATION AREA
JUNE 14, 1945
—— CORPS BOUNDARIES
---- DIV. BOUNDARIES

SCALE OF MILES
0   20   40   60   80 100

In the process of redeployment and withdrawal to permanent national occupation zones, by June 14 the Army area had been reduced to that shown on Map No. 18, and the Army organization of major units was as follows:

VIII Corps
  30th Infantry Division
  76th Infantry Division
  89th Infantry Division (at Le Havre)
  102d Infantry Division
  6th Armored Division
XIX Corps
  70th Infantry Division
  78th Infantry Division
  3d Armored Division
XXI Corps
  69th Infantry Division
  5th Armored Division
  7th Armored Division
29th Infantry Division—Task Force Bremen
2d Armored Division—Task Force Berlin
75th Infantry Division (at Reims)
95th Infantry Division (en route to Camp Old Gold)

In the meantime, by 12th Army Group Letter of Instructions No. 24, dated May 30, 1945, Ninth Army had been directed to turn over its entire area and all troops to Seventh Army not later than June 15. After a number of conferences with 12th Army Group and Seventh Army, all details had been arranged for the mass transfer, and at one minute after midnight on the night of June 14-15, all Ninth Army forces were transferred to Seventh Army. Thus, after nine months and ten days of active operations Ninth Army wrote "Finis" to its task in the European Theater.

CHAPTER 9
THE END OF THE STORY

HEADQUARTERS Ninth Army had turned over its area of occupation in Germany in preparation for being redeployed to the Pacific war zone through the United States. Such a mission had been anticipated by General Simpson, and even before the conclusion of its occupational duties the Army was preparing for combat operations against Japan. The headquarters had its share of high-point personnel to return to the United States for discharge; plans were made to fill vacancies thus created. Studies were undertaken of the climate and terrain in the Pacific theaters, of Japanese tactics, organization, and methods of fighting, and of the offensive operations already in progress against the Japanese. General Simpson left the headquarters on June 20 and flew to the United States to receive War Department instructions on the new Ninth Army mission. While in the United States he participated in victory celebrations at Pittsburgh, Pennsylvania, Fort Worth, Texas, and at Weatherford, Texas, his birthplace.

From the United States, General Simpson flew to China, where he visited the headquarters of Lieutenant General Albert C. Wedemeyer, Commander of the United States Forces in the China Theater. Major General James E. Moore, Ninth Army Chief of Staff, who assumed command of the Army on General Simpson's departure from Europe, joined General Simpson in China, flying direct from the European Theater. The Army Commander and his Chief of Staff observed the combat operations of Chinese forces and studied the organization and functioning of the China Theater Headquarters, its Combat Command Headquarters, and its Services of Supply with a view to determining whether or not all or a part of the Ninth Army staff could be profitably employed in the China Theater. The Army Commander met with a most cordial reception from Generalissimo Chiang Kai-shek and from General Wedemeyer, both of whom were extremely desirous of having experienced combat commanders and their staffs brought to the China Theater. It was determined that General Simpson would be assigned as Commanding General, Field Forces, China Theater, and as Deputy Theater

Commander. As Commander of the Field Forces, he would command two groups of armies—one on the north under Lieutenant General Lucian K. Truscott, Jr., Commander of the U.S. Fifth Army in Italy, and one on the south under Major General Robert B. McClure, who was already commanding the Chinese Combat Command in that area.

In the meantime, Ninth Army Headquarters, under Brigadier General Roy V. Rickard, Assistant Chief of Staff, G-4, who had assumed command on General Moore's departure, moved to Deauville, France, on July 8 to prepare for return to the United States from the near-by port of Le Havre. In Deauville, fashionable peace-time seaside resort, the headquarters offices occupied the Hotel Royal, and the officers were quartered in the Hotel Normandie, both overlooking the famous beach. The enlisted men were quartered in the Golf Hotel, on the edge of the golf course which extended to the sea. Deauville had suffered, like all France, under the German occupation. Most of the beautiful trees and flowers that justified the French name of "Deauville, *Plage-Fleurie*"—Deauville, the Flower Beach—had been uprooted to make way for trenches, barbed wire, and machine-gun emplacements. But the fine weather remained unchanged, and the beautiful beaches—once they had been de-mined—remained undamaged. The French people were hospitable and friendly, and the headquarters personnel enjoyed the recreation facilities, both of Deauville and of the adjoining resort town of Trouville, while they prepared the headquarters equipment for the return trip to the United States. An advance party, under command of Brigadier General Armistead D. Mead, Jr., Assistant Chief of Staff, G-3, left for the United States from Le Havre on the Army Transport *Santa Maria* on July 18. The main body of the headquarters sailed from the same port on July 27, on the Army Transport *John Ericsson*. Bearing two great banners displaying the Ninth Army insignia, the *John Ericsson* sailed into New York harbor on the morning of August 6, bringing to most of the Army Headquarters personnel their first sight of America in over thirteen months.

From New York City, the headquarters was taken immediately to Camp Shanks, New York, where the personnel were processed before taking thirty days' leave prior to the reassembly of the headquarters at Fort Bragg, North Carolina. At Camp Shanks, too, provision was made for the assembly of an advance party of the headquarters at Washington, D. C., on August 10. For even as the *John Ericsson* reached New York, word had been received that General Simpson had returned from China, that key personnel of the headquarters would be assembled in Washington for orientation on the new mission, and that this same key personnel would constitute an advance party to fly to China in mid-September. The remainder of the headquarters would follow at a later date.

While the advance party was assembled in Washington came the news of the Japanese surrender proposal, and with the acceptance of the surrender Ninth Army's prospective mission in China was cancelled. The headquarters personnel, less those discharged at the various separation centers after their leave, reassembled at Fort Bragg in mid-September. There, provision was made for the discharge or transfer of the remainder of the headquarters personnel. Headquarters Ninth Army was officially inactivated at Fort Bragg on October 10, 1945.

The United States Ninth Army had a life span of 16 months 19 days. For nine months and ten days of this time, it engaged in active operations on the continent of Europe, culminating in the complete defeat and occupation of Germany. Highlights of Ninth Army's accomplishments in Europe:

Reduced the stronghold of Brest.

Received the surrender of 20,000 German troops at Beaugency, France, on September 16, 1944, the largest capture of German troops up to that date.

Fought in five countries—France, Belgium, Luxembourg, the Netherlands, and Germany—and at one time operated concurrently in all five.

Fought in Germany from west of the Siegfried Line to within 53 miles of Berlin.

Made an assault crossing of the flooded Roer River and reached the Rhine River in seven days. Within sixteen days after crossing the Roer River, Ninth Army held the west bank of the Rhine from Neuss to Wesel.

Made an assault crossing of the wide lower Rhine River and, in conjunction with U.S. First Army, encircled and reduced the Ruhr, Germany's greatest industrial area.

Drove 230 miles into Germany in 19 days. Ninth Army was the first Allied Army to reach and cross the Elbe River, and its bridgehead across the Elbe was being developed to continue the attack to Berlin when orders were received to stand fast.

Occupied some 30,000 square miles of Germany—from the Rhineland to the Elbe.

Liberated nearly 600,000 Allied prisoners of war and more than 1,250,000 displaced persons.

Captured 758,923 German prisoners of war.

Reached its greatest strength on May 21, with 5 corps, 22 divisions, and over 650,000 troops.

General Simpson commended the men of Ninth Army after they had smashed their way to the Elbe:

"Your exploits will rank among the greatest of military achievements.

"My congratulations to each and every officer and man upon your brilliant accomplishments and my heartfelt thanks for your never-failing support.

"Command of the Ninth Army I consider a great privilege. Service in it, along with you, is a great honor."

APPENDIX I

Chronology

1944

May 22   Headquarters U.S. Ninth Army activated at Fort Sam Houston, Texas.

May 11-12 Advance Party of Army Headquarters flew to the United Kingdom.

June 10   Main body of Army Headquarters departed Fort Sam Houston, Texas.

June 12   Main body arrived at Camp Shanks, New York.

June 22   Main body sailed from New York City on the *Queen Elizabeth.*

June 28   Main body disembarked at Gourock, near Glasgow, Scotland.

June 29   Army Command Post opened at Clifton College, Bristol, England.

Aug 27   Army Headquarters initiated movement from Bristol, England to France.

Aug 29   Army Command Post opened at St. Sauveur-Lendelin, France.

Aug 30   Rear Echelon of Army Headquarters opened at Périers, France.

Sept 3   Army Command Post opened at Mi-Forêt, near Rennes, France.

Sept 4   Rear Echelon opened at Mi-Forêt.

Sept 5   Ninth Army became operational at 12:00 noon, taking over the operations against Brest, the protection of the south flank of 12th Army Group along the Loire River, and command of the VIII Corps, the 2d, 8th, 29th, and 83d Infantry Divisions, and the 6th Armored Division.

Sept 8   Attack on Brest renewed.

Sept 16   20,000 Germans surrendered to Ninth Army at Beaugency, France.

Sept 18   Brest fell to VIII Corps.

Oct 2   Army Command Post opened at Arlon, Belgium.

Oct 4   Ninth Army, with VIII Corps and the 2d and 8th Infantry Divisions, took over sector between First and Third Armies.

Oct 14   Rear Echelon opened at Maastricht (Wijk), Netherlands.

Oct 22   Army Command Post opened at Maastricht, Netherlands. VIII Corps, with the 2d, 8th, and 83d Infantry Divisions, and the 9th Armored Division, passed to control of First Army. XIX Corps with the 29th and 30th Infantry Divisions, and 2d Armored Division, passed from First Army to Ninth Army.

Nov 8   XIII Corps became operational at 12:01 A.M., assuming command of the 84th and 102d Infantry Divisions.

Nov 16   November offensive began; Ninth Army attacked at 12:45 P.M.

Nov 28   Ninth Army units reached the Roer River.

Dec 16   Germans began the Ardennes counteroffensive. Ninth Army began relinquishing units to move south and organizing its sector for defense in depth.

Dec 20   Ninth Army placed under command of British 21 Army Group at 2:00 P.M.

Dec 21   XIII Corps took over the XIX Corps sector and troops. XIX Corps took over First Army's VII Corps sector and troops. VII Corps remained under command of First Army.

1945

Jan 26   102d Infantry Division under XIII Corps staged limited objective attack along Army north flank in support of British Second Army attack to clear to the Roer River in the British zone.

Jan 30   78th Infantry Division under XIX Corps began attack along Army south flank in conjunction with First Army's attack on Roer River Dams.

Feb 6   XIX Corps zone and troops taken over by VII Corps of First Army. XIX Corps took over a portion of XIII Corps zone and troops. XVI Corps became operational at 12:00 noon and took over a portion of British Second Army's zone and command of the 35th Infantry Division and the British 7th and U.S. 8th Armored Divisions.

Feb 9   Roer River dams blown by Germans, causing Roer River to be flooded for two weeks.

Feb 23   Ninth Army attacked across Roer River with XIII, XVI, and XIX Corps.

Mar 1   München-Gladbach fell to XIX Corps.

Mar 2   The Rhine River was reached at Neuss by the 83d Infantry and 2d Armored Divisions of XIX Corps.

Mar 3   Krefeld cleared by XIII Corps.

Mar 10   Army Command Post opened at München-Gladbach.

Mar 11   XVI Corps wiped out last organized resistance west of the Rhine in the Army zone.

Mar 20   Rear Echelon of Army Headquarters opened at Rheydt.

Mar 24   Ninth Army attacked over Rhine River using XVI Corps and the 30th and 79th Infantry Divisions to make the assault crossing.

Mar 30   XIX Corps attacked east of Rhine out of the XVI Corps bridgehead.

Mar 31   XVI Corps secured complete bridgehead as designated in Rhine River attack order.

Apr 1   Ninth Army and First Army made contact at Lippstadt, encircling the Ruhr Valley and industrial area. XIII Corps attacked east of Rhine.

Apr 3   Munster cleared by XIII Corps.

Apr 4   Ninth Army reverted to U.S. 12th Army Goup at 12:01 A.M. Weser River reached by XIII and XIX Corps. Hamm cleared by XIX Corps. Army Command Post opened at Haltern.

Apr 11   Hannover cleared by XIII Corps. Essen cleared by XVI Corps. Elbe River reached by the 2d Armored Division of XIX Corps.

Apr 12   Army Command Post opened at Gutersloh. Braunschweig cleared by XIX Corps. Elbe River reached by XIII Corps. XIX Corps' 2d Armored Division established bridgehead over Elbe.

Apr 13   Duisburg taken by XVI Corps. XIX Corps' 83d Infantry Division established a second bridgehead over Elbe.

Apr 14   XVI Corps cleared last resistance from its zone in the Ruhr pocket. 2d Armored Division bridgehead over Elbe withdrawn.

Apr 17   Ruhr pocket eliminated, as First Army completed junction with XVI Corps.

Apr 18   Magdeburg taken by XIX Corps.
            Rear Echelon of Army Headquarters opened at Munster.

Apr 21   Harz Mountains cleared by XIX Cops. XIII Corps launched attack northeast in area taken over from the British, to clear additional portion of the west bank of the Elbe.

Apr 23   Army Command Post opened at Braunschweig.

Apr 25   XIII Corps cleared last resistance from additional Ninth Army zone west of Elbe.

Apr 30   Russian forces contacted by 113th Cavalry Group of XIX Corps.

May 1   Elements of 95th Infantry Division under XVI Corps moved to Bremen–Bremerhaven Enclave area.

May 6   Ninth Army took over VII and VIII Corps, their divisions, and Corps and army troops from First Army.

May 8   Elements of 29th Infantry Division relieved elements of 95th Infantry Division in the Bremen area. 2d Armored Division passed to direct control of Ninth Army, in preparation for the division's mission as Task Force Berlin.

May 9   European War ended. Ninth Army had under command VII, VIII, XIII, XVI, and XIX Corps; the 9th, 29th, 30th, 35th, 69th, 70th, 75th, 76th, 78th, 79th, 83d, 84th, 87th, 89th, 95th, 102d, and 104th Infantry Divisions; the 2d, 3d, 5th, 6th, and 8th Armored Divisions; reaching a peak troop-strength of over 650,000 on May 20.

May 15   Rear Echelon of Army Headquarters opened at Gutersloh.

May 24   29th Infantry Division assumed responsibility for Bremen–Bremerhaven Enclave Area from the British, and the division passed from XVI Corps to direct Ninth Army control.

May 25   British units began relief of XIII Corps.

May 29   British units began relief of XVI Corps.

June 7   British forces completed relief of XVI Corps.

June 11   British forces completed relief of XIII Corps.

June 13   Russian units began relief of VII Corps.

June 15   Ninth Army's area and troops passed to U.S. Seventh Army at 12:01 A.M.

July 8   Army Command Post closed at Braunschweig, Germany, and opened at Deauville, France.

July 28   Army Headquarters sailed from Le Havre for the United States on the *John Ericsson*.

Aug 6   Army Headquaters disembarked at New York City and proceeded to Camp Shanks, New York.

Sept 4   Army Command Post opened at Fort Bragg, North Carolina.

Oct 10   Headquarters U.S. Ninth Army inactivated.

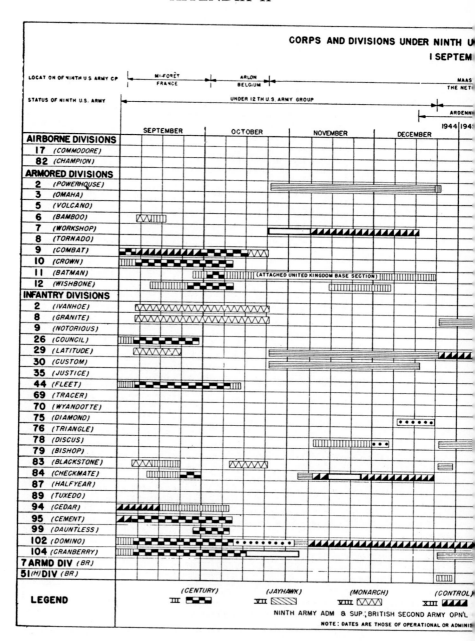

APPENDIX II

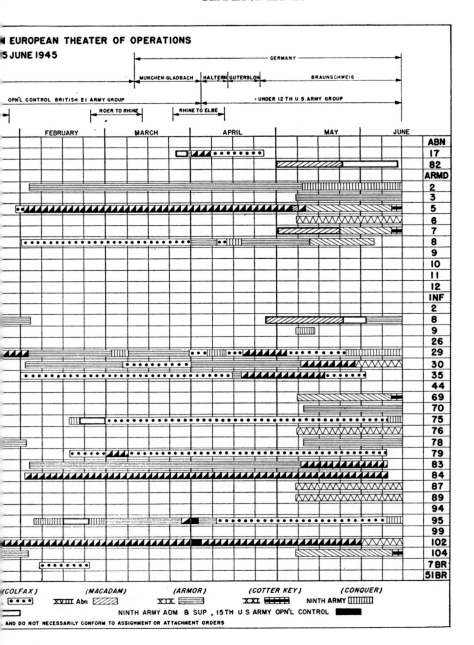

APPENDIX III

Non-Divisional Units Operational Under Ninth Army
5 September 1944—5 May 1945, inclusive

ANTIAIRCRAFT ARTILLERY

Antiaircraft Artillery Brigade Headquarters: 55th.

Antiaircraft Artillery Group Headquarters: 2d, 12th, 18th, 19th, 26th, 38th,, 105th, 113th.

Antiaircraft Artillery Gun Battalions: 124th, 127th, 131st, 132d, 135th, 141st, 749th (Less Batteries A and B).

Antiaircraft Artillery Automatic Weapons Battalions (Mobile): 379th, 430th, 440th, 445th, 446th, 448th, 453d, 459th, 462d, 463d, 531st, 547th, 548th, 552d, 553d, 555th, 556th, 557th, 559th, 562d, 563d, 580th, 597th, 635th.

Antiaircraft Artillery Automatic Weapons Battalions (Semi-mobile): 385th, 397th (Batteries B, C and D).

Antiaircraft Artillery Automatic Weapons Battalions (Self-propelled): 195th, 203d, 387th, 473d, 571st, 573d, 777th.

Antiaircraft Artillery Searchlight Battalions: 226th (Battery A), 357th (Battery B).

Antiaircraft Artillery: Operations Detachment: 154th.

ARMORED

Armored Group Headquarters: 3d, 7th, 10th.

Tank Battalions: 701st, 709th, 717th, 736th, 739th (Special-Mine Exploders), 740th, 741st, 743d, 744th (Light), 747th, 750th, 761st, 771st, 774th, 781st, 784th.

ARTILLERY

Corps Artillery Headquarters: VIII, XIII, XVI, XIX, XVIII Airborne.

Field Artillery Brigade Headquarters: 34th.

Field Artillery Group Headquarters: 40th, 119th, 174th, 196th, 202d, 210th, 211th, 219th, 228th, 252d, 258th, 333d, 349th, 401st, 402d, 404th, 407th, 411th, 422d, 472d.

Field Artillery Observation Battalions: 8th, 12th, 14th, 16th, 285th, 290th, 291st, 294th.

Field Artillery Battalions (105mm Howitzer): 25th, 70th, 252d, 280th, 283d, 687th, 688th, 690th, 691st, 692d.

Armored Field Artillery Battalions (105mm Howitzer, self-propelled): 65th, 83d, 275th, 695th, 696th.

Field Artillery Battalions (4.5 inch gun): 199th, 211th, 259th, 770th, 771st, 774th, 777th, 959th.

Field Artillery Battalions (155mm Howitzer): 2d, 81st, 203d, 215th, 228th, 254th, 333d, 349th, 351st, 666th, 751st, 753d, 754th, 755th, 758th, 768th, 808th, 809th, 963d, 965th, 967th, 969th.

Field Artillery Battalions (155mm Gun): 261st, 516th, 547th, 548th, 549th, 559th, 561st, 978th, 979th.

Field Artillery Battalions (155mm Gun, Self-propelled): 174th, 258th, 557th.

Field Artillery Battalions (8 inch Howitzer): 207th, 264th, 578th, 739th, 740th, 743d, 745th, 748th, 787th, 788th, 793d.

Field Artillery Battalions (8 inch Gun): 256th.

Field Artillery Battalions (240mm Howitzer): 265th, 269th, 272d.

CAVALRY

Cavalry Group Headquarters, Mechanized: 11th, 14th, 15th, 102d, 113th.

Cavalry Reconnaissance Squadron, Mechanized: 15th, 17th, 18th, 32d, 36th, 38th (Troop A), 44th, 86th (Troop F), 102d, 113th, 125th.

CHEMICAL

Chemical Battalions, Motorized: 3d, 86th, 89th, 90th, 92d, 94th.
Chemical Smoke Generator Battalion: 27th.
Chemical Decontamination Company: 30th.
Chemical Depot Companies: 64th, 222d.
Chemical Maintenance Companies: 19th, 57th.
Chemical Smoke Generator Companies: 74th, 83d.

ENGINEER

Engineer Combat Group Headquarters: 1102d, 1103d, 1104th, 1105th, 1106th, 1107th, 1110th, 1115th, 1117th, 1120th, 1124th, 1128th, 1130th, 1132d, 1141st, 1142d, 1143d, 1144th, 1145th, 1146th, 1147th, 1148th, 1149th, 1152d, 1153rd, 1160th, 1163d, 1186th.
Engineer Combat Battalions: 5th, 35th, 37th, 44th, 49th, 61st, 82d, 138th, 147th, 148th, 149th, 158th, 159th, 164th, 167th, 168th, 171st, 172d, 184th, 187th, 188th, 202d, 203d, 207th, 208th, 234th, 237th, 238th, 243d, 244th, 245th, 246th, 247th, 248th, 250th, 251st, 252d, 253d, 256th, 257th, 258th, 260th, 276th, 277th, 278th, 279th, 280th, 281st, 282d, 288th, 292d, 294th, 295th, 297th, 298th, 336th, 348th, 381st, 1251st, 1253d, 1254th, 1255th, 1256th, 1257th, 1260th, 1262d, 1263d, 1264th, 1265th, 1276th, 1343d, 1695th, 1698th, 1699th, 3051st, 3052d, 3053d.
Engineer Camouflage Battalions, Army: 84th (Company C), 602d, 604th (Company D), 606th.
Engineer Heavy Ponton Battalions: 180th, 181st, 551st, 552d, 554th.
Engineer Topographic Battalions, Army: 654th, 655th.
Engineer Base Depot Companies: 395th (2d and 3d Platoon), 440th (Parts Supply Platoon), 459th (Detachment only), 465th, 729th (3d Depot Platoon), 1961st (Aviation).
Engineer Dump Truck Companies: 582d, 767th, 793d, 1353d, 1354th, 1355th, 1363d, 1365th, 1368th, 1369th, 1370th, 1451st, 2705th, 2707th.
Engineer Harbor Craft Companies: 329th (Detachment C), 344th.
Engineer Light Equipment Companies: 574th, 611th, 612th, 625th, 626th, 627th, 628th, 630th, 631st, 632d, 633d, 634th, 678th, 2726th, 2729th, 2733d.
Engineer Light Ponton Companies: 70th, 73d, 74th, 500th, 503d, 507th, 508th, 511th, 512th, 527th, 536th, 539th.
Engineer Maintenance Companies: 467th, 962d, 969th, 977th, 978th, 981st, 982d, 1468th, 1473d, 1477th, 1479th.
Engineer Topographic Companies, Corps: 62d, 663d, 665th, 667th, 669th, 672d, 3060th.
Engineer Treadway Bridge Companies: 989th, 990th, 997th, 999th, 1000th, 1013th.
Engineer Water Supply Companies: 1501st, 1503d, 1510th.
Engineer Firefighting Platoons: 1214th, 1219th, 1236th, 1238th.
Engineer Spare Parts Platoons: 440th.
Engineer Map Depot Detachment: 1608th.
Engineer Searchlight Maintenance Detachment: 1410th.
Engineer Survey Liaison Detachments: 1677th, 1682d.
Engineer Utility Detachments: 1091st, 1641st, 1663d.
Engineer Technical Intelligence Teams: 2889th, 2893d, 2894th, 2895th, 2902d, 2941st, 2943d, 2944th, 2945th, 2950th.
Engineer General Service Regiment: 356th (3d Platoon Company C).
Engineer Survey Regiment: 11th (Detachment).

MEDICAL

Medical Group Headquarters: 1st, 30th, 31st, 64th.
Medical Battalion Headquarters: 62d, 86th, 169th, 170th, 174th, 178th, 183d, 184th, 185th, 188th, 240th, 241st, 242d, 426th, 430th, 432d.
Medical Gas Treatment Battalion: 95th.
Convalescent Hospitals: 8th.
Evacuation Hospitals: 24th, 41st, 91st, 100th, 102d, 105th, 107th, 108th, 111th, 113th, 114th, 115th, 119th, 129th.
Station Hospitals: 127th (Detachment A), 152d (Detachment of Detachment C).
Field Hospitals: 20th, 48th, 53d, 63d, 67th.

Medical Ambulance Companies, Motor: 417th, 471st, 472d, 488th, 489th, 564th, 565th, 566th, 574th, 580th, 581st, 588th, 590th, 595th, 597th.
Medical Base Depot Companies: 28th, 33d (Advance Section II), 35th.
Medical Clearing Companies: 609th, 620th, 621st, 623d, 625th, 626th, 627th, 629th, 634th, 635th, 640th, 643d, 658th, 660th, 666th.
Medical Collecting Companies: 396th, 415th, 419th, 420th, 421st, 422d, 423d, 426th, 429th, 439th, 442d, 445th, 446th, 448th, 457th, 459th, 462d, 463d, 465th, 481st, 483d, 497th, 499th, 500th, 501st, 502d, 508th.
Medical Dental Prosthetic Detachments: 461st, 462d, 463d, 464th, 465th, 473d.
Mobile Dental Units: 500th, 542d.
362d Medical Composite Detachment (Laboratory).
5th Auxiliary Surgical Group.

MILITARY POLICE

Military Police Battalions: 505th, 507th (Company C), 510th, 511th (Company A), 524th (Company B), 795th.
Military Police Companies (Corps): 817th, 822d, 823d.
Military Police Escort Guard Companies: 472d, 554th, 620th.
Military Police Criminal Investigation Detachments: 4th, 28th.

ORDNANCE

Ordnance Group Headquarters: 59th, 60th, 79th.
Ordnance Battalion Headquarters: 48th, 65th, 172d, 178th, 185th, 187th, 260th, 312th, 320th, 328th, 330th, 334th, 335th, 340th, 592d.
Ordnance Ammunition Companies: 316th, 583d, 584th, 586th, 588th, 593d, 598th, 599th, 637th, 640th, 657th, 658th, 665th, 697th.
Ordnance Depot Companies: 181st, 314th, 329th, 333d, 342d, 346th, 348th, 349th, 839th, 954th.
Ordnance Evacuation Companies: 422d, 464th, 475th, 482d, 483d, 485th, 486th.
Ordnance Heavy Maintenance Companies (Field Army): 124th, 138th, 216th, 295th, 519th, 545th, 547th, 548th, 567th.
Ordnance Heavy Maintenance Companies (Tank): 503d, 536th, 538th, 553d, 554th, 555th, 561st, 566th.
Ordnance Heavy Automotive Maintenance Companies: 220th, 447th, 853d, 866th, 869th, 903d, 911th, 916th, 927th, 3561st.
Ordnance Maintenance Companies (Antiaircraft): 300th, 351st, 352d, 353d, 367th.
Ordnance Medium Automotive Maintenance Companies: 3419th, 3422d, 3445th, 3499th, 3508th, 3510th, 3512th, 3513th, 3522d, 3525th, 3526th, 3530th, 3532nd, 3535th, 3546th.
Ordnance Medium Maintenance Companies: 6th, 7th, 16th, 18th, 92d, 104th, 107th, 111th, 128th, 130th, 132d, 134th, 135th, 293d, 294th, 302d, 308th, 3464th, 3468th.
Ordnance Motor Vehicle Distributing Company: 3081st.
Ordnance Tire Repair Company: 158th (Detachment 4).
Ordnance Bomb Disposal Platoon: 233d.
Ordnance Bomb Disposal Squads: 38th, 39th, 51st, 52d, 53d, 91st, 110th, 111th, 112th, 115th, 116th, 117th, 121st, 122d.
Ordnance Ballistics and Technical Service Detachments: 2d, 9th, 282d.
Ordnance Service Detachment (Mess): 262d.

QUARTERMASTER

Quartermaster Group Headquarters: 543d, 544th, 550th, 559th.
Quartermaster Battalion Headquarters: 1st, 2d, 3d, 6th, 7th, 24th, 63d, 80th, 166th, 185th, 228th, 236th, 467th, 476th, 512th, 520th, 548th, 559th, 563d, 587th, 588th, 628th, 688th.
Quartermaster Bakery Companies: 268th, 3007th, 3013th, 3017th, 3023d, 3026th, 3038th, 3062d, 4370th.
Quartermaster Car Companies: 23d, 122d (2d Platoon), 506th (3d Platoon), 6804th (later became 506th).
Quartermaster Depot Companies: 80th, 346th, 488th, 543d.
Quartermaster Fumigation and Bath Companies: 823d, 852d, 856th, 864th, 866th, 872d.
Quartermaster Gas Supply Companies: 195th, 837th, 3860th, 3877th, 3916th, 3920th, 4298th, 4399th.

Quartermaster Graves Registration Companies: 605th, 608th, 611th, 3042d, 3046th.

Quartermaster Laundry Companies: 463d, 479th (less 3d and 4th Platoons), 550th, 598th, 599th, 629th, 633d.

Quartermaster Railhead Companies: 44th, 87th, 307th, 526th, 562d, 571st, 574th, 4286th, 4300th.

Quartermaster Refrigeration Companies: 485th (1st Section), 626th.

Quartermaster Sales Company: 582d.

Quartermaster Salvage Collecting Companies: 231st, 674th, 3052d, 3053d.

Quartermaster Salvage Repair Companies: 532d, 540th, 946th.

Quartermaster Service Companies: 960th, 970th, 972d, 974th, 3121st, 3127th, 3128, 3130th, 3133d, 3136th, 3173d, 3200th, 3203d, 3218th, 3222d, 3223d, 3225th, 3238th, 3246th, 4057th, 4084th, 4093d, 4130th, 4176th, 4177th, 4204th, 4404th, 4405th, 4450th, 4451st.

Quartermaster Service Detachments (Petroleum Products Laboratory): 928th, 940th.

Quartermaster Truck Companies: 131st, 134th, 378th, 382d, 398th, 402d, 428th, 432d, 439th, 446th, 447th, 646th, 648th, 649th, 651st, 652d, 662d, 663d, 664th, 665th, 666th, 667th, 668th, 669th, 670th, 3326th, 3343d, 3415th, 3416th, 3420th, 3435th, 3439th, 3454th, 3455th, 3456th, 3479th, 3496th, 3497th, 3533d, 3574th, 3584th, 3598th, 3599th, 3616th, 3620th, 3622d, 3623d, 3631st, 3658th, 3675th, 3694th, 3695th, 3696th, 3698th, 3699th, 3700th, 3738th, 3803d, 3806th, 3864th, 3907th, 3912th, 3965th, 3967th, 4030th, 4041st, 4044th, 4045th, 4046th, 4252d.

SIGNAL

Signal Battalions: 2d, 4th, 54th, 59th, 66th (Company A), 97th.

Signal Light Construction Battalions: 38th, 39th.

Signal Operation Battalion: 310th.

Signal Service Battalion: Detachments A and E, 3187th.

Signal Depot Company: 578th.

Signal Heavy Construction Company: 535th.

Signal Motor Messenger Company: 3137th (Detachment A).

Signal Photographic Companies: Detachments 167th and 168th.

Signal Pigeon Companies: 278th.

Signal Radio Intelligence Company: 137th.

Signal Repair Companies: 179th (Detachment C), 188th.

Signal Service Companies: 3132d, 3163d, 3252d, 3257th, 3258th, 3262d, 3282d (Film Library—Type B).

Signal Service Companies (Radio Intelligence): 3254th, 3259th.

Signal Center Team: 4th.

Signal Radar Maintenance Units: 13th, 215th, 216th, 237th, 238th, 240th, 447th, 448th, 449th, 450th.

Enemy Equipment Intelligence Service: 9th.

TANK DESTROYER

Tank Destroyer Brigade Headquaters: 1st.

Tank Destroyer Group Headquarters: 2d, 6th, 7th, 12th, 16th, 20th.

Tank Destroyer Battalions: 603d, 605th, 612th, 628th, 638th, 643d, 644th, 654th, 692d, 702d, 705th, 771st, 772d, 801st, 802d, 807th, 809th, 813th, 814th, 817th, 821st, 823d, 893d.

MISCELLANEOUS UNITS

Army Air Forces Liaison Squadron: 125th.

Army Air Forces Mobile Communication Squadron: 40th (Detachment YC, YI, ZP, ZQ, ZU).

Army Air Forces Mobile Reclamation and Repair Squadron: 50th.

Army Air Forces Weather Squadron: 21st (Detachments YC, YI, ZP, ZQ, ZU).

Army Ground Forces Bands: 66th, 88th, 112th.

Army Photographic Interpretation Detachment.

Army Postal Units: 145th, 175th, 177th, 202d, 231st, 232d, 266th, 267th, 553d, 555th, 576th, 577th, 599th, 647th.

Counterintelligence Corps Detachments: 1st, 2d, 8th, 29th, 30th, 75th, 83d, 84th, 102d, 208th, 213th, 216th, 219th, 309th, 502d, 506th, 507th.

Criminal Investigating Section 28.

1st European Civil Affairs Regiment (Detachments): A1C1, B1B1, B1F1, C1A1, C1E1, D1G1, D2G1, D5A1, D5E1, D5G1, D6B1, D6D1, D6E1, D6G1, D10B1.

2d European Civil Affairs Regiment (Detachments): Headquarters, Company D; Headquarters, Company H; 3d Section, Service Platoon, Headquarters and Service Company; A1A2, B1A2, C1A2, C2A2, D1A2, D3A2, D5A2, D6A2, D7A2, E1C2, E1H2, F1C2, F1G2, F1H2, G1H2, H1C2, H1G2, H1H2, H2H2, H3H2, H5H2, H6H2, H7H2, I1C2, I1G2, I1H2, I2C2, I2G2, I2H2, I3C2, I3G2, I3H2, I4C2, I4H2, I5C2, I5H2, I6C2, I6H2, I7C2, I8C2, SRA2.

3d European Civil Affairs Regiment (Detachment): Headquarters, Company D; Headquarters, Company E; Headquarters, Company H; F1D3, F1H3, H1D3, H1E3, H1H3, H2D3, H2E3, H2H3, H3D3, H3E3, H3H3, H4D3, I1D3, I1E3, I1H3, I2D3, I2E3, I2H3, I3D3, I3E3, I3H3, I4D3, I4E3, I4H3, I5D3, I5E3, I5H3, I6D3, I6E3, I6H3, I7D3, I7E3, I7H3, I8D3, I8E3, I8H3, I9E3, I10E3, I11E3, I12E3.

Finance Disbursing Sections: 4th, 7th, 12th, 42d, 54th, 58th, 59th, 63d, 64th, 71st, 123d, 167th.

Information and Historical Service: 4th.

Interrogation Prisoner of War Teams: 28th, 81st, 105th, 144th.

Machine Records Units: 11th, 13th, 46th, 47th, 48th, 49th, 54th.

Military Intelligence Interrogation Teams: 452-G, 453-G, 454-G, 492-G, 494-G, 495-G.

Military Intelligence Service Liaison Section.

Mobile Radio Broadcasting Companies: 4th (Detachment C), 5th (Detachment A).

Office of Strategic Services Detachment: Special Force 13.

Order of Battle Team Number 3.

Photographic Interpretation Team Number 96.

Postal Regulating Section: 20th.

Provisional Document Team.

72d Public Service Battalion:
3d Service Group, Headquarters Platoon, Headquarters Company.
3d Army Group Communication Platoon, Headquaters Company.

Radio Controlled Aerial Target Detachment.

Ranger Battalions: 2d, 5th.

Special Service Companies: 15th, 16th, 19th, 24th, 35th.

Static Staffs: 4th, 5th.

Traffic Regulating Group: 38th.

Transportation Corps Amphibious Truck Companies: 458th, 459th, 461st, 469th.

Transportation Corps Harbor Craft Companies: 329th (Detachment C), 344th (Detachment).

United Nations Relief and Rehabilitation Administration Teams: 7th, 13th, 38th, 39th, 40th, 57th, 58th, 59th, 60th, 170th.

United States Navy LCVP Unit Number 3.

War Crimes Investigation Team: 6825th.

APPENDIX IV

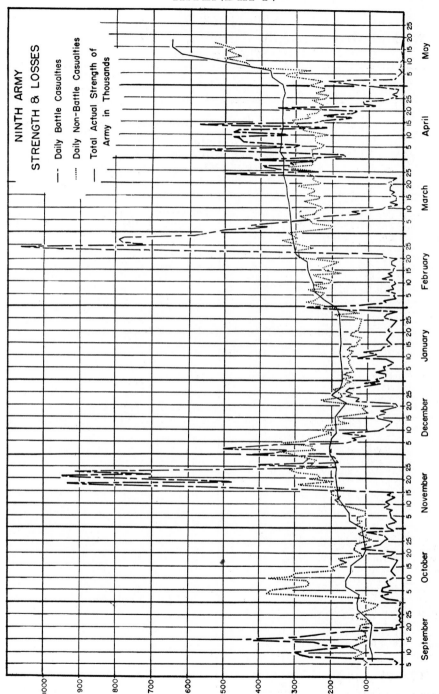

NINTH ARMY
STRENGTH & LOSSES

--- Daily Battle Casualties
.... Daily Non-Battle Casualties
—— Total Actual Strength of
     Army in Thousands

APPENDIX V
Weekly Army Strength, Casualties, Gains, and Prisoners of War Captured

Date	Average Effective Strength	Casualties						Gains		PW's
		Battle					Non-battle	Reinforcements	Returned to Duty	Captured
		Killed	Wounded	Missing	Captured	Total				
5 Sep —11 Sep	86426	169	900	43	7	1119	787	910	489	8391
12 Sep —18 Sep	90917	252	1324	177	0	1753	790	549	476	39094
19 Sep —25 Sep	99432	21	87	10	0	118	755	2131	765	3728
26 Sep — 2 Oct	121809	12	33	19	0	64	642	79	27	165
3 Oct — 9 Oct	169006	41	206	76	0	323	2165	137	378	223
10 Oct —16 Oct	138769	25	128	13	0	166	1712	320	323	91
17 Oct —23 Oct	104120	41	243	52	0	336	951	946	608	175
24 Oct —30 Oct	109007	50	308	35	2	395	753	917	222	135
31 Oct — 6 Nov	147547	23	185	7	0	215	816	674	458	57
7 Nov —13 Nov	170932	22	205	26	0	253	1088	1294	801	73
14 Nov —20 Nov	183228	336	2140	579	2	3057	1466	2329	1301	4731
21 Nov —27 Nov	182697	393	2749	947	16	4105	1899	3782	1103	2525
28 Nov — 4 Dec	200304	309	1767	447	15	2538	1946	1923	1095	1040
5 Dec —11 Dec	187300	125	489	191	0	805	1725	933	1225	168
12 Dec —18 Dec	180685	39	226	77	4	346	1085	462	929	219
19 Dec —25 Dec	173855	78	504	26	3	611	1038	424	635	251
26 Dec — 1 Jan	169355	139	461	115	10	725	1144	471	774	178
2 Jan — 8 Jan	170650	60	268	10	0	338	1036	3145	954	53
9 Jan —15 Jan	174723	62	381	54	0	497	991	1410	855	85
16 Jan —22 Jan	175556	46	194	18	0	258	966	1661	808	43
23 Jan —29 Jan	179866	24	187	19	0	230	931	959	981	117
30 Jan — 5 Feb	219933	109	574	23	0	706	1539	912	1055	903
6 Feb —12 Feb	251954	31	168	28	0	227	1572	1424	2224	4
13 Feb —19 Feb	270216	28	165	1	0	194	1445	2515	1810	11
20 Feb —26 Feb	302435	454	2844	198	0	3496	1961	5190	2202	5855
27 Feb — 5 Mar	310113	446	2318	333	9	3106	1884	3284	1836	19470
6 Mar —12 Mar	317406	148	574	113	0	835	1701	2228	1591	4303
13 Mar —19 Mar	326084	33	150	13	1	197	1782	1585	1563	227
20 Mar —26 Mar	331749	146	980	57	6	1189	1697	1228	1884	4530
27 Mar — 2 Apr	336219	242	1694	147	3	2086	1691	1578	2899	13274
3 Apr — 9 Apr	339112	439	2328	162	3	2932	1745	1429	1510	90234
10 Apr —16 Apr	335176	340	1775	389	2	2506	1887	1788	1882	131735
17 Apr —23 Apr	333743	406	560	152	31	1149	1746	1761	1807	39386
*24 Apr—30 Apr	332453	55	221	14	1	291	1625	1980	2413	49242
1 May— 7 May	392827	45	200	144	1	390	2036	1688	3007	543039
8 May—14 May	609974	5	15	1	0	21	3132	3226	5017	149640
15 May—21 May	645222	0	4	0	0	4	1954	5263	2764	10400
22 May—28 May	629518									
29 May— 4 Jun	569504									
5 Jun —11 Jun	464689									
12 Jun —14 Jun	386393									
TOTALS[1]		5194	27555	4716	116	37581	54083	62535	50671	1123795

*[1]—Figures subsequent to April 27 and the totals include strength, casualties, gains, and PW's captured by XVIII Airborne Corps, which was attached to the British for operations and to Ninth Army for administration and supply. Prisoners taken by Ninth Army totaled 758,923.

APPENDIX VI

Key Personnel, Headquarters Ninth Army, on V-E Day, May 8, 1945.

Commanding General	Lieutenant General William H. Simpson
Chief of Staff	Major General James E. Moore
Deputy Chief of Staff	Colonel George A. Millener
Secretary of the General Staff	Colonel Art B. Miller, Jr.
Assistant Chief of Staff, G-1	Colonel Daniel H. Hundley
Assistant Chief of Staff, G-2	Colonel Harold D. Kehm
Assistant Chief of Staff, G-3	Brigadier General Armistead D. Mead, Jr.
Assistant Chief of Staff, G-4	Brigadier General Roy V. Rickard
Assistant Chief of Staff, G-5	Colonel Carl A. Kraege
Adjutant General	Colonel John A. Klein
Antiaircraft Officer	Colonel John G. Murphy
Artillery Officer	Colonel Laurence H. Hanley
Armored Officer	Colonel Claude A. Black
Chaplain	Colonel W. Roy Bradley
Chemical Officer	Colonel Harold Walmsley
Engineer	Brigadier General Richard U. Nicholas
Finance Officer	Colonel John L. Scott
Headquarters Commandant	Colonel James A. Warren, Jr.
Inspector General	Colonel Perry L. Baldwin
Judge Advocate	Colonel Stanley W. Jones
Ordnance Officer	Colonel Walter W. Warner
Publicity and Psychological Warfare Officer	Colonel Kern C. Crandall
Provost Marshal	Colonel Robert C. Andrews
Quartermaster	Colonel William E. Goe
Signal Officer	Colonel Joe J. Miller
Special Services Officer	Lieutenant Colonel Kenneth K. Kelley
Surgeon	Colonel William E. Shambora

APPENDIX VII

Officers, Headquarters Ninth Army

(Assigned, attached, or attached unassigned during the existence of the headquarters. Rank as of October 10, 1945, or the latest date the individual served with the headquarters).

Lieutenant General
Simpson, William H.

Major General
Moore, James E.

Brigadier Generals
Mead, Armistead D., Jr.
Nicholas, Richard U.
Rickard, Roy V.

Colonels
Adler, Eugene T.
Anderson, Norman W.
Andrews, Robert C.
Baldwin, Perry L.
Beishline, John R.
Berry, William L.
Bixel, Charles P.
Black, Claude A.
Bradley, W. Roy

Brill, Clinton B. F.
Cave, John W.
Crandall, Kern C.
Cunningham, John K.
Dallmer, Rolf
De Rohan, Frederick J.
Dennis, Chester I.
Doherty, Harold A.
Epperly, James M.
Fagg, William L.
Flaherty, Francis F.
Fraser, William B.
Fuge, Wilfred W.
Gill, Louis J.
Goe, William E.
Grace, Charles O.
Hanley, Laurence H.
Heintz, Leo H.
Holman, John A.
Hundley, Daniel H.

Ingalls, Robert D.
Jennings, William A.
Jones, Stanley W.
Kaiser, Clifford A.
Kehm, Harold D.
Kennedy, Grafton S.
Kennedy, John P., Jr.
Klein, John A.
Kraege, Carl A.
Leone, Louis P.
Linehan, Francis B.
McCoach, David III
Millener, George A.
Miller, Joe J.
Morgan, Lewis D.
Murphy, John G.
Parker, Theodore W.
Reinstein, Herman
Roosma, John S.
Schulze, Hartwin A.

Scott, John L.
Sexton, Laurence R.
Shambora, William E.
Simon, Leslie E.
Smith, Russell O.
Smith, Gordon K.
Smith, Herbert H.
Sperry, James R.
Sprague, John T.
Thompson, William J.
Tibbetts, Ralph E.
Walmsley, Harold
Warner, Walter W.
Warren, James A., Jr.
Weber, Milan G.
Werner, Richard J.
Williams, John F.
Young, Frederick R.

Lieutenant Colonels
Abbott, James P.
Agnew, Russell P.
Aldredge, William J.
Amps, Lewis C.
Andrews, Charles H.
Ashworth, Ray
Bailey, George W.
Baltzall, Ernest R.
Bartosik, Matthew J.
Baxter, Charles E.
Bertolett, Arthur D.
Bishop, Loren E.
Blankenhorn, Heber
Boardman, Thomas G.
Booth, Bruce G.
Brion, Clay W.
Burns, Kenneth P.
Bush, Robert B.
Callanan, William A.
Cavell, Roscoe W.
Clark, Lymon J.
Clement, Richard W.
Conner, Ray C.
Connor, William M., Jr.
Cragholm, E. A.
Crawford, Harry
Cruise, Edward E.
Darling, Clarence K.
Davidson, Maurice C.
Deisher, Francis
De Pasqual, Francis
Dick, Allan
Dickey, Laurence W., Jr.
Downing, Wayne E.
Dunnington, Frank P.
Egan, John B.
Ehrmann, Martin L.
Ennals, Berl E.
Feckter, John A.
Fickett, Thomas H.
Fisher, Carleton R.
Fisher, Lynwood W.
Gilfoil, Floyd R., Jr.
Goodrich, Raymond H.
Gould, Edward A.
Haight, Lloyd E.
Hardcastle, Robert D.
Harding, George H.
Hart, James P., Jr.
Hatcher, Howell J.
Haynes, Delbert L.
Heimerdinger, Earl H.
Heisler, Emil M.
Hensel, Joseph W.
Holland, Miller
Jackson, William C., Jr.
Johnson, Kermit M.
Jones, Howard P.
Jones, William B.
Jordan, Herbert A.
Kahn, Edgar V.
Keck, John A.
Keith, Francis C.
Kelley, Kenneth K.
Kenney, John J., Jr.
Kirchner, William B.
Kirks, Rowland E.
Koch, Edward F.
Langdell, Ralph E.
Larson, Randell J.
Leich, Robert M.
Lindsay, Donald E.
Logan, George A., Jr.
Mace, Wallace P.
Maginnis, John J.
Manning, John G.
McClenaghan, Robert
McKee, John B.
Meadors, Howard C.

Miller, Art B.
Mitchell, Melvin V.
Mize, Henry H.
Moore, James A.
Murphy, Matthew F.
Mursell, George R.
Muth, Roy W.
Nelson, Carlton W.
Newville, Jack R.
Nielson, David J.
Norris, Ned T.
Osborne, Harold F.
Oshields, Edward P.
Ottoman, Charles F.
Parker, Henry S.
Perry, Robert L.
Pharr, Marion M.
Poore, Archie P.
Pope, Lemuel E.
Purdy, Edward
Raymer, Felix A.
Read, Lathrop B., Jr.
Riddinger, Philip H.
Ryder, Frank J., Jr.
Scott, Jean D.
Shinn, Frank R., Jr.
Shoemaker, Joseph J.
Smith, Alpheus W.
Smith, Ernest M.
Smith, Jack C.
Snyder, Robert L.
Spackman, Jestin L.
Spinrad, William M.
Stephens, Charles H.
Stover, William J.
Street, Frank L.
Sutherland, Arthur E.
Swoboda, Leo A.
Swoger, Frank R.
Taylor, James C.
Thames, William M., Jr.
Tiffany, Kenneth E.
Tindall, Robert F.
Troy, Smith
Truly, Merrick H.
Turner, Robert O.
Urban, Charles R.
Usher, John P.
Voorhees, John S.
Walsh, James M.
Warren, Frederick M.
Williams, John B.
Wood, August R.
Wynn, William J.

Majors
Aaronson, Nils
Adams, Bennett, R., Jr.
Aldrich, Eugene V.
Anderson, Bolton G.
Armstrong, Leslie R.
Bagley, Leo W.
Bailey, William R.
Barnes, James A.
Bates, Richard F.
Baxter, Leroy J.
Bean, Wyont B.
Becker, Loftus E.
Bergman, John L.
Bernard, Edward
Bever, Clarence L.
Blum, John
Bost, James W.
Bostwick, Allan H.
Bowman, Clair F.
Boyer, Donald P., Jr.
Boyle, Joseph A.
Bratton, Willard L.
Briggs, Ernest A. H., Jr.
Brink, Johnnie C.
Brown, Thomas W.

Brown, William R.
Brue, Leif J.
Buchanan, Earl K.
Burke, Robert E.
Burns, Frederick A.
Burns, Eugene J.
Burrell, Walter E.
Button, Robert E.
Carey, George T.
Carlisle, Gerald
Carter, Philip R.
Caskey, Edward A.
Cawthorne, Templar S.
Chilton, Elmore F.
Cilley, George E.
Coffey, Carol T.
Coney, John D.
Cooper, David K., Jr.
Crawford, Kenneth C.
Crismon, Paul M.
Daigre, Joseph B.
D'Andrea, Maurice J.
Davis, Hugh O.
Davis, Rockwell A.
Davis, Edward S.
Dawson, Hobart S.
Day, John A.
Deemer, George A.
Dodds, Robert J., Jr.
Dodge, Clarence, Jr.
Dodge, Elmer W.
Drewry, Thomas W.
Droke, Alfred B.
Durrenberger, William
Dwyer, Charles F., Jr.
Dyer, William B.
Earley, Douglas C.
Eisel, Joseph B.
Evans, Jack C., Jr.
Evans, Cecil F.
Ferguson, John F.
Field, Winston L.
Fields, Walter S.
Filer, Burt K., Jr.
Fisher, George W.
Foster, Virgil P., Jr.
French, Dexter S.
Gault, George W.
Gaynor, Samuel L.
Geiwitz, Herbert J.
Glasgow, Ralph E.
Gordon, Harold L., Jr.
Gove, John E.
Gray, Herbert C.
Gregory, John M.
Griswold, Alexander B.
Groves, Claire E.
Hammell, Glenn R.
Hansin, Ervin D.
Harden, John M.
Hartzell, Herbert F.
Hayes, Joseph P.
Heegaard-Jensen, P. A.
Heuck, Robert
Hoadley, John A.
Hoge, Arthur G., Jr.
Hollander, William V.
Holm, Leroy G.
Hopkins, James D.
Horn, John D.
Hurley, John C.
Johnson, Clarence E.
Johnson, Bertil A.
Johnston, Thomas A.
Judelsohn, Louis
Kamena, Marshall T.
Kapplin, Irving J.
Kaufman, Russell E.
Kelly, Edward J.
Kelsey, Lee C.

Keresey, Jerome D.
Kimball, Curtis Y.
Knoche, Henry G.
Korb, William C.
Koivisto, Alfred K.
Krawetz, Isreal E.
Kring, Hugh E.
La Brecque, Earl V.
Landis, Warren C.
Lanham, Clyde B.
Lawes, Charles O.
Leader, William J.
Ledgerwood, Howard G.
Levin, Albert D.
Linton, Donald H.
Littlejohn, Charles A.
Lockland, Harry
Lounsberry, Arthur E.
Lytle, Byron H.
Mackey, Harold V.
Magruder, Lloyd B., Jr.
Maloit, Robert J.
Markley, Sidney M.
McBee, Howard M.
McBride, James C.
McCausland, Charles
McCormick, J. E., Jr.
McDaniel, Alva T.
McDonnell, Owen T.
McEniry, Murray W.
McGrady, Harper L.
McKee, Gregg L.
McNeel, William D.
Meseck, Walter T.
Meyer, Arthur L.
Middleton, John S.
Miller, Whiteside
Mitchell, Burt L., Jr.
Molyneux, Robert E.
Morley, Howard P.
Morris, Ben S.
Morse, Henry P.
Morse, Ulrich J.
Mullen, John C.
Mundy, Woodie, Jr.
Murphy, Robert J.
Nader, Kenneth D.
Napper, Fay H.
Neel, Robert W., Jr.
Nelson, Rehnon D.
Nelson, Alex N.
Norris, William Y.
Norris, Clovis B.
Oldfield, Arthur B.
Ostrom, C. D. Y., Jr.
Overholtzer, Harry A.
Owendorff, Robert A.
Parks, William H.
Peckham, John A.
Penny, George C.
Peterson, Alden E.
Pierce, Joseph A., Jr.
Pike, William W.
Plummer, Kenneth C.
Porter, James F., Jr.
Potts, Robert L.
Prunty, Francis C.
Reymann, Bernard A.
Reynolds, Jay F.
Rife, John W.
Riley, Harley M.
Rushton, Benjamin W.
Rutherford, Paul A.
Rutledge, Fred R.
Sandusky, William R.
Schauers, Charles J.
Schroeder, Hal L.
Sebastian, T. B., Jr.
Seiller, Edward F.
Sessions, Marion B.

Shallcross, L. B.
Shanks, James C.
Shirley, Fred V.
Shoemaker, C. R.
Shope, Frederick L.
Simpson, Vernon R.
Sloan, William N., Jr.
Smith-Peterson, F. A.
Smith, Boise B
Smith, Thurmond S.
Smith, Anson H.
Snegireff, Leonid S.
Sorrells, Russell B.
Spahn, Otto J., Jr.
Sperlin, Edmund G.
St. Claire, William K.
Steenrod, Robert L.
Stegner, Cecil R.
Strang, Arthur L.
Sullivan, Cornelius D.
Sweeney, Edward C.
Taylor, Tazewell, Jr.
Thorn, Arthur K., Jr.
Timmons, Kenneth E.
Tyner, Layton C.
Upton, Ralph R.
Van Hardeveld, Jacob
Waara, Tarmo
Wagner, Richard F.
Wallace, Edward F.
Ward, John C.
Watson, Frank
Weinberger, Rudolph F.
Welling, Richard M.
West, John L., Jr.
Whitney, Walter N.
Wiggin, Arnold T.
Wiley, John E.
Wilkey, Malcolm R.
Wilson, Frederick G.
Wisnioski, Stanley W.
Yarrington, Paul T.
Yearous, Glenn
Zimmerman, Morris L.

Captains
Adams, John C.
Anderson, Vincent L.
Armstrong, Fred G.
Atkinson, Robert A.
Atwell, Charles R.
Audet, George A.
Bader, John A.
Bailey, John T.
Bailey, Fred J.
Bardwell. David W.
Barnes, Charles De M.
Barrett, Robert E.
Barsy, Solbert J.
Bartee, Harvey E.
Bayle, Frank R.
Beamer, Scott
Becnel, Morris G.
Belcher, John R.
Belluscio, Lawrence G.
Bender, Kenneth M.
Benton, Thomas L.
Bivins, Robert R.
Black, Kirtley E.
Black, Dale W.
Blinder, Samuel
Boesel, Kenneth S.
Bolin, Kenneth L.
Bolton, William W.
Boyce, Wallace C.
Braswell, John T., Jr.
Braswell. Roger E.
Braud, Weston M.
Broms, Nelson
Bryant, William C.
Burdick, James R.

Burke, Robert K.
Cameron, Robert G., Jr.
Capelle, Louis C.
Carlson, Robert J.
Carney, Gerard J.
Carroll, William R.
Casey, Daniel W.
Ceaser, Paul G.
Cholis, Alexis
Christensen, James C.
Clement, Richard E.
Clifford, Austin V.
Cocoros, Anthony E.
Cole, Neemias B.
Coler, William B.
Conner, Robert O.
Cook, George L.
Cook, Carl M.
Cooney, William H.
Cope, William W.
Copenhaver, Luther M.
Cutshaw, Jay M.
Dammen, Arnold H.
Dana, Raymond E.
Dennis, Raymond L.
Diehl, Edward L.
Dishong, William W.
Donaldson, T. Q., IV
Dorsett, Lloyd G.
Drew, Horace R., Jr.
Dubois, Ramon B.
Ducker, Malcolm D.
Ebert, Ralph M.
Emerson, John D.
Ephrussi, Ignace L.
Ewing, Charles H.
Fadler, William F., Jr.
Fain, Weldon R.
Fay, Robert A.
Feinman, Milton
Fellouris, John H.
Ferrall, Samuel B.
Ferris, Bernhardt L.
Field, George A.
Ford, Joseph A., Jr.
Forman, Jerome F.
Foster, Amurice C.
Foster, Howard J.
Fowler, Joseph O.
Frangedakis, P. E.
Freeman, John J.
Furr, Jones B.
Gallant, Alyre J.
Gardner, Lamar W.
Garrison, Arthur M., Sr.
Gegus, Stephen E.
Gilbert, Lloyd C.
Gilliland, J. L., Jr.
Gores, Landis
Grant, Paul S.
Grant, Joseph H., Jr.
Green, Wade M.
Green, Harry
Griffin, Louis H.
Griffith, James A.
Gripenstraw, Louis L.
Groh, Edwin G.
Gussman, Ralph J.
Hagins, Leroy R.
Haley, Austin
Hall, Winfield E., Jr.
Harless, Robert W.
Hayes, Arthur E.
Herro, Marshall J.
Herthel, Stephen W.
Hicks, William E.
Hodge, Carl P.
Hodges, Henry F., Jr.
Hoffman, John L.
Hofman, Godfried J.
Holdsworth, Wallace G.

Holm, George P.
Honsa, William M.
Hope, Thomas W.
Horan, Charles H.
Houck, Jerry L.
Howard, Alice G.
Hubbard, Allen S.
Hurley, Joseph C.
Husch, Arthur A.
Hutter, Karl G.
Hvass, Baldwin C.
Ingalls, Robert L.
Jacobson, Richard C.
Johnson, Mannon A.
Jones, Albert W.
Jones, Robert C.
Jones, Samuel G.
Joseph, Franklin A.
Jost, Charles F.
Kalbfleisch, Harry D.
Kane, Bertram J.
Keating, Paul J.
Kelley, James L.
Kelso, Rupert E
Kemp, Jason W.
Kilburn, Friend L.
Kingdon, Frederick T.
Kirwan, William E.
Konecky, William S.
Krenik, George J.
Kubicek, William F.
Kuhfeld, Frank W.
La Farge, Louis B.
Lane, Roger F.
Lapitino, Alfred G.
Larsen, Harold R.
Lavelle, Edward C.
Lee, Carl D.
Leight, George S.
Lewis, Charles A.
Lewis, Donald N.
Lounsberry, Ralph F.
Lowd, Judson D.
Lowe, Jerome A.
Lyon, James B.
Mack, Edward N.
Mann, Benjamin F.
Manning, Charles W.
Marazzini, Bernard J.
Markhart, Lyle M.
Marks, Roger J.
Marquardt, Erwin G., Jr.
Martin, Henry H., Jr.
Mathews, W. R., Jr.
McCain, James L.
McIntosh, Alexander
McKenzie, Robert E.
McKeever, R. L., Jr.
McNamara, John G.
Meinzer, George C.
Meiselman, Sumner
Melfi, Joseph L.
Metz. Leroy L.
Middlebrooks, John T.
Miller, Robert A.
Misner, Elza L.
Moody, William J.
Moore, Randolph W.
Morgan, George A., Jr.
Morris, Charles E., Jr.
Morton, Richard F.
Mueller, Elmer D.
Munn, Thelma
Murray, Vernon M.
Nelson, Jesse R.
Nordyke, Dalton L.
Okeefe, Arthur M.
Olson, Elmer H.
Ormsbee, John M., Jr.
Osborne, Albert B.
Paddenburg, John A.

Pallman, George H.
Palmeiro, Manuel
Panneck, Theodore W.
Payne, Bernard
Peirano, Joseph M.
Pendley, Dee F.
Peoples, Roy A., Jr.
Percival, Spencer M.
Peterson, Robert B.
Phillips, Noel F.
Pokerr, Leo A.
Poole, Allen H.
Popham, John S. R.
Preston, Harlow L.
Prevatt, Myron C.
Rhead, Roland F.
Rhodes, John M.
Rich, Earle L., Jr.
Riddler, Garth A., Jr.
Rising, Caroll A.
Rispoli, Milano
Robbins, James A.
Robinson, James W.
Roser, John R.
Ross, Ernest
Samson, David H.
Scannell, Richard J.
Scarborough, Oscar L.
Schacter, Hershel
Schaeffer, Albert M.
Scharf, Arthur
Scheuing, Fred R., Jr.
Schmahl, John, Jr.
Schmitt, Bernard L.
Schoenholz, S. M.
Scott, Arnold E.
Seale, William D.
Seemiller, Joseph C.
Shondel, George W.
Shugart, Henry H.
Shultz, John J., Jr.
Shultis, Samuel
Simons, Charles J.
Simpkins, Gouverneur
Sincavich, Leon E.
Slater, John P.
Smith, Almoth E.
Sneden, Robert W.
Snyder, Paul C.
Sorensen, Wendell H.
Spofford, Homer
Stafford, John M.
Steagald, Ray L.
Stewart. John H.
Story, Noel E.
Straiton. Kenneth E.
Strehle, Theodore C.
Sugarman, Benjamin E.
Sullivan. William H.
Sulzer, Walter G., Jr.
Talbott, Raymond L.
Taylor, Robert S.
Taylor, Harold W.
Taylor, Nobel E.
Templeton, Ames B.
Temple. Robert L.
Terry, Mack W.
Theodore, Andrew
Todd, James G., Jr.
Todd, John T.
Townsend, Robert E.
Treadway, James L.
Trullinger, Frederick
Tsoulas. George L.
Uhler, David M.
Van Horn. Robert M.
Verheyden, Clyde J.
Vick, Thomas M., Jr.
Vineyard, Hodge J.
Vondrasek. Earl A.
Wadham, Lester B.

Ward, James H.
Weiss, Samuel G.
Wiggins, Richard B.
Wilkinson, Robert L.
Williams, Edwin H.
Williams, Robert M.
Wilson, Philip M.
Wintman, Melvin R.
Wiswell, Leslie C.
Witte, Carl G.
Witzler, Julius L.
Wolff, William M.
Wood, Carl E.
Wrigley, Winship G.
Zicard, Frederick A.
Ziegel, Donald L.
Zimmer, Charles R.

1st Lieutenants
Adair, Alexander M.
Andrews, Schofield
Anseaume, Walter J.
Antognoni, Guido J.
Arrowsmith, Roland J.
Badura, John
Bailey, John W., Jr.
Beardsell, Wallace A.
Beck, Joseph A.
Bergmann, John E.
Berman, Jack C.
Beverly, Harold B.
Black, Ralph M.
Blackwell, John R.
Bloeman, Rene J.
Boswell, William F.
Bovie, Fred E.
Breen, Myer
Broom, Harold J.
Brown, William R., Jr.
Byrne, Robert E.
Byron, Thomas F.
Caplan, Richard
Capps, William B.
Carter, Alfred H.
Clarkston, Orvil A.
Coffman, Ray H.
Collier, George W.
Collins, Rodney J.
Comita, Gabriel W.
Conger, Robert D.
Cooke, Herbert E.
Coonan, Patrick M.
Coppock, Henry, Jr.
Craighill, James B.
Czepiel, Charles P.
Daniels, William F.
Darling, Dudley V.
Di Giovanni, Gregory
Diffey, John A., Jr.
Dolsen, Charles R.
Donnelly, Charles G.
Downey, Glanville
Duffy, Jack W.
Duryea, Henry A.
Dziduch, Frank A.
Eades, Virgil O.
Egan, Robert B.
Eliot, Mather G.
Ellinger, Emanuel
Erickson, Leonard A.
Ernst, Gerald E.
Etchison, Charles E.
Evans, John M.
Faust, Bernard A.
Fleming, Robert O.
Floyd, Samuel R., Jr.
Ford, Merril H.
Forsyth, John
Freeman, Donald E.
Freier, Rudolph C.

Friis, Fred P.
Fuller, George E., Jr.
Funk, Herbert W.
Gauthier, Frederick O.
Gemmer, Gerald M.
Gerrish, Howard H.
Gibson, Henry H.
Girlamo, Robert A.
Gordon, Jack E.
Guthmann, Henry J.
Haertig, Norman R.
Haney, George J.
Hansen, Horace R.
Harbaum, Donald J.
Harper, Robert O.
Harris, Milford D., Jr.
Harwell, Horace F., Jr.
Hasley, Frederick E.
Hastall, Frank A., Jr.
Headlee, Frank M.
Heineman, Frank J.
Heiple, Loren R.
Helms, Walter B.
Helwig, Robert J.
Hering, Robert L.
Herman, Bernard K.
Higby, John B.
Hcffman, Roy A.
Hogan, John F.
Hoorn, Richard F.
Horst, Herman H.
Howell, Robert W.
Hunter, John C.
Isabell, James C.
Isenberg, Harold
Jameson, Merril E.
Kent, Charles S.
Kershaw, Charles H., Jr.
Kitt, Walter R.
Knuti, Leo L.
Kopp, William T.
Kreinberg, Herman G.
Lacour, Joseph
Lane, John C.
Lawrence, James P.
Leveque, Madeline
Levy, Gilbert A.
Light, Robert K.
Lloyd, Robert O.
Loeffler, Irwin J.
Logan, Thomas P.
Lovanyak, Ernest J.
Lowe, Robert
Lynch, Dan T.
MacKie, James C.
Maher, John J.
Maranagella, Joel B.
Mastin, John B.
McAllister, Paul W.
McBride, R. B., III
McCann, Thomas A.
McDougal, John A.
McDougal, Herbert D.
McDonald, Eugene P.
Meyer, Edward J.
Michau, Werner T.
Miles, Jack R.
Millar, John R.
Miller, Willis T.
Mitchell, William R.
Mondell, William H.
Montgomery, Leverette
Morey, Johnathon T.
Morgan, Joseph F.
Morrill, Robert C.
Murov, Lazar M.
Netzorg, Richard W.
Nikirk, Ernest E.
Nolan, Paul F.
Noland, John N.

Ogg, Joseph
Ohringer, Joachim
Olson, Willard A.
Ordower, Sidney L.
Otto, Frank
Parker, Henry M.
Pasander, Sylvia S.
Pasnik, Joel
Patrick, Hal T., Jr.
Patterson, William E.
Patterson, Tom M.
Perkins, John R.
Perrault, Frank R.
Pfreimer, Harold A.
Pilus, Myron R.
Plumb, Frank A.
Potts, Richard H.
Pride, Richard
Raulerson, Preston A.
Rebholv, Anthony C.
Reece, Isadore
Rees, Roger W.
Reinheimer, Martin
Richardson, Erle R.
Riggs, Stanley A.
Rogers, Leslie C., Jr.
Ross, Darrel E.
Ross, Fred R.
Sanders, Frederick J.
Schenck, Wolcott L.
Schmidt, George E.
Scott, James C.
Search, Harry K., Jr.
Selleck, Lyle
Sereiko, Stanley G.
Setzekorn, Melvin C.
Sharp, Jim B.
Shaw, Robert L.
Shea, Hartley S.
Silber, Osie M.
Simmons, Richard R.
Sinex, Gene O.
Skydell, Harry A.
Smith, Lena M.
Sola, Dominic A.
Sosnove, William
Spillane, Edmund
Stepanchev, Stephen
Stevenson, Millard G.
Sullivan, Dennis R.
Swelbar, William A.
Swisher, Ovid A.
Sword, Earl F.
Syperski, Florence B.
Teague, Julian H.
Thatcher, Charles M.
Thompson, Lester J.
Tichy, Michael W.
Tilson, John B.
Toronto, John S.
Townsend, Richard T.
Urtes, John N.
Vreeland, John B.
Weaver, Myles R.
Weick, Fred D.
Whiddon, Oslin D.
Whipple, T. W., Jr.
Williams, George K.
Williams, William C.
Wilson, William M.
Winkler, Wallace R.
Winkler, Harlan R.
Winter, Carl G.
Wolters, Arnold M.
Wozencraft, Frank M.
Yarborough, Kemp P.

2d Lieutenants
Andrews, John H.
Asher, Alan F.

Auerbach, Solley
Ball, Fred N.
Barnes, Wilmot L., Jr.
Beal, William V.
Bergmann, Carl W.
Bernheim, Philip J.
Bienvenu, Gerard J.
Bodenman, Paul S.
Breckinridge, John
Broderick, Andrew I.
Buck, Mary E.
Buckley, Jack C.
Cleaver, Paul C.
Collier, Dillard M.
Correa, Harry R., Jr.
Crocker, Julian
Crouser, Harold L.
Daniel, Thomas N.
De Farkas, Louis T.
De Luca, Frank
Dean, James G.
Dewey, Lester M.
Donovan, Eileen R.
Donovan, Edward G.
Drysdale, James D.
Ehlinger, Gerard A.
Evans, Allen V.
Everitt, Vernon C.
Ferguson, Richard M.
Fisher, Erwin B.
Fitzpatrick, M. M.
Fletcher, Allen D.
Frojd, Mary E.
Fulkerson, Hubert H.
Furstenthal, Robert E.
Goettle, James W.
Gordon, Joseph F.
Guile, Dickson B.
Haag, Roy W.
Hammarstrom, Arthur F.
Hammond, William L.
Herlihy, William J.
Hinman, George T.
Hone, Robert E.
Jacob, Norbert
Kabler, Hugh E.
Kaiser, Harold A.
Kapser, Joseph W.
Kilgore, John B., Jr.
Klein, Henry
Koch, David
Kotleroff, Irwin
La Palme, Majorie E.
Langhals, Jerome H.
Leefe, Guy F., Jr.
Linder, Medric I.
Lipschultz, Irving N.
Lissy, Lee W.
MacKirdy, Robert K.
Marak, George E.
McInnis, Jane K.
McMorrow, Gertrude A.
Melford, Walter R.
Michael, Walter O.
Miller, Henry D.
Miller, Eugene H.
Missimer, Martin F.
Moore, Lamont
Moran, William P.
Morrow, Warren J.
Mueller, Gustave C.
Myers, Johnnie W. R., Jr.
Neilsen, Marcella C.
Norton, Thomas R.
Ojdana, Edward S.
O'Neal, John K.
Paul, Philip R.
Pechar, Godfrey J.
Pecor, John H.
Petty, George R.

Prosser, Elizabeth M.
Putt, Wilma M.
Radcliffe, William E.
Rittman, William
Robinson, Lillian L.
Rogin, Martin
Roos, Edwin G.
Ryan, Mary E.
Sanders, Neal W., Jr.
Schlund, Maxine C.
Scott, Edith A.
Sellers, Henry C.
Shafter, Alfred M.
Sherrill, Woodrow W.
Shive, Eleanor L.
Shuman, Philip B.
Smith, Calvin D.
Sprague, Edward L.
Steidinger, Robert R.

Stern, Julius
Swanton, Willis C.
Tannenbaum, Emanuel
Theune, Herbert H.
Tucker, John K.
Tuel, Houston N.
Von Oder, Eugene W.
Warner, Theodore M.
Webb, Earl W.
Weber, Arthur J.
Weisskopf, Leon J.
Wilmoth, Carl L.
Wilson, Ruth A.
Wimberley, Albert S.

Chief Warrant Officers
Bullard, Robert A.
Burns, Francis H.
Cooke, Charles V.

Ebert, Kenneth W.
Edwards, Joel H.
Farquhar, William G.
Federspiel, John A.
Fennimore, Earle E.
Hoffman, Charles J.
Miller, Frank P.
Nelson, John L.
Olsen, Earl
Rankine, William F.
Redd, Samuel C.
Rossman, Aaron
Sinclair, Jack W.
Wakefield, Harry T.
Wilson, James W.
Witmeyer, Carl J.

Warrant Officer Junior Grade
Auerbach, Herman L.

Barnett, George H.
Chekel, Martin A.
Cobb, Samuel B.
Collins, Lawrence
Gibbons, Miles F.
Greengard, Jay J.
Harker, Glenn H.
Kaufmann, Mayer D.
Minichiello, Arthur F.
Moore, William C.
Morgan, Charles S.
Muscio, Melvin
Rosenberg, Abram
Ward, John E.
Washburn, Leroy F.
Watson, Hughitt H.
Wiese, Clemens J.
Wilson, Clarence L.

APPENDIX VIII

Enlisted Personnel, Headquarters Ninth Army

(Assigned, attached, or attached unassigned during the existence of the headquarters. Rank as of October 10, 1945, or the latest date the individual served with the headquarters).

Master Sergeants
Alexander, James E.
Algozer, John D.
Allen, Arthur M.
Azarian, Garo S.
Bartelli, Lindo J.
Bigler, Keith C.
Boissenin, Robert P.
Bowden, Troy C.
Bushon, Herman J.
Caccese, Charles A.
Campbell, Clinton
Cardwell, George J.
Carey, John J.
Cassidy, Jerome R.
Codd, Arthur B.
Dobin, Ben
Doherty, Columkille
Dunn, David C., Jr.
Eakin, Kenneth L.
Ehring, William H.
Eisenberg, Nathaniel
Elliott, Francis J.
Ellis, Joseph C.
Garbs, Alvin
Greene, Bradford M.
Gubacz, Mathew C.
Hapli, Lawrence J.
Harner, Carroll A.
Jansen, Daniel E.
Kenny, Richard F.
Kirshners, Eugene J.
Klug, Armin G.
Litwack, Abner
Logan, Milon G.
McNally, Arthur J.
Meier, John M.
Miller, George
Miller, Hugh R.
Moran, Clifford J.
Morgan, Charles S.
Morris, Robert O.
Oliveau, Roy H.
Parker, Alva M.
Paschkewitz, Otto J.
Penny, Roy V.

Pepin, Nelson A.
Revitz, Irving
Rimer, Wendell D.
Romano, Salvatore
Roman, John A., Jr.
Rosenberg, Abram
Salopek, Thomas
Shriner, Marquis A.
Sichel, Rudolf D.
Sponholz, Kuno A.
Stewart, Raymond L.
Sumner, Willis A.
Sweeney, Michael F.
Trumbla, Wayne W.
Turner, Ralph S.
Vuille, Pierre A.
Wacker, Emil, III
Williams, Austin F.
Williams, Harry E.

First Sergeants
Brockway, Robert L.
Fisher, Randolph L.
Litow, Max
Pentecost, Art L.
Shaw, Edward J.
Yancey, William R.

Technical Sergeants
Adseh, Ted W.
Allen, Edward A.
Arbesman, Harold J.
Bejesky, Anthony L.
Brannigan, Thomas J.
Broderick, Andrew I.
Bruden, Philip O.
Burmeister, Henry J.
Callahan, Lydon E.
Coambs, Harry A.
Coffey, Howard D.
Courlter, Thomas H., Jr.
Coutrell, William D
Cupit, Wallace E.
DeWall, Walter A.
Dennis, Lesley W.
Dobbins, Paul G.

Ehler, Erwin H.
Ehrman, Le Roy G.
Ellis, Joseph C.
Erickson, Milton E.
Fales, Donald J.
Ferringer, Reuben P.
Friedlander, Bernard
Gibson, Billie L.
Gillis, Albert H.
Girard, Alfred M.
Gray, John F.
Greenwalt, Stanley E.
Hansen, Jack P.
Henderson, Urban H.
Hendricks, Ford D.
Hubbard, Woodhull R.
Hunman, George T.
Jessee, Albert W.
Kahn, Joseph
Kahn, Fred
Kerch, Earl J.
Kewman, Joseph
King, Ralph J., Jr.
Kowalsky, William
Leace, David
Lehmann, Andrew R.
Leonard, Robert E.
Lesser, Sidney
Lozier, Earl J.
Madden, William L.
Marsh, Wyman L.
Miller, Bennett M.
Million, Raymond G.
Mitchell, John C., Jr.
Mount, Thomas L., Jr.
Norr, Wayne D.
Owen, Alva Q.
Page, Rodney C.
Page, Jesse T.
Plotkin, Albert H.
Ragg, Ronald M., Jr.
Ricker, Henry F.
Skaggs, Joseph H.
Steiner, Robert P.
Stoddard, Robert W.
Stoffel, Bernard A.

Stuersel, William P.
Sullivan, John J.
Tobin, Peter A.
Toht, Stephen J.
Trawick, Lloyd W.
Turner, Robert E.
Vargas, John J.
Wells, Raymond I.
Wiese, Clemens J.
Wilburn, Roy S.
Williams, Walter J.
Wilmers, Wilmer A.
Woods, James T.

Staff Sergeants
Achoa, Alfred F.
Aikman, James S.
Arnold, Norman N.
Baxter, Barker
Bednar, Edward J.
Benson, Thomas R.
Berkelman, Donald R.
Berman, Fred
Bilks, Emmanuel A.
Blatti, Joseph R.
Bragon, Roland M.
Brewer, Glenn M.
Butts, Ora J.
Cahn, Meyer M.
Caywood, Thomas S.
Colby, Kendall G.
Connor, V. K.
Corco, Miguel, Jr.
Cross, Fred M.
Curley, Robert L., Jr.
De Shazer, Leo V.
Dininsky, Steve
Edwards, Leslie S.
Egan, William J.
Elsesser, Harry C.
Failing, Robert A.
Falkenstein, Ralph S.
Fussnecker, August W.
Galbraith, Alex
Gardner, Ayers D.
Geeser, John H., Sr.

Gleeson, Robert E.
Gordon, Charles E.
Graca, Joseph G.
Hammerstrom, Robert M.
Hanf, Arthur H.
Harrison, Newton J.
Hat, Lucas G
Heard, Albert S.
Hill, William A.
Hopper, James H.
Howard, Harry C.
Hunt, Edward J.
Imler, Harry J.
Jaeger, Hubert T.
Juge, Angus J.
Kane, Frank P.
Kaplan, Philip
Kelly, Robert S.
Kendall, Paul
Kerchaearl, J.
Krause, Karl E.
Kreinberg, Herman G.
Krueger, Arthur C.
Lane, Albert L.
LeClair, Ernest J.
Lyon, Henry
Madden, Dale A.
Madison, Gerald C.
Marcus, Edward M.
Marmorek, Franz
Mazzei, Joseph D.
McCormick, John F.
McPherson, George W.
Miinikel, Eugene P.
Miller, Donald G.
Mohr, Rudolph A.
Mosell, Albert L.
Nelson, Edward M.
Noggle, John M.
Oglesby, David F.
O'Leary, George B.
Orr, John H.
Palicki, Stanley R.
Parkison, Arthur R.
Pastor, William H.
Pederson, Lawrence T.
Peoples, Eugene
Peraino, Matthew M.
Petrone, Nebo R.
Phillbrook, Clyde H.
Powell, Neil H.
Pryer, Maynard M.
Quigley, Clyde
Reed, Walter E.
Rupp, Theobald J.
Sakheim, George A.
Sanucci, James R.
Schmidt, Norvin T.
Schmous, Walter
Schoenbachler, L. C.
Schultz, Robert W.
Selm, Robert E.
Shulenberger, R. J.
Sindlinger, William J.
Smith, Karl G.
Sprenger, Eugene W.
Szege, George C.
Toomey, Harvey T., Jr.
Vogel, Frank S.
Von Henke, Vincent A.
Wasilczyk, Stanley P.
Wells, Earnest D.
Werkheiser, Vernon R.
Wilser, Karl O.
Winn, Claud R.
Winter, Henry F.
Zimner, Bernard J.

Technicians, Third Grade
Abrahamson, Albert L.
Agnew, Harold F.

Allen, Frank W.
Alvarado, Louis C.
Amunrud, Sever B.
Barritt, Carlyle W.
Bell, Tyree F., Jr.
Bienfang, Woodrow F.
Birk, Irvin F.
Bobrow, Lucien R.
Bonet, Sebastian, Jr.
Brennan, Edwin L.
Briand, Robert E.
Broden, Gerald D.
Burkholder, Glenn W.
Caffrey, Robert G.
Calamar, Donald B.
Capetz, John G.
Cardozo, Ezekiel
Carlisle, Benjamin H.
Carson, Dudley W.
Corbett, Morton
Corsiglia, John B.
Craig, John W., Jr.
Cravens, Donald H.
Crooks, Bruce R.
Czygan, Wolfgang C.
DaVee, William L.
Durham, Roger
Edvall, Arthur B.
Eproson, John W.
Feldman, Horace J.
Ferguson, Claude L.
Fontana, Elio A.
Fuld, Jacob
Giovanetti, Corado
Godins, Frederick K.
Goff, Charles H.
Goldsmith, Gilbert V.
Grzeskowiak, Ben F.
Hagen, Boyd B.
Harper, Cecil R.
Herndon, Charles A., Jr.
Hilland, Earl E.
Hirsch, Paul T.
Holmer, Roland C.
Hoyt, Daniel B.
Hutter, Victor
Jones, John P.
Karlin, Myron
Kaufman, Stuart F.
Knudsen, Marvin
Landman, Otto E.
Lissance, Arnold
McMahon, Robert W.
McMahon, Samuel P.
Miller, Robert A.
Moore, Dale E.
Moulder, Fred W.
Nathan, Eric
Newman, Ralph E.
Nordlinger, Walter
Parks, Lowell F.
Pederson, Harold P.
Peebles, Allen W.
Peightal, Robert L.
Plomondon, Walter P.
Pontarelli, Arthur R.
Reuther, John A.
Ricard, Guy R.
Richstein, Abraham R.
Roehrich, Otto F.
Ryan, Edward J. C.
Sacco, Angelo W.
Salam, Joseph E.
Sands, Roy A.
Scharff, David P.
Schmalkuche, Idale F.
Schmidt, William L.
Scullion, James E.
Seyler, Karl W.
Shaw, Horace D.

Simon, George A.
Slade, John H.
Soldinger, Herman
Sommerfield, Gunther
Strauss, Frederick L.
Strehecker, Louis H.
Surdam, Harvey J.
Thompson, Raymond E.
Tierman, Andrew J., Jr.
Trimble, Peter G.
Tye, Cecil E.
Ullman, Walter
White, Henry H.
Witt, Franz A.
York, Wilford E.
Young, Arthur C.
Young, Richard
Zachary, Roger H.

Sergeants
Alexander, John P.
Amidon, Roger W.
Andrada, Claude V.
Aycock, Edward L.
Azarenok, Michael D.
Baldwin, Allan R.
Barmantje, John A.
Becwar, George J.
Benko, John E.
Boerner, Eugene H.
Bossert, Eugene
Brasfield, Granville
Brodt, Ray H.
Buckler, William G.
Burns, Herbert I.
Burrill, Carleton P.
Bush, Warren E.
Bush, Millard
Cannerday, Elbern R.
Collins, Donald G.
Conerly, Robert H.
Coniff, Edgar J.
Conti, Peter
Cordisco, Mario V.
Coulbourne, Thomas W.
Daugherty, Joseph V.
Deschenes, Philip A.
DiBonato, Carmine C.
DiGiovanna, Vincent
Dill, Harry O.
Diorio, Michael L.
Douglas, Charles H., Jr.
Dunn, William
Dymoski, Carl
Eaton, Max M.
Eck, Charles M.
Edmondson, Samuel R.
Emling, Maurice W.
Fay, Lucien W.
Finnegan, John J.
Fisher, Willis W.
Fitzgerald, Joseph E.
Foss, Victor O.
Franks, Herbert L.
Frey, John M.
Gauger, John H.
Gibbons, John B.
Giehls, Russel C.
Givan, John M.
Gordon, Walter S.
Graham, Wallis A.
Griffin, Edward L.
Griffin, Frederick W.
Gros, Roy J.
Gudger, Lawrence W.
Gutmann, Walter M.
Hand, James H.
Hawkins, Bruce C.
Hegarty, Vernon F.
Henifin, Lyle L.

High, William A.
Hiller, Leo
Holland, James T.
Holrayd, Harold R.
Hughes, Charles C.
Jamesgaard, Alvin F.
Kiewlen, Alexander M.
Kirkland, William E.
Klimowicz, Edward J.
Knight, William R.
Lavalle, Leo L.
Leabo, Jesse D.
Lindzon, Louis
Litthe, Thunder H.
Logan, Regis F.
Luciano, Frank
Macklin, Charles R.
Main, Bradford T.
Maxwell, Harold
McCord, Walter R.
McKay, Charles A., Jr.
McKinnon, Lloyd L.
McNamara, Michael E.
Merkel, James R.
Merrell, Frederick E.
Miller, Ellwood W.
Miller, Dwight W.
Mummert, Harold Y.
Narland, Kenneth E.
Nees, Glenn R.
Neher, Dean J.
Paroutaud, Henry D.
Petrosky, Leo A.
Pickett, Herbert I.
Pickett, Melvin L.
Prevost, Cuthbert B.
Reiter, Robert J., Jr.
Renucci, Valdo M.
Reuber, August E.
Riddell, John G.
Roberstad, Harold E.
Rollins, Frank C., Jr.
Romandi, Sam R.
Roper, Jack R.
Rubin, William A.
Samaklis, John A.
Samuels, Emory B.
Schwab, Eugene O.
Siegel, Stanley
Simko, Steve G.
Simon, Joseph
Simonian, Simon
Smith, Clyde B.
Smith, Willard M.
Smith, Frank W.
Smith, Clyde B.
Starkel, Melvin B.
Stringer, Carl V.
Thomas, Anthony P.
Tiura, Einard E.
Truche, Romulus A.
Tweddell, Pearl D., Jr.
Tyrrell, Robert E., Jr.
Urias, Emigdio N.
Wang, Harold O.
Willoughby, Thomas L.
Wilson, James H.
Winkler, Richard E.
Wither, John N.
Wright, Durrant E.
Wyszka, John A.

Technicians, Fourth Grade
Alholm, Roy L.
Babb, Oscar S.
Baker, Earl J.
Barber, Almon
Barry, James E.
Basarab, Michael
Bialecki, Donald W.

Bone, Robert M.
Bonwitt, Bernard
Brewer, Wesley M.
Brobst, Pierson T., Jr.
Brower, Wesley M.
Brown, Willett J.
Brown, Garland J.
Carberry, Robert H.
Carrere, Fernande
Cartwright, Elton A.
Chutroo, Louis
Clark, Edward F.
Cobyrn, Ralph L.
Collins, Daniel E.
Cook, Joel J.
Cox, John E.
Creel, Ivy R.
Crofoot, Maurice O.
Curcio, Vito
Czubiak, Walter C.
Daniel, George M.
Danke, Joseph P.
Daum, Joel
Daum, Raymond W.
Day, Joseph A., Jr.
Davis, John T. P.
Dean, Wiley J.
Dill, Archie R.
Donahey, Max R.
Dorfer, Stanley I.
Doty, Donald O.
Drake, Robert J.
Duganski, Edwin J.
Eddings, Norman J.
Einig, Stephen E.
Fernandes, Joseph A.
Finkels, Eliot S.
Fitzsimmons, George J.
Fox, Donald R.
Furton, Walter J.
Gabriel, Donald E.
Gamulis, George
Garber, Martin
Garrett, Clifford N.
Geist, Faylon W.
Gelfius, Charles E.
Gellhaus, Verlin L.
Getze, Frank
Gilmore, Robert C.
Ginsburg, Harold B.
Gitlin, Benjamin
Glauser, Marvin
Golf, Alexander P.
Gordon, Robert A.
Grant, Thomas I.
Greco, James A.
Greenleaf, Willard A.
Griffin, Henry A.
Grosz, Harold C.
Gruenhagen, Robert H.
Grunow, Glenn C.
Gwin, Lawrence Q.
Hager, George, Jr.
Hamblen, William B.
Hammersley, F. H.
Hamilton, John J.
Hancox, Ernest, Jr.
Harris, Samuel
Henry, Fred C.
Hodgdon, Virgil A.
Hoff, Finn E.
Holcomb, Maurice E.
Holland, Leroy E.
Holley, Thomas G.
Holliway, Robert E., Jr.
Hubbard, James E.
Jaimerena, Louie A.

Johnson, Leland L.
Kaska, Earl F.
King, Harry
Kirschner, Elwood D.
Kopp, Dale F.
Korostoff, Abe B.
Kucher, Frank J.
Kunkle, Maurice G.
Landis, Robert F.
Larson, Clarence W.
Larson, Charles H.
Lash, Vernon W.
Latham, James, E., Jr.
Lerman, Sidney
Levin, Leon
Levine, Samuel M.
Linger, Harry C.
Lofgren, David E., Jr.
Logan, Herman, Jr.
Logan, Dale E.
Lowney, Patrick A.
Manbey, David J. S.
Marx, Kenneth H
Mastrosimore, Frank R.
Mattus, Albert H.
May, Wallace C.
McBride, Thomas P.
McCarthy, Roland J.
McNamee, John P.
Meister, Jack H.
Mendelson, Robert R.
Minghini, Benjamin B.
Monroe, Kermit K.
Monson, Otto J.
Morris, William H.
Moses, Max H.
Mowry, Richard S.
Moyer, Woodrow C.
Mueller, Gus, Jr.
Mulhern, John R.
Myers, Ben M.
Neilson, Robert D.
Neuman, Herbert F.
Nicklaus, Norman C.
Ochab, Frank S., Jr.
Oczke, Francis G.
O'Neill, Martin V.
Opperman, Kermit E.
Otremba, Edward T.
Parker, Lloyd E.
Parks, Frank S.
Pater, Franz
Pendry, Floyd J.
Perryman, Donald E.
Pinner, John B.
Plamp, Richard W.
Potts, Donald B.
Proulx, Howard T.
Puckett, Charles G.
Rayburn, Bill E.
Reich, John V.
Reimer, Richard J.
Resner, William A.
Richardson, Gerald W.
Rigden, Lawrence A.
Robinet, Edwin
Roche, Robert E.
Rosenberg, Curtis
Sarafian, Azad O.
Sauer, George
Sawyer, William H.
Sell, Jesse D.
Sellars, Giroux D.
Sherman, Victor V.
Sinclair, Howard A.
Skinner, Russell E.
Slater, Denver P.

Smith, Luther C.
Smith, Jack P.
Standish, Peter L.
Stanley, Joe
Stanse, Hugh V.
Starnowsky, Roy A.
Stecker, Fred P.
Tesser, Charles
Thomas, Wayne E.
Touche, Fuad J.
Towne, Frank M.
Towsley, Glenn O.
Trachte, Eugene W.
Triscik, Michael J.
Trucksis, Robert C.
Untiedt, Roger H.
Vail, Thornton P.
Vinyard, Arlice C.
Watt, James G.
Weller, Kenneth J.
Westfall, Raynal W.
Wheeler, John O.
Winkler, Henry P.
Wood, Malcolm
Wood, Raymond J.
Wren, James H.
Young, Robert E.
Zera, Charles J.
Zielinski, Theodore J.
Zuck, David L.

Corporals
Altman, Carl
Anderson, Milford L.
Anderson, Carl W.
Anderson, Keith E.
Arch, Francis L.
Arthur, William B.
Auerbach, Isidor
Bandur, Michael R.
Beauden, Arthur H.
Behringer, Robert O.
Bernstein, Irving
Bilancini, Rocky T.
Binger, Cecil A.
Birdsong, Olen A.
Blumenthal, Hymen
Bourgeois, Wilfred A.
Bruce, James M.
Bullar, Carl
Bupp, William H.
Burak, Joseph J.
Busby, Marvin R.
Buttins, Joseph P.
Campione, Jim
Cantwell, John A.
Carroll, Joseph P.
Carson, Charles H.
Celmo, Paul
Champion. Richard S.
Chandler, Dean L.
Chester, Hazen E.
Chivington, Elmore B.
Clark, Donald L.
Coggins, Walter W.
Cohen, Benjamin L.
Cross, Harry T., Jr.
Dainsberg. Marshall S.
De Witte, Clifford H.
Degen, Leroy W.
Diglia. Patrick V.
Doar, William F.
Domato, Joseph A.
Dubitsky, Nicholas M.
Duncan. David M.
Duran, Barnabe G.
Elgin, Eugene A.

Engel, Owen L.
Fedor, John
Frkovich, Charley
Funaro, Frank M.
Gaes, Philip B.
Garves, Bennie E.
Gaut, Robert L.
Giffin, Francis W.
Gill, Chester W.
Graham, Stewart W.
Graham, James R.
Gregory, James O.
Gutmann, Walter M.
Gwiazdon, Harry H.
Hagen, Everett L.
Haines, Lester S.
Hermann, Harold B.
Hile, John B.
Hoover, Robert H.
Jabara, Wilfred G.
Jackson, James J.
Jackson, George J.
Jacobs, Jesse B.
Janney, George H.
Kahn, Hugo
Keen, Stewart, Jr.
Keller, Arthur F.
Kemorer, Floyd E.
Kenney, John J.
Keppler, Carl T.
Kessler, Julius W.
Kliebert, Maurice J.
Kloster, Andrew M.
Klugh, Arthur M., Jr.
Kocurek, Willie
Kosydar, Theodore P.
Kreuscher, Kenneth C.
Kruzic, Anton J.
Kyle, Robert E.
Lawrence, Harold W.
LeBlanc, Elmo, Jr.
Leaply, Andrew O.
Lebold, Stanley C.
Lege, Francis M.
Lind, Clifford M.
Little, Daniel T., Jr.
Lubrant, Adam F.
Lucas, Donald
Luna, Joe W., Jr.
Malehorn, Walter K.
Markus, Joseph J.
Marma, Edward K.
Martin, William T., Jr.
Martin. Granville M.
McAuliffe, John P.
McCormick, John F.
McConnell, Robert T.
McGarry, William H.
McHenry, Jesse D.
McKnight, Arthur, Jr.
McMillian, John G.
Meehan, James F.
Midkiff, Robert H.
Mittelmaier, F. E., Jr.
Moore, Floyd J.
Munro, Robert E.
Myers, Harry C.
Nagle, John M.
Neal, Harold H.
Newom. John T., Jr.
Odonnell, James F.
Oettinger, Richard P.
Oppenheim, Leopold
O'Shea, John J.
Oshin, Saul
Ott, Gilbert E.
Pearson, Henry D.

Phillips, Thomas J., Jr.
Pisciotta, Joseph E.
Place, Gene E.
Pliske, James E.
Potash, Leon
Puckett, Hugh W.
Raettig, Edward A.
Richardson, Andrew L.
Riley, Virgil R.
Robertson, Ernest, R.
Robinson, Walter A.
Rochna, John J., Jr.
Ruff, Wilbur A.
Sandstrom, William R.
Sarofeen, Joseph J.
Schmitt, John
Schmidt, John L.
Schultz, Carl E.
Sebastiao, Antone C.
Seeger, Glenn F.
Serigos, Alexander
Shaughnessy, John J.
Sienicki, Theodore E.
Simon, Elwood L.
Slack, Franklin J.
Smith, Harrison H.
Smith, Kenneth
Smith, Harold E.
Snow, Leslie E.
Sommers, Albert K.
Spear, Archer L.
Stewart, Earl S.
Stewart, William D.
Stitz, William
Sugg, Norman
Sullivan, Gerald J.
Swiderski, Felix H.
Tannenbaum, David
Taylor, James E.
Tenuta, George
Terek, George A.
Tetreault, Leo C.
Thaxton, Elgin H.
Thompson, Edwin S.
Thrash, Marion M.
Tobler, Ralph O.
Treherne, William V.
Tucker, William A.
Underwood, Robert R.
Van Lacys, Edward J.
Vukodinavich, George
Waid, Emerson S.
Weeds, Raymond E.
Weiler, James D.
Welch, Edmund E., Jr.
Williams, Richare N.
Williams, Earl E.
Woltman, James H.
Yokum, Calvin L.
Young, Andrew A.

Technicians, Fifth Grade
Addison, Fleet S.
Akins, James L.
Amick, Clyde L.
Apostolico, Catello J.
Autoy, Joseph F.
Baggs, Leonard F.
Barklow, Carl A., Jr.
Becker, Robert C.
Bell, William D.
Beller, Francis A.
Berth, Merton F.
Bice, Oscar W.
Black, Richard W.
Blitstein, Joseph
Boettger, Earl H.
Bombenger, James P.
Bork, Louis H.
Bowling, George S.

Bowman, Woodrow C.
Boyd, Harry L.
Brocaw, Roy B., Jr.
Brock, Clifton J.
Burcham, Victor W.
Calderon, Santiago M.
Caquias, Joseph R.
Cardinalli, John
Carpenter, Thomas W.
Cecil, Virgil L.
Chusid, Monte
Chutroo, Louis
Chutree, Louis
Cluck, Daniel
Connell, James E.
Corhan, Joseph D.
Corrado, Carmen A.
Cortez, James J.
Cotten, Elmer W.
Crawford, Donald A.
Croker, Charles D.
Cross, Albert L.
Crotinger, Howard B.
Daily, John J.
Dakunchak, George A.
Dalessio, Gennaro P.
Davis, Kenneth H.
Delaney, Lawrence F.
Delay, Lester W.
Des Jardins, Philip C.
Deweese, Roger C.
Dowling, Ernest D.
Dring, Philip J.
Drummond, Aubrey J., Jr.
Dukehart, Charles E.
Ebers, Gideon F., Jr.
Eiden, Donald B.
Fairbairn, Charles L.
Falkenhager, Lloyd C.
Felch, Frederick C.
Ferrick, George F.
Figueroa, Alfred A.
Finch, Ward J.
Fordham, George W., Jr.
Foreman, Richard R.
Foster, Gaylon A.
Frangipane, Frank A.
Frank, Irving C.
Franz, George A.
Freudenstein, Charles
Fromer, George
Froment, Frank L.
Fugeman, John H.
Gabrial, Harry G.
Gagnon, Marcel J.
Gallagher, Henry N.
Gerald, Fred S.
Gibbney, John J.
Gibson, Frank R.
Glaseman, William
Gmeinweiser, John
Goldman, Morris W.
Gordon, Melvin J.
Gottlieb, Saul F.
Green, George N.
Griffin, Max C.
Griffin, Harold D.
Griffin, Oliver E.
Guillory, Nolan J.
Guinn, Armand R.
Gwiazdowski, John R.
Hacker, William E., Jr.
Haight, Paul J.
Hamil, Leon B.
Hanrahan, John R.
Hanson, Virgil G.
Hardin, George G.
Harison, William B.
Harrison, William B.
Hartwyk, Robert T.

Heineman, Charles E.
Heiser, William E.
Hersom, Ernest W.
Hessing, Roger S.
Higginbotham, Paul C.
Hitz, Carl R.
Holtzman, Jaob M.
Hon, Woo S.
Honeywell, Curtis A.
Hood, Fred M., Jr.
Hopkins, Charles A., Jr.
Inglot, Adolf A.
Jacknowitz, Sol
Jackson, Russell P.
Jansen, Henry J.
Johnson, Robert L.
Karp, Philip
Karr, Joseph D., Jr.
Katz, Max
Kayden, John J., Jr.
Keck, Sheldon W.
Keiley, Joseph B.
Kettering, Carl R.
Kieffer, Charles A.
Kilian, Arthur H.
Kirk, Francis J.
Kirton, Joseph W.
Knight, Johnie B.
Kollar, Frederick S.
Koveleski, Leo L.
Kraus, Stefan
Kupper, Martin J., Jr.
La Bonne, William J.
La Fuente, Severino
Lancaster, Wallace H.
Landers, Charles L.
Lange, Lawrence R.
Laveroni, Audel F.
Leonard, Laurence R.
Leveillee, Edgar
Levine, Seymour M.
Liebman, Benjamin E.
Lilley, Arthur W.
Lindberg, Carl R.
Lindeheimer, Alfred
Little, Arthur J.
Lokey, James W.
Loverin, Milton
Lucas, Clifford K.
Lueck, Lloyd N.
Lynam, Joseph J., Jr.
Lynn, Joseph E.
Makarewicz, Zigmund J.
Malancon, Leonidas
Mandis, Emanuel M.
Marsters, Henry E.
Martell, Maxwell J.
Martin, Elmore L.
Marx, Kenneth H.
Matrian, Herman L.
May, James M.
Mayer, Rolf J. F.
McAvoy, Richard G.
McCann, Herbert C.
McClelland, B. E.
McConnaha, Harold R.
McElroy, A. L., Jr.
McHugh, Neal J.
Melinger, Paul
Menshek, Richard L.
Meslin, Jerome
Meyers, William G.
Milburn, William I.
Miller, Samuel J., Jr.
Minnick, Leon A.
Minor, John R.
Mireles, Alfredo
Mischnick, Robert D.
Mitchell, Robert F.

Morris, Thomas L.
Morse, Junior F.
Mullane, Donald P.
Murner, Fred O.
Murphy, Glen E.
Nelson, Elmer O.
Nerman, Jerome S.
Nicholson, Merle A.
Niemann, Hilbert H.
Oldham, Jimmy B.
Oliphant, Cecil H.
Onorato, Joseph F.
Patrone, Joseph
Patterson, Wilford R.
Patton, Jack
Pearson, Charles R.
Pederson, Harold G.
Peisak, Herbert A.
Pfeiffer, John F.
Phelan, Fredrickar
Porter, Tracy W., Jr.
Portillo, Carmen N.
Potocnik, Edward G.
Potter, Vance E.
Powers, Thomas A.
Powley, Clarence M.
Presyon, Ivan L.
Radman, John J.
Raduenz, Harold W.
Raskin, Normah H.
Reed, Tom W.
Reed, Russell T.
Reese, Garmen D.
Reilly, Raymond N.
Renda, George J.
Reynolds, Leon H.
Reynolds, C. W., Jr.
Richards, Maurice B.
Righto, Louis C., Jr.
Romanos, Nicholas D.
Rosenberg, Abe
Rucker, Arthur L.
Samuel, Joseph M.
Sawyer, Allen C.
Sawyers, Rush A.
Schatz, Leo A.
Schroeder, Robert J.
Seifert, Howard V.
Shader, Everett R.
Shearer, Larry K.
Sill, Jack M.
Simco, Joe S.
Slowinski, Joseph S.
Smith, William R.
Soares, Alvin C.
Spatcher, Francis
Spencer, Arthur W.
Spilos, Harvey A.
Staiger, Eugene L.
Standley, Bernard J.
Stanley, Harold J.
Stark, William S.
Stevens, Norman W.
Stickle, Wilhelm F.
Stonaker, Paul
Stroebel, Warren P.
Sutton, Donald R.
Sutton, Homer G., Jr.
Sykes, Rupert
Tallmadge, Burdette E.
Tardio, Francis J.
Taylor, Lyle S.
Taylor, John S., Sr.
Thomas, Charles G.
Thomas, Clyde O.
Tippens, Frank H.
Tisiniai, George F.
Toms, Robert
Townsend, Clarence A.

Trimble, Peter
Underwood, Harland R.
Unite, Joe O.
Valleau, Russell F.
Van Slyke, Bobbie D.
Vesey, Henry H.
Vinyard, Arlice C.
Visel, Charles H.
Wagner, Richard H.
Warner, Edward
Weideman, Leslie E.
Weinstein, Milton
Weiss, Julius G.
White, Adrian O.
White, Harold B.
Williams, John G.
Williams, Freddie F.
Willi, Kenneth G.
Witwer, Alvin E.
Wong, Gim Y.
Wong, Wing Y.
Woodbury, Alva A.
Word, William H.
Wormser, Stephen P.
Yarley, Earle J.
Yeagle, Allison A.
Young, Benamin R.
Youngren, Shannon C.
Zembovictz, Joseph A.

Privates First Class

Acord, Willard J.
Adams, John W.
Affholder, George M.
Allen, Wilmer V.
Allen, Charles L.
Allred, Lewis H., Jr.
Ambers, Henry J.
Amer, Ely
Anderson, Clarence S.
Anderson, Elmo E.
Angotti, Joseph A.
Armstrong, Edward D.
Aronson, Jacob I.
Asbell, Crawford O.
Bagnall, Jack R.
Bailey, Lloyd B.
Bailey, John S., Jr.
Bailey, Floyd J.
Bain, Walter D.
Baker, Chester
Balaga, Frank W., Jr.
Banks, Chester W.
Basial, George J.
Batts, Grover C.
Baucom, Thomas H.
Baus, Elmer N.
Bays, Dennis C.
Bazemore, John C.
Beaven, Thomas M.
Beckman, Frank H.
Beckman, Robert T.
Beggs, Roy J.
Benke, John J.
Benoit, Roland J.
Bentel, George E.
Benton, Thomas H., Jr.
Bergeon, Anthony H.
Berlin, Joseph D.
Bernot, Anthony A.
Bice, Oscar W.
Birn, Erwin
Bisese, Robert J.
Blake, Robert S.
Bland, Mike M.
Bockerman, Mervin G.
Bondy, Delmont J.
Borst, Lewis J., Jr.
Bouchard, Maurice R.

Boulden, Clayton T.
Bowen, Frank C.
Bowers, Anthony J.
Brammeier, Herbert J.
Brance, Manuel J.
Brandt, Carl F.
Brann, Arthur L.
Brennan, Donald P.
Brewster, Robert S.
Browning, Cal
Brown, James R.
Brown, Charles M.
Brumley, Coolidge A.
Brundage, Theodore S.
Bryant, William E.
Bryant, Henry G.
Bunce, Kenneth L.
Burbank, Brigham O.
Burley, Albert L.
Bush, Carlos B.
Cairns, Richard S.
Camack, Kenneth W.
Campbell, Robert R.
Cardwell, Robert T.
Carius, Donald M.
Carleton, Clifford C.
Carlin, Joseph S.
Casey, John T.
Cason, Richard K.
Chamberlain, Leroy H.
Chambers, Talmage
Chandler, Clarence O.
Cheatham, Robert J., Jr.
Cheesman, Chester H.
Chevarie, Edward H.
Childers, Paul P.
Chojnacki, Bruno C.
Cipriano, Raymond
Clancy, Edward K.
Clements, John H., Jr.
Clingman, Marvin E.
Clinton, Leo L.
Cody, William P.
Cole, Edric C., Jr.
Concienne, Daniel L.
Cone, Jay
Cones, Gregory J.
Connor, Eugene R
Cook, Edward M.
Costello, Cornelius J.
Cotler, Gerald
Cox, Joseph E.
Coyne, George P., Jr.
Curtis, Paul A.
Cuthbert, Samuel H.
Dahlberg, Bruce T.
Davidson, Delbert E.
De Bullet, F. A. E.
De Frehen, Albert T., Jr.
Demeo, Silvio A.
Dennis, Thomas S.
Deshinsky, Edward J.
Dhu, Benjamin F.
Diaz, Victor R.
Dinnesen, Martin H.
Dinnsen, Martin H.
Dirolf, William E.
Dore, Vincent R.
Dudeck, Reinhold
Duerksen, Ernest J.
Duffy, Thomas G.
Dufur, James A.
Dunigan, John L.
Dyer, Stanley F.
Eck, Dale C.
Edelstein, Leonard J.
Edelstein, Nathan S.
Elias, Armando F.
Ellis, Frank B.
Enlow, Gilbert R.

Ennis, Rufus D.
Fahey, John W.
Farrick, Daniel J.
Fincham, Kenneth S.
Ford, Cornelius M., Jr.
Forgey, Clarence P.
Fortune, Hugh W.
Fowler, Charles H.
Frase, Joseph A.
Fredericks, Thomas E.
Frey, Edward W.
Friedman, Elliott B.
Fry, Harold E.
Galanty, Daniel D.
Galbawy, Ira G.
Gallagher, Thomas F.
Gans, Julius R.
Gargan, William D., Jr.
Garland, Carl G.
Gates, John F.
German, Leo J.
Giangreco, William F.
Gilbert, Herman
Gilbreath, Woodrow
Giles, Robert S.
Glass, James R.
Gloudeman, Bernard F.
Godbold, Lawrence R.
Golodetz, Alexander
Gomberg, Elbert
Gosser, William H.
Gotlob, Jack L.
Grafton, William
Graham, Charles S.
Grandolfo, Anthony J.
Gresham, James C.
Griffin, Carroll C.
Grizzard, James F.
Group, Donald S.
Grundle, Joseph G., Jr.
Haegele, Fred L.
Haines, Francis D.
Hall, Edgar H.
Hamann, William H.
Hamilton, Herman L.
Hannon, James J.
Harding, William C.
Harmic, William R.
Harmon, James S.
Harthausen, Wilbert P.
Hartle, George A.
Hauman, David P.
Havey, Robert E.
Heemskerk, Peter
Heffran, John E.
Helgeson, Raymond S.
Hendrickson, John A.
Herkeim, Harold R.
Hermansen, Kenneth L.
Hindelang, Robert L.
Hintchel, Arvel H.
Hodges, Jack W.
Hoffmann, Norman G.
Holmes, Harry W.
Holt, Don R.
Houger, Wesley L.
Houghton, James F.
Houghland, James E., Jr.
Houser, John H.
Hughes, Howard B., Jr.
Hughett, Leon
Huntworth, George N.
Imes, Loren G.
Irelan, Dayton V.
Jatczak, Edmund J.
Jesberger, Paul B.
Jindra, Charles C.
Johannes, Frank F.
Johnson, David J.
Johnson, Davis J.

Johnson, Kenneth M.
Johnson, Charles M., Jr.
Johnson, Kenneth M.
Johnston, Hugh L.
Johnson, Burdette R.
Jones, Euel B.
Jones, Irvin N.
Judson, Eugene F.
Junkins, Clarence E.
Kageff, Richard O.
Kaiser, Kenneth A.
Kamphuis, Wilbur H.
Katzer, Albert E.
Keating, John R.
Keegl
Kemper, Richard L.
Kendrick, Elton N.
Kennedy, Andrew T., Jr.
King, Jack M.
Klaus, Verne J.
Kolecki, Chester A.
Koontz, Lloyd H.
Kotis, John
Kovac, Andrew, Jr.
Krah, Joseph R.
Krauss, Theron F.
Krieger, John
Krieger, Michael W.
Kuchta, Walter J.
Kullman, George W.
Kyde, Richard Y.
La Rocque, Henry P.
Landvater, Harry E.
Lapoczka, Steve J., Jr.
Lauffer, Harold A.
Laughery, William R.
Lawrence, Edward D.
Lee, Dale D.
Lee, Silas R.
Leighton, Evan E.
Lester, Richard A.
Lewis, Sumner D.
Lewis, Solomon
Lewis, Lawrence H.
Lilley, James F.
Lingl, Russell E.
Lipman, David
Litcher, Benjamin
Lithvay, Albert
Lockhart, Leo B.
Loeb, Morris J.
Lykens, Victor L.
Madsen, Theodore F.
Mainville, Frank W.
Majure, Henry C., Jr.
Mannino, Rosario
Marasca, Frank
Margiotta, Charles W.
Mark, Nile G.
Martin, Floyd L., Jr.
Martinez, Inez
Mason, Owen M., Jr.
Master, Louis F.
Mayer, Bernard H.
McCall, Robert B.
McCraine, Bennett O.
McFarland, Robert E.
McMahon, Roger W.
McWherter, Gorman G.
Meadows, Thomas W.
Meek, William R., Jr.
Melliand, Robert F.
Memberg, Albert
Michael, John F.
Michael, Jack H.
Milby, Ralph
Miles, Ben D.
Miller, Bernard R.
Miller, Clyde
Miritello, Michael S.

Mitchell, John S.
Moncey, George W.
Moravitz, John E., Jr.
Moses, Mitchell
Muehe, Robert P.
Mullican, Howard C.
Murphee, James E.
Myers, John J.
Nelson, R. L.
Nicholas, Talmage D., Jr.
Niehaus, Charles L.
Nielson, Charles F.
Norris, William L.
Oates, Gaylon D.
Odynecky, Martin M.
Oliver, Howard
Opdahl, Elmer M.
Opper, William J.
Ounly, Ralph
Oxe, Walter R.
Patterson, Earle T., Jr.
Pefley, Robert L.
Pena, Vincent E.
Pennington, Bruce R.
Periera, Woodrow H.
Perlman, Melvin M.
Perry, John C.
Petit, Prosper R.
Pettit, Richard A.
Pfaff, Robert J.
Phelps, Carl F.
Pinsonneault, Armel J.
Pool, Jack C.
Poplin, James T., Jr.
Potashnick, Samuel A.
Powell, Donald O.
Powell, Robert G.
Preiner, George P.
Prendergast, Edward B.
Prendergast, Edward F.
Prendergast, Frank E.
Prenguber, John C.
Preuninger, Frank A.
Pringle, Bruce M.
Pritchard, Carl A.
Pritchard, Robert E.
Pruitt, Alonza H.
Pryor, James J., Jr.
Pyer, Wayne H.
Quagliana, Melvin J.
Raan, Odin G.
Rachal, Burk J.
Rachel, Norman E.
Rankin, William A. L.
Rano, Clyde A.
Raper, Charley B.
Rath, John H.
Reed, Marvin J.
Reese, Eddie A., Jr.
Reeves, Jeptha P.
Reynolds. James H.
Richard, Elias
Richardson, John C.
Ringo, Odell
Rinke, John
Ripley, Paul E.
Roadifer, Clarence E.
Robley, Kenneth W.
Rodriguez, Paul A.
Rohde. Kenneth L.
Roni, Louie
Ropelski, Edwin S.
Rosenstern, Herbert J.
Rotenberg, Leonard A.
Rouleau, Colin J.
Ruble, Joseph S.
Rumpf, Frederick A.
Russo, George L.
Rutenberg. Morten A.
Ruth, Roy L.

Sabel, Seymour
Sagnella, Frank V.
Salacinski, Michael W.
Salsgiver, Cecil O.
Santen, James R.
Satterwhite, George W.
Scanlen, John H.
Schaefer, Melvin C.
Schirl, Emil J.
Schoonover, L. W.
Schulbaum, Marcel M.
Schwartz, Byron
Schwalb, William R.
Schwalb, William B.
Schwartz, Sidney C.
Selepak, John
Sendroff, Ira L.
Severini, Vincent J.
Shamis, Charles
Shanley, William T.
Sharpe, Boyd V.
Shaw, Joseph L.
Sheedy, John F.
Shell, Dudley P.
Simcoke, Verne L.
Sims, Merle N.
Skaggs, Fordyce Y.
Smith, Harold F.
Smith, James C.
Smith, William M.
Smith, Marvin C.
Soha, John P.
Solomon, Philips
Soper, Robert A.
Spagno, Tony A.
Speelman, James F.
Spencer, Virgil E.
Stahl, Percy W.
Standridge, Gilbert
Steinhaufel, James A.
Stewart, Donald E.
Stewart, James E.
Stewart, Richard B.
Stillwell, Coy
Stolle, Carl
Strauss, Lewis H.
Streeter, Marion F.
Subotnik, Myron
Suciu, Nick
Sullivan, Gerald P.
Sussner, John H.
Sutherlan, James P.
Swanger, Johnnie R.
Swarner, Wesley T.
Swink, Lee R.
Szczesniewski, Walter
Taylor, William A.
Tenore, Angelo
Testa, Vincent
Tharp, Edgar E.
Thiess, Richard L.
Thomas, George A.
Thompson, Joseph L.
Thorsheim, Laurence M.
Thursten, Donald R.
Tiables, Frank H.
Todd, Walter L., Jr.
Toney, Earl G.
Tongring, Jack L.
Trost, John M.
Tucker, Ralph G.
Valdez, John J.
Van Orden, Theodore M.
Vasques, Manuel C.
Vick, William J.
Villarrubia, James A.
Vizzard, James P.
Waddle, Harry E.
Walker, William M.
Walker, Frank H.

Walsh, Edward D., Jr.
Walter, Frederick J.
Warren, Richard H.
Warren, George E.
Waterson, James G.
Watson, Abraham L.
Weiser, Samuel F.
Weiss, Edward A.
Wells, Charles B.
Wernersbach, Joseph
Wesley, William A.
Westmoreland, John W.
Weston, Ronald L.
Wheelock, Robert B.
Whitcomb, Sheldon A.
White, Harold B.
Wicks, Raymond E.
Wierzbicki, Benjamin
Wilday, Howard J., Jr.
Wilkins, Lester C.
Williams, Chester W.
Williams, Robert A.
Williams, William R.
Winthrop, Allen B.
Wishni, Sidney L.
Woo, Fook N.
Wright, Jack E.
Wuertenberg, W. E.
Wynn, Herman L.
Ybarra, Ralph R.
Zaentz, Bernard
Zajal, Eugene H.
Ziejeski, Henry F.

Privates
Abbott, Chadwell O.
Abele, Frederick C.
Acosta, John M.
Adams, Delbert L.
Adams, James T.
Aisenberg, Manuel
Albert, William O.
Alexander, Clarence L.
Allstead, Rudolph C.
Alton, Woodford K.
Ambrozy, Stanley
Anderson, Alfred
Anderson, Edwin O.
Anderson, Renhold L.
Andoire, Jean J.
Andrews, Joseph C.
Andrews, Charles E.
Apmann, George H.
Armentrout, Roscoe A.
Aronson, Jacob I.
Attix, Paul R.
Baggett, Jim E.
Baker, Morris D.
Banach, Martin
Bankston, Ralph E.
Barkey, Patrick W.
Barnes, Albert H.
Bartlett, George G.
Bazdarich, Robert M.
Beal, William V.
Beaudrie, Charles R.
Becker, Elmer M., Jr.
Bedig, Edward C.
Belensky, Edward F.
Beller, John J.
Bendekovich, Joseph N.
Bennett, Billy F.
Bergmayr, Robert D.
Bettmann, James J.
Bevensee, Leo T.
Bickett, Paul S.
Bieber, Wallace J.
Bigelman, Charles T.
Binder, Victor J.
Bires, Robert E.

Bittle, Augustus L.
Blackmon, Eugene
Black, Thomas J., Jr.
Blair, Byron L.
Blasdale, Daniel T.
Blaszkiewicz, B. M.
Blonski, John F.
Bodenhorn, Max E.
Bohmann, Lawrence J.
Bolz, Lovell M.
Boosel, Harry X.
Borkland, Alfred G.
Bosco, Anthony L.
Boudreau, Herman F.
Bowers, Ernest, Jr.
Bowman, Louis P.
Brabant, Raymond G.
Brackin, Harold P.
Breen, Robert J.
Brown, Emory L., Sr.
Brown, George
Brown, Robert J.
Brown, Roy M., Jr.
Brown, Thomas L., Jr.
Brunet, Eldeon A.
Bubka, Tony
Bublitz, Vern A.
Bundschu, Charles C.
Bupp, Francis H.
Burger, Clifford V.
Burke, James F.
Burney, Donald E.
Burnett, Harold C.
Burns, Harry E.
Burton, John B.
Busching, Howard W.
Busher, Pino J.
Busichio, Daniel D.
Callaway, Jewett A.
Campbell, Howard H.
Carle, Walter D.
Carlisle, Melvin L.
Carmasine, Frank F.
Carter, Dalton F.
Casaletto, Robert R.
Caselli, William A.
Casey, Thomas L.
Cavanaugh, Floyd V.
Cawood, Ernest J.
Chapman, Wilbur E.
Charboneau, Edward J.
Chase, Howard F.
Chenault, Joseph H.
Chewning, Jimmy R.
Cistola, Lawrence
Clark, Allen M.
Coakley, Timothy L.
Coby, Fred
Conforti, Remo L.
Connelly, Brian T.
Connelly, John C.
Contreras, Henry C.
Cormier, Leonard J.
Cottrill, Ross H.
Coulter, Woodrow W.
Cowan, Daniel A.
Coyne, John J.
Crandall, Robert S.
Crenny, John F.
Crisp, Aurba E.
Crowley, Sammie R.
Cudney, Owen D.
Culver, Elmer G.
Cuper, Bazil C.
Dalby, Melvin S.
Dalton, William J.
Damon, Dennison
Daniel, Byron G.
Davidson, Raymond
Davis, Burl B.

Davis, Robert R.
Davis, Royce E.
DeBaer, Donald
DeFosse, Roland
DeLuca, Joseph A.
DePaul, John L.
DeVries, Henry
Deford, Howard W.
DelCastello, Alfredo
Delarosa, Gregory
Delia, Arthur A.
Della Valle, Louis
Dennis, Hubert D.
Desiderio, Dominick M.
Desmarais, Albert J.
Dhoneau, Owen E.
Dillon, Oscar E.
Dine, Robert A.
Dirvanowski, W. J.
Drumm, Kenneth T.
Dubois, Arthur H.
Duffy, Edward F.
Dugan, John A.
Dunbar, Everett C.
Eastop, James E.
Edmonds, Carl W.
Eisele, Garnett T.
Ekstrand, Kenneth P.
Elenbass, Henry R.
Elkins, Max A.
Ellis, Dwight R.
Ellison, George W. L.
Enfield,Marley
Epperson, Richard S.
Erdner, Martin
Estermann, Lionel J.
Esterkes, Herbert
Evans, Earl S.
Eysman, Theodore E.
Ezor, Frederick A.
Fagan, Lloyd E.
Fantanetta, Anthony R.
Farnsworth, Roland W.
Fay, William S.
Feddock, Thomas J.
Fend, John D., Jr.
Fennessy, William J.
Fetter, Samuel
Fike, Ronald E.
Fink, Charles F., Jr.
Finn, Kenneth M.
Fleming, Raymond P.
Foard, Louis P.
Formaro, Charlie P.
Foster, Carl C.
Fowler, John I.
Fowler, Le Roy
Fox, Cecil C.
Fox, Francis F.
Fredrickson, Alfred N.
Friedman, Harold J.
Fuchs, Eugene W.
Fuller, Ralph H.
Gagliano, Santo C.
Gallaghan, John W.
Gallegly, Harrison L.
Garland, Carl G.
Garner, Roy B.
Garner, William G.
Garza, Anestacio S.
Gasiorek, Aloysius R.
Gates, Roy A.
Gaudynski, John P.
Gearinger, Charles R.
Gerkardz, Vincenz
Geyer, William F., Jr.
Giambalvo, Leonard
Giles, Benjamin F., Jr.
Giles, John E.
Gillette, Frank R.

Gillman, Philip
Glein, Arnold G.
Godde, Joseph H., Jr.
Golodetz, Alexander
Gonzales, Manuel C.
Goodman, Abraham A.
Gorman, Kenneth
Gorski, Frank P.
Gosse, Robert C.
Goyda, Nick
Graf, George W.
Graham, Charles S.
Granholm, Elmer
Grant, Edward L.
Graves, Drew
Greenway, David E.
Griffin, Russell H.
Grillo, Anthony J.
Groh, Alexander
Gross, Robert E.
Grundle, Joseph G., Jr.
Gryder, Robert
Guitar, Oden
Gummeson, Axel M.
Gutmann, Karl H.
Hacker, Richard E.
Hagerty, William D.
Hagerman, Arthur M.
Hamilton, Edward W.
Hammerstad, Sam J.
Handelman, George
Hanson, Bernard E.
Hardick, Michael
Harmon, James S.
Harney, Harold L.
Harry, Thomas F., Jr.
Harsh, Donald R.
Hart, Robert A.
Hartford, Harvey E.
Harwell, Lester L.
Hastings, Forrest V.
Hatchman, Frank P.
Hatschek, Robert L.
Hausbeck, John W.
Haynes, Reuben H.
Hayslip, Milton W.
Hein, Kenneth J.
Held, Robert C.
Henderson, Allen R.
Herman, Robert
Herman, Harold
Herring, Vergil F.
Herring, Lewis B., III
Hess, Robert O.
Hetz, Charles L.
Hewell, Hewitt C.
Hilger, Glenn N.
Hochalter, Howard R.
Hogan, Richard V.
Hohl, Robert J.
Holland, Benjamin F.
Holmes, Andrew B.
Honeycutt, Julias C.
Hoover, Harry L.
Hoover, John E.
Hopkins, John J.
Hopmann, Russell R.
Horn, James R.
Horton, Frederick L.
Hudson, Howard E.
Huffman, Rob L.
Hurd, Robert M.
Hurst, Lewis E.
Iacobucci, Edmund F.
Innes, Roy L., Jr.
Iron, Mocassin L.
Jacobs, Arthur J.
Jarrell, Jack R.
Jennings, Allan H.
Johnson, Theodore E.

Jones, Joseph T.
Jones, Oliver H., Jr.
Jones, W. B.
Joslyn, Edward R.
Julian, James L.
Junkins, Roland H.
Kachiroubas, Thomas
Kampfer, Carl H.
Kane, Robert R.
Kaplan, Albert S.
Kaplan, Leon
Karpac, Michael, Jr.
Karslo, William E.
Kastrul, Sidney
Kathrein, Henry R.
Kaufler, Peter H. .
Kawesch, Stanley M.
Keene, Kenneth K.
Kelly, Mitchell S.
Kennedy, Floyd M.
Kent, Lawrence B.
Kent, John H.
Keogh, John F.
Kernan, John R.
Kerner, Sal
Key, Herbert H.
Kime, Glenn E.
Kindhart, Leo C.
Kinney, Thomas, Jr.
Kirkpatrick, Greely C.
Klann, William T.
Kleinfeld, Immanuel
Klinner, Robert W.
Kmola, Leonard M.
Knight, Chester D.
Koehler, Edward E.
Konnacki, Alfred J.
Kotis, John
Kotiz, John
Kovac, Nicholas
Kowalski, Emil S.
Kowalski, Joseph F.
Kraus, James F.
Krolikowski, Eugene R.
Kroll, Kenneth G.
Kuhn, Helmut A.
Lacy, Gene A.
Lambert, Frank B.
Lang, Leslie F.
Langham, James B.
Lantz, James R.
Laporte, Vincent F.
Laughlin, Martin L.
Lawrimore, Marvin W.
Lawson, Curtis
Lee, Arthur
Lee, Ging
Legasse, Donald J.
Lentine, John
Leo, Wallace
Levi, Berthold
Lewis, Donald C.
Lieberman, Jacob
Liess, John
Lippincott, David M.
Long, Wesley W.
Loomis, Robert F.
Losh, Hobert S.
Lother, Elmwood H.
Lowary, Thomas B.
Lozo, John W.
Lukens, Harry L., Jr.
Lundeen, Eugene R.
Lykens, Victor L.
Lynton, Paul J.
Lyons, Alvin J.
Madden, Patrick J.
Maddox, Richard
Madry, Thomas O.
Main, Tom T., Jr.

Malanson, Joseph J.
Maloney, Harold J.
Maloney, James E.
Maloney, John A.
Maloney, John J.
Man, Joseph
Manheim, Ralph F.
Maniaci, Anthony
Manning, Joseph H.
Manning, John W.
Maples, J. J.
Marasca, Frank
Maretsky, Nathan
Markis, Thomas A.
Maroney, Mike
Marowitz, Harry J.
Martin, William L., Jr.
Martz, Charles W.
Mason, Erskine C., Jr.
Mason, Duane G.
Masse, William F.
Matkovic, Marvin P.
Matthews, Arthur R.
Mattie, Fullio
Mattie, Tullie
Maunsy, John W.
Maxwell, Robert G.
Maynard, Lester B.
McCament, Le Roy D.
McCoy, John F.
McCraine, Bennett O.
McDaniels, James E.
McDowell, Donald M.
McLaughlin, John J.
McNab, Maurice W.
McNeil, Robert J.
McPeak, Truman T.
McPhee, Thomas L.
McShaffery, John P.
Medlin, Eugene C.
Meinberg, Paul
Menard, Lawrence I.
Mestas, Sam
Mewbourn, Loyd E.
Meyers, Ralph
Meyer, Frank L.
Mihala, Edward B.
Miller, George W.
Miller, John E.
Miller, Mayard
Miller, Ronald N.
Miller, Thomas E.
Monnin, Cecil S.
Monroe, Harry C.
Moody, Milburn L.
Moon, Lester L.
Moreno, Domitilo H.
Moore, George W.
Moore, Lester R.
Moore, Richard C., Jr.
Moore, Robert R., Jr.
Morgan, Ralph C.
Moriarity, Robert W.
Morris, J. L.
Mounts, Allen
Murch, Howard N.
Nearing, Dudley W., Jr.
Neibauer, Rollin H.
Nelson, Howard R.
Neuberger, Leo
Newman, Vernon C.
Nink, John V.
Nollkamper, Leroy E.
Norris, William L.
Norwood, Samuel L., Jr.
Nugent, Francis E.
O'Brien, Leslie F.
O'Connor, Kenneth C.
O'Leary, Timothy J.
Orahood, Walter L.

Orr, Nick
Ott, James O., Jr.
Owen, Hurst, Jr.
Pace, Jerry M.
Pace, William H.
Pamella, Michael
Panella, Michael
Panettiers, John
Pangburn, Robert E.
Panlenner, Robert A.
Parela, Frank J.
Parker, Rowell
Pasterczyk, Rudolph A.
Pate, John W.
Patro, Edward V.
Patton, John D.
Payne, Robert C.
Pearson, Emmit
Pedersen, Peter M.
Pencak, Frank C.
Perkins, Russell C.
Perkins, Willis H.
Perlmutter, Sivien
Peters, Robert O.
Pettinelli, John J.
Pieczynski, Norbert J.
Pilat, Albert W.
Pilkinton, John L.
Pingree, William V.
Polder, John F.
Polito, Bruno
Pope, Robert R.
Porter, Paul R.
Powell, Leonard L.
Pratt, Milton S.
Pray, Willard L.
Price, Eugene D.
Prodonovich, Peter
Progar, Edward J.
Przyblski, Edwin J.
Purdy, Theodore H.
Quiram, Roy P.
Rabey, Floyd J.
Randall, James C.
Rauner, Louis D.
Reape, John P.
Reed, George W., Jr.
Reed, Shelby M.
Reynolds, Benjamin T.
Rice, James M., Jr.
Richardson, Robert P.
Richardson, William L.

Riegel, Russell L.
Rivera, Carlos
Roadcup, Harry
Roberts, Harry H.
Robertson, Fletcher A.
Robinson, Cleveland
Rona, Ernest P.
Rotell, Joseph F.
Roth, Joseph G.
Rounds, Harold H.
Rowell, Richard D.
Rubinstein, Emil
Ruppert, Charles E.
Russo, Jack J.
Ryan, Gerald P.
Sabin, Robert R.
Sackett, Gordon S.
Sadlowski, Chester J.
Salyers, Ernest
Sanderson, William C.
Sandoval, Armando V.
Sanger, Edward H.
Sannino, Salvatore J.
Sanservino, Joseph A.
Sansone, Michael C.
Saul, Kenneth J.
Saur, Kenneth E.
Scaglione, Joe
Scattoreggio, John J.
Schauer, William C.
Schmidt, Paul
Schmitz, Fred A.
Schnabel, Frederick
Schneider, Leonard L.
Schneidman, Stanley B.
Scholl, Robert R. H.
Schuetze, Hilmer O.
Schultz, Kenneth A.
Sculos, Byron S.
Seeger, Walter F., Jr.
Seiberlich, Robert E.
Seif, Samuel
Sendt, Norman H.
Sheats, James, Jr.
Shell, Dudley P.
Shellenberger, R. D.
Sherman, Henry B.
Shook, Ernest R.
Shupp, Danny E.
Siegel, Jacob
Simmons, Clifford, L.
Simmons, Harvey L.

Simon, Gerald H.
Sizemore, Clifford
Skinner, Thomas E.
Smith, Estle H.
Smith, Ellis R.
Smith, Albert L.
Smith, Faridon J.
Smith, Richard L.
Smith, Roy O.
Sokalski, Stanley A.
Sonnen, Lloyd C. A.
Southwick, Enoch I.
Spaulding, George W.
Spears, Fred W.
Stagg, Robert L.
Stillman, George F.
Stocker, Albert B.
Strada, Charles J.
Stramaglen, Joseph
Stretz, Elmer W.
Strzelecki, Edmund J.
Stuart, Thomas B.
Stull, Harry L.
Sullivan, Raymond J.
Summers, Murray P.
Swarner, Wesley T.
Sweeney, John M.
Swenson, John W.
Swenson, Menvel W.
Szczygiel, Stephen F.
Tagland, Francis J.
Taylor, Edward
Taylor, Johnie A.
Taylor, Vernon E.
Teel, Willis M.
Tempofasky, Robert C.
Tezak, Marcelen J.
Thomas, Rudolph
Thommen, Clyde W.
Thompson, Charles O.
Thompson, Earl T.
Tinsler, Dale J.
Tom, Wing G.
Townsend, George E.
Trent, George W.
Turnage, William E.
Unnerstall, Maurice L.
Urbanczyk, Ben F.
Valachovic, Andrew, Jr.
Valentic, Joseph
Valin, Bernard J.
Van Ranst, Gerald P.

Vanatta, Leonard F.
Vanhonsebrouck, H. F.
Varga, Ernest
Vargo, Walter P.
Varhol, Stanley C.
Vecchio, Anthony
Viola, Louis L., Jr.
Viscome, Joseph R.
Volkman, Alfred A.
Waddle, Harry E.
Walker, Davis
Walker, Douglas V.
Walker, Parks W., Jr.
Wallinger, Robert
Walmer, Glenn B.
Warnol, Earl J.
Warrant, Charles B.
Weatherford, Francis
Weaver, Benjamin F.
Weaver, Joe W.
Webb, Clarence E.
Webber, Lewis W.
Weger, Dennis D.
Wells, Flawrence B.
Werkmeister, Hans W.
Werner, Walter G.
Werner, Ralph W.
Wertz, Gerald W.
Whisenant, Carl N.
White, John V.
White, Wesley D.
Whitney, Maynard H.
Wilger, Bernard P.
Williams, John R.
Williams, Ola R.
Wilson, Albert C.
Wisman, Harold O.
Wisneski, Leonard B.
Wodarczyk, Richard E.
Wollner, Herman
Wood, Cecil W.
Woods, Charles M.
Wootton, Velmon E.
Worley, Henry M.
Worman, Robert W.
Zapata, Ernesto S.
Zavodnick, Anthony P.
Zielinski, Edward W.
Zimmerman, Fred
Zimmerman, Joseph

APPENDIX IX

Selected Artillery Ammunition Expenditures

The figures on artillery ammunition below are intended to show relative expenditures of ammunition during several operations and to show the difference between expenditures in an attack as compared to those during a static situation or a pursuit.

1. *November Offensive (by XIX Corps)*

From 6:00 AM November 16 to 6:00 AM November 18, the first two days of the operation. The attack began at 12:45 PM on the 16th.

Type	Total Rounds	Rounds Per Gun Per Day
105 H	28,672	72
4.5 G	4,575	48
155 H	8,646	40
155 G	2,639	27
8″ H	1,307	18
8″ G	216	18
240 H	386	16

2. *Static Situation in Ninth Army Area.*

Week ending at 6:00 AM January 22, 1945. These figures show expenditures in Ninth Army for a week as the Ardennes counteroffensive was in progress to the south of Ninth Army.

Type	XIII Corps Rds	XIII Corps R-G-D	XIX Corps Rds	XIX Corps R-G-D
105 H M2	9,511	10.3	8,871	7.5
4.5 G	2,706	16.1	697	4.2
155 H	5,579	11.1	2,902	4.3
155 G M1	2,352	14.0	636	3.8
155 G M12	805	9.6	446	5.3
8″ H	917	10.9	377	4.5
8″ G	120	2.9	----	----
240 H	186	4.4	76	1.8

3. *Crossing the Roer and the advance to the Rhine.*

a. 6:00 AM, February 21, to 6:00 AM, February 22. These figures show the very small expenditure of ammunition the day before the attack started.

Type	XIII Corps Rds	XIII Corps R-G	XVI Corps Rds	XVI Corps R-G	XIX Corps Rds	XIX Corps R-G	34 FA Brig Rds	34 FA Brig R-G
25 pr	----	----	545	22.7	----	----	----	----
105 H (German)	----	----	565	56.5	----	----	----	----
105 H M2	764	3.8	466	3.2	481	2.2	----	----
4.5 G	39	3.2	35	1.5	----	----	----	----
155 H	861	9.0	129	2.7	795	7.4	----	----
155 G M1	162	6.7	49	2.0	49	2.0	----	----
155 G M12	81	6.8	----	----	24	2.0	----	----
8″ H	72	6.0	----	----	80	3.3	----	----
8″ G	----	----	----	----	----	----	81	13.5
240 H	----	----	----	----	----	----	39	2.2

b. 6:00 AM, February 22, to 6:00 AM, February 23. These figures reflect the artillery preparation and other fires in support of the Army attack launched at 3:30 AM, February 23.

Type	XIII Corps		XVI Corps		XIX Corps		34 FA Brig	
	Rds	R-G	Rds	R-G	Rds	R-G	Rds	R-G
25 Pr	—	—	187	7.8	—	—	—	—
105 H M2	13,715	67.2	1,497	10.4	21,049	94.8	—	—
4.5 G	645	53.8	412	17.2	604	50.2	—	—
155 H	6,488	71.4	582	12.2	7,042	65.2	—	—
155 G M1	1,385	55.8	380	15.8	1,435	59.8	—	—
155 G M12	692	57.6	—	—	443	36.9	—	—
8″ H	369	30.6	—	—	1,204	51.9	—	—
8″ G	—	—	—	—	—	—	283	47.2
240 H	—	—	—	—	—	—	371	20.6

Other weapons in an artillery role.

Type	XIII Corps Rds	XVI Corps Rds	XIX Corps Rds
3″ G	627	—	4,476
75 H	—	—	1,508
75 G	2,922	—	—
90 G AA	1,342	—	—

c. 6:00 AM, February 23, to 6:00 AM, February 24. These figures show expenditures for the first full day of the attack.

Type	XIII Corps		XVI Corps		XIX Corps		34 FA Brig	
	Rds	R-G	Rds	R-G	Rds	R-G	Rds	R-G
25 pr	—	—	2,600	108.5	—	—	—	—
105 H M2	19,588	96.0	9,016	63.2	30,056	135.2	—	—
4.5 G	340	28.4	789	32.8	847	70.6	—	—
155 H	8,142	84.8	2,500	52.2	12,222	113.1	—	—
155 G M1	1,183	49.2	704	29.4	2,572	107.2	—	—
155 G M12	723	56.2	—	—	634	52.8	—	—
8″ H	375	31.3	—	—	2,172	90.5	—	—
8″ G	—	—	—	—	—	—	271	45.2
240 H	—	—	—	—	—	—	479	26.6

Other weapons in an artillery role.

Type	XIII Corps Rds	XVI Corps Rds	XIX Corps Rds
3″ G	869	—	7,633
75 H	—	—	4,100
75 G	873	—	—
76 G	597	301	—
90 G AA	278	102	—

4. *Crossing the Rhine and the pursuit in central Germany.*

a. 1:00 AM, March 24, to 6:00 AM, March 25. These figures reflect expenditures during the preparation prior to the attack and the first complete day of the operation.

Type	XIII Corps		XVI Corps		XIX Corps		34 FA Brig	
	Rds	R-G	Rds	R-G	Rds	R-G	Rds	R-G
25 pr	—	—	6,757	563.0	—	—	—	—
105 H M2	11,391	82.5	81,669	267.0	4,734	29.2	—	—
4.5 G	1,172	97.7	5,911	164.2	—	—	—	—
155 H	5,125	61.0	34,871	207.5	1,246	34.6	—	—
155 G M1	2,143	89.3	12,015	333.8	—	—	5,062	140.1
155 G M12	85	7.1	2,206	183.9	—	—	—	—
8″ H	931	38.8	8,583	143.0	—	—	—	—
8″ G	—	—	—	—	—	—	812	135.2
240 H	—	—	—	—	—	—	1,829	101.7

Other weapons in an artillery role.

Type	XIII Corps Rds	XVI Corps Rds	XIX Corps Rds
3" G	—	13,093	132
76 G	534	386	—
90 G	1,070	4,295	57
75 G (German)	135	—	—
88 G (German)	163	—	—

b. 6:00 AM, April 6, to 6:00 AM, April 7. These figures reflect, in the case of XIII and XIX Corps, the small artillery expenditures during the pursuit across central Germany and, in the case of XVI Corps and the 34th Field Artillery Brigade, the much larger expenditures fired in the reduction of the Ruhr industrial area.

Type	XIII Corps Rds	XIII Corps R-G	XVI Corps Rds	XVI Corps R-G	XIX Corps Rds	XIX Corps R-G	34 FA Brig Rds	34 FA Brig R-G
25 pr	—	—	2,591	216.0	—	—	—	—
75 H (A/B)	—	—	977	32.6	—	—	—	—
105 H M2	706	4.2	12,468	115.4	4,759	16.2	—	—
105 H M3 (A/B)	—	—	414	34.5	—	—	—	—
4.5 G	—	—	1,188	49.5	16	0.7	—	—
155 H	120	1.4	6,022	72.0	2,824	26.1	—	—
155 G M1	142	5.9	1,700	141.6	1,200	50.0	1,413	39.5
155 G M12	32	2.7	—	—	209	17.4	—	—
8" H	46	1.9	1,339	37.2	255	7.1	—	—
8" G	—	—	—	—	—	—	130	21.7
240 H	—	—	—	—	—	—	404	22.4

APPENDIX X

Supply Tonnages Received in Ninth Army Area

Week Ending	Rail	Truck	Air	Total
OCT 1944				
7	3264	495	106	3865
14	6640	154	818	7612
21	4539	995	989	6523
28	12960	1872	72	14904
NOV 1944				
4	17502	4256	73	21831
11	26837	4254	746	31837
18	13331	1443	650	15424
25	17170	1976	552	19698
DEC 1944				
2	19788	2377	614	22769
9	18094	1492	840	20426
16	18748	6505	547	25800
23	16990	3411	83	20484
30	11170	2031	153	13354
JAN 1945				
6	14789	1599	0	16379
13	19717	1906	4	21627
20	18164	1732	8	19859
27	19098	1981	5	21084
FEB 1945				
3	17435	2491	9	19935
10	34924	3472	0	38396
17	44555	3745	10	48374
24	27091	2870	32	29993
MAR 1945				
3	32237	4502	2	36741
10	28057	4656	2	32715
17	19099	2004	2	21105
24	51092	2839	5	53936
31	34712	2544	0	37256
APR 1945				
7	36896	3382	14	40294
14	44184	1528	7	45719
21	22174	2755	13	24942
28	41183	4341	481	46005
MAY 1945				
5	29591	12052	40	41686
12	34789	7374	313	42476
19	49410	14259	132	63801
26	26007	8422	4	34433
JUNE 1945				
2	27692	5321	3	33016
9	30150	1187	0	31337
14	18243	350	0	18593
TOTAL	908,303	128,597	7,329	1,044,229

GRAND TOTAL (period 1 Oct 1944 to 14 June 1945)—1,044,229 tons

APPENDIX XI

Rations, Gasoline, and Diesel Oil Received in Ninth Army Area

Week Ending	Rations Number	Rations L-Tons	Gasoline Gallons	Gasoline L-Tons	Diesel Oil Gallons	Diesel Oil L-Tons
SEP 1944						
23	789,491	2,668	652,335	5,030	9,611	38
30	634,315	1,867	353,630	1,262	7,390	29
OCT 1944						
7	402,298	1,180	273,632	977	16,390	15
14	657,921	1,930	419,558	1,499	14,940	58
21	751,688	2,182	593,070	2,120	23,228	90
28	1,010,507	2,963	335,345	1,268	8,745	34
NOV 1944						
4	1,412,483	4,143	744,350	2,656	22,820	91
11	1,441,629	4,229	969,930	3,464	28,935	113
18	1,657,387	4,860	1,494,620	5,337	33,880	142
25	1,710,756	5,019	975,485	3,494	47,400	172
DEC 1944						
2	1,852,219	5,432	1,098,265	3,922	92,450	199
9	1,837,661	5,394	1,061,650	3,790	49,340	193
16	1,701,025	4,989	1,436,546	4,052	51,110	198
23	1,489,791	4,370	1,410,059	3,965	34,595	135
30	1,896,226	5,563	1,181,670	4,221	47,550	184
JAN 1945						
6	1,675,454	4,625	1,090,480	3,888	66,320	258
13	1,595,488	4,680	1,107,950	3,956	49,840	195
20	1,541,946	4,523	1,197,940	4,279	49,160	191
27	1,580,994	4,637	1,267,110	4,526	63,305	245
FEB 1945						
3	1,695,159	4,973	1,387,660	4,957	65,800	258
10	2,492,332	7,310	2,246,995	8,025	62,145	261
17	2,382,381	6,988	1,766,205	6,307	67,535	264
24	2,687,637	6,779	2,030,961	7,264	83,571	327
MAR 1945						
3	2,793,825	8,194	2,632,685	9,761	81,285	316
10	2,996,780	8,791	2,543,440	9,076	97,910	382
17	2,935,286	8,609	2,547,130	9,097	121,800	474
24	3,144,427	9,223	2,540,210	9,072	123,195	481
31	3,371,705	9,890	3,379,565	12,071	1,321,555	516
APR 1945						
7	3,558,029	10,436	4,251,270	15,183	134,681	525
14	3,518,239	10,906	4,496,330	16,046	122,835	478
21	3,903,887	11,439	4,353,520	15,567	118,060	461
28	4,516,424	13,247	3,511,760	12,542	113,680	442
MAY 1945						
5	5,130,496	15,247	4,198,340	14,984	138,840	542
12	6,027,879	17,689	3,824,530	13,660	96,655	377
19	8,245,702	24,185	5,230,736	18,681	125,580	490
26	8,257,558	24,241	5,524,685	19,732	184,205	719
JUN 1945						
2	8,227,668	24,131	4,940,570	17,644	74,360	282
9	4,935,206	14,475	4,000,006	14,285	56,000	217
14	2,514,612	7,375	2,150,000	7,680	40,000	155

APPENDIX XII

Selected Weapons, Vehicles, and Signal Equipment in Ninth Army

(Note: Total quantities in the Army area on the date shown, including depot stocks and items in the hands of troops.)

Item	20 Nov '44	20 Feb '45	20 Mar '45	5 May '45	Average
Rifles, M1	50,900	100,950	111,519	124,184	96,888
Rifles, .03	6,720	7,426	7,224	8,153	7,381
Rifles, .03A4	469	792	729	1,018	752
Pistols	12,809	19,506	23,704	25,658	20,419
BAR	1,216	5,070	4,781	5,276	4,086
Carbine	84,594	138,044	142,804	171,125	134,142
Sub MG	13,909	24,970	25,712	27,914	23,126
TOTAL (Individual Weapons)	170,176	296,758	316,473	363,328	286,794
Rocket Launcher	7,489	13,129	14,020	16,126	12,691
Grenade Launcher	16,194	33,264	35,751	42,641	31,962
Cal .30, MG	2,299	7,799	8,405	9,512	7,004
Cal .50, MG	5,151	9,868	10,493	11,331	9,211
Mortars, 60mm	551	1,440	1,561	1,740	1,323
Mortars, 81mm	336	633	669	757	599
40mm AA Guns	324	565	582	582	513
90mm AA Guns	103	107	106	107	106
Carriage, Multiple Gun, AA	308	819	903	725	689
57mm AT Gun	275	648	635	788	586
3" AT Gun	107	186	199	139	158
105mm Howitzer, M2	234	422	409	467	383
105mm Howitzer, M3	77	173	173	208	158
4.5" Gun	59	50	53	41	51
155mm Howitzer	176	282	287	327	268
155mm Gun	37	72	84	107	75
8" Howitzer	36	38	74	98	61
8" Gun	6	6	7	7	6
240mm Howitzer	12	18	18	19	17
SP Artillery	240	383	365	438	356
SP Tank Destroyer	244	397	590	612	461
Light Tanks	395	703	792	965	714
Medium Tanks	507	1,433	1,423	1,746	1,277
Heavy Tanks	----	---	—	78	—
Half Tracks	1,705	2,382	2,516	3,230	2,458
Armored Cars	466	1,015	1,076	1,079	909
Scout Cars	31	28	68	39	41
Tank Recovery Vehicles	100	211	194	220	181
Tank Transporters	59	103	126	157	111
4-Ton Wreckers	89	157	181	176	151
10-Ton Wreckers	164	259	279	324	256
High Speed Tractors	572	803	899	869	785
6-Ton Prime Movers	71	141	257	206	168
7½-Ton Prime Movers	24	82	119	147	98
2½-Ton Shop Trucks	249	380	419	481	382
2½-Ton Tank Trucks	15	30	30	35	28
DUKWs	6	173	217	225	155
Semi-Trailers (Van)	215	271	308	339	283
Cargo Carriers, M29 and M29C	51	347	598	666	415
Ambulances	591	890	916	1,060	864

Item	20 Nov '44	20 Feb '45	20 Mar '45	5 May '45	Average
Motorcycles	307	328	331	372	334
Trucks, ¼-Ton	7,312	13,396	14,226	16,522	12,864
Trucks, ¾ T Command	793	1,092	1,106	1,133	1,031
Trucks, ¾ T WC	3,018	5,684	5,869	6,886	5,364
Trucks, 1½ T Cargo	721	1,312	1,332	1,502	1,217
Trucks, 2½ T Cargo	8,419	13,870	14,677	15,929	13,224
Trucks, 2½ T Dump	505	1,214	2,116	1,986	1,455
Trucks, 4 T Cargo	228	354	354	344	320
Trailers, ¼ Ton	2,861	5,100	5,393	5,880	4,808
Trailers, 1 Ton (all types)	6,678	11,625	12,329	13,340	10,993
Trailers, 4 Ton, M21	12	62	70	106	62
Trailers 8 Ton, M23	—	46	80	106	58
Cable Assm'y CC-358					
(¼ Mi. reel, Spiral-4 Cable)	10,303	29,780	29,107	27,860	24,262
Mine Detectors	2,128	2,810	2,909	2,726	2,643
Radio Sets, all types	8,850	12,265	12,863	14,444	12,105
Switchboards, field type	832	1,125	1,225	1,384	1,141
Telegraph Sets	322	419	491	487	430
Telephones, field type	7,605	14,276	14,095	16,707	13,146
Teletype Equipment	64	98	108	112	95
Wire, field type (miles)	18,073	24,964	20,394	33,066	24,124
100 mi. Radio VHF Relay Equipment	3	6½	8	9	7
100 mi. Carrier Systems	15	18	19	23	19

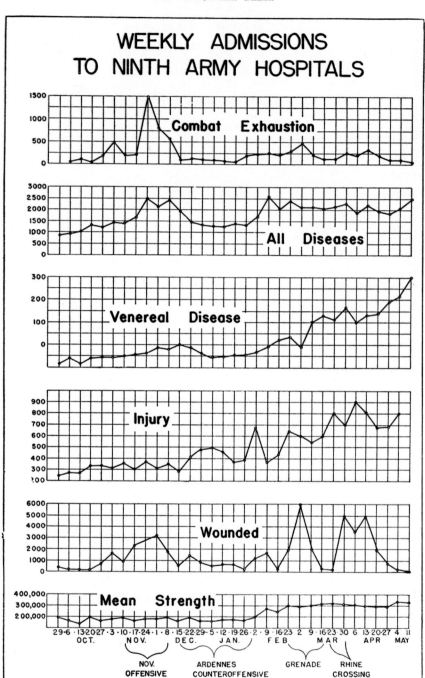

WEEKLY ADMISSIONS TO NINTH ARMY HOSPITALS

MONTHLY ADMISSIONS TO NINTH ARMY MEDICAL INSTALLATIONS

	ARMY STRENGTH
Sept 1944	115,423
Oct.	162,701
Nov.	173,408
Dec.	176,227
Jan.1945	169,067
Feb.	252,638
Mar.	301,806
Apr.	308,063
May	455,602

WOUNDS

INJURIES

DISEASE

COMBAT EXHAUSTION

TOTAL ADMISSIONS TO NINTH ARMY MEDICAL INSTALLATIONS SEPT. 1944—MAY 1945

TOTAL 113,630

DISEASE 55,508

WOUNDED 34,387

INJURY 17,658

COMBAT EXHAUSTION 6,077

= 10,000 CASES

INDEX

INDEX OF NUMBERED UNITS[1]

[1]German units are in *italic*.

PHOTOGRAPHS

Major General James E. Moore
Chief of Staff

Colonel George A. Millener
Deputy Chief of Staff

Colonel Art B. Miller, Jr.
Secretary of the General Staff

Brigadier General Armistead
D. Mead, Jr.
Assistant Chief of Staff, G-3

Brigadier General Roy V. Rickard
Assistant Chief of Staff, G-4

Colonel Charles P. Bixel
Assistant Chief of Staff, G-2
(May 22, 1944 to February 22,
1945)

Colonel Harold D. Kehm
Assistant Chief of Staff, G-2
(March 3 to October 10, 1945)

Colonel Daniel H. Hundley
Assistant Chief of Staff, G-1

Colonel Carl A. Kraege
Assistant Chief of Staff, G-5

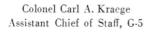

Colonel John A. Klein
Adjutant General

Colonel John G. Murphy
Antiaircraft Officer

Colonel Laurence H. Hanley
Artillery Officer

Colonel Claude A. Black
Armored Officer

Colonel W. Roy Bradley
Chaplain

Colonel Harold Walmsley
Chemical Officer

Brigadier General Richard U.
Nicholas
Engineer

Colonel John L. Scott
Finance Officer

Colonel James A. Warren, Jr.
Headquarters Commandant

Colonel Perry L. Baldwin
Inspector General

Colonel Stanley W. Jones
Judge Advocate

Colonel Walter W. Warner
Ordnance Officer

Colonel Kern C. Crandall
Publicity & Psychological
Warfare Officer

Colonel Robert C. Andrews
Provost Marshal

Colonel William E. Goe
Quartermaster

Colonel Joe J. Miller
Signal Officer

Lt.Colonel Kenneth K. Kelley
Special Services Officer

Colonel William E. Shambora
Surgeon

The railway station at the hamlet of Mi-Forêt, near Rennes, France. In the surrounding forest was located the Army command post during the reduction of Brest and the operations on the Brittany Peninsula.

General Simpson, General Middleton, VIII Corps Commander, and General Stroh, 8th Infantry Division commander, discuss the plans for the capture of Brest.

The Catholic school in Maastricht, Netherlands, occupied by the General Staff sections of Army headquarters during the winter of 1944-45.

Typical road signs around Maastricht

General Bradley, General Eisenhower, and General Simpson at Maastricht

General McLain, commanding XIX Corps, General Simpson, and Brig.Gen. William K. Harrison, Assistant Division Commander of the 30th Infantry Division, discuss coming operations.

General Gillem, XIII Corps commander, General Simpson, Field Marshal Montgomery, and General Keating, 102d Infantry Division commander, discuss the plans for crossing the Roer River.

General Simpson and Field Marshal Montgomery with Ninth Army corps and division commanders after a conference at the command post of XIII Corps just before the crossing of the Roer River and the drive to the Rhine. Left to right: Brig.Gen. Hamilton E. Maguire, Chief of Staff, XIX Corps; General Devine, 8th Armored Division commander; General Oliver, 5th Armored Division commander; General McLain, XIX Corps commander; General Simpson; General White, 2d Armored Division commander; Field Marshal Montgomery; a British staff officer; General Gillem, XIII Corps commander; General Baade, 35th Infantry Division commander; General Bolling, 84th Infantry Division commander; General Anderson, XVI Corps commander; General Twaddle, 95th Infantry Division commander; General Gerhardt, 29th Infantry Division commander; Brig.Gen. R. M. Montague, Division Artillery Commander and Acting Division Commander, 83d Infantry Division; Col. George B. Peploe (behind General Montague), Assistant Chief of Staff, G-3, XIII Corps; Brig.Gen. W. K. Harrison, Assistant Division Commander, 30th Infantry Division; General Moore, Chief of Staff, Ninth Army.

The massive Schwammenauel dam and reservoir which controlled the waters of the Roer River

A flooded street in Weisweiler, Germany

An antiaircraft gun crosses the still flooded Roer River on a treadway bridge

A portion of the buildings occupied by Army headquarters in München-Gladbach, Germany. Note the painted signs exhorting the German people to further efforts for the Fatherland. The one just right of center asks, "What have *you* done for Germany today?" Similar signs, including many protestations in large capital letters saying, "We Love Our Führer," were characteristic of this part of Germany.

Infantry advances in the rubble just east of the Rhine

Airplane vapor trails in the skies
over Germany

Maintaining some of the hundreds
of field telephone wire lines

Prime Minister Winston Churchill crosses the Rhine in a landing craft just after Ninth Army's assault over the river. General Anderson, XVI Corps commander (extreme left), General Simpson, Field Marshal Montgomery, and Field Marshal Viscount Alan Brooke, Chief of the British Imperial General Staff (extreme right in visored cap) accompanied him.

Floating bridges constructed by Ninth Army engineers over the Rhine at Wesel. Bottom to top: Demolished railroad bridge; 25-ton ponton bridge; class 40 floating Bailey bridge; and M2 treadway bridge. Note the Lippe River and the ruins of Wesel in the left background.

The white flags of surrender are hung out in the town of Tangermünde on the Elbe River

Some of the hundreds of thousands of Germans who made their way across the Elbe River to surrender to Ninth Army

At his headquarters in Braunschweig (Brunswick) General Simpson entertains Colonel General Alexander Gorbatov, Russian Third Army Commander

A German underground aircraft factory in a salt mine near Engels, Germany

General Simpson with his corps and division commanders in Braunschweig just after the surrender of Germany. First row: General McLain, XIX Corps commander; General Gillem, XIII Corps commander; General Simpson; General Anderson, XVI Corps commander. Second row: General Twaddle, 95th Infantry Division commander; General White, 2d Armored Division commander; General Wyche, 79th Infantry Division commander; General Gerhardt, 29th Infantry Division Commander; General Devine, 8th Armored Division commander. Third row: General Oliver, 5th Armored Division commander; General Moore, Chief of Staff, Ninth Army; General Hobbs, 30th Infantry Division commander; General Baade, 35th Infantry Division commander; General Macon, 83d Infantry Division commander; General Porter, 75th Infantry Division commander; General Keating, 102d Infantry Division commander. General Bolling, 84th Infantry Division commander, was not present.